But not you kids. I'm not worried about y'all.
y'all are good kids.

Texas Border Patrol to International School of the Americas High School Students in McAllen, Texas. The Agent was telling the stories of three Latino teenagers who had been tried and convicted of drug smuggling, human smuggling and capital murder in Texas border towns. He also demanded that the students should not show sympathy or an ounce of compassion for the criminals.

McAllen, Tx February 19. 2016

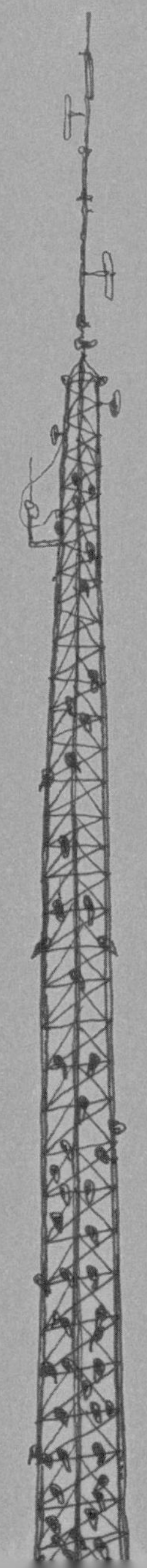

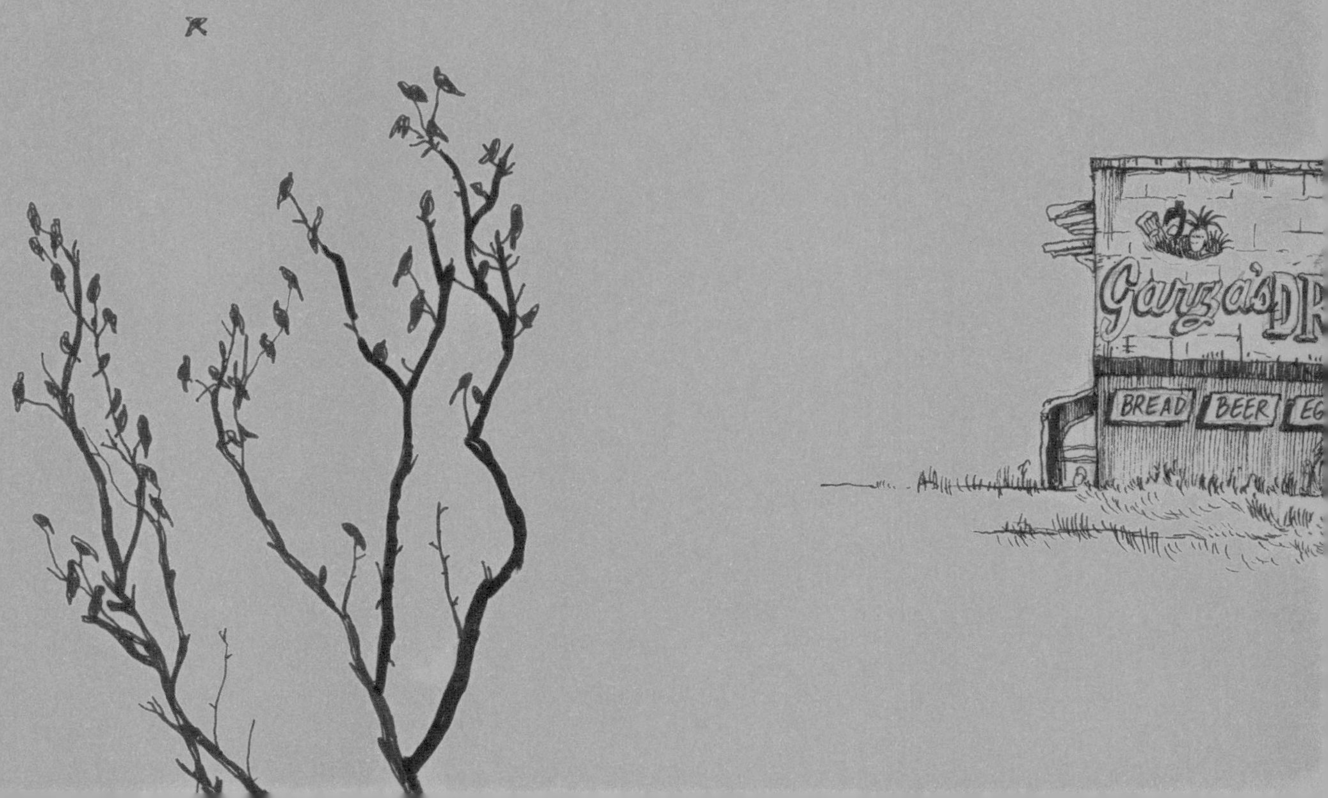

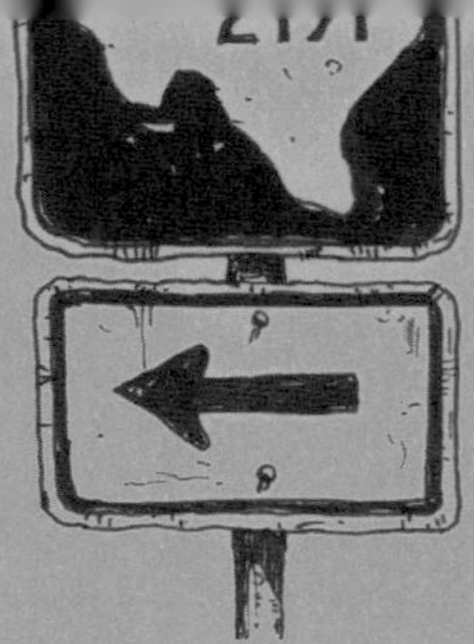

If it's not right for you,

leave.

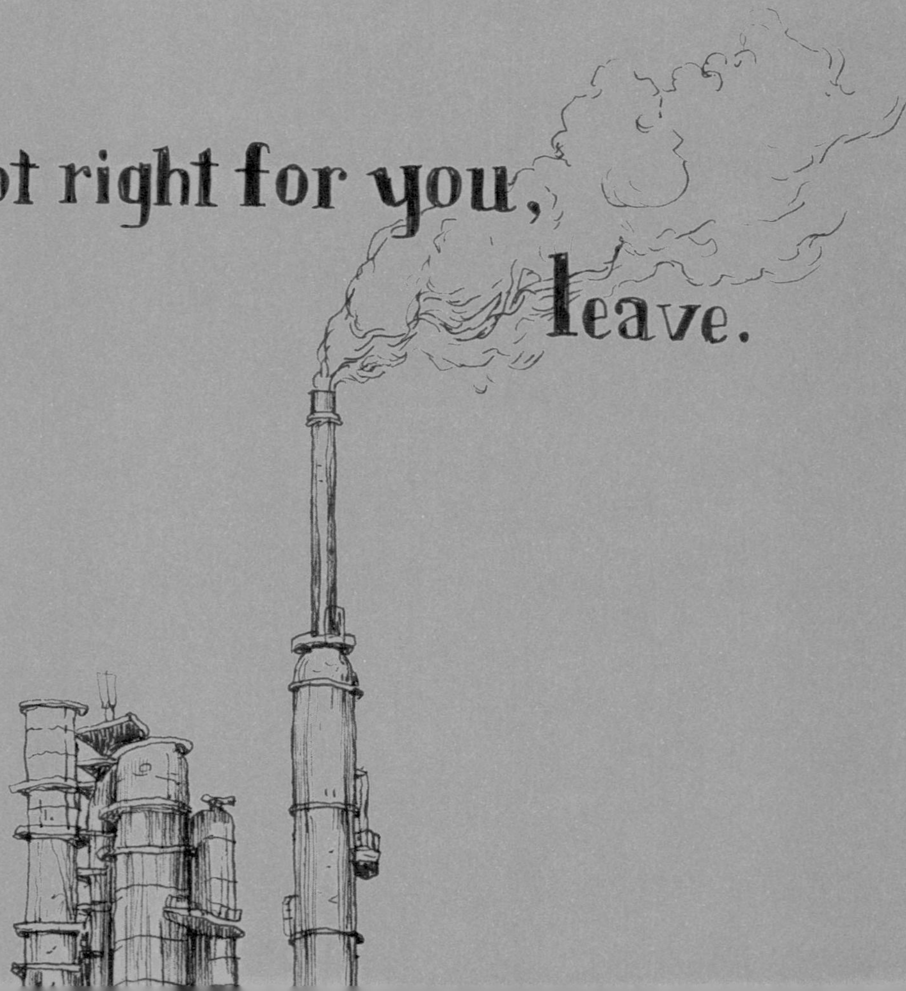

Here is my visual testimony.
A tale of love, struggle and survival
in twenty-first-century America.

—V.V.

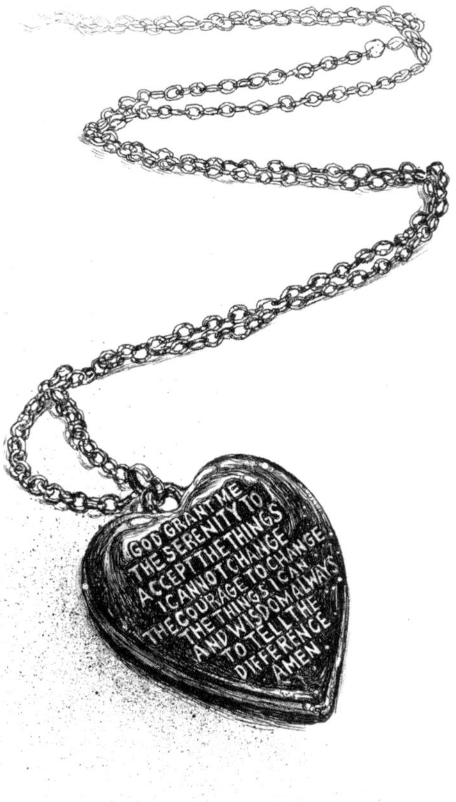

(cover) ***Eaten*, 2018–19**
Oil on canvas and bronze
Photo: Paul Salveson

(endpapers) ***Somewhere In South Texas*, 2016**
Ink on paper

(this page)
***The Slaughterhouse Five Drawings*, 2023**
Ink on paper,
published by Arion Press

(p 4–5)
It Was a Very Good Year (Nineteen Eighty Seven)
(work-in-progress), Valdez studio, 2024
Oil on canvas
Photo: Vincent Valdez

(p 6–7) ***Supreme***
(work-in-progress), Valdez studio, 2024
Oil on canvas
The Spectacle
(work-in-progress), Valdez studio, 2024
Oil on canvas
Photos: Vincent Valdez

(p 8–9) ***Hello America*, Valdez studio, 2024**
Ink and pencil on paper
Photo: Timothy Doyon

(p 10–11)
It Was a Very Good Year (Nineteen Eighty Eight)
(work-in-progress), Valdez studio, 2024
Oil on canvas
Photo: Robert LeBlanc

X ARTISTS' BOOKS

MASS MoCA

Contemporary Arts Museum Houston

Published on the occasion of *Vincent Valdez: Just a Dream...*
Contemporary Arts Museum Houston
November 15, 2024 – March 23, 2025
MASS MoCA
May 24, 2025 – April 5, 2026

Published by X Artists' Books
PO Box 3424, South Pasadena, CA 91031
www.xartistsbooks.com

Co-published by MASS MoCA
1040 MASS MoCA Way, North Adams, MA 01247
www.massmoca.org

Co-published by CAMH
5216 Montrose Blvd., Houston, TX 77006
www.camh.org

Edited by Denise Markonish
Copyediting by L. Jane Calverley
Proofreading by Paulette Wein
Spanish translations: Victoria Principi and Verónica Visgarra (Eriksen Translations); Nicole Hervás Ibañez and Gwen Davis-Barrios (X Artists' Books); and José Arconada (Penguin Random House Grupo).
Joyce Carol Oates credits: © 1987 by The Ontario Review, Inc. Reprinted by permission of John Hawkins & Associates, Inc., pp. 8–29. Spanish version, *Del boxeo* by Joyce Carol Oates © 1987, The Ontario Review, Inc. Licencia editorial otorgada por Penguin Random House Grupo Editorial, S.A.U.
Book design by Bob Faust
Printed in Italy by O.G.M. SpA

Library of Congress Cataloguing-in-Publication
Data available upon request

Library of Congress Control Number: 2024938767

Presenting sponsorship for *Vincent Valdez: Just a Dream...* is provided by the Henry Luce Foundation and the Terra Foundation for American Art. Major exhibition support is provided by the Ford Foundation, the Jacques & Natasha Gelman Foundation, and Judy and Charles Tate. Generous support is provided by the National Endowment of the Arts, The Andy Warhol Foundation for the Visual Arts, Beverly and Howard Robinson, and Mid-America Arts Alliance, and the state arts agencies of Arkansas, Kansas, Missouri, Nebraska, Oklahoma, and Texas. Additional support is provided by Nicole Deller and Matt Bliwise, Lisa Rich and John McLaughlin, Meridee Moore, Weingarten Art Group Fund, and Ric and Tina Whitney. Special thanks to Jon Cooper, Enrico Encarnacion, Janet Flohr, Tessa Ferreyros, Jan Greenberg, Clara Ha, Glenn Ligon, Mary Maas, Anne Parke, and Elizabeth Tenenbaum.

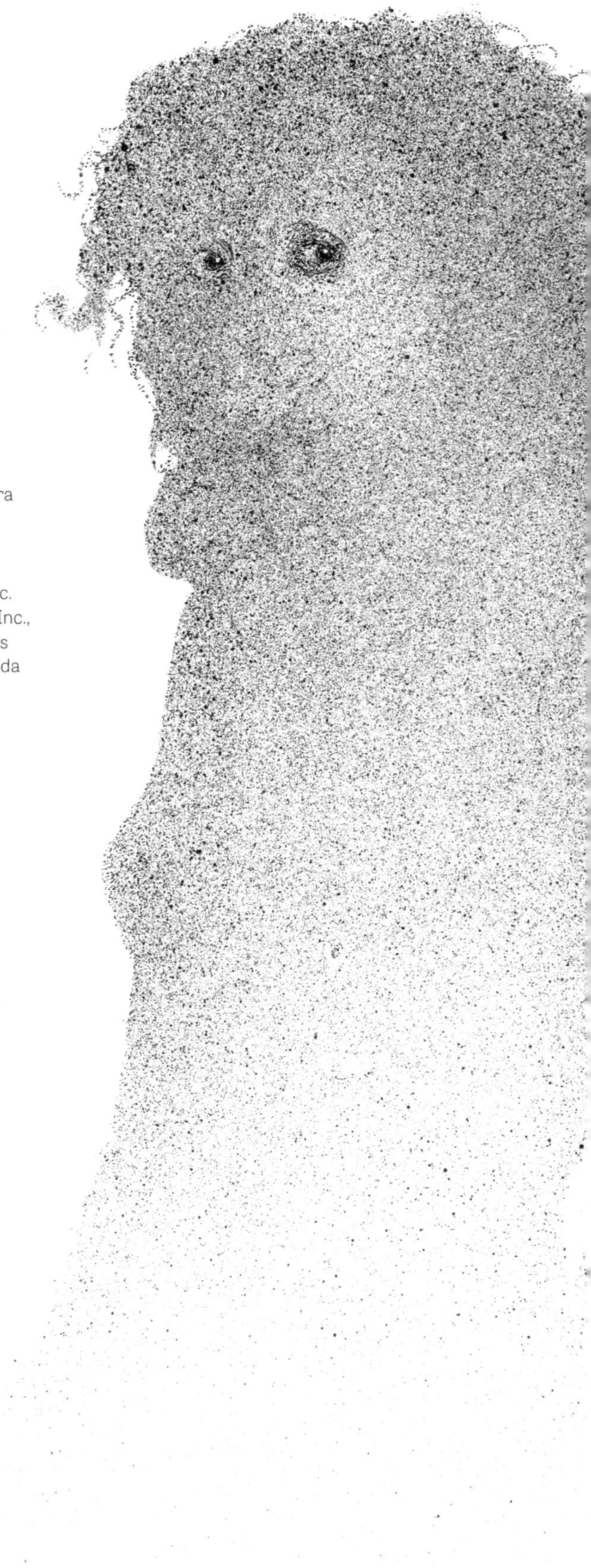

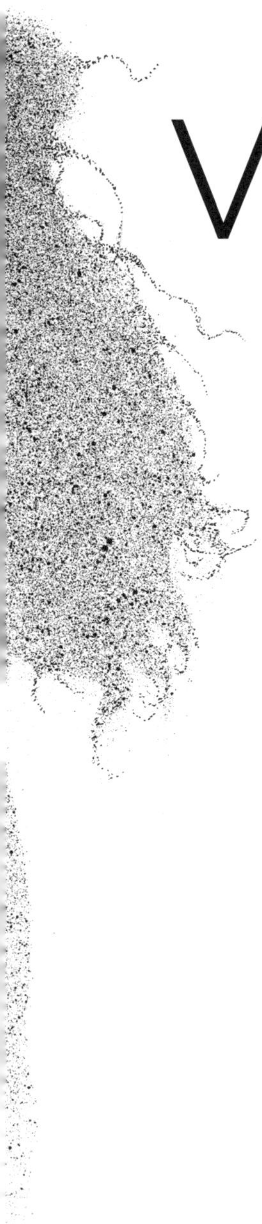

Vincent Valdez

JUST A DREAM ...

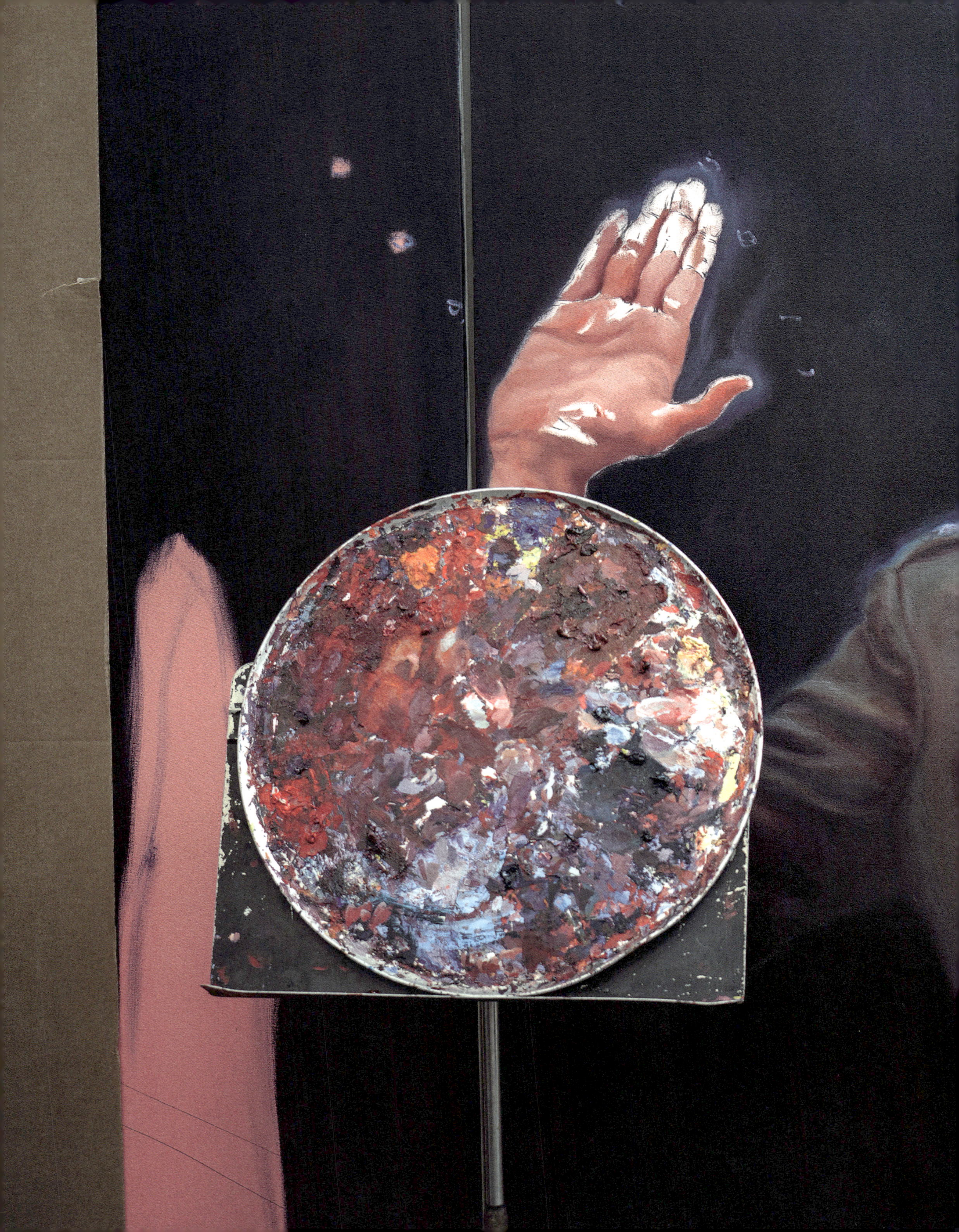

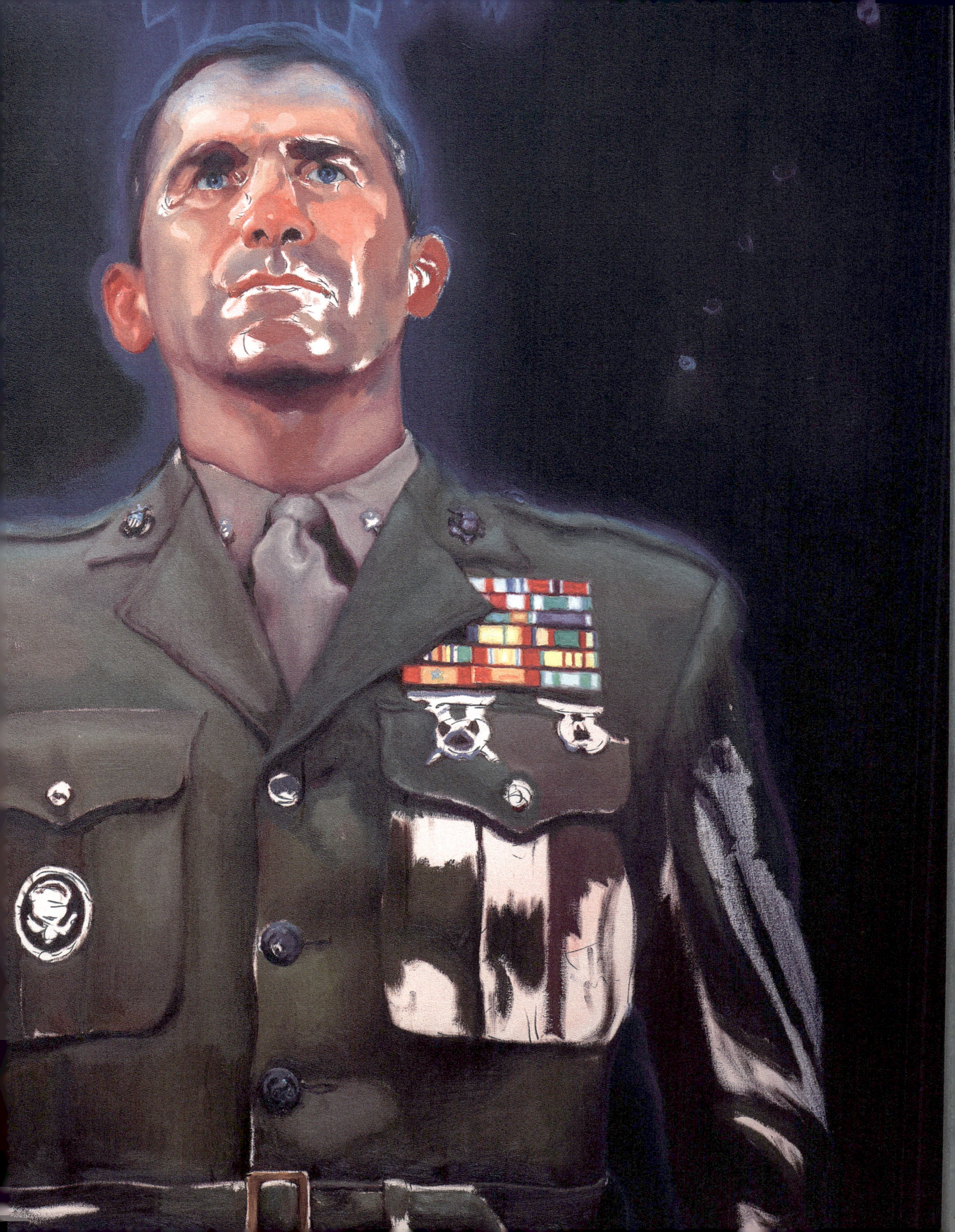

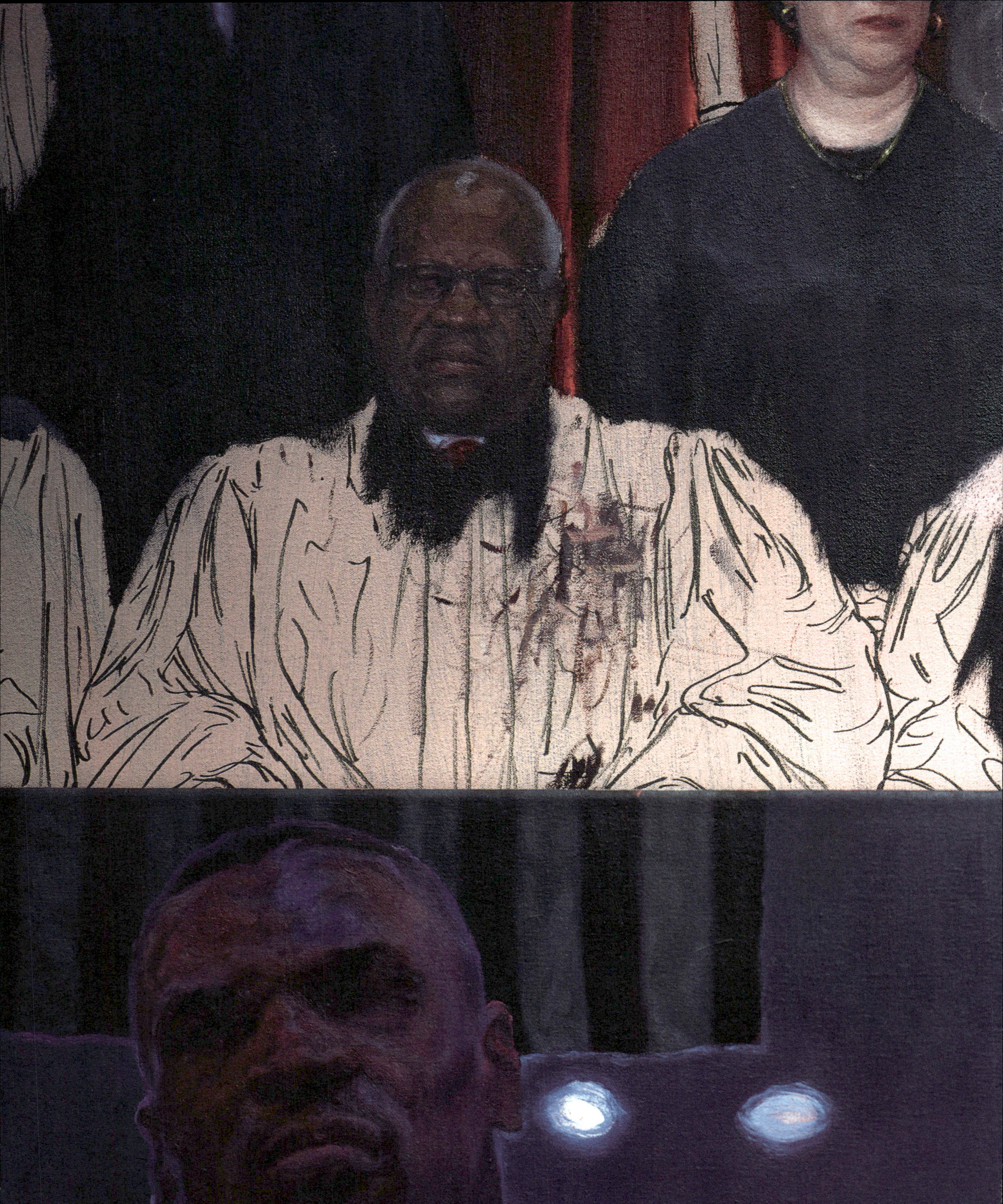

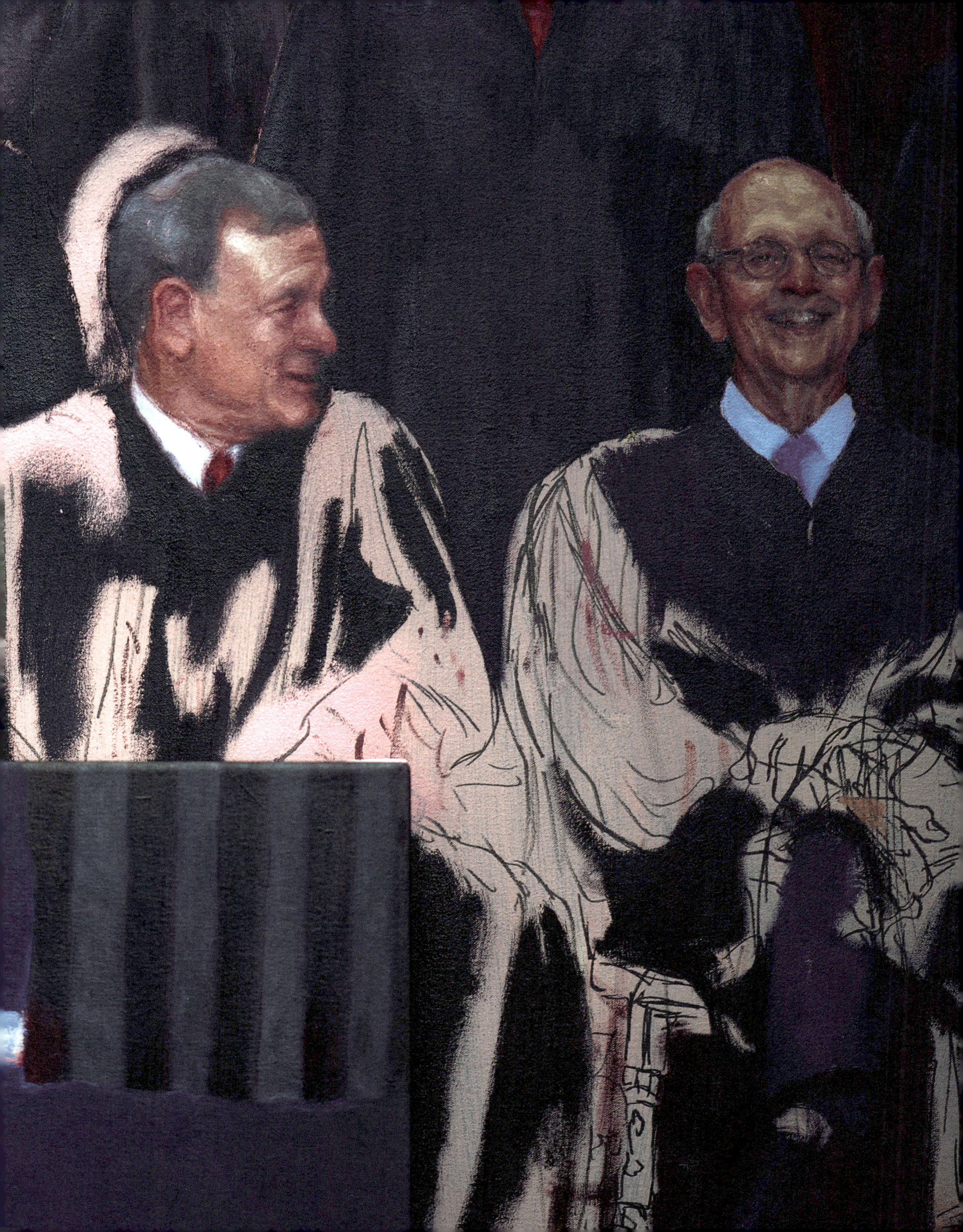

Contents

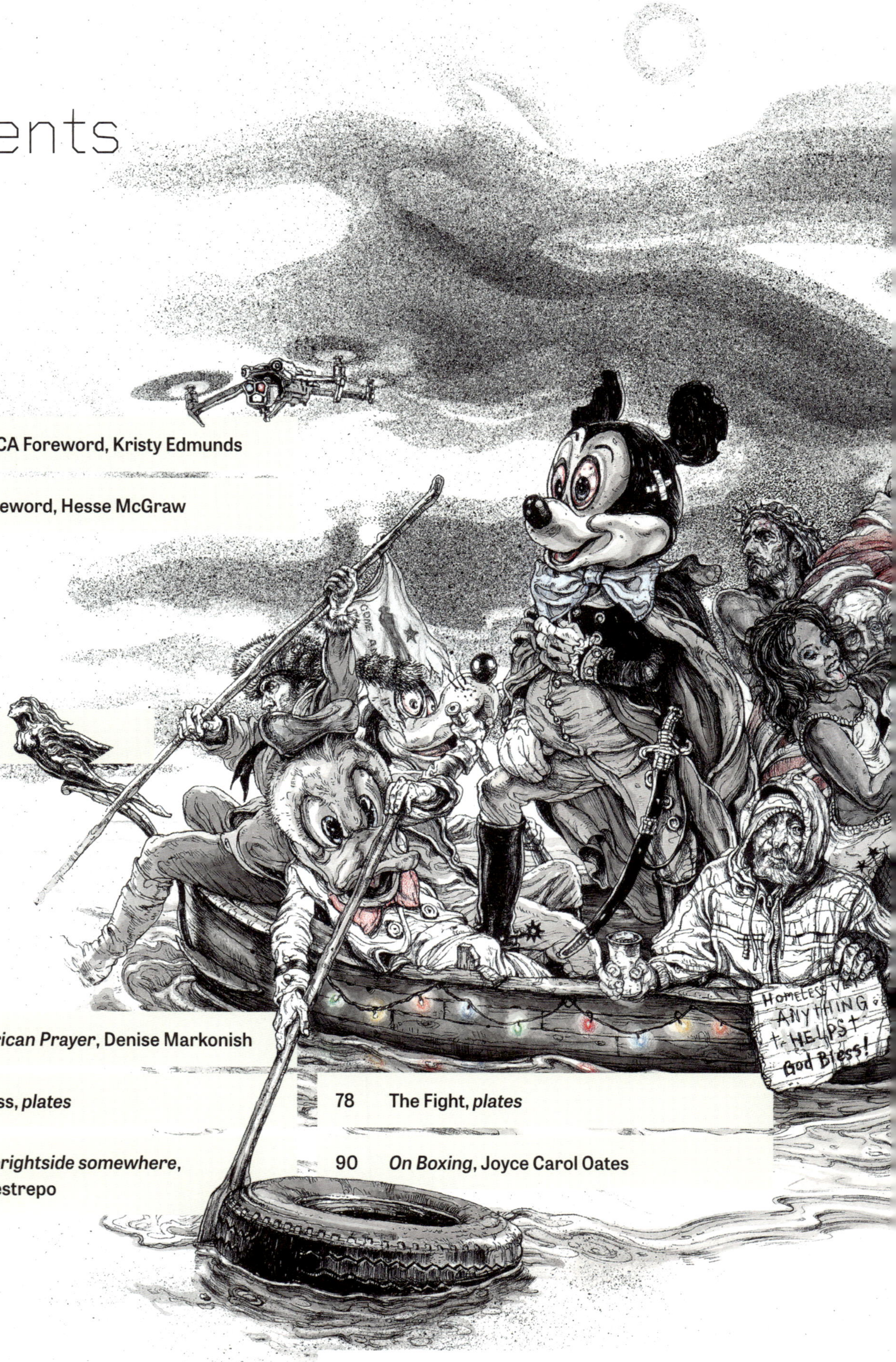

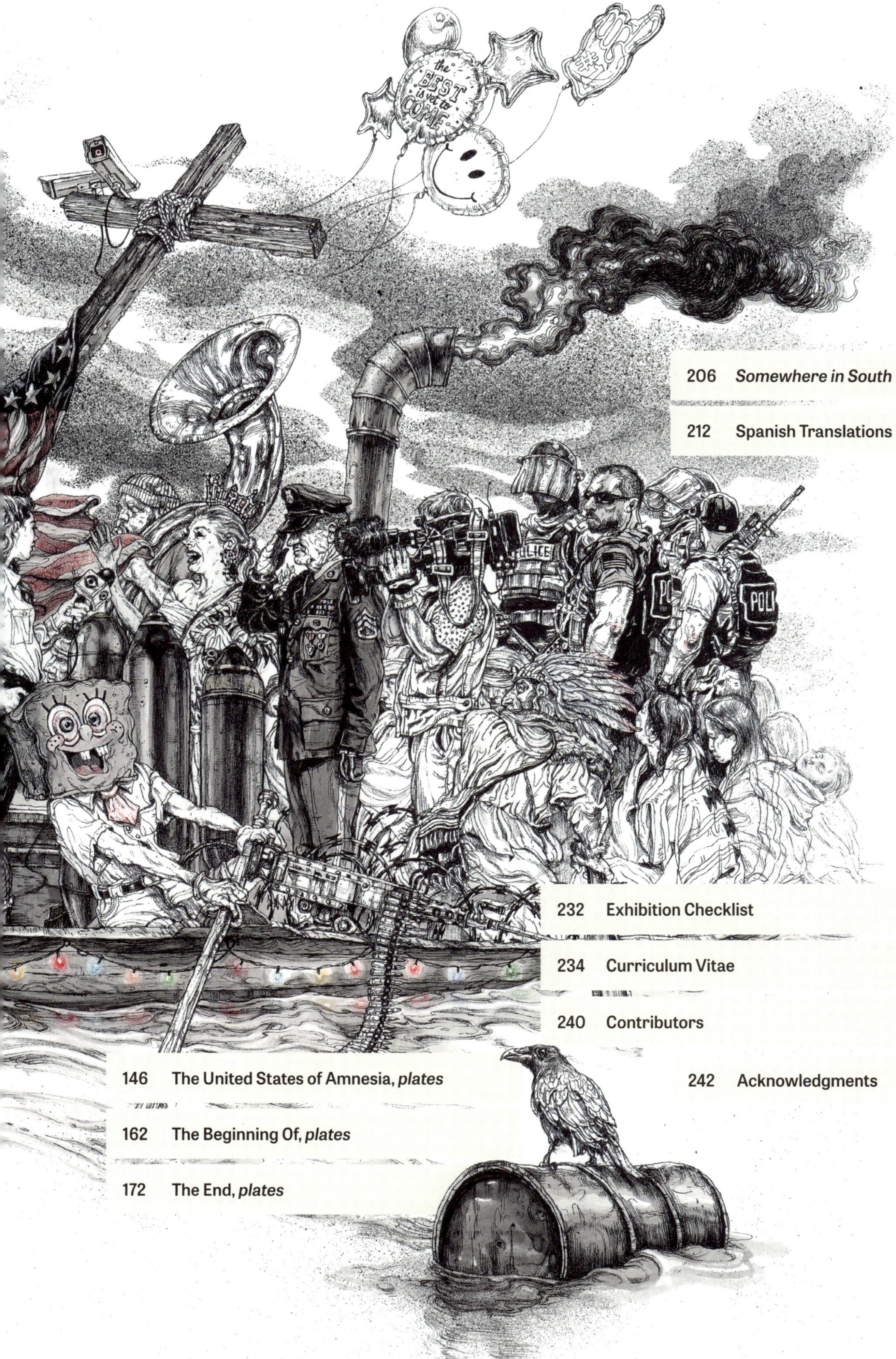
the BEST is yet to COME
POLICE

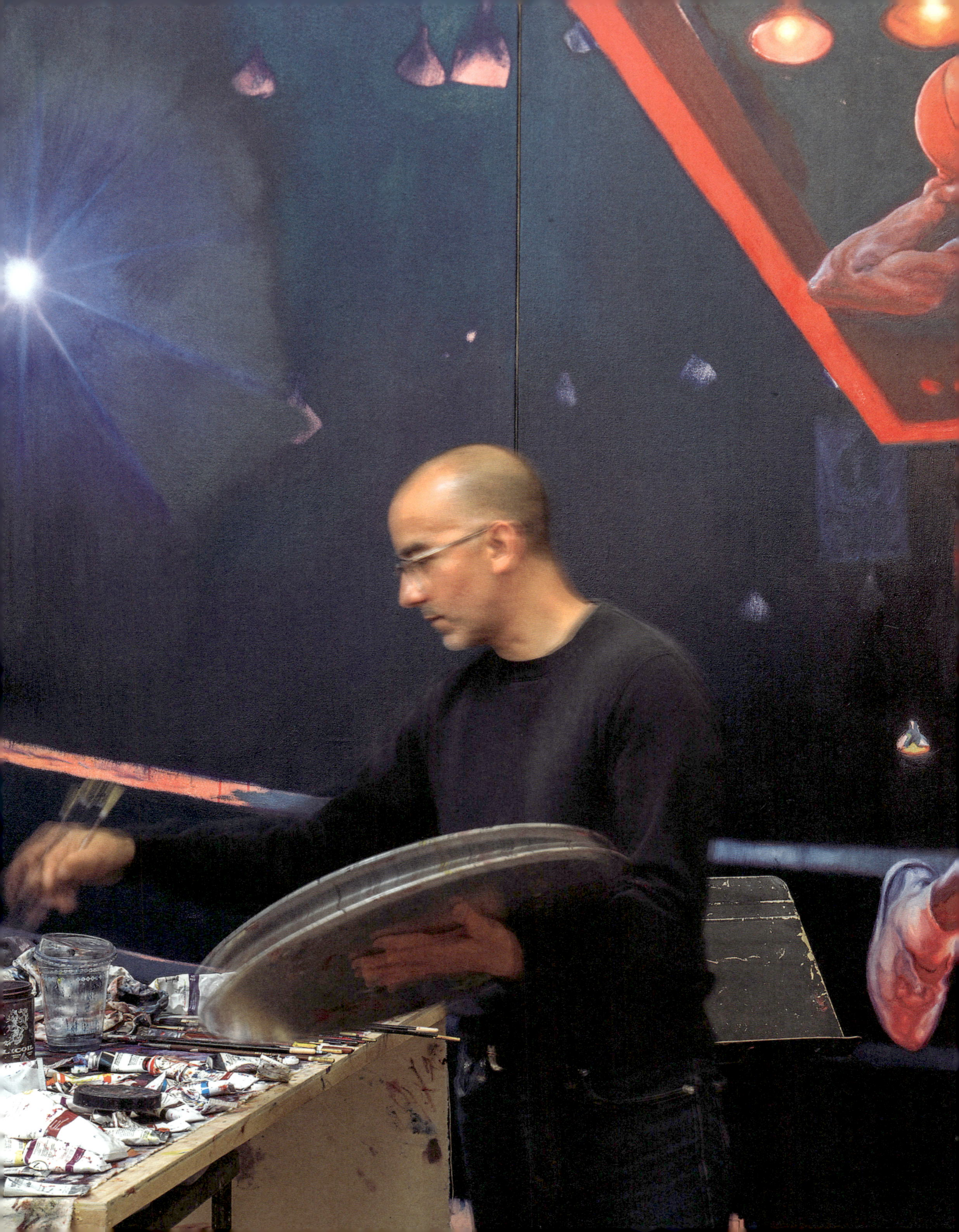

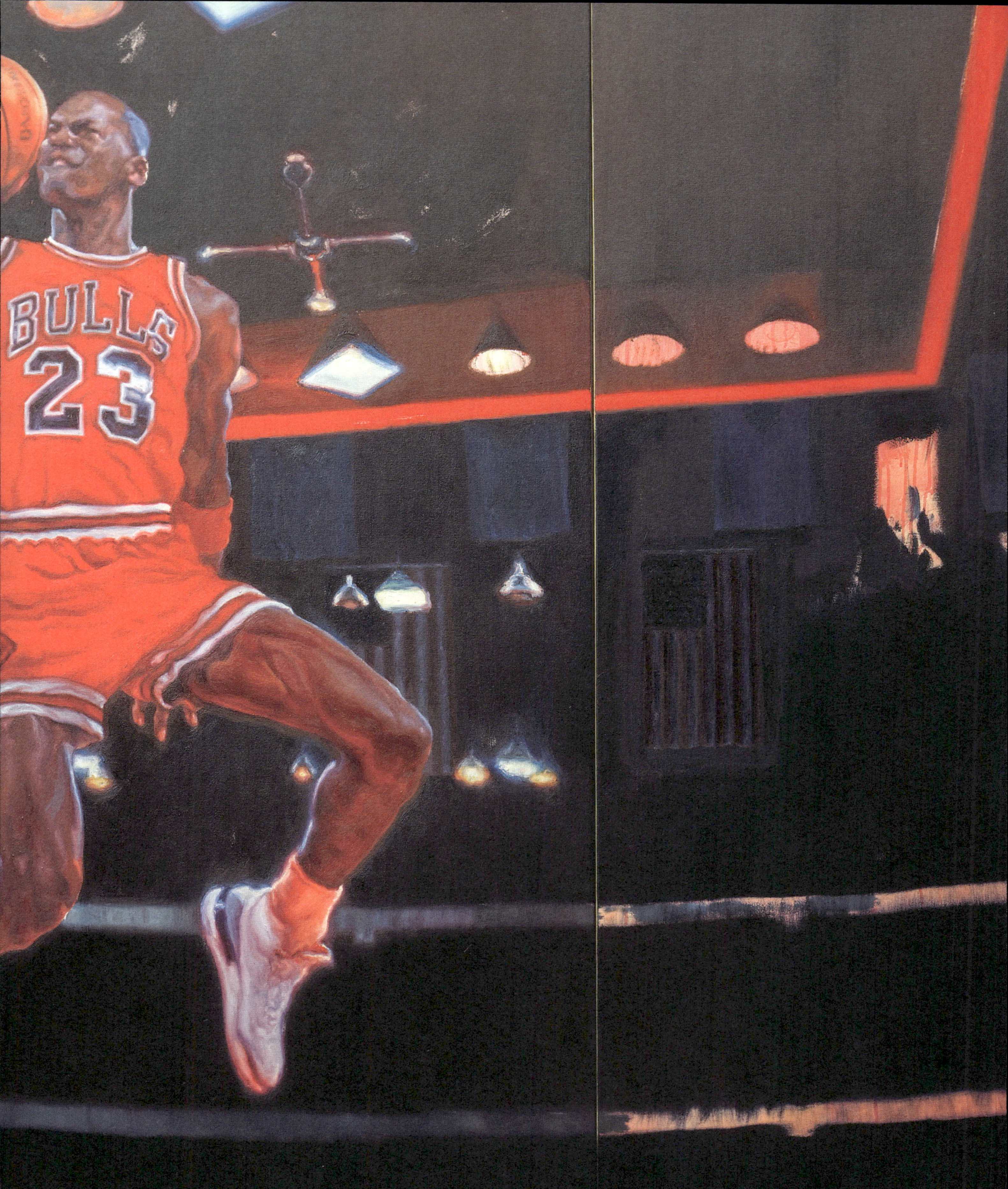
BULLS
23

Foreword

KRISTY EDMUNDS
DIRECTOR, MASS MOCA

My first encounter with the art of Vincent Valdez was in 2007, when I was listening to Ry Cooder's album *My Name Is Buddy* in my flat in Melbourne, Australia. I was drawn in by Vincent's sleeve art, featuring completely arresting images of a bedraggled cat, looming large against its landscape. Over subsequent years in Los Angeles, my exposure to his practice became more frequent. In every memorable encounter I was struck by a kind of bruising elegance in his work that seemed to emanate from an enormous capacity to both see and act with unflinching care in each painting. His visual narratives, subjects, and perspectives are always rendered into unforgettable imagery that is so singularly and vividly alive.

Just A Dream... is the first career survey of Vincent's art. In an exhibition that not only brings together decades of his artistry—from his boyhood in San Antonio to the most recent series of paintings made for MASS MoCA—but also traverses the extensive explorations and dialogues between two curators who know Vincent well: Denise Markonish, MASS MoCA's chief curator, and Patricia Restrepo, CAMH's curator. There is no doubt that their approach to co-curating adds to the richness of how we will come to more deeply recognize Vincent's art and the generous humanity that informs it.

MASS MoCA and our audience are no strangers to Vincent and his work. Denise, in her 2019 exhibition *Suffering from Realness*, presented his *Requiem*, which was done in collaboration with Adriana Corral. The piece featured stories contributed by hundreds of people and a fallen eagle made of bronze. This sculpture was carried in procession through our galleries, accompanied by a series of South Texas musicians, with Vincent joining in on trumpet. We are thrilled to welcome him back to North Adams.

We are also thrilled to collaborate again with CAMH after Cauleen Smith's *We Already Have What We Need* exhibition, curated by MASS MoCA's Susan Cross, traveled to Texas in 2021. Now, Vincent's ambitious project brings us together again, uniting our two non-collecting contemporary art museums at a time when the questions posed to cultural institutions could not be more important in a highly fractured political landscape. While Massachusetts and Texas carry distinct histories, geographies, and political strata, MASS MoCA and CAMH share the common bond of elevating the critical and creative dialogues

Mi primer encuentro con el arte de Vincent Valdez fue en 2007, mientras escuchaba el álbum de Ry Cooder *Mi nombre es Buddy* en mi departamento de Melbourne, Australia. Me llamó la atención el arte de Vincent en la portada, donde se presenta la imagen increíblemente cautivante de un gato desaliñado, que aparece allí imponente delante del paisaje. Durante los años que siguieron, en Los Ángeles, mi contacto con su práctica se volvió más frecuente. En cada encuentro memorable, me impresionaba la elegancia contundente de su obra, que parecía emanar de una enorme capacidad para ver y actuar con un cuidado inquebrantable en cada pintura. Sus narrativas visuales, sus personajes y sus perspectivas se traducen siempre en imágenes inolvidables animadas de una manera muy singular y vívida.

Solo un sueño... es la primera exposición retrospectiva en la carrera de Vincent. Se trata de una muestra que no sólo reúne décadas de arte — desde su infancia en San Antonio hasta la serie de pinturas más reciente que hizo para el Massachusetts Museum of Contemporary Art (MASS MoCA)—, sino que también atraviesa las extensas exploraciones y diálogos entre dos curadoras que conocen muy bien a Vincent: Denise Markonish, jefa de curaduría del MASS MoCA, y Patricia Restrepo, curadora del Contemporary Arts Museum Houston (CAMH). No cabe duda de que su enfoque como curadoras adjuntas enriquece la forma en que podremos reconocer con más profundidad el arte de Vincent y la generosa humanidad que le da forma.

El MASS MoCA y nuestro público no son ajenos a Vincent y su obra. En su exposición *Sufro de realidad* (2019), Denise presentó *Réquiem*, la obra que el artista creó en colaboración con Adriana Corral. La pieza presentaba historias aportadas por cientos de personas y un águila caída hecha de bronce. Al águila se la llevó en procesión por nuestras galerías, acompañada por una banda de músicos del sur de Texas, a quienes Vincent se unió como trompetista. Nos encanta volver a recibirlo en North Adams.

También nos complace volver a colaborar con el CAHM después de haber trasladado a Texas la exposición *Ya tenemos lo que necesitamos* de Cauleen Smith, curada por Susan Cross del MASS MoCA en 2021. Ahora, el ambicioso proyecto de Vincent nos reúne de nuevo, y unimos los esfuerzos de nuestros museos de arte contemporáneo sin colección propia en un momento en el que las preguntas que se les plantean a las instituciones culturales son realmente importantes, debido al escenario político enormemente fracturado que nos

of our communities: both institutions are dedicated to the creation of new history through supporting the work, and working ideas, of artists. It is a pleasure and honor to collaborate in this mutual endeavor to present *Just a Dream...*, and to support this extraordinary artist who so astutely and evocatively envisions the very idea of America.

I join my colleague, CAMH's executive director Hesse McGraw, in appreciation of—and admiration for—the tremendous work of co-curators Denise and Patricia in realizing this first survey with Vincent. My gratitude to the team at CAMH, and those I have the joy of working with at MASS MoCA, with special acknowledgement to the Visual Arts team: Zoe Berg, Spencer Byrne-Seres, Meghan Claire Considine, Tavish Costello, Rory Coyne, Evan Garza, Martin Gonzalez, and Andy Slemenda; the Buildings and Grounds crew; Paige Bartles, Ellen Beck, and Elizabeth Smith in Advancement; Amy Chen and Jen Falk in Communications and Content; and Lisa Dent and Chris Conti in Public Programs. Special thanks also to Bob Faust for his book design and our co-publishing partners, X Artists' Books.

So, thank you to the Henry Luce Foundation, Terra Foundation for American Art, Ford Foundation, Jacques & Natasha Gelman Foundation, Judy and Charles Tate, National Endowment of the Arts, The Andy Warhol Foundation for the Visual Arts, Beverly and Howard Robinson, Mid-America Arts Alliance, the state arts agencies of Arkansas, Kansas, Missouri, Nebraska, Oklahoma, and Texas, Nicole Deller and Matt Bliwise, Lisa Rich and John McLaughlin, Meridee Moore, Weingarten Art Group Fund, and Ric and Tina Whitney, Jon Cooper, Enrico Encarnacion, Janet Flohr, Tessa Ferreyros, Jan Greenberg, Clara Ha, Glenn Ligon, Mary Maas, Anne Parke, and Elizabeth Tenenbaum.

Above all, my profound gratitude to Vincent, whose expansive art calls us to examine the essential facts and falsehoods of inequitable American histories, as well as the unrealized dreams being continuously pursued, so that through his work we can be accelerated toward new futures.

rodea. Si bien Massachusetts y Texas tienen historias, geografías y estratos políticos diferentes, tanto el MASS MoCA como el CAMH comparten el vínculo común de elevar los diálogos críticos y creativos de nuestras comunidades: ambas instituciones están abocadas a la creación de una nueva historia mediante el apoyo a las obras y las ideas de trabajo de los y las artistas. Es un placer y un honor colaborar en este esfuerzo común para presentar *Solo un sueño...*, y apoyar a este artista extraordinario que imagina la idea misma de Estados Unidos de una manera tan astuta y evocadora.

Me uno a mi colega, Hesse McGraw, director del CAMH, en su reconocimiento —y admiración— por la enorme labor de las curadoras adjuntas Denise Markonish y Patricia Restrepo para la organización de la primera exposición retrospectiva de Vincent. También deseo expresar mi gratitud con el equipo del CAMH y con las personas del MASS MoCA con quienes tuve la dicha de trabajar. Además, quisiera reconocer especialmente el trabajo del equipo de Artes Visuales: Zoe Berg, Spencer Byrne-Seres, Meghan Claire Considine, Tavish Costello, Rory Coyne, Evan Garza, Martin Gonzalez y Andy Slemenda; del personal de las instalaciones; de Paige Bartles, Ellen Beck y Elizabeth Smith de Promoción; de Amy Chen y Jen Falk de Comunicaciones y Contenido; y de Lisa Dent y Chris Conti de Programas Públicos. Un agradecimiento especial a Bob Faust por diseñar el libro y a nuestros socios editoriales, X Artists' Books.

Las generosas personas que nos apoyan son fundamentales para cualquier institución cultural, sin ellos no sería posible organizar una exposición de esta magnitud y ambición. Es evidente, pero hace falta decirlo: los recursos destinados al arte y la cultura garantizan que las alternativas audaces se oxigenen y puedan levantar vuelo. Por eso, gracias a la Henry Luce Foundation, la Terra Foundation for American Art, la Ford Foundation, la Jacques & Natasha Gelman Foundation, Judy y Charles Tate, el Fondo Nacional para las Artes, la Andy Warhol Foundation for the Visual Arts, Beverly and Howard Robinson, Nicole Deller y Matt Bliwise, Lisa Rich y John McLaughlin, Meridee Moore, el Weingarten Art Group Fund, y Ric y Tina Whitney.

Sobre todo, mi profunda gratitud a Vincent Valdez, cuyo arte expansivo nos llama a examinar los hechos esenciales y las falsedades de las historias injustas de Estados Unidos, junto a los sueños sin cumplir que se persiguen continuamente para que, a través de su obra, podamos acelerar nuestro viaje hacia nuevos futuros.

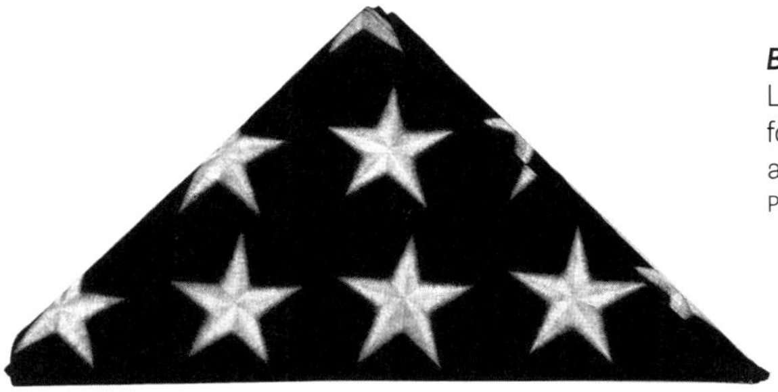

***Black Flag*, 2012**
Lithographic crayon on folded canvas, pedestal, and lucite vitrine
Photo: David Shelton Gallery

Foreword

HESSE MCGRAW
EXECUTIVE DIRECTOR, CAMH

Vincent Valdez's survey exhibition, *Just a Dream...*, is the exceedingly rare presentation that implants itself into one's memory as a marker of how to understand our world. I believe it was in my first week at CAMH, in January 2020, when our curator Patricia Restrepo shared her dream of organizing the first survey of the work of this Houston-based artist. Patricia imparted her vision with bright-eyed enthusiasm and articulated the importance of this project for both Vincent and CAMH. I left that meeting, just a few weeks shy of COVID's onset, feeling buoyed by this museum's unique ability to elevate artists who help us clearly see our past while envisioning a shared future.

In the years since, I've watched the development of *Just A Dream...* alongside the increased fracturing of our society and have come to understand the extraordinary power of Vincent's work as a brace against divisions. Vincent sees both seemingly intractable fault lines across the American landscape and the possibility for common ground, crystallized through images such as a sun rising above a pile of rubble. His work directly confronts complex realities and opens new paths to collective hope.

The development of this exhibition accelerated through our partnership with MASS MoCA and particularly the deep knowledge and collaboration of MASS MoCA chief curator Denise Markonish, Patricia's co-curator, whose long-standing dialogue with Vincent added layers of complexity that you'll experience both in this publication and the exhibition. *Just A Dream...* spans twenty-five years of Vincent's work—yes, he produced his first work at twenty-two years of age—and it's also the first time CAMH has devoted the entire Museum, encompassing both the Brown Foundation and Nina and Michael Zilkha Galleries, to the presentation of a single artist.

La exposición retrospectiva *Solo un sueño...* de Vincent Valdez es una presentación sumamente excepcional que se implanta en nuestra memoria como un indicador de la forma en que debemos comprender el mundo. Creo que fue en mi primera semana en el Contemporary Arts Museum Houston (CAMH), en enero de 2020, cuando la curadora Patricia Restrepo compartió su sueño de organizar el primer recorrido por la obra de este artista de Houston. Patricia transmitió su visión con los ojos brillosos de entusiasmo y manifestó con claridad la importancia de este proyecto tanto para Vincent como para el CAMH. Salí de esa reunión, allí por los inicios del COVID, fascinado con la capacidad única de este museo para enaltecer a los y las artistas que nos ayudan a ver con claridad nuestro pasado al tiempo que vislumbramos un futuro compartido.

Desde entonces, he observado el desarrollo de *Solo un sueño...* junto con la fracturación cada vez más grande de nuestra sociedad, y he logrado comprender el extraordinario poder que tiene la obra de Vincent como amalgama contra estas divisiones. Vincent imagina tanto líneas divisorias aparentemente insolubles en el paisaje americano como la posibilidad de un terreno común, y eso se materializa a través de imágenes, como la de un sol naciente sobre una pila de escombros. Su obra confronta de manera directa con realidades complejas y abre nuevos caminos a la esperanza colectiva.

El desarrollo de esta exposición se aceleró gracias a nuestra asociación con el Massachusetts Museum of Contemporary Art (MASS MoCA) y, en particular, gracias al profundo conocimiento y la colaboración de Denise Markonish, jefa de curaduría del MASS MoCA y curadora adjunta con Patricia, cuyo diálogo de largo plazo con Vincent, sumó capas de complejidad que se podrán apreciar tanto en esta publicación como en la muestra. *Solo un sueño...* abarca las obras creadas por Vincent durante veinticinco años —sí, realizó su primera obra a los veintidós años—. Además, es la primera vez que el CAMH dedica el museo entero, incluidas las galerías The Brown Foundation y Nina and Michael Zilkha, a la presentación de un solo artista.

It's important to share the catalytic effect solo exhibitions at CAMH often have – this same venue staged the pivotal launch of many internationally recognized artists, including Nan Goldin, Ernesto Neto, and Julian Schnabel, and similarly served to showcase Houston-based artists such as Trenton Doyle Hancock and Dorothy Hood.

As this is a non-collecting museum, the exhibition is core to our belief in supporting the creation of new work and in bringing it to new audiences. CAMH is not a place that simply presents art; we are a museum where contemporary art *happens*.

CAMH is exceptionally grateful for the support of our Board of Trustees and the sponsors who made this exhibition possible. The Museum also thanks the lenders to this exhibition for sharing their treasured works with all of us.

We thank our MASS MoCA colleagues for their partnership in organizing the exhibition, tour, and publication. Patricia and Denise worked tirelessly over the past few years to assemble a stunning and rich representation of Vincent's work in a dynamic and reflective installation.

Patricia's vision led our exhibitions team—Tim Barkley, Kenya Evans, Marcelina Guerrero, and Jeff Shore—to transform the entirety of CAMH's galleries for this presentation. I'd also like to acknowledge Felice Cleveland, Director of Learning and Engagement, for her essential work in developing the interpretive materials and stewarding an advisory committee to better connect the exhibition's themes with our diverse community. Their work facilitates our audiences' deep engagement with the work on view.

Finally, we are profoundly grateful to Vincent Valdez for entrusting us with this first solo museum survey of his work, enabling CAMH to fulfill our mission of bringing extraordinary, thought-provoking art to Houston audiences and beyond.

Es importante destacar el efecto catalizador que suelen tener las exposiciones individuales del CAMH: este mismo sitio fue escenario del lanzamiento crucial de muchos artistas con reconocimiento internacional, como Nan Goldin, Ernesto Neto y Julian Schnabel, además de que sirvió para promover a artistas de Houston como Trenton Doyle Hancock y Dorothy Hood. Dado que somos un museo sin colección propia, las exposiciones son fundamentales para respaldar nuestra convicción de apoyar la creación de nuevas obras y de acercarlas a nuevas audiencias. El CAMH no es solo un lugar donde se presentan obras de arte, el CAMH es donde el arte contemporáneo sucede.

El CAMH agradece enormemente el apoyo de nuestra Junta Directiva y de los patrocinadores que han hecho posible esta exposición. El Museo también agradece a los prestamistas por compartir sus valiosas obras con todos nosotros.

Agradecemos a nuestros colegas del MASS MoCA por su colaboración en organizar la muestra, la visita guiada y la publicación. Patricia Restrepo y Denise Markonish trabajaron incansablemente durante los últimos años para reunir una representación rica y asombrosa de la obra de Vincent en una instalación cargada de dinamismo y reflexión.

La visión de Patricia llevó a que nuestro equipo de exhibición —Tim Barkley, Kenya Evans, Marcelina Guerrero y Jeff Shore— transformaran todas las galerías del CAMH para esta presentación. También quisiera agradecer a Felice Cleveland, directora de Educación y Participación, por su trabajo esencial en el desarrollo de materiales interpretativos y en la administración de un comité asesor para lograr una mejor conexión entre los temas de la exposición y nuestra diversa comunidad. El trabajo de estas personas posibilita que el público se vincule en profundidad con la obra expuesta.

Finalmente, estamos profundamente agradecidos a Vincent Valdez, por confiar en el CAMH para organizar esta primera retrospectiva individual de su obra en un museo. Esa confianza nos permite cumplir nuestra misión de llevar arte extraordinario y de reflexión al público de Houston y más allá.

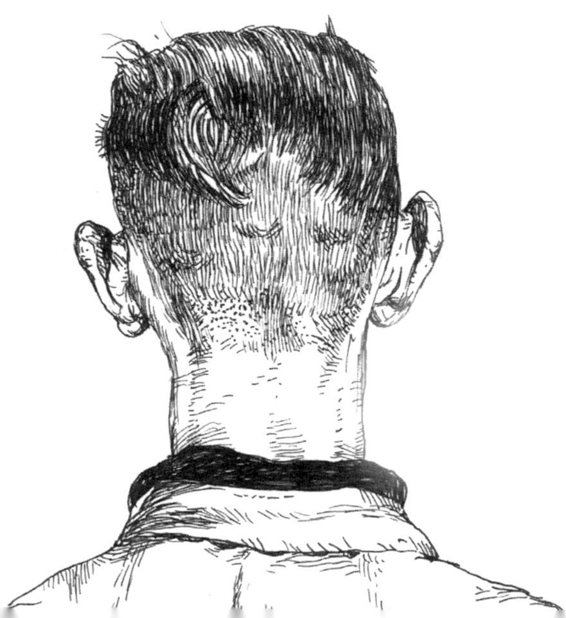

***Berlin series*, 2015**
Ink on paper

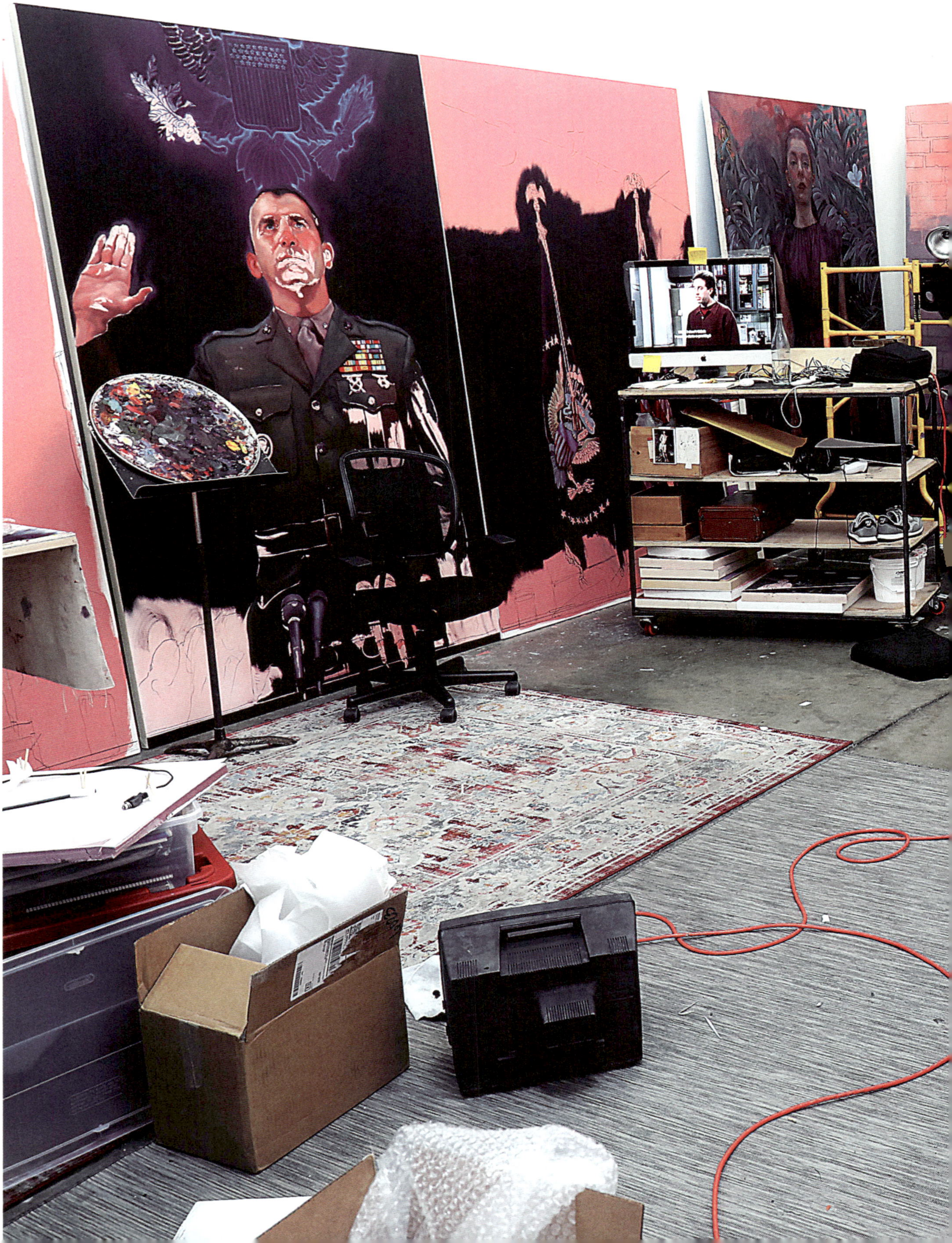

Vincent Valdez studio, Los Angeles, 2024 Photos by Rich Nielsen and Robert LeBlanc

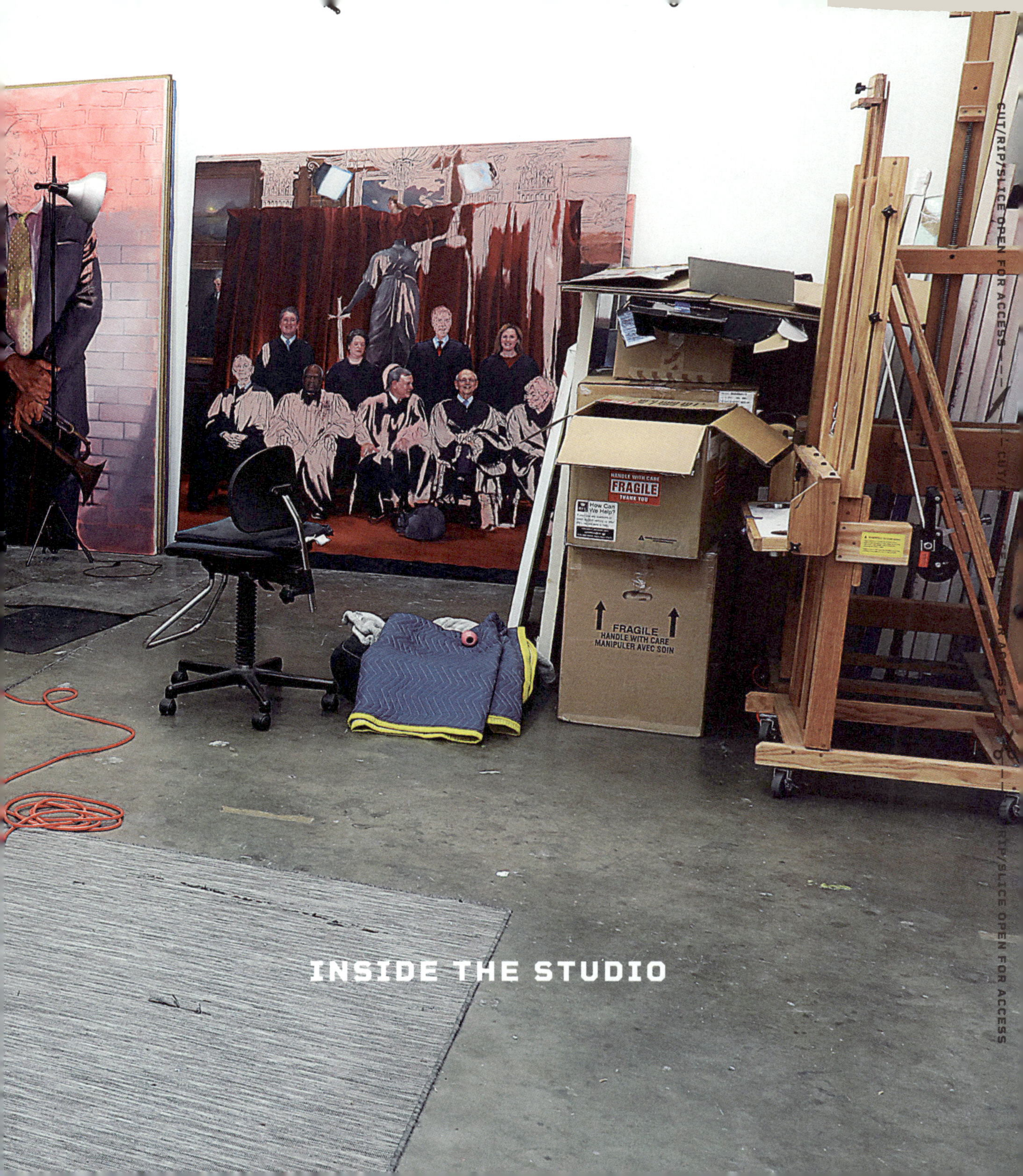

INSIDE THE STUDIO

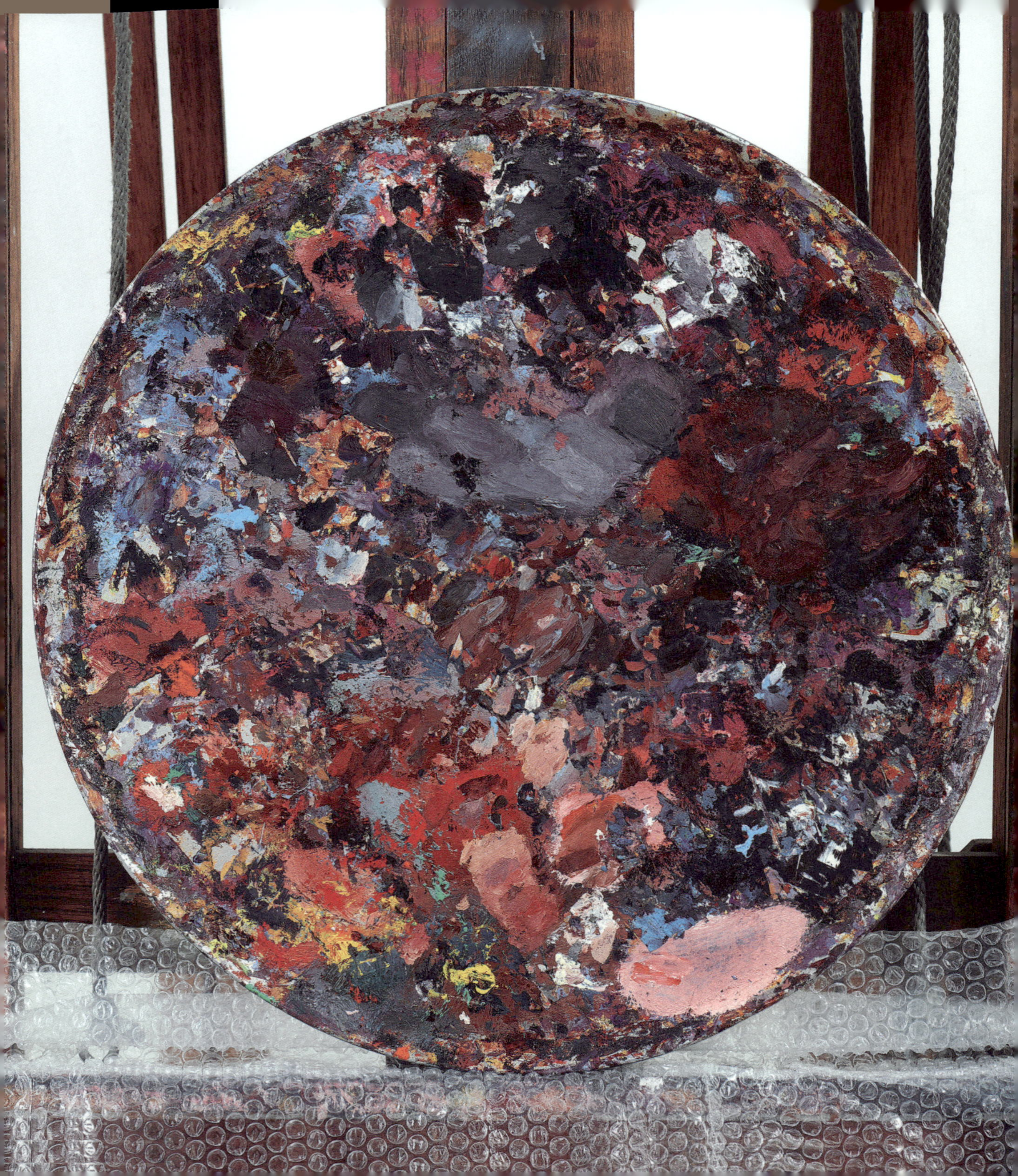

'What do you expect me to see when I look in the mirror? This empty world, like a hastily deserted room with a torn book on the floor, with everything torn . . . What has become of that nineteenth-century universe where we paid in sous and crossed every frontier where we liked and as we liked? It was to no avail to see the clouds on the horizon, to prophesy disaster. Who, living in his own home, could imagine what it would all lead to—the broken doors, the exasperation, those poor objects which we thought were ours? And we stood there, terrified or rebellious, hanging on to those values which we had never questioned, still finding the strength to survive in our old trust.'

LOUIS ARAGON
La Mise à mort

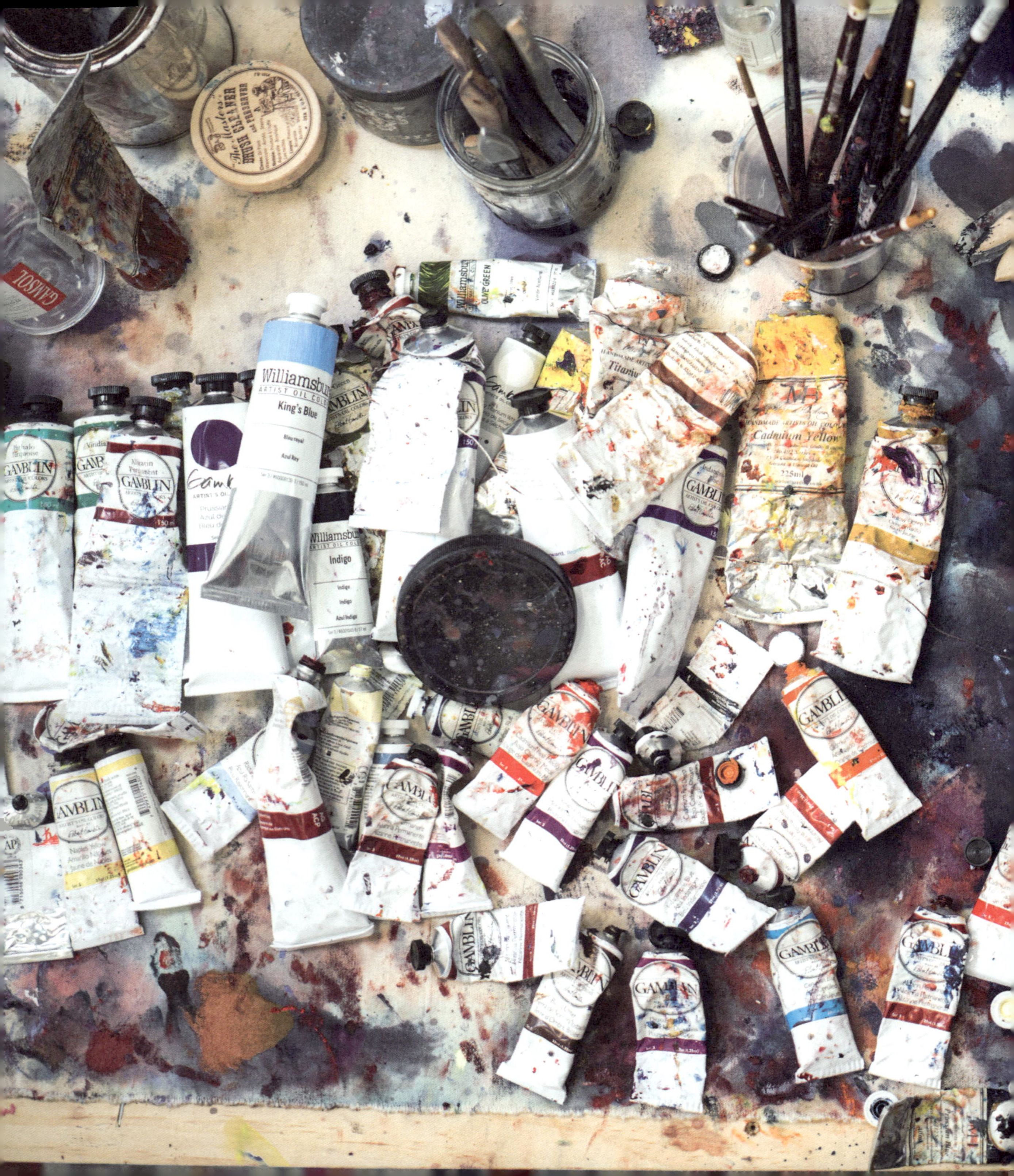

Williamsburg
ARTIST OIL COLORS
King's Blue
Bleu royal
Azul Rey
Williamsburg
Indigo
OLIVE GREEN
GAMBLIN
Cadmium Yellow
225ml
GAMSOL
The Masters
BRUSH CLEANER

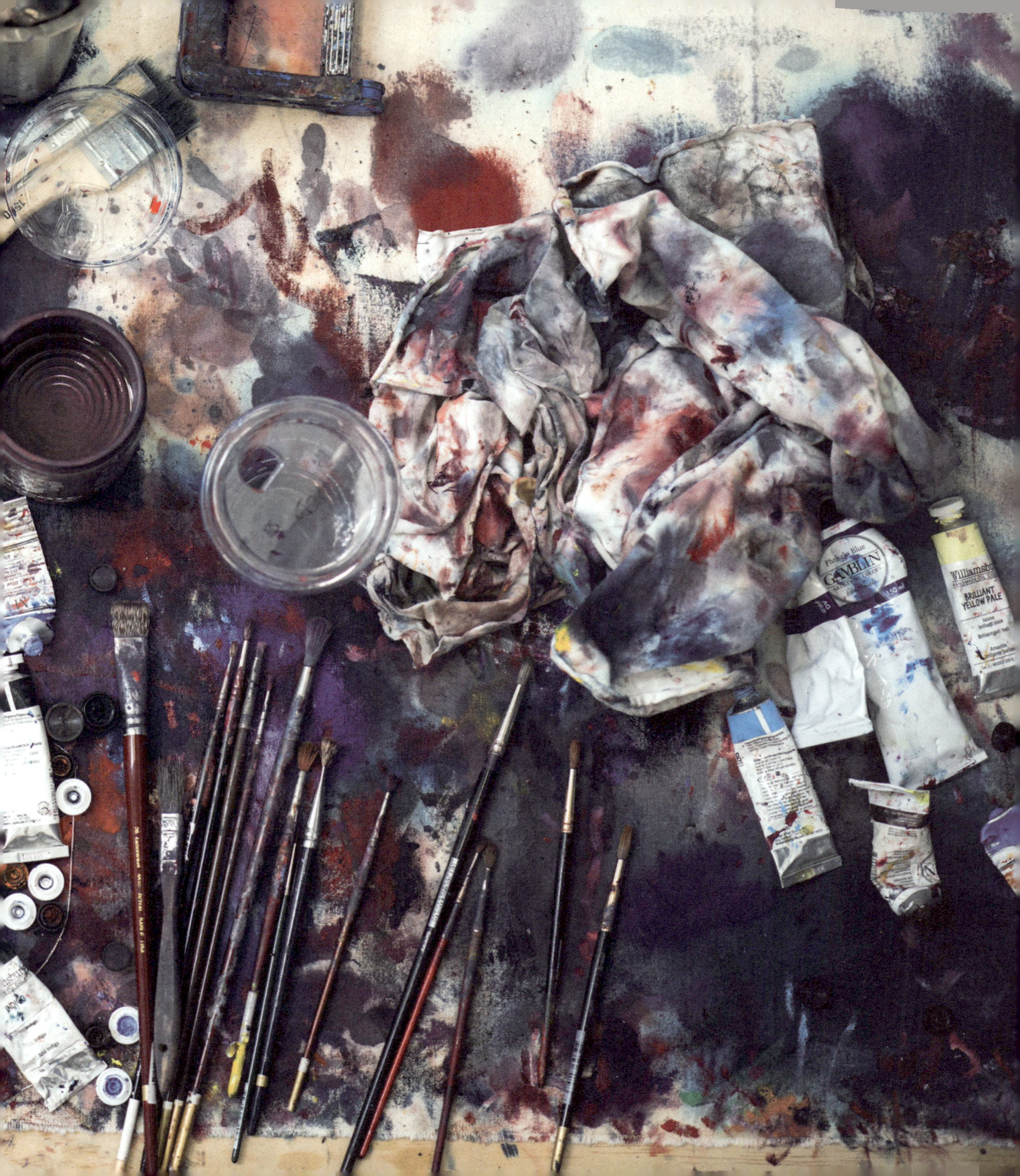
Phthalo Blue
GAMBLIN
BRILLIANT YELLOW PALE

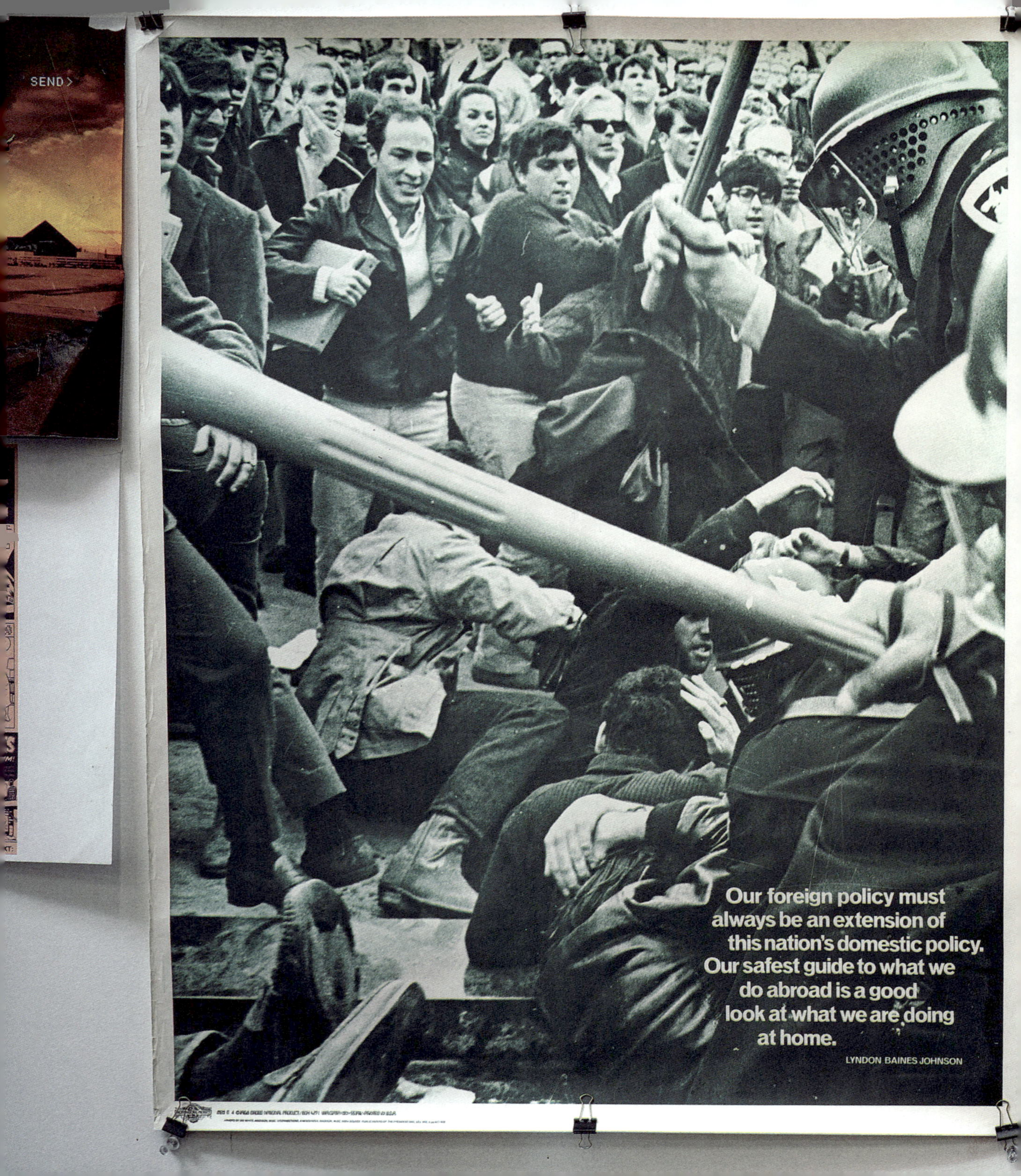
SEND >
Our foreign policy must always be an extension of this nation's domestic policy. Our safest guide to what we do abroad is a good look at what we are doing at home.
LYNDON BAINES JOHNSON

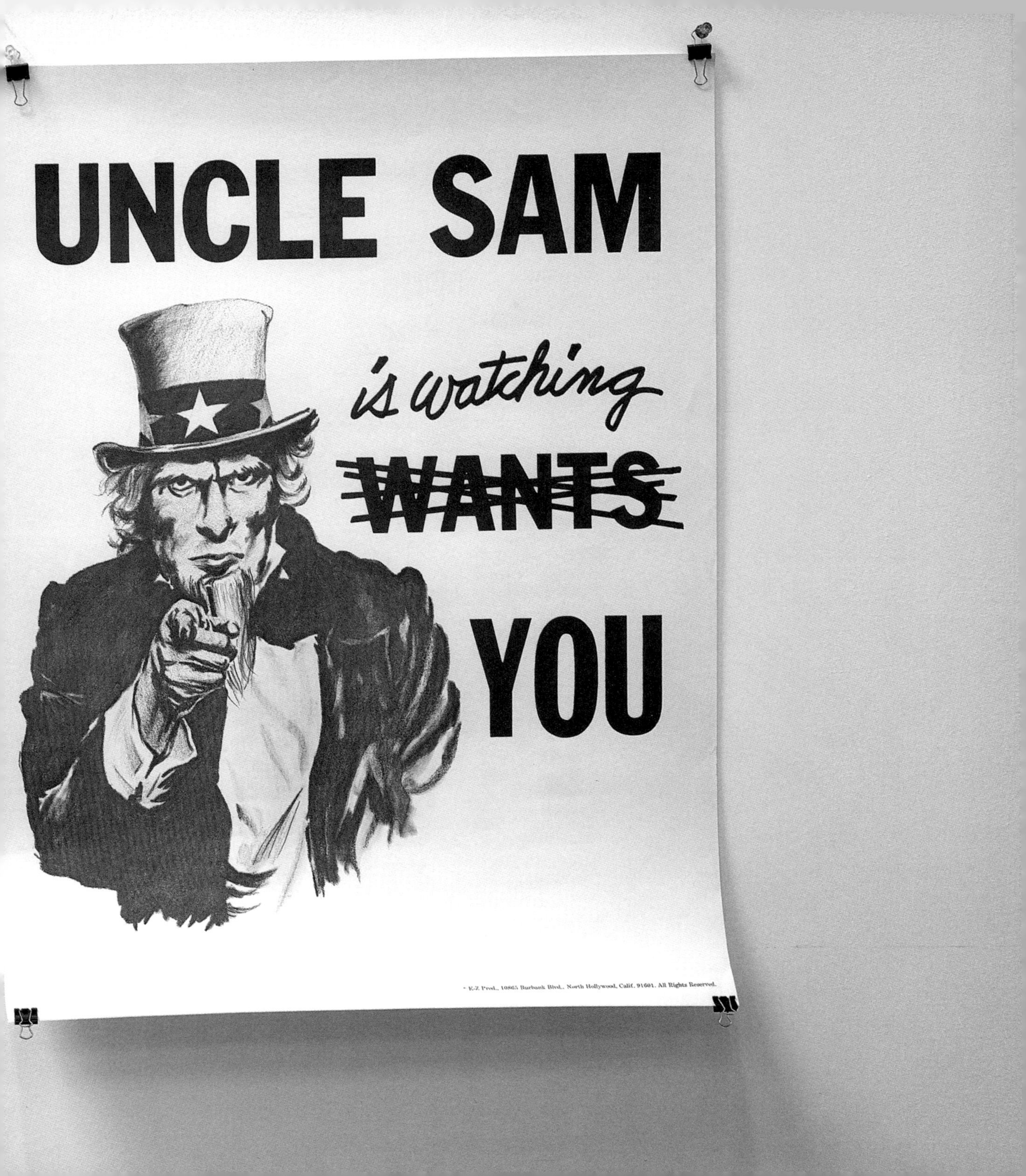
UNCLE SAM
is watching
WANTS
YOU
© E-Z Prod., 10865 Burbank Blvd., North Hollywood, Calif. 91601. All Rights Reserved.

CUT/RIP/SLICE OPEN FOR ACCESS
CUT/RIP/SLICE OPEN FOR ACCESS
CUT/RIP/SLICE OPEN FOR ACCESS
CUT/RIP/SLICE OPEN FOR ACCESS
CUT/RIP/SLICE OPEN FOR ACCESS

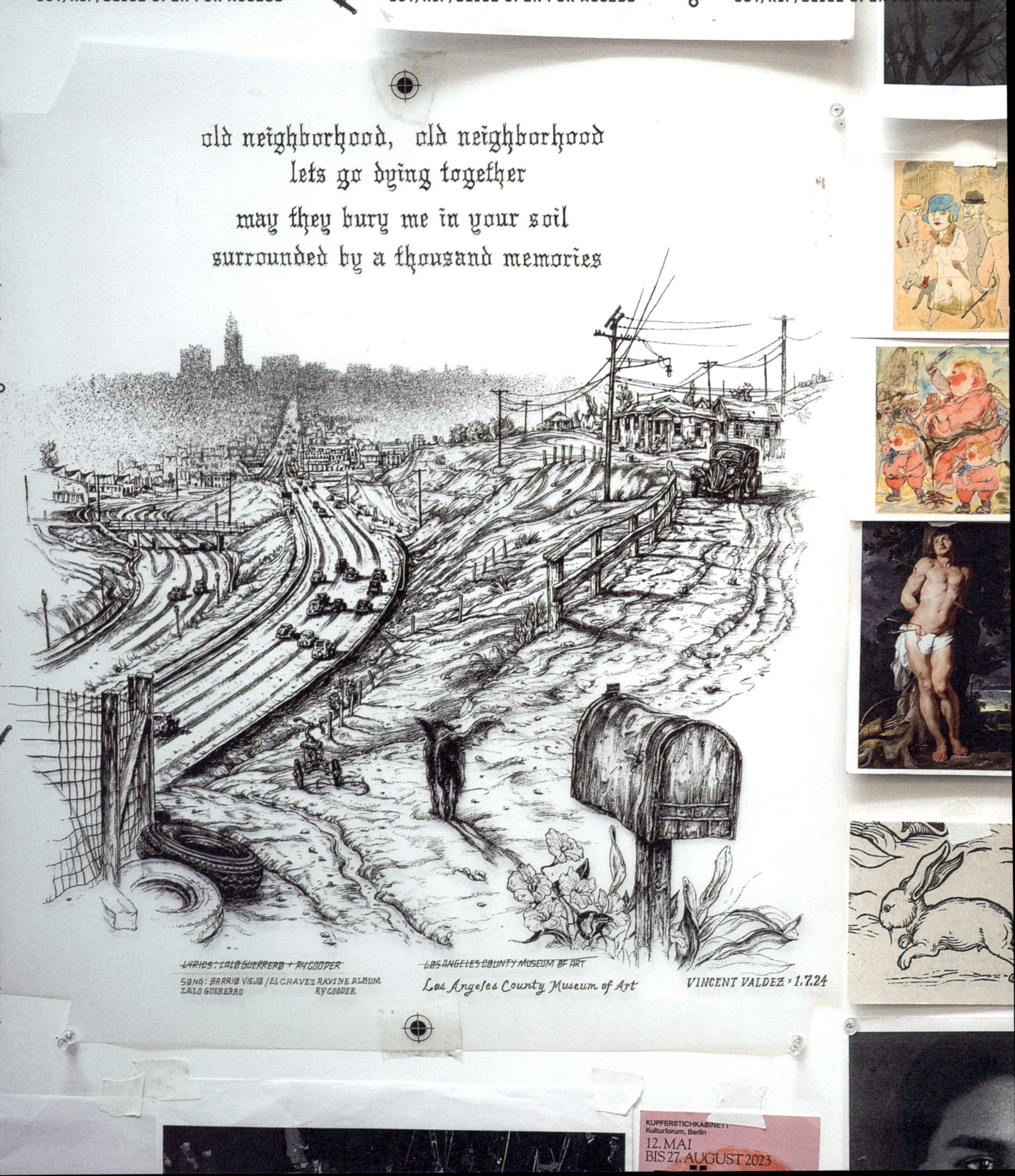

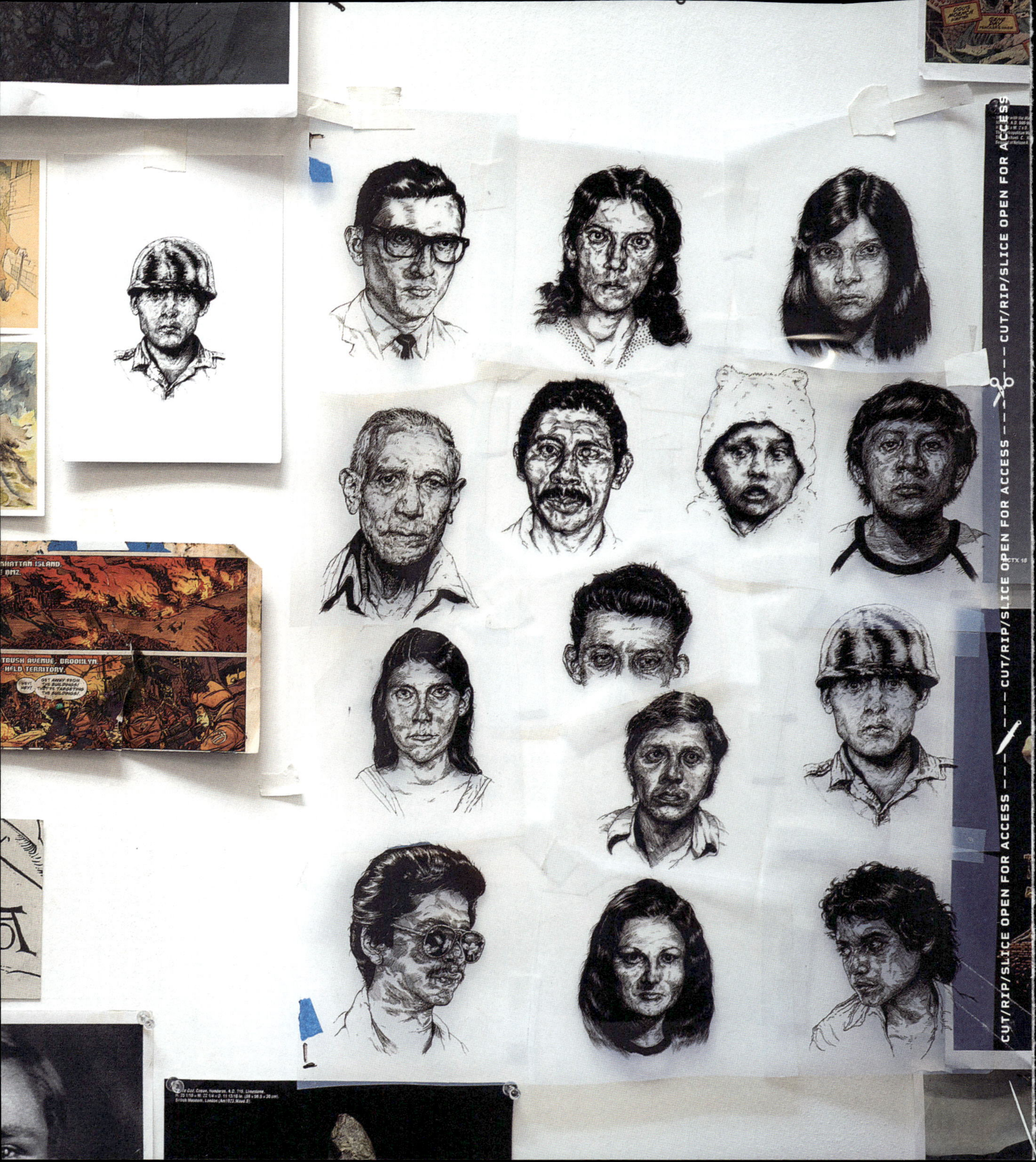
CUT/RIP/SLICE OPEN FOR ACCESS

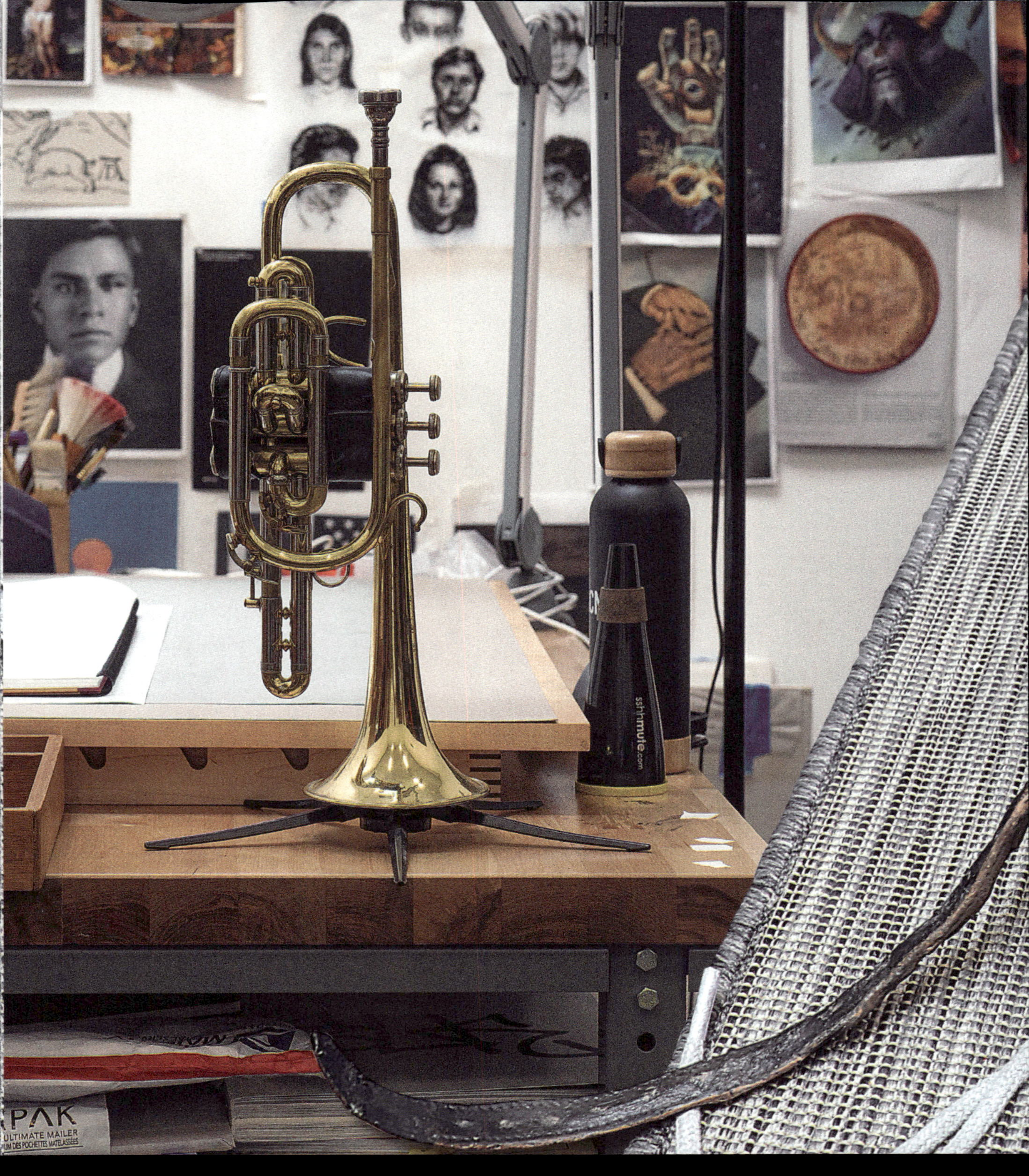
sshhmute.com
PAK
ULTIMATE MAILER

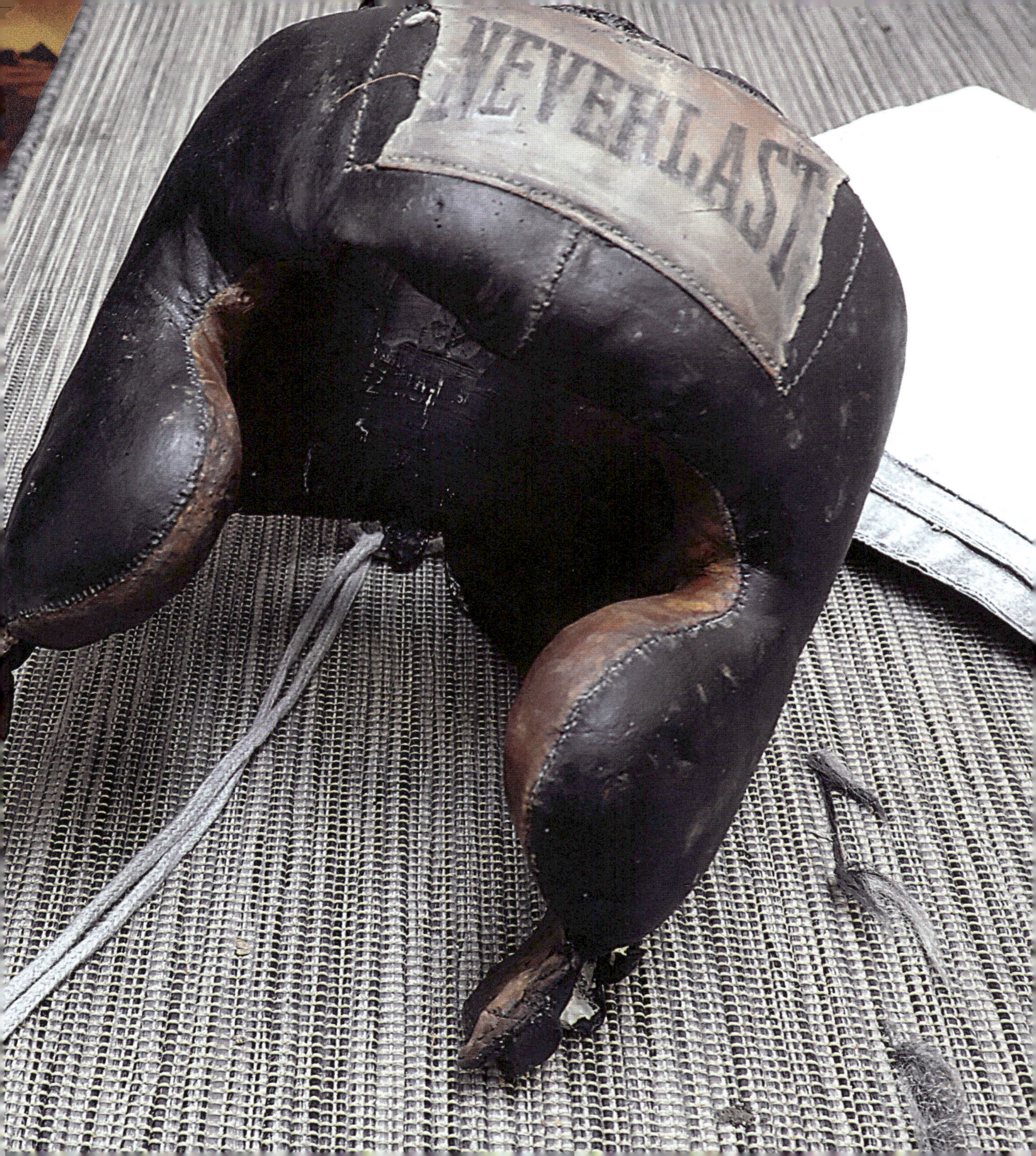
EVERLAST

Lost Angeles

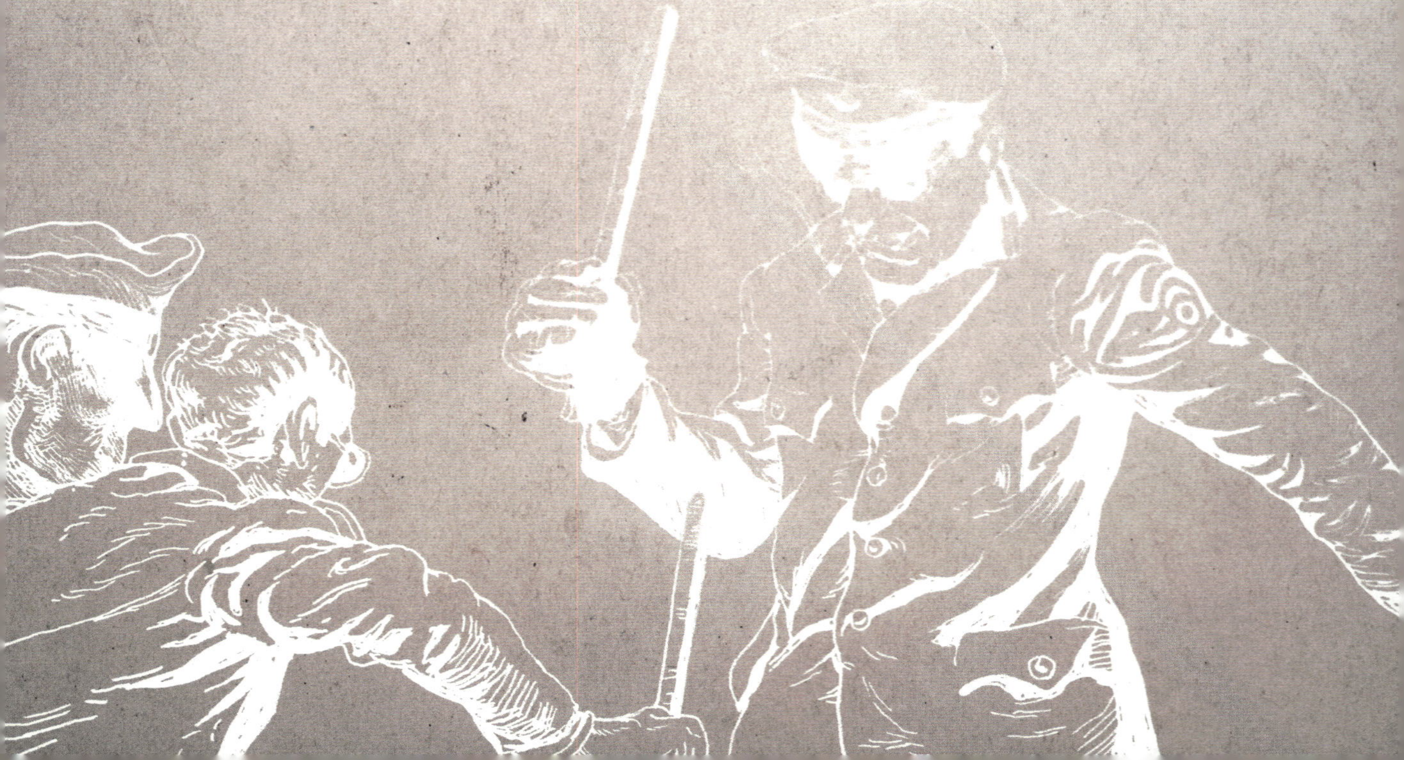

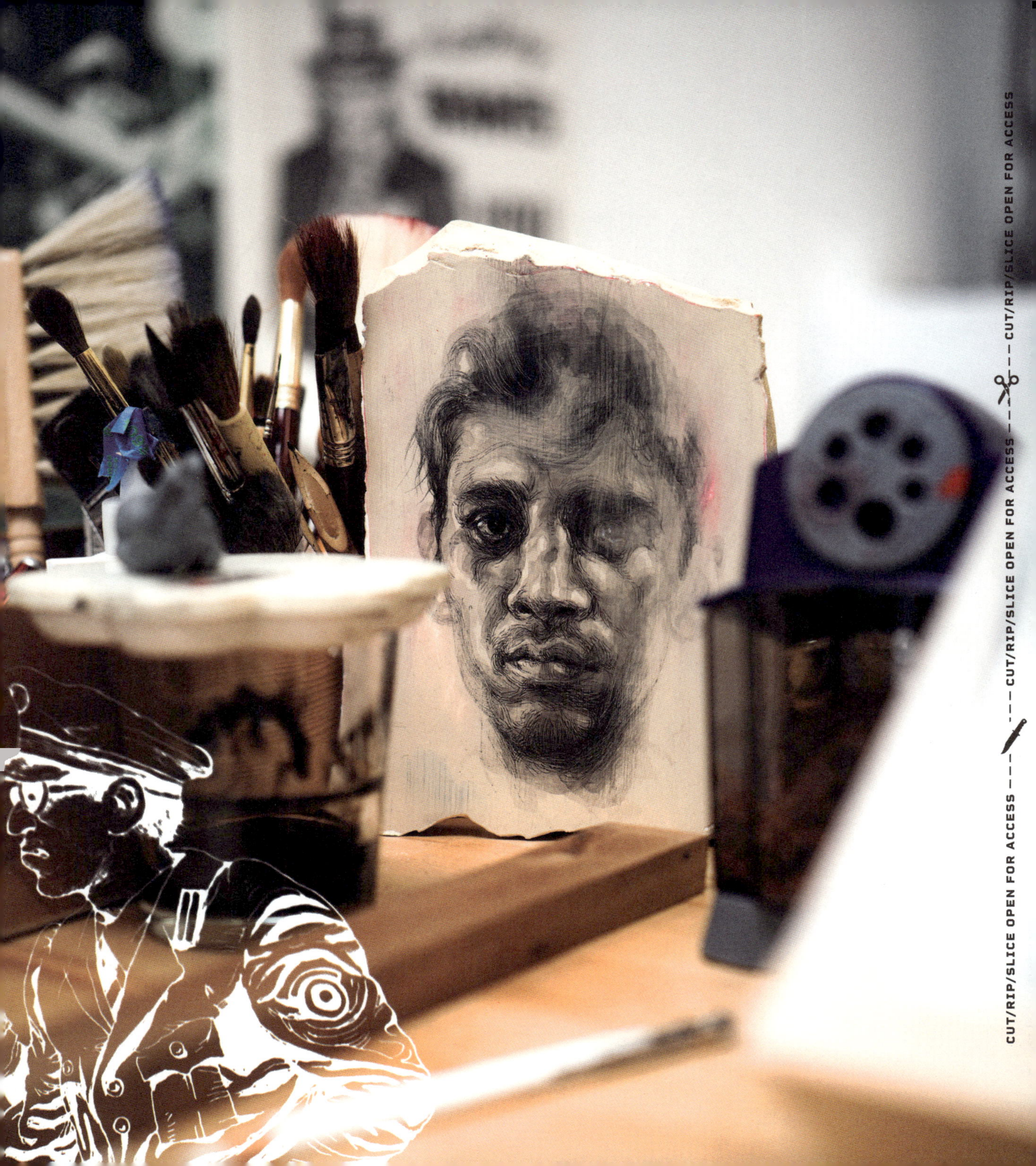
CUT/RIP/SLICE OPEN FOR ACCESS
CUT/RIP/SLICE OPEN FOR ACCESS
CUT/RIP/SLICE OPEN FOR ACCESS

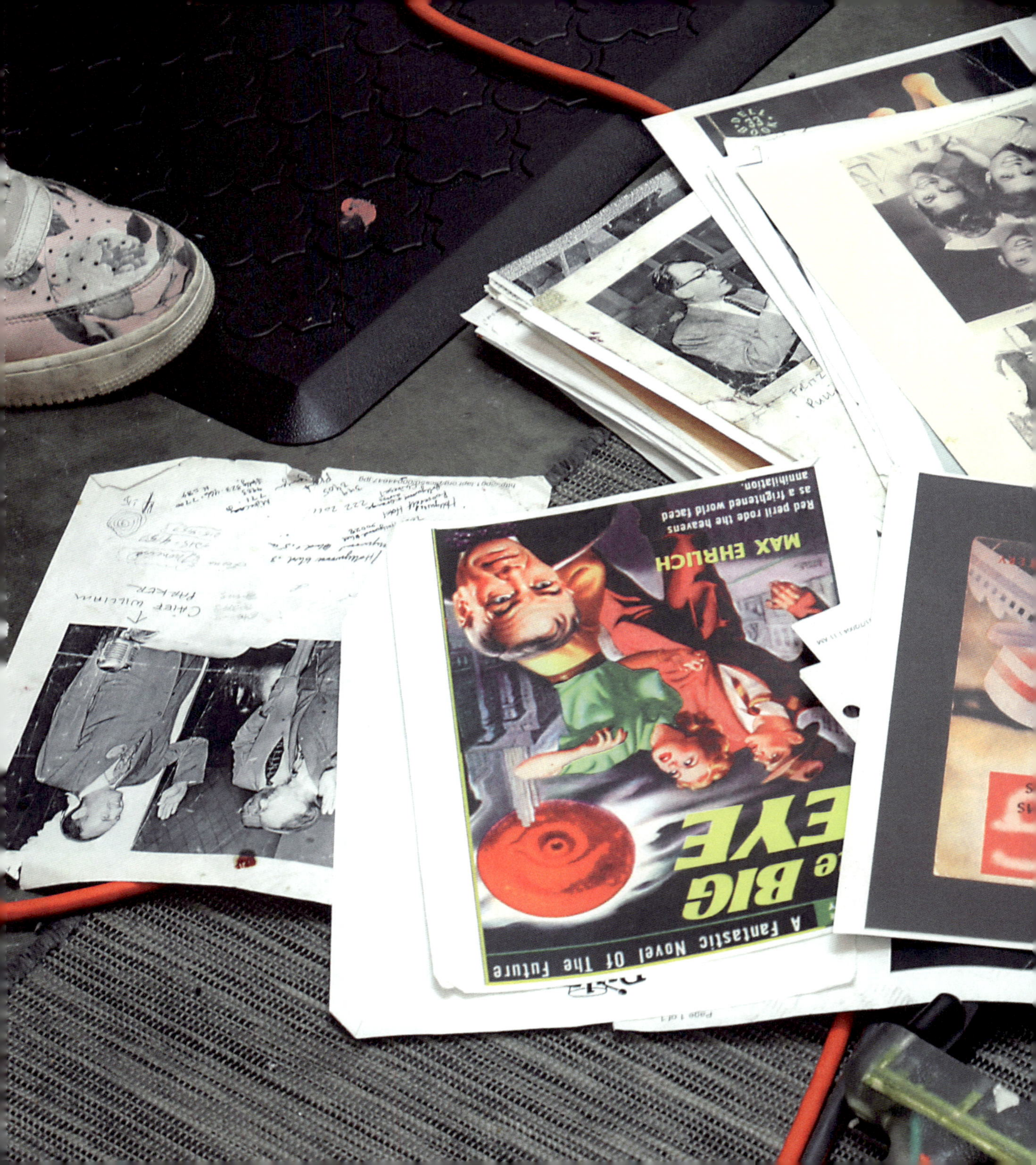
MAX EHRLICH
Red peril rode the heavens
as a frightened world faced
annihilation.
BIG
EYE
A Fantastic Novel of the Future

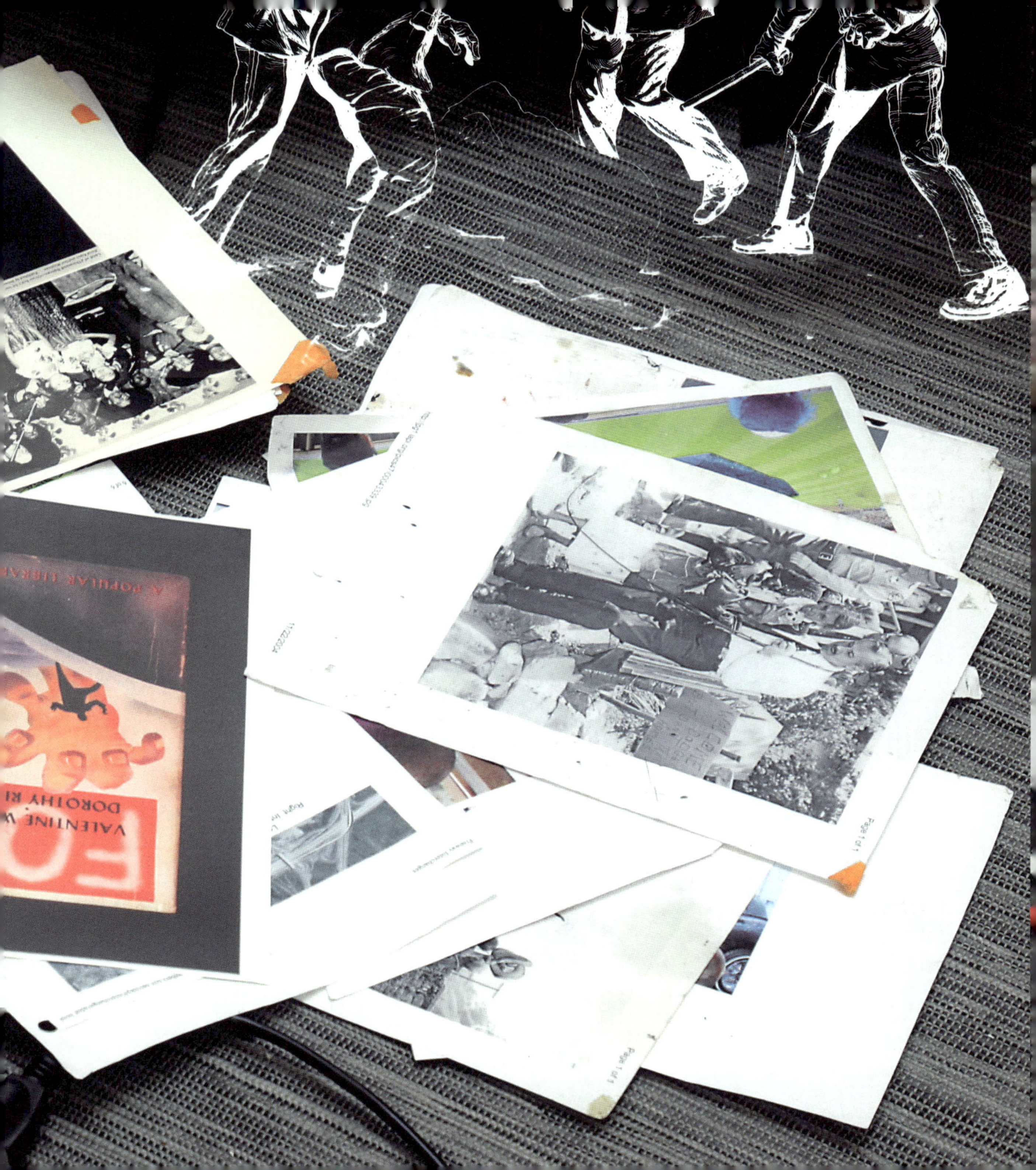

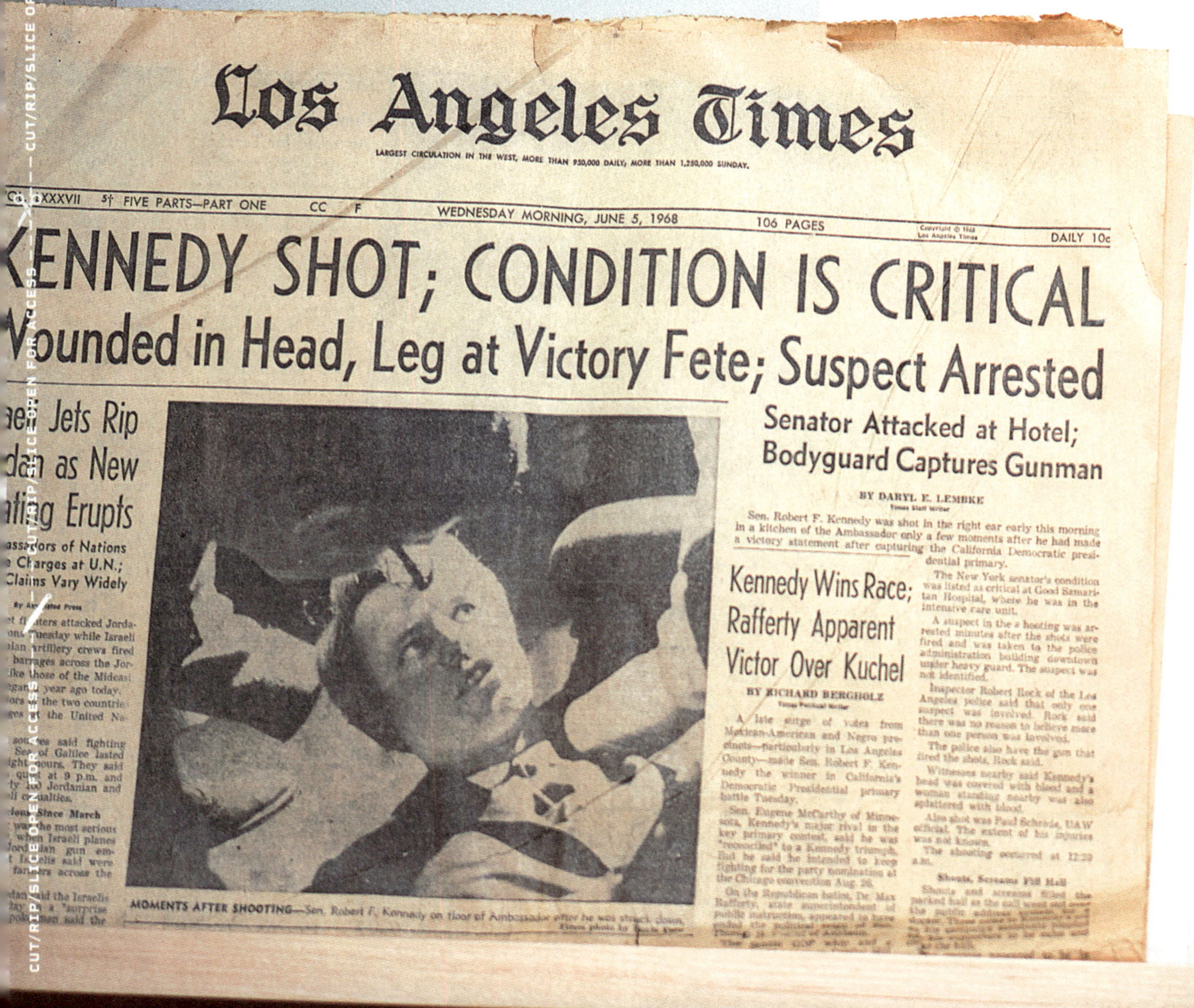

Los Angeles Times

LARGEST CIRCULATION IN THE WEST, MORE THAN 950,000 DAILY; MORE THAN 1,250,000 SUNDAY.

...LXXXVII 5¢ FIVE PARTS—PART ONE CC F WEDNESDAY MORNING, JUNE 5, 1968 106 PAGES Copyright © 1968 Los Angeles Times DAILY 10c

KENNEDY SHOT; CONDITION IS CRITICAL

Wounded in Head, Leg at Victory Fete; Suspect Arrested

...aeli Jets Rip ...dan as New ...ting Erupts

...assadors of Nations ...e Charges at U.N.; ...Claims Vary Widely

By Associated Press

...et fighters attacked Jorda... ...ons Tuesday while Israeli ...nian artillery crews fired ... barrages across the Jor... ...like those of the Mideast ...egan a year ago today. ...ors of the two countries ...ges at the United Na...

...sources said fighting ... Sea of Galilee lasted ...ight hours. They said ... quiet at 9 p.m. and ...ly 100 Jordanian and ...li casualties.

...ious Since March

... was the most serious ... when Israeli planes ...Jordanian gun em... ...t Israelis said were ... farmers across the

...dan said the Israelis ...day in a "surprise ... policeman said the

MOMENTS AFTER SHOOTING—Sen. Robert F. Kennedy on floor of Ambassador after he was struck down. Times photo by Boris Yaro

Senator Attacked at Hotel; Bodyguard Captures Gunman

BY DARYL E. LEMBKE
Times Staff Writer

Sen. Robert F. Kennedy was shot in the right ear early this morning in a kitchen of the Ambassador only a few moments after he had made a victory statement after capturing the California Democratic presidential primary.

The New York senator's condition was listed as critical at Good Samaritan Hospital, where he was in the intensive care unit.

A suspect in the shooting was arrested minutes after the shots were fired and was taken to the police administration building downtown under heavy guard. The suspect was not identified.

Inspector Robert Rock of the Los Angeles police said that only one suspect was involved. Rock said there was no reason to believe more than one person was involved.

The police also have the gun that fired the shots, Rock said.

Witnesses nearby said Kennedy's head was covered with blood and a woman standing nearby was also splattered with blood.

Also shot was Paul Schrade, UAW official. The extent of his injuries was not known.

The shooting occurred at 12:20 a.m.

Shouts, Screams Fill Hall

Shouts and screams filled the packed hall as the call went out over the public address system ...

Kennedy Wins Race; Rafferty Apparent Victor Over Kuchel

BY RICHARD BERGHOLZ
Times Political Writer

A late surge of votes from Mexican-American and Negro precincts—particularly in Los Angeles County—made Sen. Robert F. Kennedy the winner in California's Democratic Presidential primary battle Tuesday.

Sen. Eugene McCarthy of Minnesota, Kennedy's major rival in the key primary contest, said he was "reconciled" to a Kennedy triumph. But he said he intended to keep fighting for the party nomination at the Chicago convention Aug. 26.

On the Republican ballot, Dr. Max Rafferty, state superintendent of public instruction, appeared to have ended the political career of Sen. Thomas H. Kuchel of Anaheim.

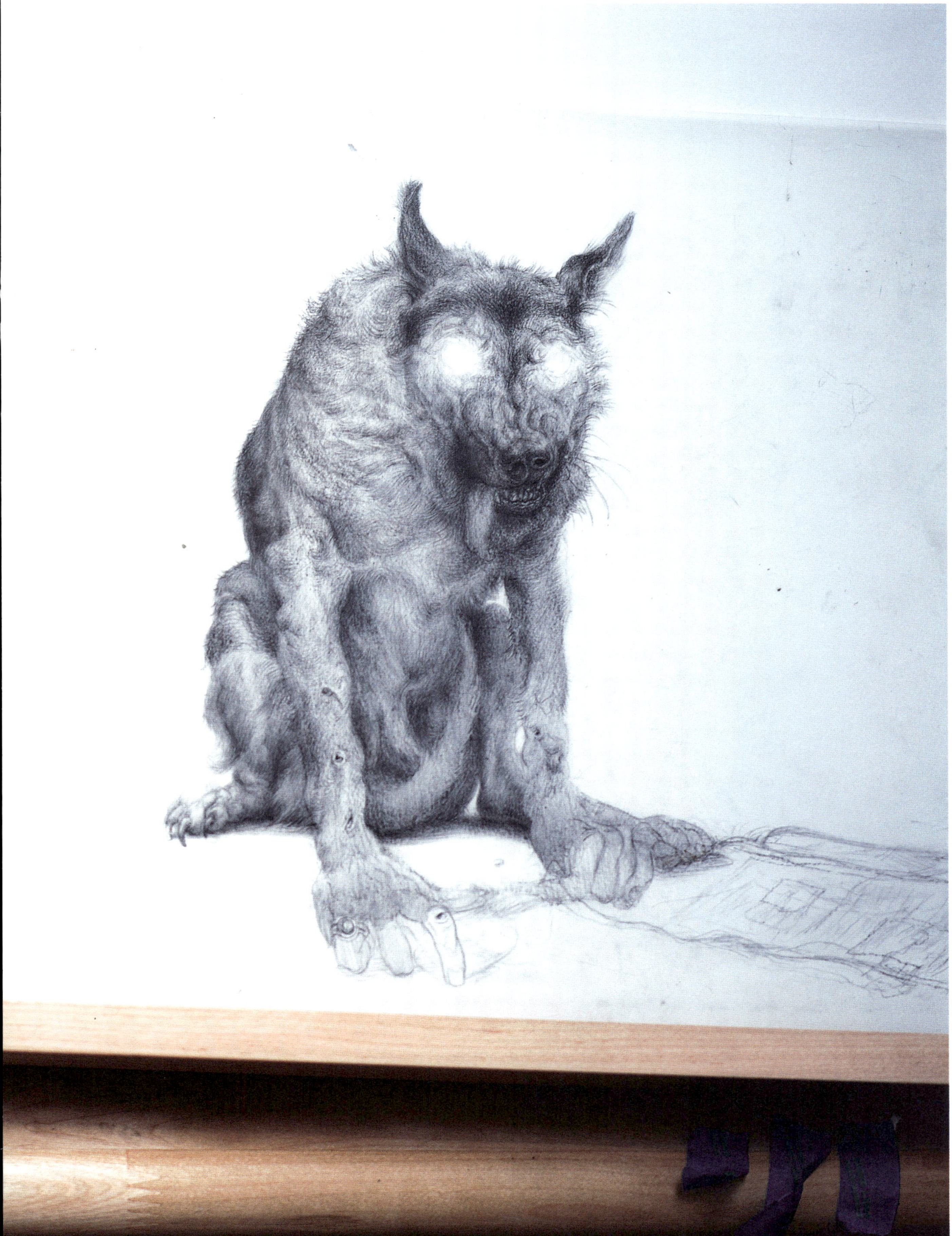

***Requiem I*, 2014**
Graphite on paper
Photo: David Shelton Gallery

"The future is dark, which is on the whole, the best thing the future can be, I think." — VIRGINIA WOOLF[2]

"Only those who still have hope can benefit from tears. When they finish, they feel better. But to those without hope, whose anguish is basic and permanent, no good comes from crying. Nothing changes for them. They usually know this, but still can't help crying." — NATHANAEL WEST[3]

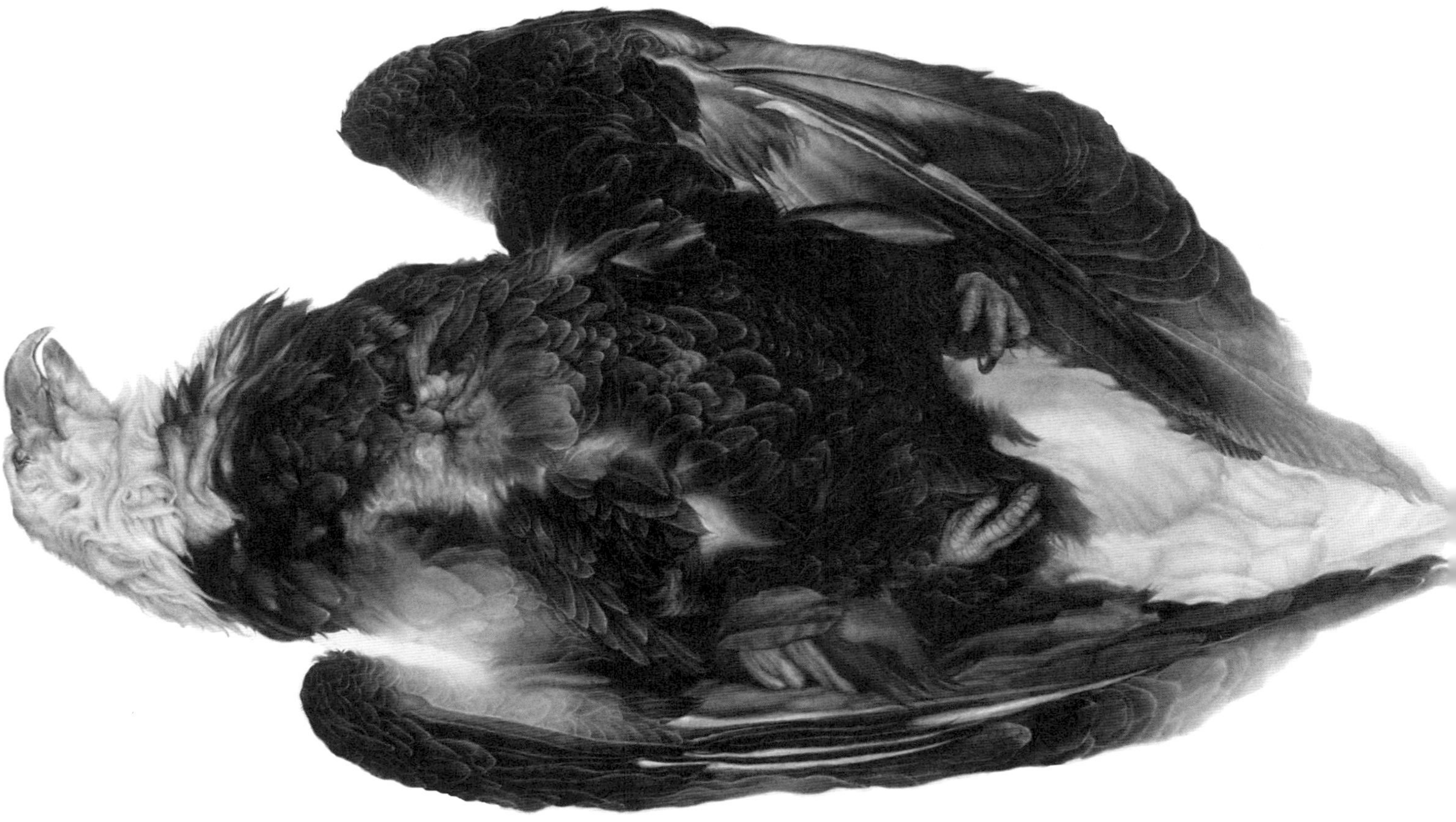

New American Prayer[1]

DENISE MARKONISH

The future felt dark and the tears hot. It was November 9, 2016, a day when many woke to news that would change the course of the United States. I arose that morning in San Antonio, Texas, getting ready to open a trio of exhibitions at Artpace. Falling asleep the night prior, I thought, "Maybe it will be OK?" When I looked at my phone at 3 a.m., I realized that was far from the truth. So, bleary eyed, weepy, and generally befuddled, I made my way to Vincent Valdez's studio. I had met his partner Adriana Corral (an amazing artist in her own right) a year before, and when I showed up at the converted fire station where they lived and worked, the first thing I saw was a large drawing lying on the floor. Rendered in black and white, the image that confronted me was of a supine American Bald Eagle, lifeless, yet with its downy feathers still somehow animated, as if it had just taken its last breath. Luckily it was framed, or the tears that formed in my eyes would have stained its surface.

Seeing *this* drawing at *that* time felt as if Vincent had pulled off a tremendous illusion. To present, after a tragic election, an image of our country vulnerable and dying, seemed almost too much to bear. Over the ensuing years Vincent and I have become great co-conspirators, friends, and colleagues, which is why, in this essay, you will unusually see a shift from the personal "Vincent" to the professional "Valdez." This encompasses the deeply entwined ways in which artists and curators exist in each other's lives.

Titled *Requiem*, after rites meant to honor the dead, the image endures nearly eight years later. In 2019, I invited Vincent and Adriana to present a new version of this piece for the MASS MoCA exhibition *Suffering from Realness*. For this iteration, the eagle was cast in bronze with a soot-black patina made from the ashes of burned papers. The papers once contained stories the two artists collected from 243 Americans (the number references the age of the American Republic that year). The contributors included artists, prison inmates, activists, teachers, homeless, immigration attorneys, social workers, environmentalists, musicians, industry workers, nannies, bus drivers, immigrants, healers, store cashiers, Buddhists, journalists, civil workers, nurses, historians, yard workers, custodians, human rights attorneys, soldiers, etc. Each entry contained a date and description of a personal and/or historically significant moment, creating a people's history of America. The eagle itself was carried through the galleries in a procession before being laid to rest in front of a wall into which Adriana had painstakingly carved these dates. There was total silence in the room, except for a mournful dirge played by South Texas–area musicians, with Vincent on trumpet.

THE WITNESS

"But how does one bear witness to a world that goes to its ruin with blindfolded eyes and its face covered, a republic that collapses without lucidity or pride, in fear and abjection? The blindness is all the more desperate, for the doomed believe they can steer their own wreck, swear that everything can be kept under control technically, that there is no need for a new god or a new heaven—merely prohibitions, experts and doctors. Panic and deceit." – GIORGIO AGAMBEN[4]

This eerie conjuring of the mood of the moment led me to believe Vincent must be a magical seer, since the drawing wasn't completed that morning, and had already been in the works well before things collapsed. However, there is nothing supernatural about Vincent. Rather, he just witnesses the world, isn't afraid to peel back the veil, to pay deep attention, and to understand that history happens the moment we capture it. He knows that the past is a ghost that haunts us in the present. He states, "I am an observer. I bear witness. I am committed to putting it down on record. To testify. I choose to confront the world as opposed to turning away from it."[5]

Like the Four Horsemen of the Apocalypse, Vincent reveals what we know to be true: it is hard to find hope in a world on fire. But, at the same time, we must strive to contend with, and image, that which seems too painful to talk about, let alone reckon with.

There is a bravery in laying the world bare, in telling us we must not look away. Susan Sontag frequently spoke of this urge to see the truth. First, in *Regarding the Pain of Others*, she writes, "Let the atrocious images haunt us. Even if they are only tokens, we cannot possibly encompass most of the reality to which they refer, they still perform a vital function. The images say: This is what human beings are capable of doing—may volunteer to do, enthusiastically, self-righteously. Don't forget."[6] This compulsion to look toward rather than away is what makes Vincent the artist most adept at imagining his time. Like Goya before him—whom Sontag discusses in this book—he does not shrink away from horror; he unveils it plain as day so we, too, cannot avoid it. To use painting as his message board is complex, since the medium is essentially mute, but Vincent knows it speaks without words, with a silence that is deafening. In *The Aesthetics of Silence* Sontag addresses this need for art that can be silent, writing, "Traditional art invites a look. Art that is silent engenders a stare." Sontag goes on to state that "a stare is perhaps as far from history, as close to eternity, as contemporary art can get."[7] This call for silence is also a call to arrest time, providing the opportunity to witness. It is the chance to see the downy feathers of the eagle belly up and wonder how we got to this place and where we might go next.

What's remarkable – and unsettling – is that even as a child Vincent understood his responsibility to see for a world that frequently remains blind. He started his art career young—as a video dating from 1987 illustrates—always drawing and even getting in trouble at school for doing other kids' art-related homework assignments. When Vincent was nine years old he participated in a mural project run by Alex Rubio, a public artist and arts mentor also based in San Antonio. Rubio quickly realized that Vincent wasn't like the other kids and soon the young artist was painting alongside his mentor. In the video, a local news station interviews kids working on the original school-sponsored mural. The reporter listens to one girl describe painting idyllic scenes of flowers, harmonious homes, pets, butterflies, etc.—you know, standard ten-year-old fare. Then the reporter comes upon Vincent, who is painting the following scene: a field of workers harvesting crops as American fighter jets swoop overhead, with a text reading "Make food not war," all set against a sky that looks like the aftermath of nuclear fallout. He looks straight at her and says, "In the future will there be any animals left, any flowers or air left to breathe? Will I still be around?" You can see the reporter recoil and quickly look around for some kid painting a puppy in a desperate attempt to save her story and her soul. But what she didn't see in Vincent is that he wasn't referencing complete annihilation, but, rather, he wanted to warn us to not be complacent, because we face an uncertain future.

With this uncertainty, Vincent provides us with a new American prayer, not one based in religion but one of cautious optimism, one that reveals the truths history has obscured. What does it mean to pray for something you are not sure you believe in? Do like-minded people who are sick and tired and grieving exist? Do we see each other's eyes across the room—slightly red? Do our compatriots return our call and assure us that we are not alone? Do we confirm for one another that, as Langston Hughes wrote, "O, yes, I say it plain, America never was America to me, And yet I swear this oath—America will be!"[8] It is in this place, and this place only, the place of this prayer, the place of belief despite the odds, where paintings of both soldiers and puppies coexist, and must. This spotlight on ambiguity and bleakness, mixed with hope, is what makes Vincent's work so human, and, dare I say, hopeful, because it reminds us that we are still alive and must push through the debris of the mushroom cloud.

THE FIGHT

"Celebrating while still fighting, which is perhaps what represents the ethos of this country more than anything else. To bear witness to so much death that could easily be your own is to push towards redefining 'country,' until it becomes a place where there is both pride AND safety.... And so a community nurtures more of its own, but does not forget to celebrate, and does not forget to sing." – HANIF ABDURRAQIB[9]

It is no surprise that this fight is frequently portrayed by Valdez via the image of boxers. In *On Boxing*, Joyce Carol Oates writes about the sport as a metaphor for humanity. She states, "Considered in the abstract the boxing ring is an altar of sorts, one of those legendary spaces where the laws of a nation are suspended: inside the ropes, during an officially regulated three-minute round, a man may be killed at his opponent's hands but he cannot be legally murdered. Boxing inhabits a sacred space predating civilization; or, to use D. H. Lawrence's phrase, before God was love. If it suggests a savage ceremony or a rite of atonement it also suggests the futility of such gestures. For what possible atonement is the fight waged if it must shortly be waged again . . . and again? The boxing match is the very image, the more terrifying for being so stylized, of mankind's collective aggression; its ongoing historical madness."[10] Here we are at a site of worship again, but one that mimics the world through its endless cycle of real and performed violence. From 2001 to 2004, Valdez created the series *Stations*, chronicling the last bout of a boxer, his hopes, dreams, and possibilities, but also the ultimate end of his reality. The thirteen large-scale charcoal drawings refer to the Stations of the Cross, the traditional image cycle of Jesus Christ on the day of the crucifixion. The Stations have been depicted throughout art history, by everyone from Giotto to Picasso, but the version that resonates most in relation to Valdez is Barnett Newman's take on the subject, created from 1958 to 1966. Newman's paintings are starkly black and white, with his signature zips of paint down the canvases. The palette is akin to Valdez's charcoals, but so is Newman's abstraction of the subject, which for the artist is a meditation on humanity and a memorial to the victims of the Holocaust, just as Valdez focuses on the symbol of boxing as a struggle for dignity and survival.

In Valdez's *Stations*, just as Oates notes, the boxing ring is the stage, as we cycle through images that go from excitement to defeat, and finally despair. *Stations: The Strongest Man in the World is He Who Walks Alone* shows our protagonist entering the arena, robe hood over his head and game face on. He is the underdog, yet he walks past his opponent's adoring fans without noticing the cameras in his face. You can almost hear the din of the crowd, as loud as the sound of blood pumping through his head as he gets ready to enter the ring. At this point there is no sign of pending defeat, and like any good fighter he assumes victory. Similarly, *Stations: Main Event* shows our boxer standing tall in the ring and ready to fight. From here the tragedy unfolds. *Stations: A Fine Performance by Our Winning Fighter Tonight* depicts him on the ground, blood spewing from his head, as bystanders attend to him. *Stations: He Then Fell Once More* is an aerial view of defeat: arms and legs splayed out, a ghostly tattoo of Jesus on the boxer's chest. This piece is a precursor to *Stations IX: Laid Out*, in which the boxer lies flat on his back on a gurney (or is it an altar). It is hard to tell if he is alive or dead and Valdez isn't revealing the answer.

Nearly twenty years later, Valdez created *Just a Dream (In America)* (2020–21). The painting images a boxer, sitting on a stool, arms heavy by his side, legs akimbo. His face is badly beaten. This is where Valdez breaks the painting's gray monochrome by adding hints of red around his eyes, knees, and battered face. At his feet is the detrital residue of the event—dollar bills, coins, crushed cans, wads of paper, spilled popcorn, a bucket, etc. It is impossible to tell if we are mid-match or post, but what is clear is that despite his defeated stance and tattered body, his eyes are still open and he has not given up. It is hard not to think of Martin Scorsese's film *Raging Bull* (1980), which follows boxer Jake LaMotta's rise and fall. Valdez's rendering recalls Robert De Niro's pathos-filled portrayal of the aging fighter. Valdez instills his painting with gravitas, for unlike the traditional wall-bound display, the canvas sits on a set of bricks, only pulling the weight of the subject further to the floor. Emanating from behind the painting is a faint soundtrack of Jimmy Clanton's 1958 song "Just a Dream." The 1950s-style lilting lyrics refer to love lost, and take on a larger metaphorical context when paired with Valdez's painting, including the addition of the phrase "In America" to its title. As Clanton sings, "I know that we could never last / We just can't seem to in the past /Just a dream I dream in vain / With you I'd only live in pain"[11] it is clear that Valdez isn't speaking of love, or even boxing, but rather of the shattered dream of America, defeated, but not quite ready to give up. For as Oates observes: "The boxers make visible what is invisible in us, thereby defining us, and themselves, in a single consecrated action."[12]

Valdez's boxers represent a different kind of masculinity, one worn down and vulnerable. This anti-heroism is evident in the portrait *John* (2010–12). 2nd Lt. John R. Holt Jr., was Valdez's best friend, who, after serving as a combat medic in Iraq, lost a battle with post-traumatic stress disorder (PTSD) in 2009. Valdez's life-size painting shows John on the battlefield amid a shroud of smoke and debris. Unlike most images of war, John looks simultaneously scared and vacant, as if we are seeing him see himself in a nightmare. There is no glory here, especially when the painting is paired with *Excerpts for John* (2012), a series of intimately scaled oil paintings showing the unfolding sequence of a military funeral procession. The flag-draped coffin is the only clear image, while everything else dissolves in a haze. These drawings are about absence, about the shrouding of not just the casket but the brutal realities of war and PTSD. Of the series, Valdez writes, "The muted, dissolving, hallucinatory effects of these paintings are my attempt to translate what I experienced on that morning of his funeral. I was numb from the freezing rain and by a feeling of emotional surrender."[13]

The fading edges in *Excerpts for John* are a stylistic choice that runs through much of Valdez's work. The softness blurs figure and ground, like merging memory and reality. This comes to the forefront in his *Amnesia* drawings (2023–ongoing). Often rendered in pencil of a single color on paper (but sometimes red and blue together), these drawings feature figures who are barely there, and lines both precise and fading. Faces are rendered just enough before they fade into the paper. Bodies are barely there, as if the subjects are disappearing before our eyes. It's like the scene in *Back to the Future* (1985) when Michael J. Fox's Marty McFly plays guitar at the prom after traveling back in time to when his parents met. At risk of negatively affecting the future, McFly's hands begin to go ghost-like as he performs Chuck Berry's "Johnny B. Goode." He needs to get back to his own time before he vanishes. In her book *Hope in the Dark* (2004), Rebecca Solnit writes about the power of amnesia, stating, "The other affliction amnesia brings is a lack of examples of positive change, of popular power, evidence that we can do it and have done it." Solnit then quotes George Orwell's famous insight from *Nineteen Eighty-Four*, (1949), "Who controls the past controls the future. Who controls the present controls the past." Solnit continues, "Controlling the past begins by knowing it; the stories we tell about who we were and what we did shape what we can and will do."[14] And like McFly's hands, and Valdez's portraits, we can almost will the fading humans back to wholeness, rescuing them from disappearance by allowing them to tell their stories, as Valdez did for John.

Just as we cannot truly understand the effects of war without experiencing it, the same goes for the nuances of personal experience. To get us closer to that understanding, Valdez infuses a beautiful empathy into his portraits of the often misunderstood: the boxer is not a brute, he is fallible; the war hero is haunted; and the gang member is gentle and contemplative. *So Long, Mary Ann* (2019) shows an anonymous figure, shirtless from the waist up. He is covered in tattoos—arms, chest, face, shaven head—yet there is a gentle quality to him. His hands are clasped in front of him and he looks toward us with sympathetic eyes, standing before a perfect sunset fade of blue, pink, and purple. He glows, like a Vermeer subject, in a moment of internal reflection. Looking closely at the painting we see scars on his chest and the name "Mary Ann" tattooed across his knuckles, conjuring the 1967 Leonard Cohen song from which the painting borrows its title. In the song, Cohen sings of lost love, stating, "For now I need your hidden love I'm cold as a new razor blade / You left when I told you I was curious / I never said that I was brave / Oh so long, Marianne, it's time that we began / To laugh and cry and cry and laugh about it all again."[15] You can almost hear the refrain swirling in the head of Valdez's subject, and while we may not know his story, we do know what loss and heartbreak feel like, bringing him closer to us and us closer to empathy.

The Angustain family are evicted from their home in Chavez Ravine, Los Angeles, May 9, 1959
Los Angeles Times Photographic Archive, UCLA Library Special Collections

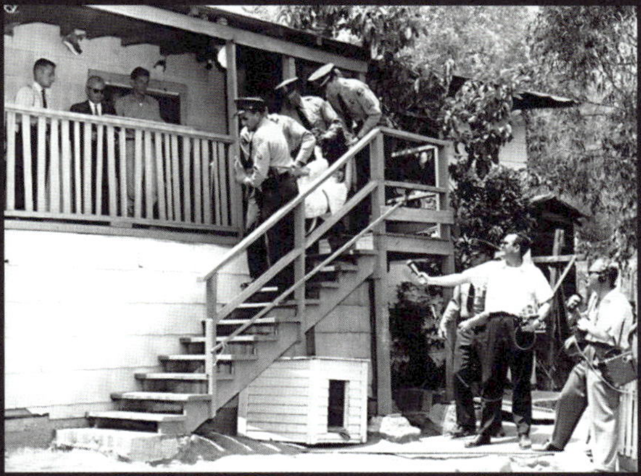

Valdez's grandfather, Arthur, and great-uncle, Ernest, during WWII

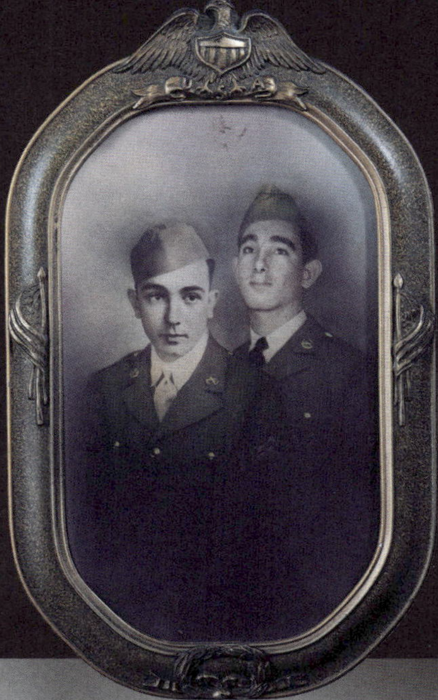

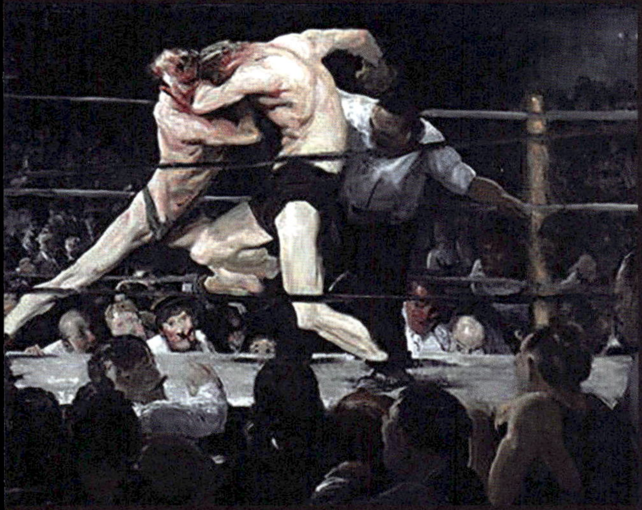

George Bellows (American, 1882–1925), *Stag at Sharkey's*, 1909
Oil on canvas
The Cleveland Museum of Art, Hinman B. Hurlbut Collection 1922.1133

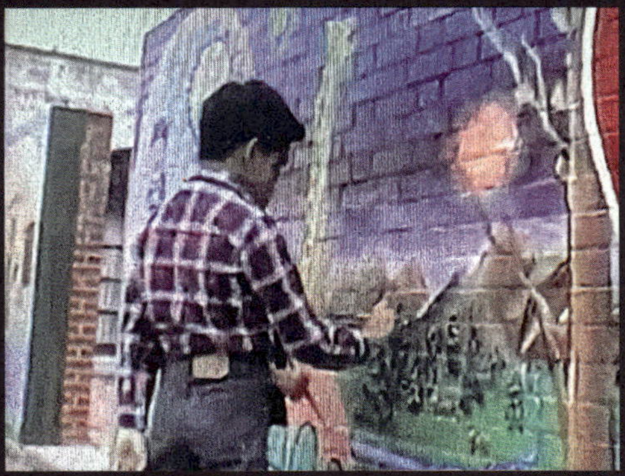

Still from video taken by his father of Valdez painting his first mural at the Esperanza Peace and Justice Center, San Antonio, TX, 1988

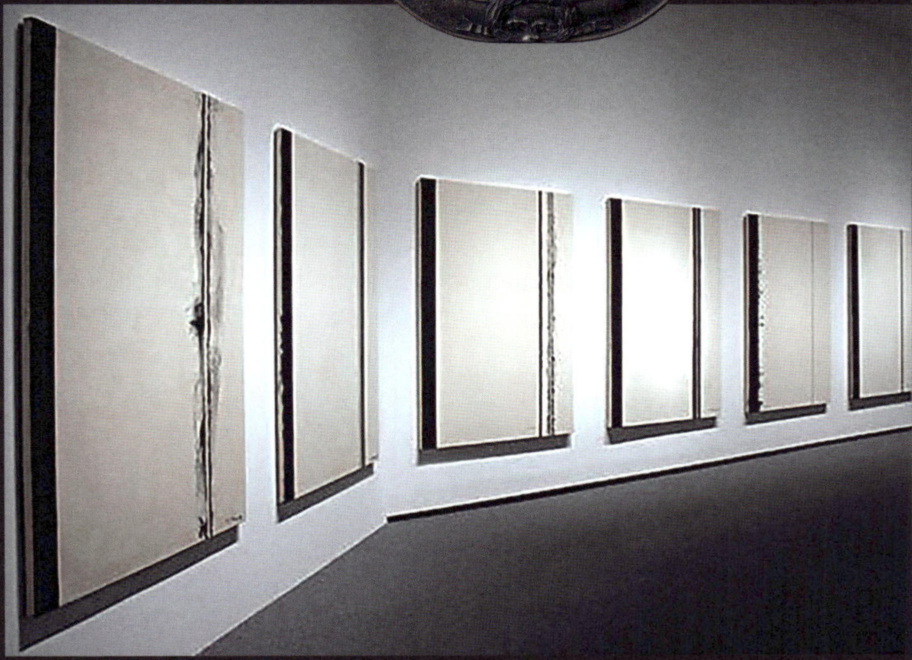

Barnett Newman, *The Stations of the Cross: Lema Sabachthani*, 1958–1966
Magna on canvas
© 2024 The Barnett Newman Foundation / Artists Rights Society (ARS), New York. Courtesy of National Gallery of Art Archives, National Gallery of Art Archives. Images—Building, Campus, and Art Installation Views

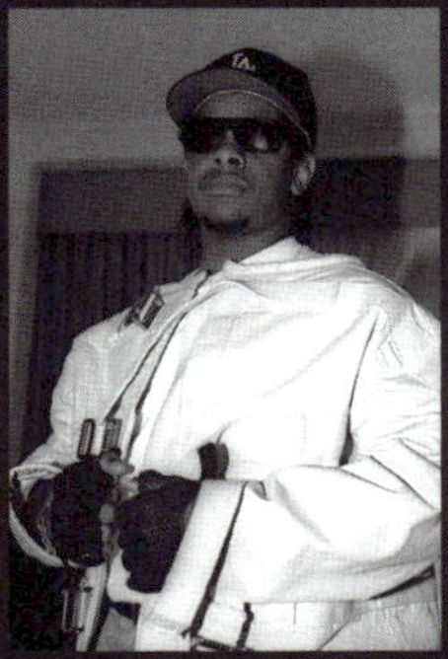

Rapper Eazy-E (aka Eric Lynn Wright) wears a straightjacket when he appears in a portrait taken on June 27, 1991, in New York City
Photo by Al Pereira/Getty Images/Michael Ochs Archives

THE REMEMBERING

"My memories don't feel as though they've been pulled up by the root. Even if they fade, something remains. Like tiny seeds that might germinate again if the rain falls. And even if a memory disappears completely, the heart retains something. A slight tremor or pain, some bit of joy, a tear." – YOKO OGAWA[16]

Empathy and amnesia are at odds with one another and the only way we can achieve the former and eradicate the latter is by telling the stories of the forgotten. This is Valdez's mission. In early works like *Kill the Pachuco Bastard!* (2001) and *El Chavez Ravine* (with Ry Cooder, 2005–7), the narrative is loud and clear: it is of the violence and erasure of Mexicans and Mexican Americans in Los Angeles. Because Valdez is a storyteller, and because he reveals frequently ignored histories, his works leave us to consider the place in which we find ourselves today: a deeply divided America at odds with who deserves to call themselves a citizen. As author, humanitarian, and holocaust survivor Elie Wiesel said in his 1986 Nobel Lecture, "Without memory, our existence would be barren and opaque, like a prison cell into which no light penetrates; like a tomb which rejects the living ... if anything can, it is memory that will save humanity. For me, hope without memory is like memory without hope."[17] By telling these stories, like Wiesel, like Valdez, we can only hope that truth can outweigh the banality of evil, and that as a result, we can strive to live rather than merely despair.

Kill the Pachuco Bastard! references the 1943 Zoot Suit Riots. From June 3 to 8 of that year, a group of American servicemen stationed in Southern California collided with young Latinos in downtown and East Los Angeles, resulting in what was essentially a race riot. Just a year before, the War Production Board had released regulations concerning the use of wool to conserve resources during World War II. A popular style of dress in the Latino community at the time was the Zoot Suit—featuring voluminous wide-cut pants, often in signature pinstriped patterns. Many American military personnel were on leave in Los Angeles in the early forties and upon seeing the Zoot Suit–wearing Latinos, or Pachucos, they became incensed at their disregard for American wartime values and began attacking them on the streets and in bars. The largest conflict took place on June 3, when even off-duty LAPD officers joined in. Miraculously, no one was killed, but hundreds were injured and arrested. Unsurprisingly, it took until 2023 for the city to publicly apologize for the riots, despite the fact that just a week after the incident, then First Lady Eleanor Roosevelt condemned the events, stating, "The question goes deeper than just suits. It is a racial protest. I have been worried for a long time about the Mexican racial situation. It is a problem with roots going a long way back, and we do not always face these problems as we should."[18] Roosevelt's statement was met with outrage and claims that she was a communist for addressing racial discord.

The composition of Valdez's painting is as chaotic as the story it depicts. A red and white checkered floor is tilted in surrealist forced perspective, as a melee of figures are scattered across the room. In the foreground, a Zoot Suit–clad man in wide striped trousers, gold chain hanging from his belt, tank top, and fedora, shoves his face into that of a naval officer who is swinging a broken bottle. Another officer is raping a woman to the right, and to the left a Pachuco takes a swift blow to the gut. The scene is reminiscent of painters like Peter Saul and Ed Paschke, whose Pop surrealism and bright colors distort and exaggerate their figures. For Valdez, this stylistic nod presents itself in the perspective of the room, the exaggerated machismo of the figures, and their sickly, greenish-hued skin. The painting also references Chicano/a artists such as Luis Jimenez, John Valadez, Esther Hernandez, Cesar Martinez, and Gaspar Enriquez. But it is American realist George Bellows who most clearly comes to mind when looking at this work. It might seem strange to bring up Bellows here, rather than in relation to *Stations*, for he was known to paint boxers. But there is something about the chaos in *Kill the Pachuco Bastard!* that, despite its surrealism, represents the reality of a bar fight, to the point where you can imagine the smell of blood. Bellows' paintings also contain this chaos, the movement of boxers and the crowd within a gritty room charged with violence.

El Chavez Ravine paints a larger picture of the tribulations faced by Mexicans/Mexican Americans in Los Angeles in the 1940s and '50s. The story of Chavez Ravine is one of erasure. Until the 1950s, the area was home to Los Angeles's largest Latine community, until the city seized the land to build Dodger Stadium, forcibly removing its population. The city's land grab brought with it the promise of the Elysian Hills Housing Development, a misplaced dream of Eden that came abruptly to a halt in 1958 when the city abandoned the project. The construction of Dodger Stadium effectively buried the community that once made the region so vibrant. From 1951 to 1961 the rightful landowners fought to save their homes, to no avail, leaving behind a story that now looms as large as the stadium.

In 2004, musician Ry Cooder reached out to Valdez and brought him to Los Angeles. Cooder asked him to collaborate on a project to accompany his upcoming record *El Chavez Ravine*. The album pays tribute to the neighborhood with lyrics like, "Chavez Ravine plugged up, / Bunker Hill ripped down / Cement mixers spreading the word around / This here is my town / It's my town."[19] To illustrate this, Valdez did not make your average painting. Instead, Cooder acquired a 1953 Good Humor ice cream truck restored by the godfathers of lowriding, Duke's Car Club, which Valdez turned into a storyboard of history. Valdez painted every inch of the truck, depicting Dodgers owner Walter O'Malley, former LAPD chief William H. Parker, Director of the FBI J. Edgar Hoover, and the displaced families. The word Elysian is written alongside plans for development, and there is graffiti, as well as nods to low rider culture. The pain of gentrification is written large across the surface of the truck, and the ice cream, meant to signal joy, is counterbalanced with strife. The presence of displaced "good humor" reminds us of resilience in the face of injustice. As Los Angeles historian Mike Davis writes in *City of Quartz*, "Los Angeles is . . . a stand-in for capitalism in general. The ultimate world-historical significance—and oddity—of Los Angeles is that it has come to play the double role of utopia and dystopia for advanced capitalism. The same place, as [Bertolt] Brecht noted, symbolized both heaven and hell."[20]

THE UNITED STATES OF AMERICA

"America I've given you all and now I'm nothing." – ALLEN GINSBERG[21]

It feels impossible to write an essay about Valdez without mentioning *The Beginning Is Near (An American Trilogy), Chapter One: The City, The City I* (2015–16), a 30-foot painting of hooded Ku Klux Klan figures in front of a background of city lights and trash piles, all lit by the headlamps of a pickup truck. It is perhaps the most written about, discussed, and controversial work of Valdez's career, bringing with it comparisons to Philip Guston. The contrarian in me is going to leave a lot unsaid about this work, but what I will say is that choosing to create an epic painting of the KKK in the twenty-first century is a bold move, but a necessary one. We naively assume these hooded figures are of the past, but if the January 6, 2021, insurrection at the US Capitol Building confirms anything, it is that these forces for evil still function proudly in America. In 1980, Gil Scott-Heron wrote "The Klan," whose lyrics state, "He who rides with the Klan / Is a devil and not a man / For underneath his white disguise / I have looked into his eyes."[22] And looking directly in their eyes is what *The City I* offers, for when you stand before the painting you are met with the figures staring at you as you stare back, making sure you know that just because they don't wear hoods doesn't mean they don't exist. Valdez countered *The City* with the series titled *The Beginning Is Near (An American Trilogy), Chapter Three: The New Americans* (2021–ongoing), which pays tribute to people trying to make change: artists Adriana Corral and Teresita Fernández, musicians Wynton Marsalis and Flaco Jiménez, and socio-political figures Mr. Checkpoint (who started AFTP—Always Film the Police and Always for the People—in an effort to create safer communities through information sharing and advocacy[23]) and civil rights attorney Juan Cartagena. These near life-sized portraits represent their subjects front on and with dignity. They too stare at us and we meet their gaze willingly, knowing that despite the ills of the world, hope still exists.[24]

By placing these two within the same series, Valdez cautions us not to approach hope blindly. Hanif Abdurraqib has written "about the value of optimism while cities burn, while people are fearing for their lives and the lives of their loved ones, while discourse is reduced to laughing through a chorus of anxiety."[25] The complication of this chorus is paramount in Kurt Vonnegut's *Slaughterhouse Five* (1969), especially when protagonist Billy Pilgrim is asked about the war. While glossing over his answer, he realizes that the perfect epitaph for his headstone would be "Everything was beautiful and nothing hurt."[26] This, of course, could not be further from the truth. Throughout the novel, Pilgrim, a prisoner of war (POW), frequently uses the phrase "so it goes," telling himself, and us, that we must move forward, despite life's realities. The similarities between *Slaughterhouse Five* and Valdez's mission are clear when Vonnegut writes, "And I asked myself about the present: how wide it was, how deep it was, how much was mine to keep."[27] Vonnegut's Pilgrim is a time traveler, claiming to be abducted by an alien race, the Tralfamadorians, who push him across time causing him to no longer feel fear because he sees what is to come. Incidentally the Tralfamadorians see through eyes in their hands—much like a painter does, much as how Valdez's witnessing is manifested. Pilgrim is therefore a seer, like Valdez, so it is apt that the artist recently created twenty-three drawings to illustrate a 2024 edition of *Slaughterhouse Five* with the Arion Press in San Francisco.[28]

Valdez was also drawn to *Slaughterhouse Five* for personal reasons. The introductory essay to the Arion Press edition states, "Vonnegut observed his twenty-second birthday in uniform as a recently enlisted soldier

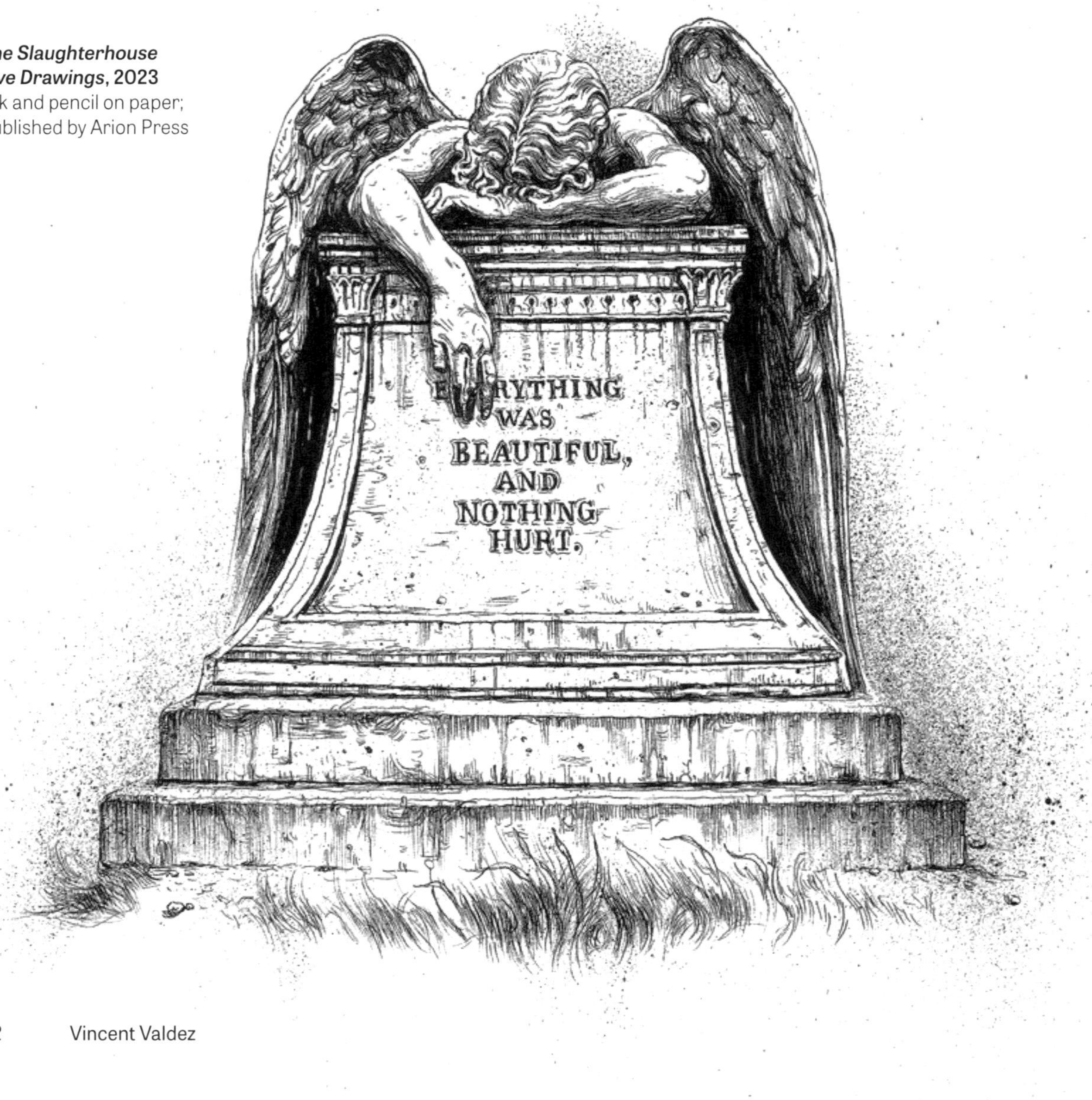

***The Slaughterhouse Five Drawings*, 2023**
Ink and pencil on paper; published by Arion Press

in the United States Army and was sent to France in the waning months of World War II, in time to be swept up in the ferocious counteroffensive launched by the German 1st Panzer Division in December of 1944 known as the Battle of the Bulge. Assigned to the US 106th Infantry Division as an intelligence scout, PFC Vonnegut was cut off from his battalion amid the ensuing chaos. He was captured on December 19 after wandering alone behind enemy lines for eleven days."[29] This is the backdrop to the experience of Pilgrim. However, it is similar to a story Valdez heard as a child, because his great uncle, Ernest Valdez, was, like Vonnegut, captured by Germans during the Battle of the Bulge and held as a POW. The recreated vintage military canister the book comes in is based on Ernest's objects from the war and the final letter he sent home before he went missing in action. Valdez's stark ink drawings illustrate various scenes from the book, always with a twist: an optometrist's machine becomes a device of time travel/state control; a boxcar turns sinister when it becomes transportation for POWs; a locket containing the Lord's Prayer sits empty on the page, divorced from its dead owner; and a gravestone with an angel draped over the top contains the "Everything was beautiful and nothing hurt" epitaph. However, there is one drawing that stands out—a silhouette of a woman in stippled ink who is seemingly vaporizing, like Valdez's *Amnesia* drawings. All we see clearly are her eyes, looking back at us from a turned head. The Vonnegut text that accompanies the image reads: "And Lot's wife, of course, was told not to look back where all those people and their homes had been. But she *did* look back, and I love her for that, because it was so human. She was turned to a pillar of salt. So it goes. People aren't supposed to look back. I'm certainly not going to do it anymore. I've finished my war book now. The next one I write is going to be fun. This one is a failure, it had to be, since it was written by a pillar of salt."[30]

Valdez will never stop looking back, and he has yet to turn into a pillar of salt, so it seems his use of time travel is suitable for now. He uses reflection to interrogate and reveal what makes America America. This is the subject of the currently in-progress works in Valdez's studio: *An American Procession* and *It Was a Very Good Year* (both 2024–ongoing). Both begin with recognizable images that many will remember seeing for the first time, thanks to the advent of television culture. In *On Tyranny: Twenty Lessons from the Twentieth Century* (2017), Timothy Snyder talks about how literature predicted our current media-saturated culture. He states, "More than half a century ago, the classic novels of totalitarianism warned of the domination of screens, the suppression of books, the narrowing of vocabularies, and the associated difficulties of thought. In Ray Bradbury's *Fahrenheit 451*, published in 1953, firemen find and burn books while most citizens watch interactive television. In George Orwell's *1984*, published in 1949, books are banned and television is two-way, allowing the government to observe citizens at all times."[31] So, for both series, Valdez combed through his own memory for stand-out images that are primarily media-based, even if he didn't directly experience them himself. *An American Procession* is focused around gatherings, movement, parades, etc. Valdez was drawn toward the idea of the procession because of its feeling of constant forward movement, which he sees as playing out through American politics, both for good and bad. The paintings in the series include O. J. Simpson's white Bronco chase as he fled the police (1994); John F. Kennedy's motorcade in Dallas on the day of his assassination (1963); the bombing of Dresden, Germany, in World War II (1945); and a Ku Klux Klan rally in Washington, DC (1925).

In *It Was a Very Good Year*—a nod to the song of the same name made popular by Frank Sinatra in 1966—these themes manifest as images that, importantly, occurred in Valdez's lifetime and have become frozen in time. He, like many of our generation, experienced the unfolding of these moments as moving images on the screen: television, theater, and home movies. Thus, the series serves as both a chronology of American life as well as Valdez's own. Subjects included are Oliver North's Iran-Contra Hearings (1987); the inauguration night when Reagan passed the baton to George H. W. Bush (1989), the Bush Dynasty (1989–2009); the invasion of Panama (1989); the space shuttle Challenger exploding (1986); Michael Jackson's burning hair while shooting a Pepsi commercial (1984); Michael Jordan's gravity defying slam dunk contest (1988), etc. The multi-panel paintings render their subjects in near life-size, pulling them off the screen and into space as free-standing objects attached back-to-back, creating a maze-like structure. In one pairing we see Lieutenant Colonel Oliver North being sworn in during the Iran-Contra Hearings. This political scandal took place when the Reagan administration brokered a deal to illegally sell

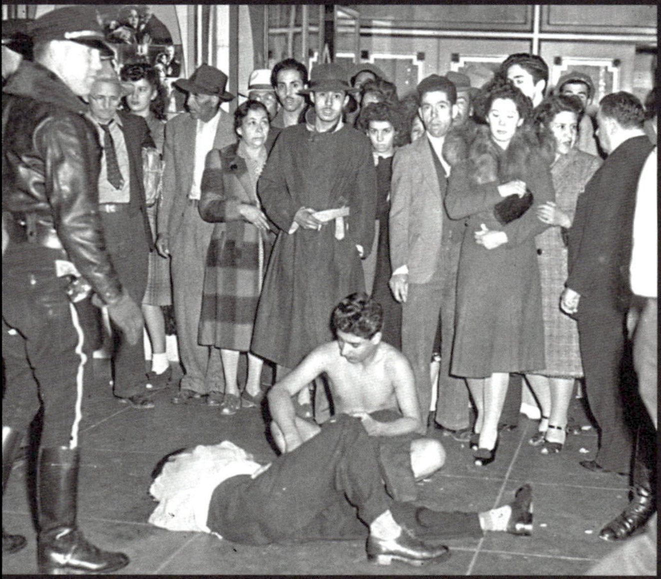

Victims of the Zoot Suit Riots, where groups of servicemen scoured the streets of Los Angeles looking for and attacking individuals wearing Zoot Suits (June 1943). The servicemen blamed the Mexican American Pachucos for numerous unprovoked assaults on their colleagues.

Niday Picture Library / Alamy Stock Photo

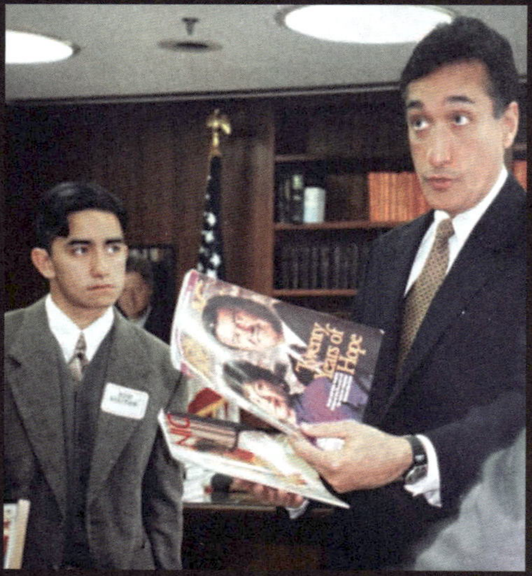

Photo of Vincent Valdez with former San Antonio mayor Henry Cisneros at the White House, 1993

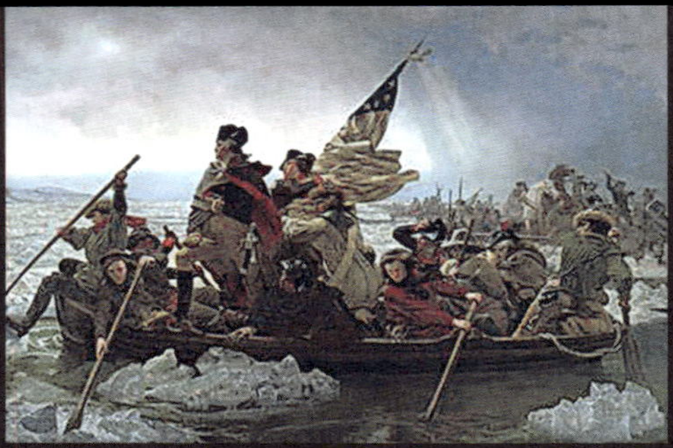

Emauel Gottlieb Leutze, *Washington Crossing the Delaware*, 1851
(post cleaning)
Oil on canvas

Image Copyright The Metropolitan Museum of Art/Image Source: Art Resource, New York

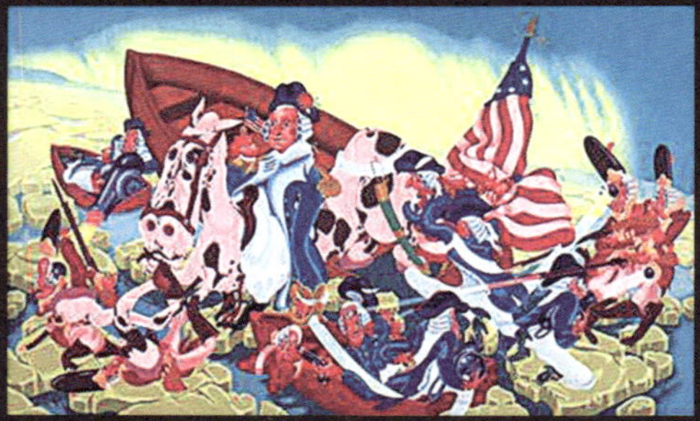

Peter Saul, *Washington Crossing the Delaware*, 1975
Oil on canvas

Collection of KAWS. Photo: Farzad Owrang © 2024 Peter Saul / Artists Rights Society (ARS), New York

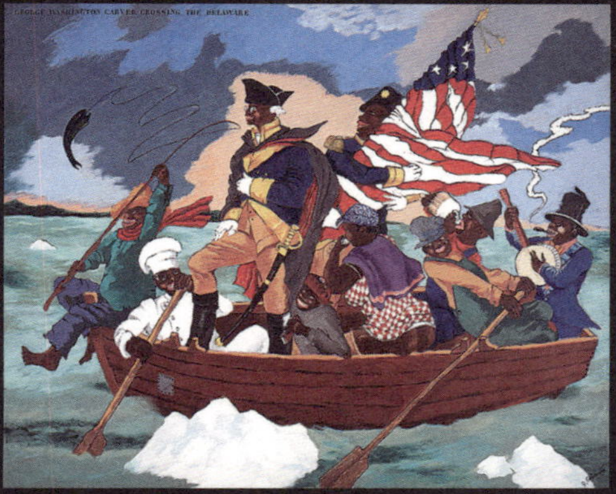

Robert Colescott, *George Washington Carver Crossing the Delaware: Page from an American History Textbook*, 1975
Acrylic on canvas

Lucas Museum of Narrative Art, Los Angeles, © 2024 The Robert H. Colescott Separate Property Trust / Artists Rights Society (ARS), New York

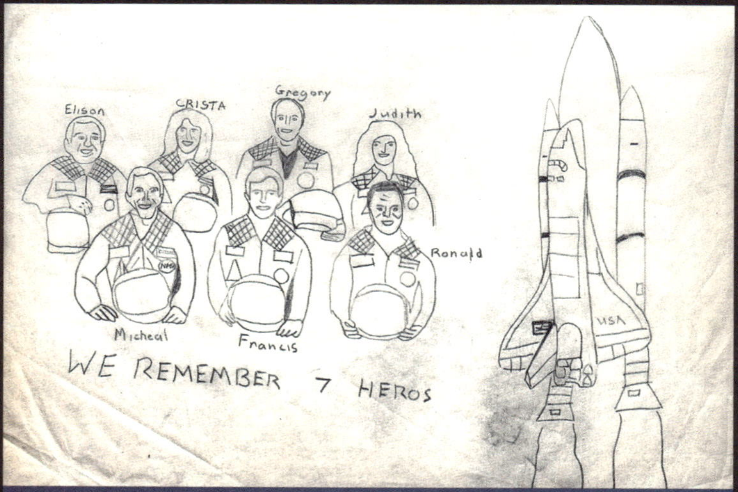

Valdez honoring those lost after the space shuttle Challenger exploded, 1986

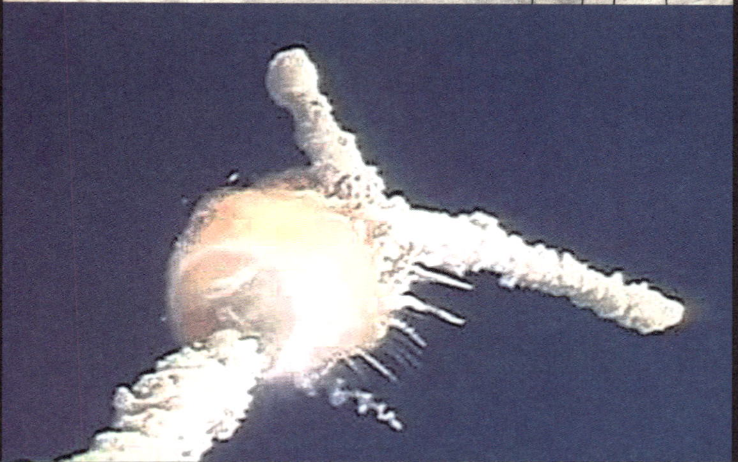

Challenger, photograph by Bruce Weaver, January 28, 1986

arms to Iran in order to fund the Contras, an anti-Sandinista rebel group in Nicaragua. They claimed this was to facilitate the release of US hostages held in Lebanon by Hezbollah, a group with ties to Iran. North testified about destroying documents related to the scandal. In Valdez's painting, North's mouth is closed as if mute to his own wrongdoing. On the opposite side is an ascension to counter North's solidity: Michael Jordan competing in a slam dunk contest, just a year after North's performance on the witness stand. In this image, Jordan defies gravity, proving to us that by striving we can stop time. In writing about a 1985 slam dunk contest Hanif Abdurraqib describes Jordan: "He started at one end of Market Square Arena in Indianapolis and ran, catapulting himself from the free-throw line (yes, the actual free-throw line!) and remaining suspended and extended, for what feels, even now, like a glorious hour. Your finest hour. The hour you've dreamed of living again ever since the final grains of it kissed the mountain of sand at the bottom of the hourglass. Have you ever been in the air so long that your feet begin to fall in love with the new familiar, walking along some invisible surface that is surely there, that must be, as there is no other way to describe what miracle keeps you afloat? How long have you been suspended in a place that loves you with the same ferocity and freedom as the ground might, as the grave might. . . . "[32] In this pairing both figures gaze up to the stars: for North they are on the American Flag and for Jordan they are arena lights, their right hands are raised, as if swearing their own oaths to the American dreams of idealism, exceptionalism, and immortality.

In a yet un-started pairing, Valdez plans to steer the series into deeply personal territory, depicting the Challenger explosion on one side, and on the other the artist's mother, in silhouette by the shore, with him as a one-year-old in her arms. For those of us who were kids in the 1980s, the story of the Challenger loomed large, as it was the first time a civilian—the school teacher Christa McAuliffe—was invited on board. TVs were rolled into our classrooms so we could view the momentous event. Shortly after launch, the rocket exploded, killing all seven on board. Most of us watching can still see the iconic shape of the explosion, and still feel the horror and inexplicability of the experience. Valdez even made a drawing of the crew and shuttle just a week after the explosion. By connecting this with such a personal image of himself and his mother (who passed away in 2020), Valdez punches us in the gut, reminding us of the loss of innocence. So, as we move around Valdez's canvases we experience the dichotomies between heaven and hell, joy and pain, and corruption and the ability to fly.

THE BEGINNING OF...

"To be honest, I expect apocalypse, or I look for and I work for defeat of international evil, indifference, and suffering, only when I am not otherwise stunned by the odds, temporarily paralyzed by the revulsion and grieving despair. but life itself compels an optimism." – JUNE JORDAN[34]

Because this is a story of cycles, I find myself back at Vincent's studio, this time in LA, on January 23, 2024. I feel déjà vu as we stare down the possibility of another Trump election. Valdez's exhibition *Just a Dream...* opens in Houston, Texas, only a week after the 2024 presidential election. We will be together again in Texas, eight years later, and while I hope we will not lament the same result, the fear is inevitable. But, as always, Valdez is preparing. His newest prophetic vision is in progress. It's not an eagle. This time around it's a re-envisioning of the founding of the American Republic through the image of George Washington crossing the Delaware River. In 1776, during the Revolutionary War, a surprise attack on Hessian forces—German auxiliary troops for the British army—took place at the Battle of Trenton in New Jersey. This moment has been captured throughout art history. Perhaps the most iconic version is Emanuel Leutze's *Washington Crossing the Delaware* (1861), a history painting with Washington at the helm of the ship heroically waving the American flag. Peter Saul's 1965 version is a pop-art masterpiece, its technicolor composition is fleshy pink, and Washington is cast as a buffoon on a sinking ship, holding a tiny flag in his hand; while Robert Colescott's *George Washington Carver Crossing the Delaware: Page from an American History Textbook* (1975) turns to African American hero and scientist George Washington Carver to lead the charge, surrounded by pre-Civil Rights era racial stereotypes such as Aunt Jemima. Both Saul and Colescott do not take the history book, or the history painting, as truth, and neither does Valdez, whose own take on the subject is the most demented yet.

Titled *Hello America* (2024), inspired by J. G. Ballard's 1980 novel of the same name, this small drawing (soon to become a large-scale canvas) casts Mickey Mouse as Washington. In front of him is Davy Crockett in his coonskin hat, waving a "Give Me Liberty or Give Me Death" flag with the "Don't Tread on Me" snake imaged on its surface; Donald Duck rows alongside Crockett and behind them is Christ carrying the cross, which doubles as a flagpole. Also on board are onlookers: paparazzi, anonymous celebrities, a marching band, Blackwater-type security agents, and a decorated yet forgotten veteran. There are planned additions to the work: the boat will be towing a stack of bombs while on the horizon is a remnant of the fallen Statue of Liberty's arm and torch, reaching toward a "promised land" of high-rise buildings, billboards, and barbed wire. When I look at this composition, so many thoughts flood my head: Elaine Benes in Seinfeld, stating to her soon-to-be boss, J. Peterman, "Oh, God. I'm so sorry. I don't even know where I'm going." As he replied, "Well, that's the best way to get someplace you've never been."[35] Or, maybe this is how the insurrectionists reached the Capitol Building on January 6. But mostly, I think of Ballard's book. *Hello America* takes place after the Bering Strait has been dammed and America is a wasteland. An expedition is undertaken that leads a team, including political hopeful, Wayne, to Las Vegas, where they come upon civilization and a man self-named Charles Manson, who claims to be the 45th president of the United States. Manson repeatedly says to Wayne that together they can "Make America Great Again," which was a slogan used by Ronald Reagan at that time, and before that by fascists in the 1930s. In one scene, Wayne wakes up in a hall of robotic presidents. Ballard writes:

"Now they were all shouting together, jostling around Wayne as if trying to win his vote, a babel of remonstrating voices that echoed off the thousands of empty seats around the arena.

> '...tanks, guns, planes...'
> '...hyphenated Americans...'
> '...safe for democracy...'
> '...too proud to fight...'
> '...Ich bin ein Berliner...'
> '...the only thing we have to fear is...'
> Wayne screamed."[36]

Ballard and Valdez show us that the ghosts of the past are alive, and that revealing their foibles is truly how we make America great again. Come gather 'round people because the times they are a-changin', or maybe a change is gonna come, but it's hard to see through the smoke of destruction. Then I remember the painting *Godspeed* (2019). It depicts another ship, this one seemingly empty of passengers, being swallowed by rough seas. The only sign of humanity is a single flare set into the sky, a beacon, and a cry for hope. Sure, Washington made it to the opposite shore, but will America? Will we, its citizens, be offered the same out? With Valdez at the helm, I think we just might.

THE END

"HISTORICAL UNDERDOSING: To live in a period of time when nothing seems to happen. Major symptoms include addiction to newspapers, magazines, and TV news broadcasts. HISTORICAL OVERDOSING: To live in a period of time when too much seems to happen. Major symptoms include addiction to newspapers, magazines, and TV news broadcasts." – DOUGLAS COUPLAND[37]

Both Vincent and I are products of Generation X, born in the 1970s and raised on MTV. We grew up with an actor turned president, Tammy Faye Bakker's mascara-streaked cheeks, Michael Jordan defying gravity, Michael Jackson's curls aflame, Oliver North, this is your brain on drugs sizzling in a frying pan, the Challenger explosion, and Monica Lewinski's blue dress, all set to a soundtrack of Run-DMC, Madonna, Milli Vanilli, Duran Duran, and the bleakness of grunge inspired by Suicide's "Dream Baby Dream." It smells like teen spirit in here. So, how could we be expected to parse the difference between truth, fantasy, and reality when we were faced with a TV full of constructed images: who shot JR, cross-dressing for cheaper housing in *Bosom Buddies*, and primetime's favorite cat-eating alien Alf? It's no surprise then, that Trump's fake news would feel normal. We were worn down by the hypernormalisation[38] of America—damn, of the world. We tried to read Bush's lips but the taxes still came; we failed to understand why his son couldn't pronounce "nuclear," but the planes still hit the twin towers; and all the "unknown unknowns" Donald Rumsfeld threw in our faces were in fact known, because America was the weapon of mass destruction. So, when we were called to "Make America Great Again," we had heard it before from the movie star president rather than the reality TV show president. Yet, as disaffected as this slacker generation is dubbed to be, we practice dark optimism, we don't let it carry us away, we still hope. We understand that fire both burns and renews. We recognize each other because, as Wisława Szymborska wrote "We are children of our age, / it's a political age. / All day long, all through the night, / all affairs—yours, ours, theirs— / are political affairs. / Whether you like it or not, / your genes have a political past, / your skin, a political cast, / your eyes, a political slant. / Whatever you say reverberates, / whatever you don't say speaks for itself. / So either way you're talking politics."[39]

I'm going to leave you with one last image pairing that may become a painting someday: two unlikely visits to the White House. In 1991, N.W.A rapper Eazy-E received a letter from Texas senator Bill Graham asking him to join a Republican-elite inner-circle dinner with George H. W. Bush. Of the $1,250 per plate dinner on March 18, Eazy stated, "They wanted to invite me to the Republican party. I'm not no fuckin' Republican, but we went there and when we got off the plane they had CBS, CNN and all these media people who blew it up saying, 'The gangbanger and drug dealer Eazy-E came down here to the President's luncheon.' Basically, what I did was pay $1,200 for a million dollars' worth of press."[40] It turned out that the organizers had sent the invitation in error, but Eazy's willingness to go could only have happened in a post-Reagan era where politics had turned into entertainment. Two years later, Vincent won a national art contest, which included a trip to the White House, this time under Bill Clinton. There is a photograph of the occasion. In it, director of the United States Department of Housing and Urban Development and former San Antonio mayor Henry Cisneros presents Vincent with a magazine, while behind him is a smiling portrait of Clinton. But the star of the show is Vincent's expression: pure suspicion. Perhaps he was thinking of the hamburger he requested; or the mural he painted of fallen soldiers; or perhaps, even at sixteen, he saw the facade of America. Part of me wishes that he and Eazy could have walked in on the same day, just to feel the seismic activity of that supernova.

Vincent Valdez is a storyteller who strips away the white noise and freezes humanity, so that we are not allowed to look away. His work is an ouroboros, a collage, a memory, a fever dream, but it's all real, just like the moon landing, or a shuttle launch denied a school teacher. Vincent's America was not made by Stanley Kubrick on a soundstage, but it occurs in a new war room, one that allows productive fighting, one free of doublethink and book burning. Vincent's war room is his studio, and while the world may never be yours, a flare will emblazon the dark sky. We still want our MTV, and know the real revolution will not be televised. We don't know if the animals will still be there, but we hear the faint song of birds: *Poo-tee-weet*. So it goes.

[1] The essay title is a nod to Jim Morrison's spoken word piece, "An American Prayer," which was set to music by The Doors after Morrison's death and recorded for the 1979 album of the same name. One pertinent lyric states, "We have assembled inside this ancient and insane theater / To propagate our lust for life and flee the swarming wisdom of the streets."

[2] Rebecca Solnit, *Hope in the Dark: Untold Histories Wild Possibilities* (Chicago: Haymarket Books, 2016), p. 1.

[3] Nathanael West, *Miss Lonelyhearts & The Day of the Locust* (Cambridge: New Direction, 1933), p. 103.

[4] Giorgio Agamben, *When the House Burns Down*, trans. Kevin Attell (London: Seagull Books, 2022), pp. 3–4.

[5] Artist Statement sent to the author.

[6] Susan Sontag, *Regarding the Pain of Others* (London: Picador, 2004), p. 115.

[7] Susan Sontag, "Aesthetics of Silence," Aspen no. 5+6, 1967, p. 6.

[8] Langston Hughes, "Let America Be America Again," from The Collected Poems of Langston Hughes (New York: Vintage Books, 1994), p. 189.

[9] Hanif Abdurraqib, *They Can't Kill Us Until They Kill Us* (Columbus: Two Dollar Radio, 2017) p. 165.

[10] Joyce Carol Oates, *On Boxing* (New York: Harper Perennial Modern Classics; Reprint edition, 2006), pp. 20–21.

[11] Jimmy Clanton and His Rockets, "Just a Dream," Ace Records, 1958.

[12] Oates, p. 170.

[13] Vincent Valdez, "Vincent Valdez on "Excerpts for John" in Home—So Different, So Appealing," *Unframed*, May 29, 2017, https://unframed.lacma.org/2017/05/29/vincent-valdez-%E2%80%9Cexcerpts-john%E2%80%9D-home%E2%80%94so-different-so-appealing.

[14] Solnit, p. xx.

[15] Leonard Cohen, "So Long, Marianne," from *Songs of Leonard Cohen*, Columbia Records, 1967.

[16] Yoko Ogawa, *The Memory Police*, trans. Stephen Snyder (New York: Pantheon Books, 2019), p. 81.

[17] Elie Wiesel, "Hope, Despair and Memory" (Nobel Lecture, December 11, 1986). https://www.nobelprize.org/prizes/peace/1986/wiesel/lecture/.

[18] "Los Angeles Zoot Suit Riots, 1943," Los Angeles Almanac, accessed June 27, 2024, https://www.laalmanac.com/history/hi07t.php.

[19] Ry Cooder, "In My Town," from *Chavez Ravine*, Nonesuch Records, 2005. Bunker Hill references another area of Los Angeles flattened to make way for development.

[20] Mike Davis, *City of Quartz* (London/New York: Verso Books, 1990), p. 15.

[21] Allen Ginsberg, "America," 1956, https://www.poetryfoundation.org/poems/49305/america-56d22b41f119f.

[22] Gil Scott-Heron, "The Klan," from *Real Eyes*, Arista Records, 1980.

[23] The acronym AFTP is a nod to the 1988 song "Fuck tha Police" (FTP) from N.W.A's *Straight Outta Compton*.

[24] *The City* and *New Americans* are Chapters One and Three respectively of *The Beginning is Near (An American Trilogy)*. Also included are the thirteen paintings that comprise Chapter Two, *Dream Baby Dream* (2015–16), which depicts mourners at the funeral of Muhammad Ali.

[25] Abdurraqib, *They Can't Kill Us*, p. 77.

[26] Kurt Vonnegut, *Slaughterhouse Five* (New York: Dial Press, 1999), p. 155.

[27] Vonnegut, p. 23.

[28] Arion Press pairs artists and literature to create limited-edition hand-made books.

[29] Kurt Vonnegut, Jr., *Slaughterhouse-Five, or— The Children's Crusade: A Duty-Dance with Death*, (San Francisco: Arion Press, 2023), p. 2, https://static1.squarespace.com/static/5c5b11c1bfba3e4a2e2cbe3a/t/6578b15f26605c4e125224e7/1702408544852/Arion.S5+prospectus.pdf.

[30] Vonnegut, p. 28.

[31] Timothy Snyder, *On Tyranny: Twenty Lessons from the Twentieth Century* (New York: Crown, 2017), p. 61.

[32] Hanif Abdurraqib, *There's Always This Year: On Basketball and Ascension* (New York: Penguin Random House, 2024), pp. 17–18.

[33] I was home sick that day and watched the event alone. I submitted this date to Valdez and Corral's *Requiem*.

[34] June Jordan, "Introduction," *Some of Us Did NOT Die: New and Selected Essays* (New York: Civitas Books, 2003), p. 4.

[35] From the episode "The Understudy," 1995.

[36] J. G. Ballard, *Hello America* (London: W. W. Norton & Co, 1981), pp. 169–70.

[37] Douglas Coupland, *Generation X: Tales for an Accelerated Culture* (New York: St. Martin's Griffin, 1991), p. 7.

[38] Adam Curtis's documentary *Hypernormalisation* (2016) takes its title from Alexei Yurchak's *Everything Was Forever, Until It Was No More: The Last Soviet Generation* (2006). Yurchak argues that the Soviet propaganda machine was so efficient that it normalized corruption. Curtis's film brings that forward to the Trump years.

[39] Wisława Szymborska, "Children of Our Age," from *view with a grain of sand: selected poems*, trans. Stanisław Barańczak and Clare Cavanaugh (Boston: Harcourt Books, 1995), p. 149.

[40] Jay Quad, "Dinner with the President: Eazy-E's Infamous Luncheon with George H.W. Bush," *Rock the Bells*, March 21, 2022, https://rockthebells.com/articles/eazy-e-lunch-with-george-bush/.

I SEE MY LIGHT COME SHININ'
FROM THE WEST DOWN TO THE EAST
ANY DAY NOW, ANY DAY NOW
I SHALL BE RELASED.

—**BOB DYLAN** excerpt from "I Shall Be Released" (1967)

THE WITNESS

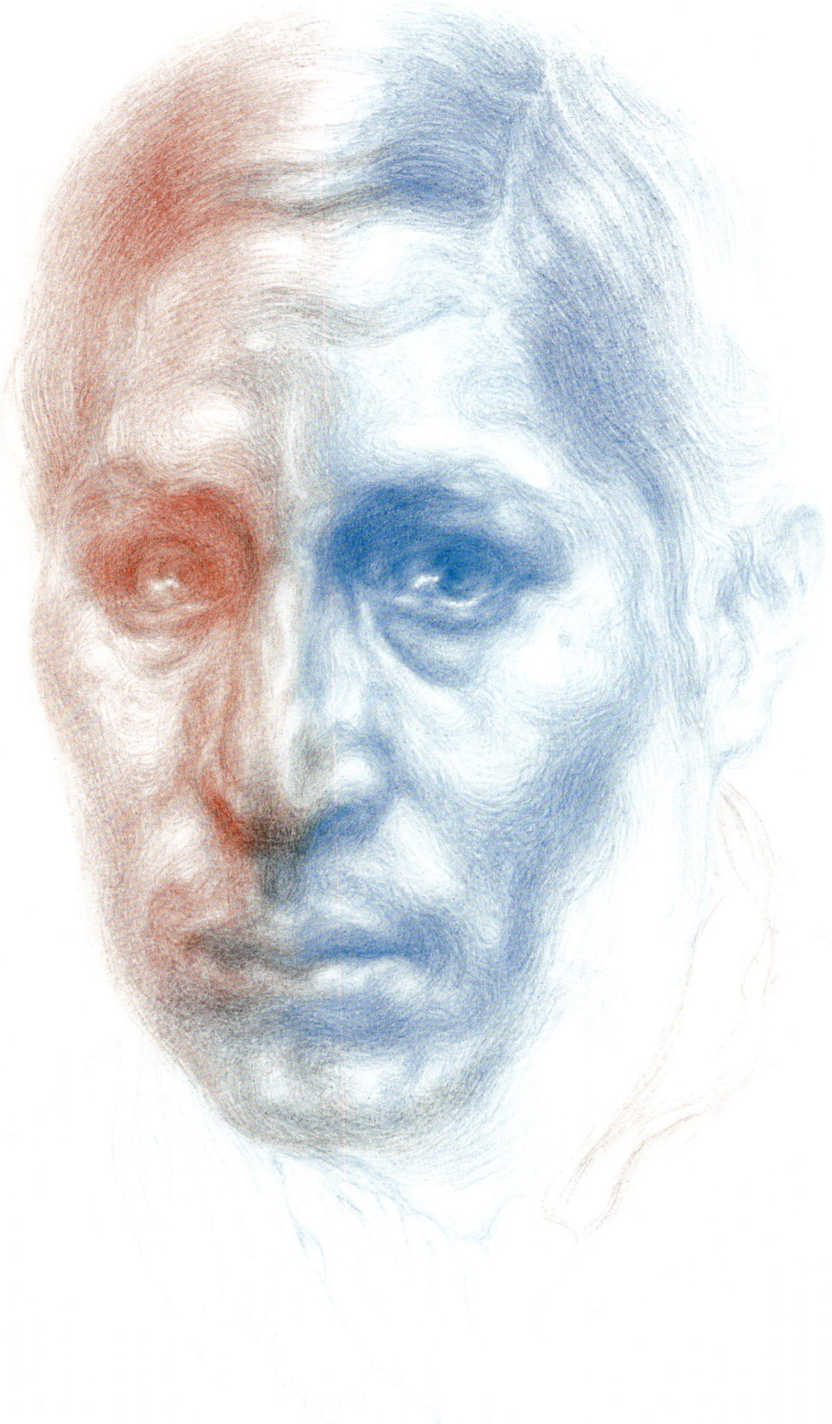

***Amnesia*, 2024**
Color pencil on paper
Photos: Elon Schoenholz

***Amnesia*, 2023**
Color pencil on paper
Photos: Elon Schoenholz

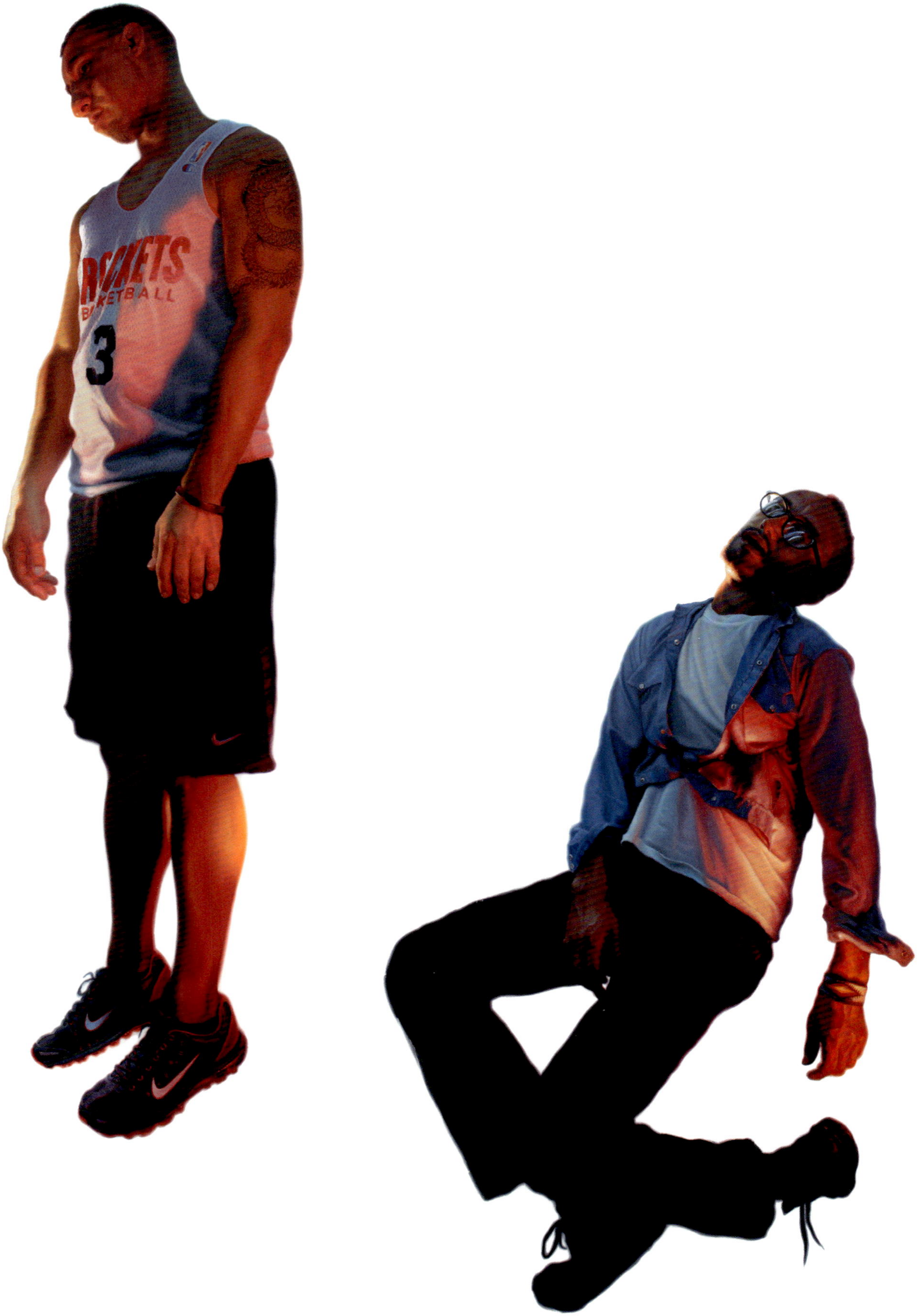

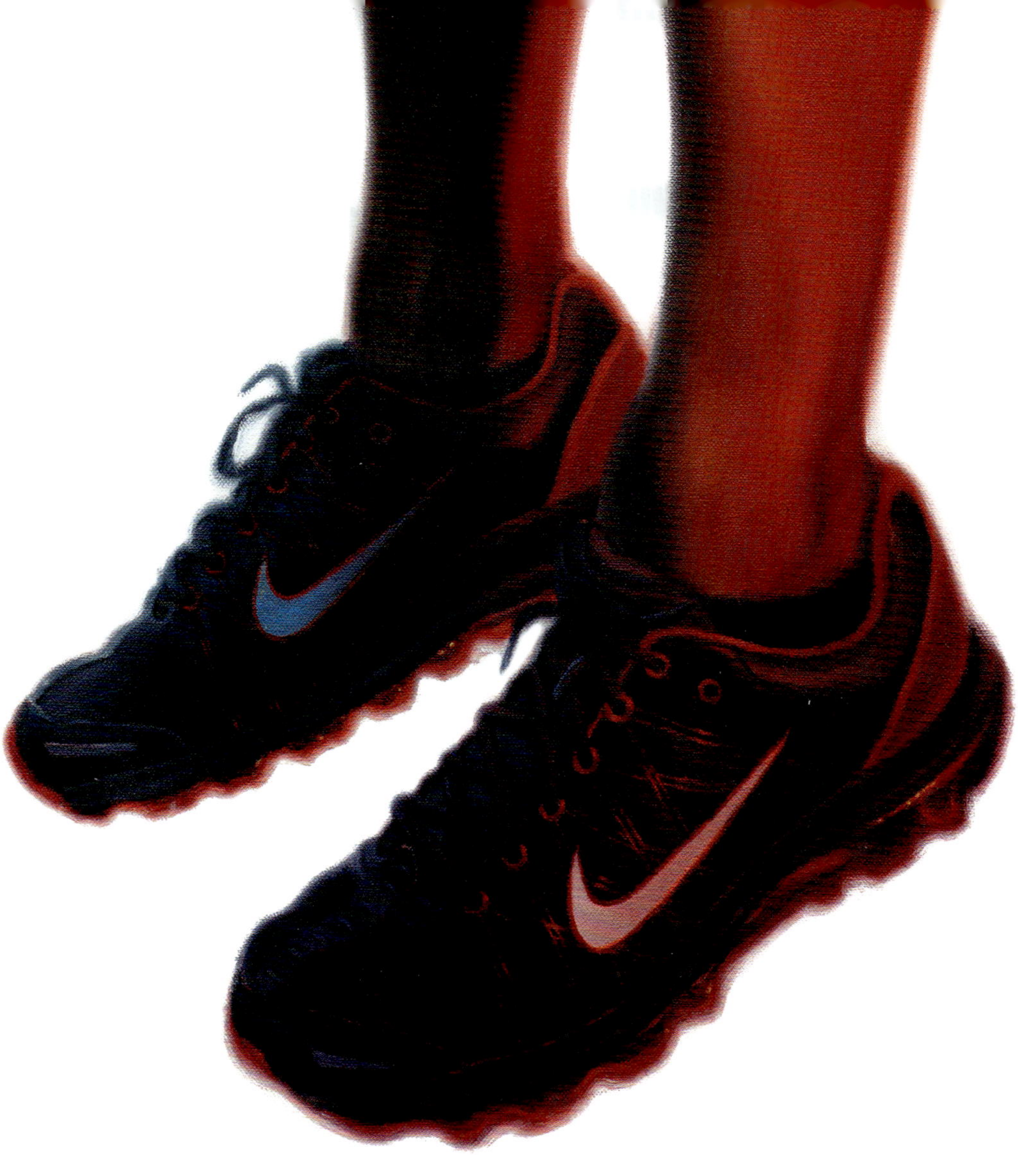

***The Strangest Fruit*, 2013**
Oil on canvas, 8 panels
Photos: Mark Menjivar

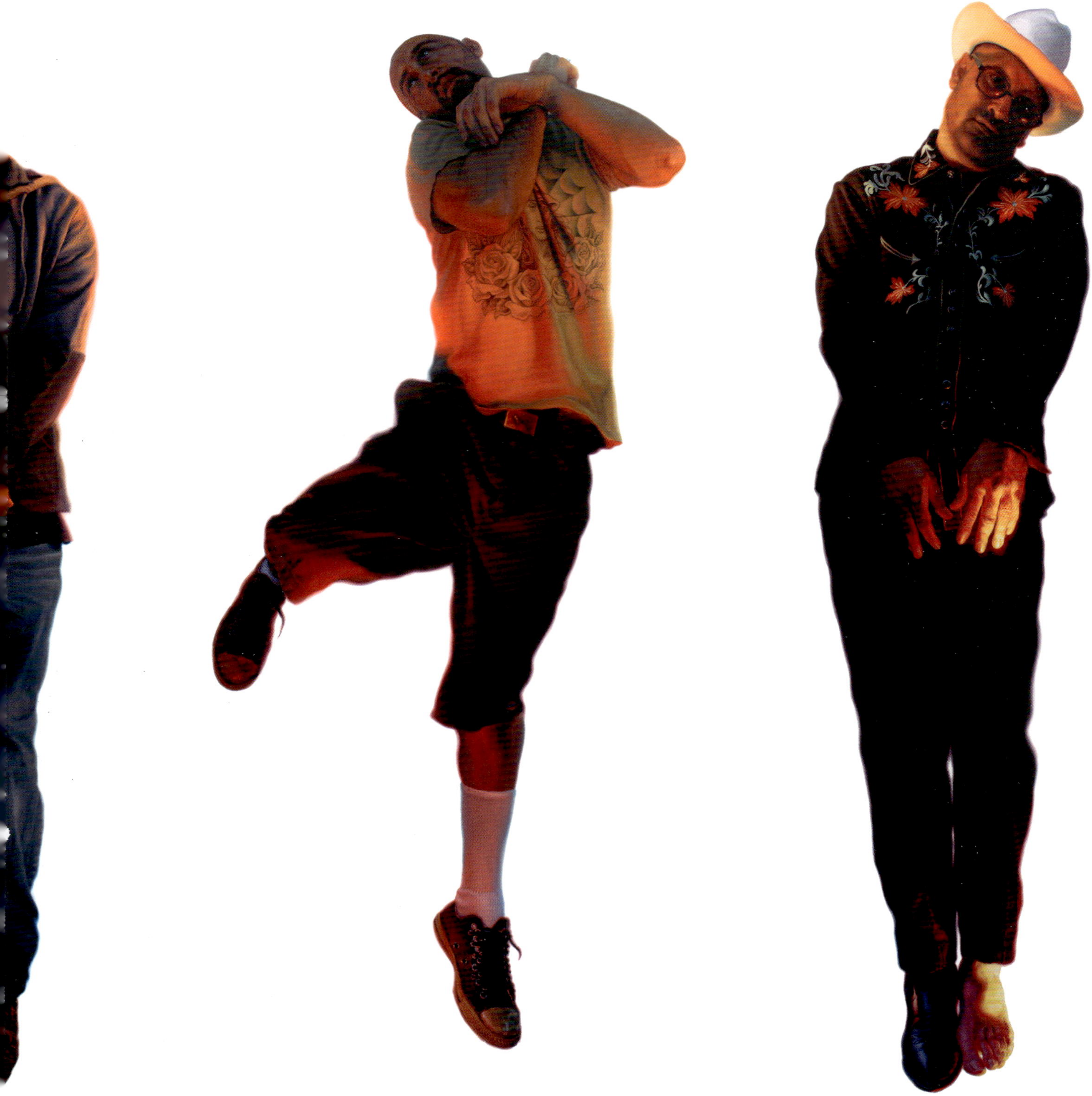

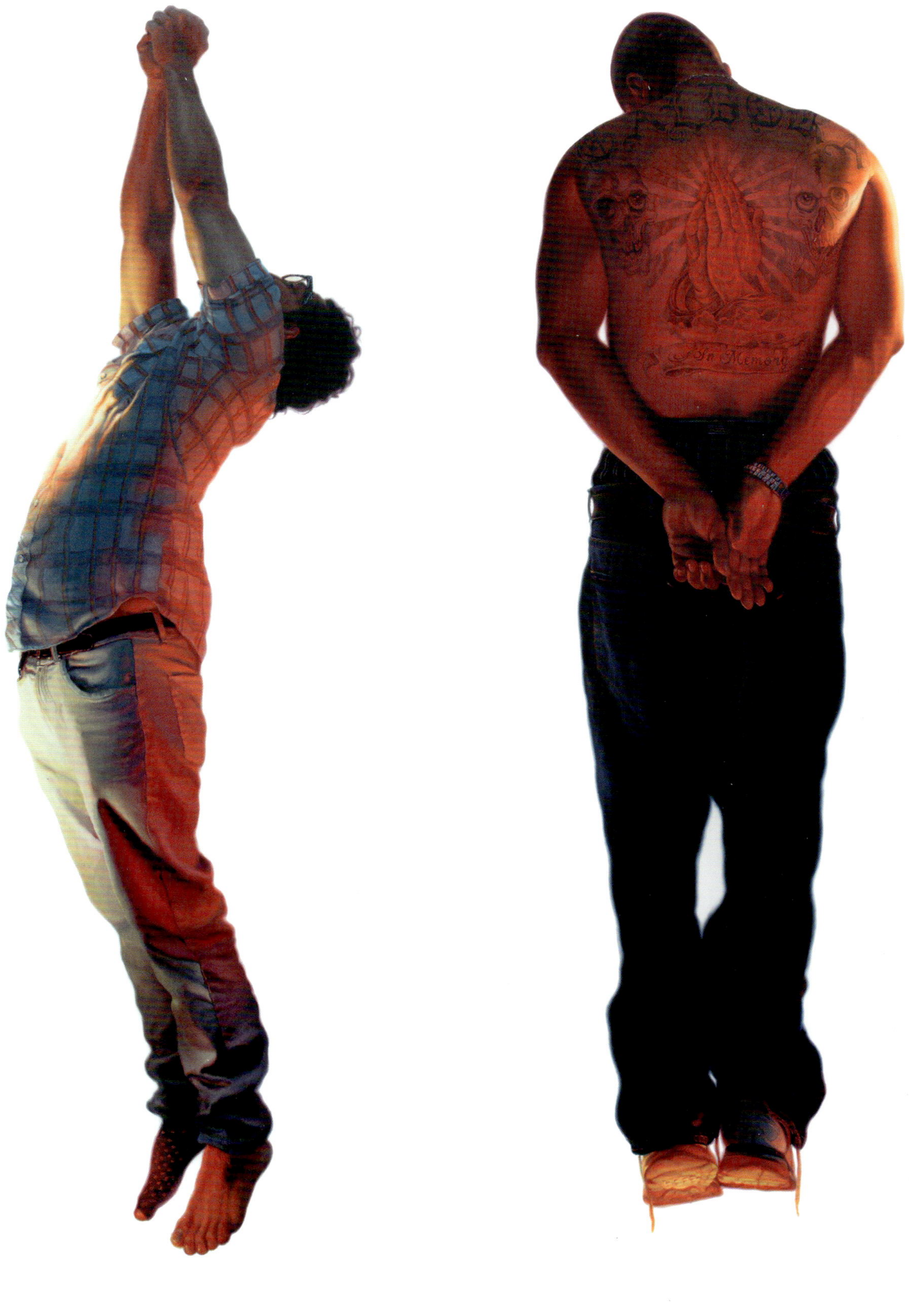
In Memory

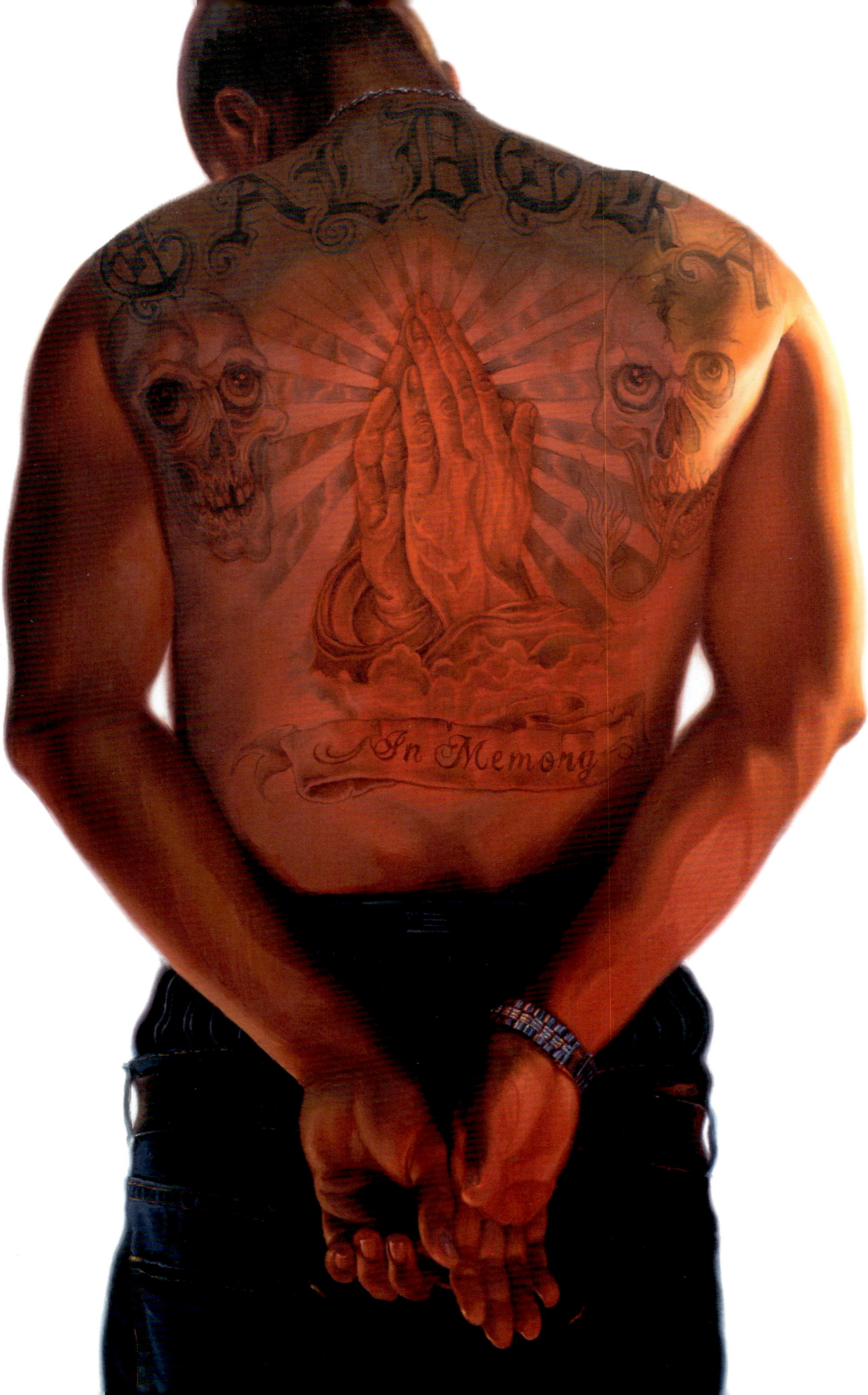
In Memory

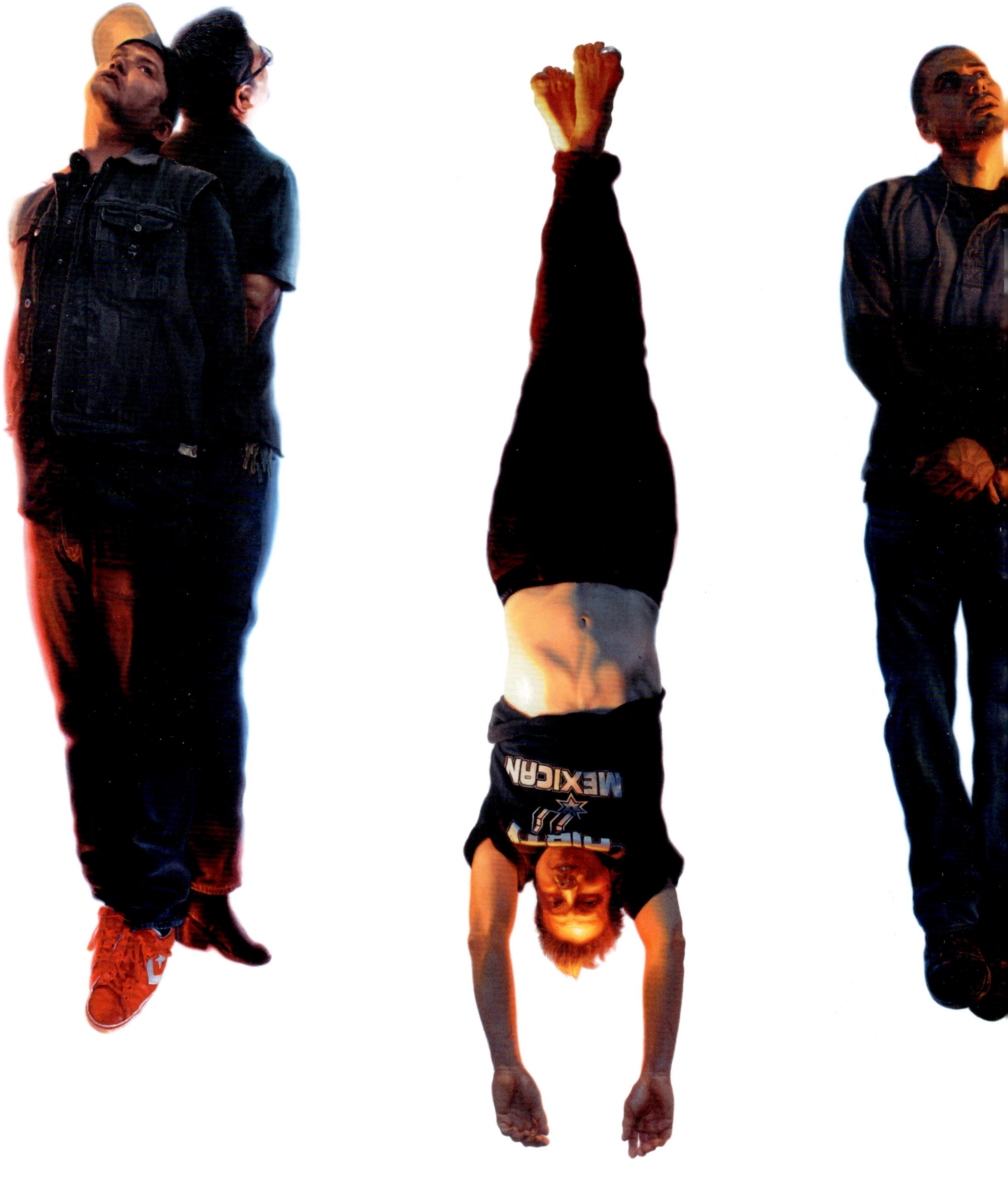
MEXICAN

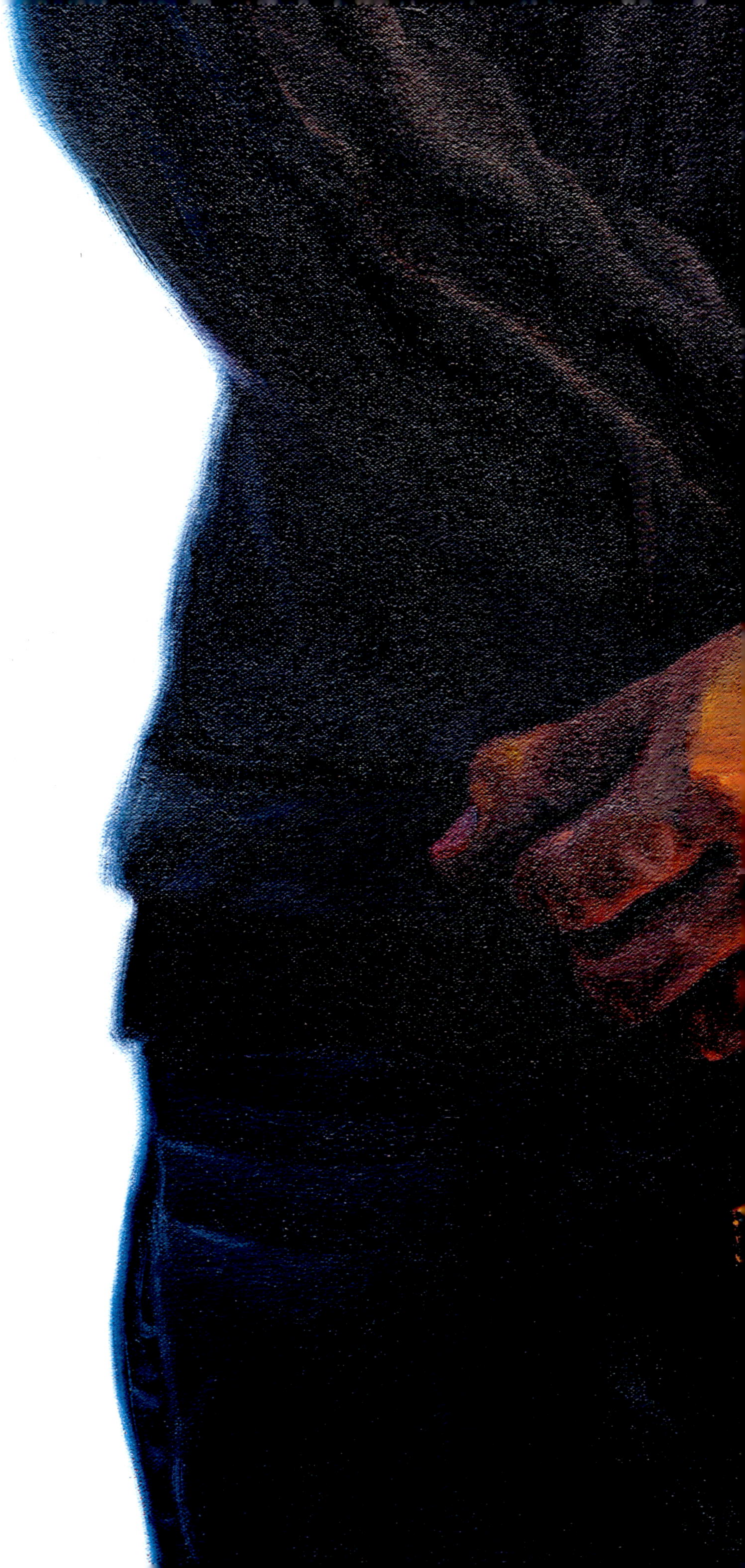

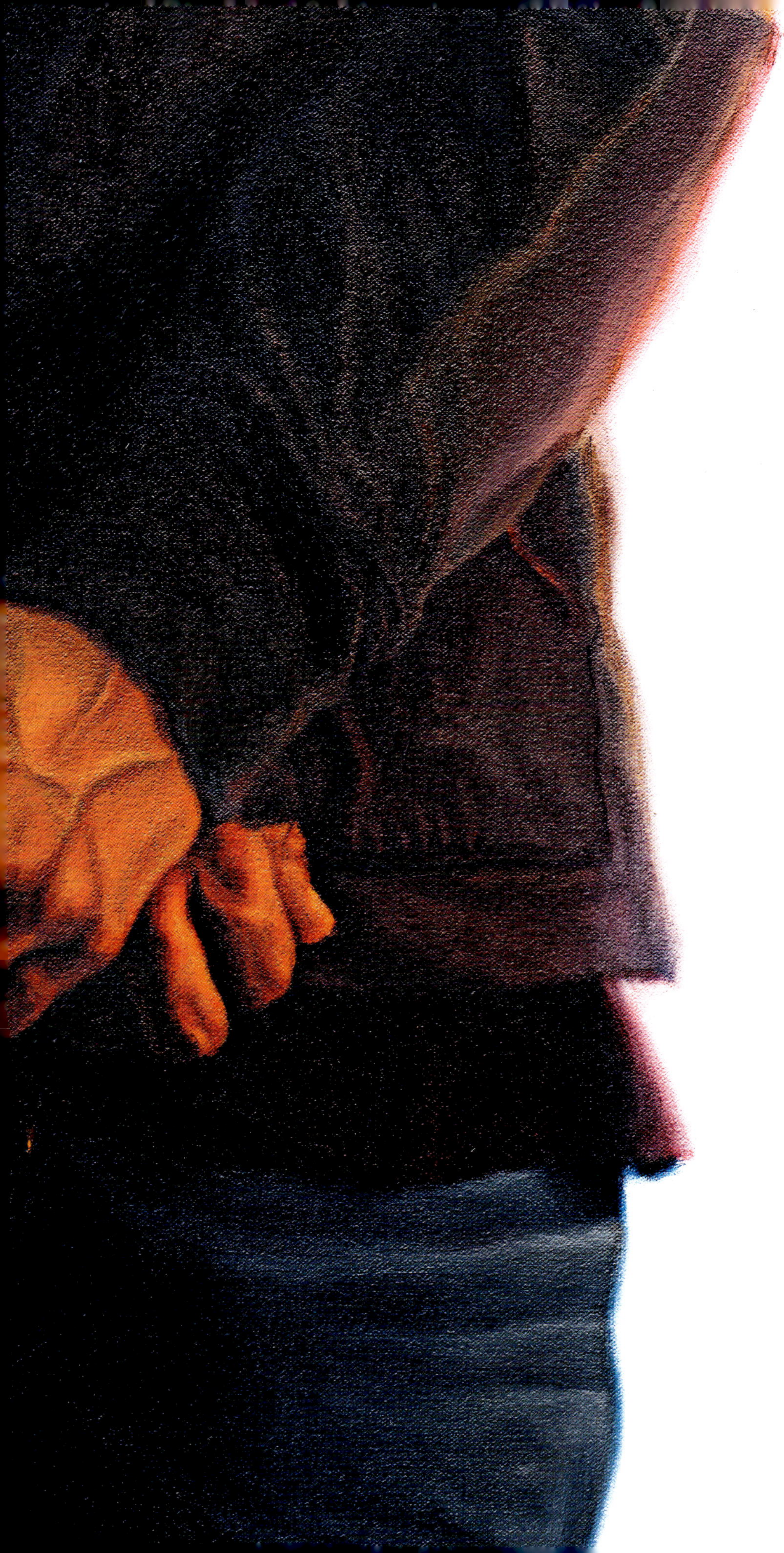

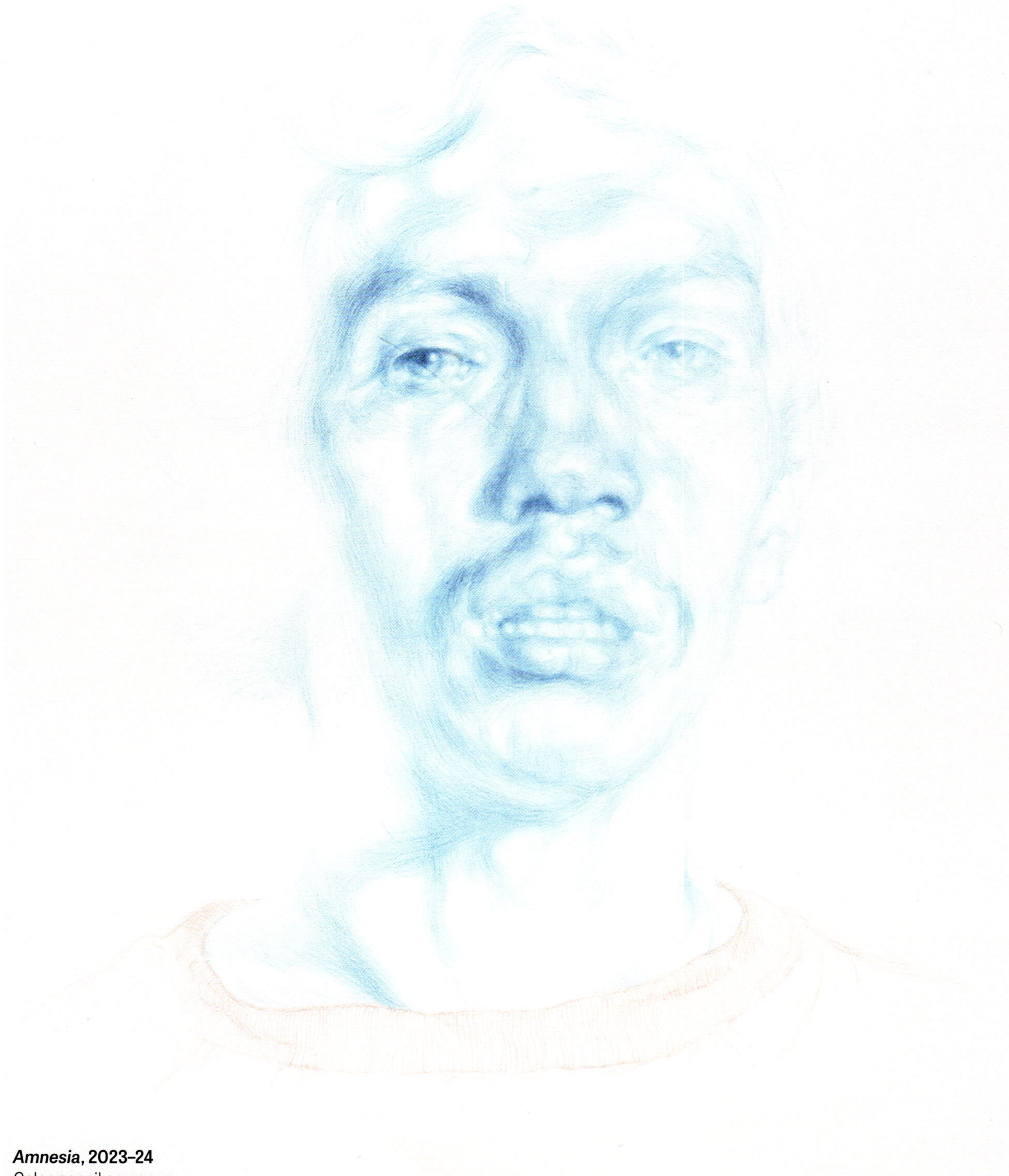

***Amnesia*, 2023–24**
Color pencil on paper
Photos: Elon Schoenholz

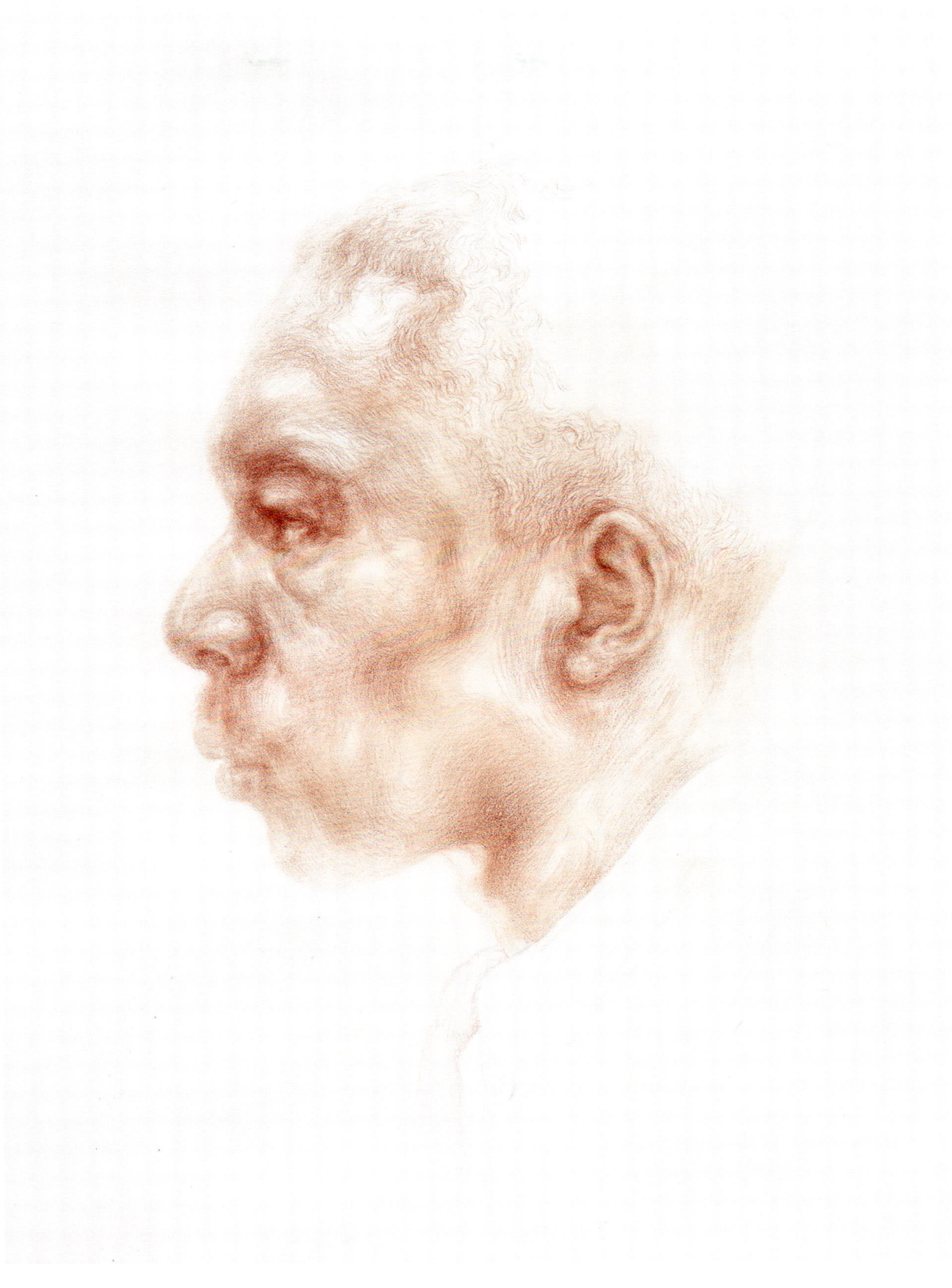

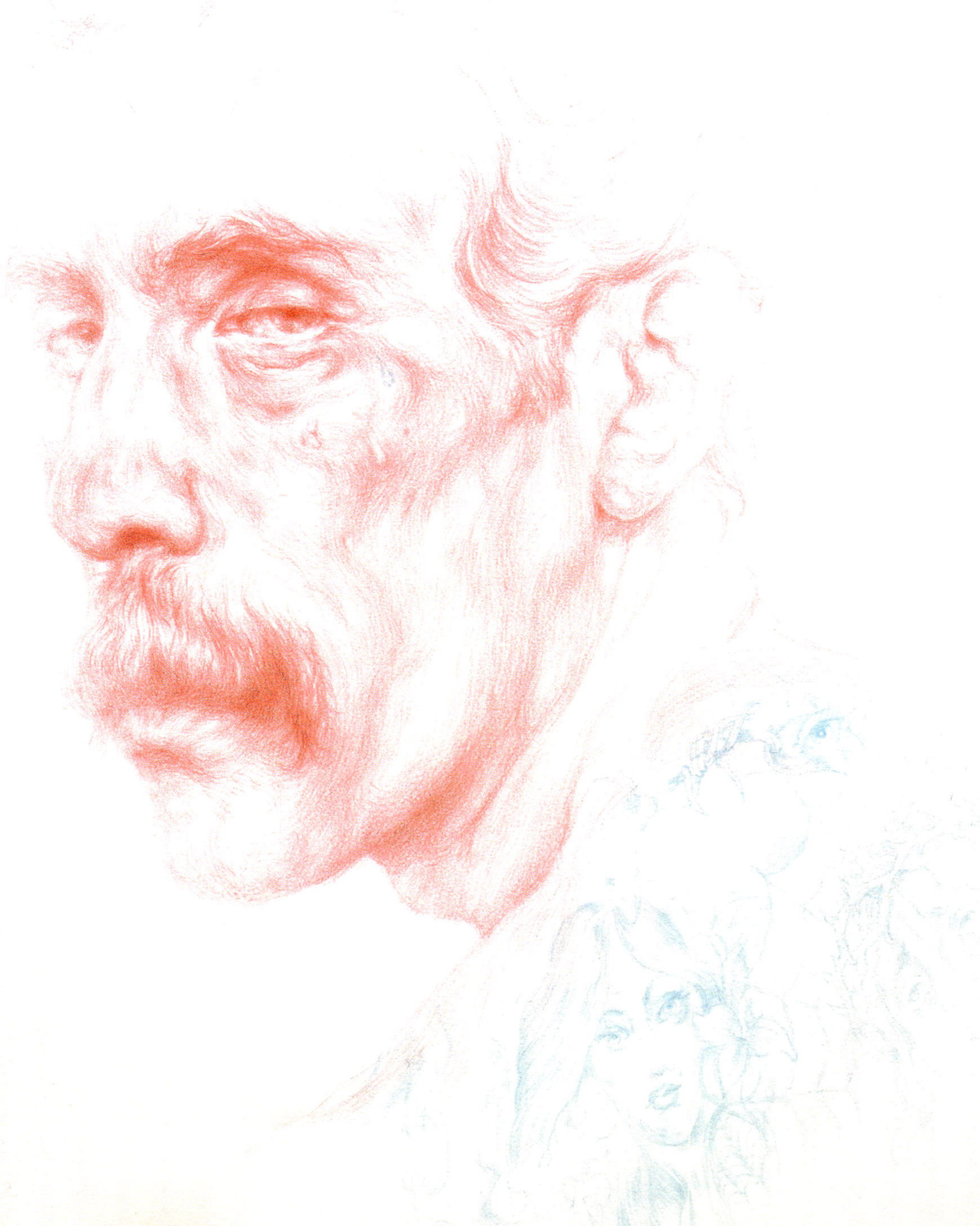

SEEMED LIKE WINTER IN AMERICA
A TIME WHEN ALL THE HEALERS
DONE BEEN KILLED.
OR BEEN BETRAYED, SAY
PEOPLE KNOW THAT SOMETHING'S WRONG
EVERYBODY OUGHTA KNOW WINTER
SEEMED LIKE WINTER IN AMERICA
THE TRUTH IS THERE AIN'T NOBODY FIGHTIN'
BECAUSE, WELL NOBODY KNOWS WHAT TO SAVE

—**GIL SCOTT-HERON** excerpt from "Winter in America" (1974)

There's a brightside

PATRICIA RESTREPO

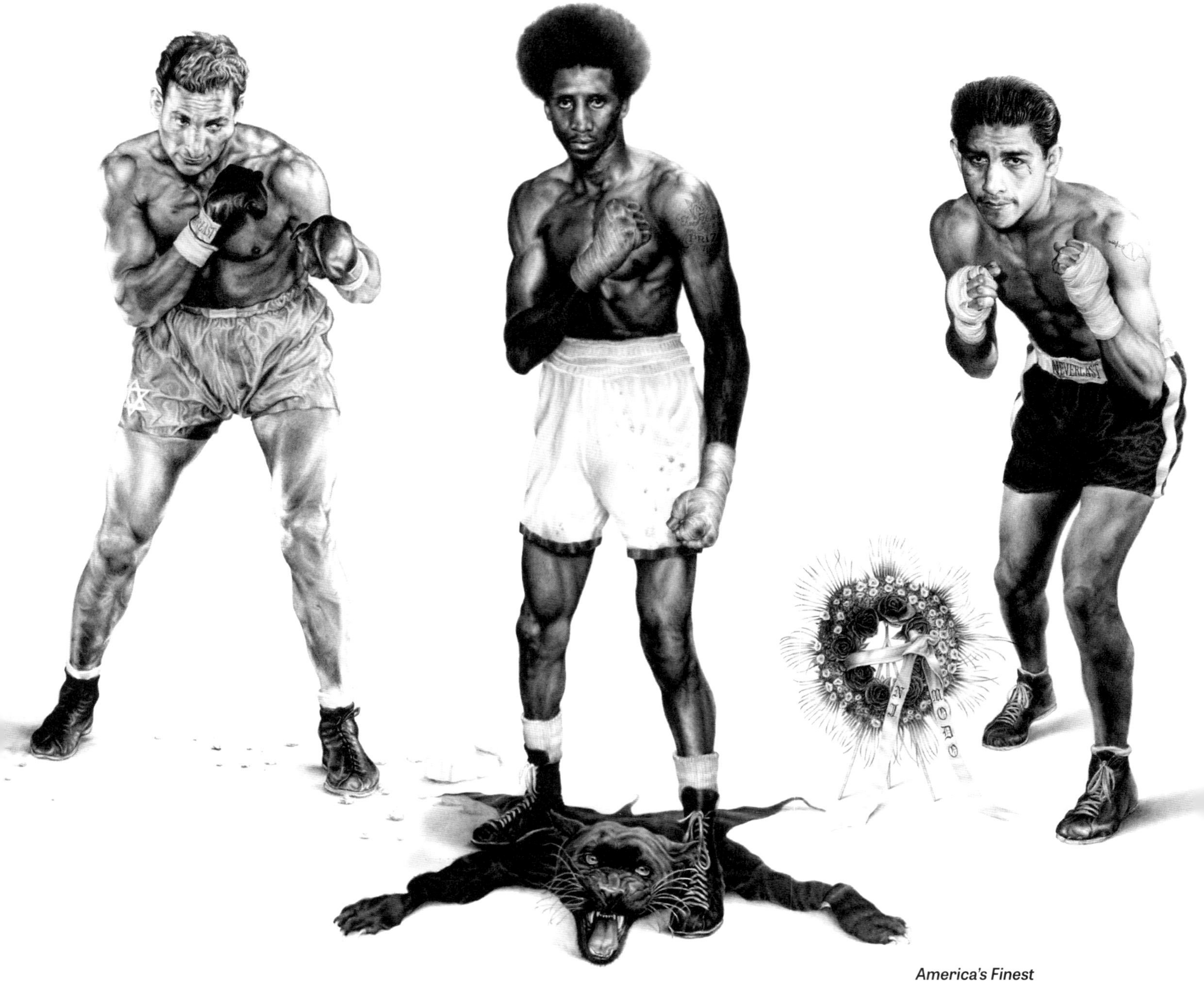

America's Finest
(detail of 6 panels), 2012
Graphite on paper
Photos: David Shelton Gallery

somewhere...

Paris, 1922. Ernest Hemingway finds himself in a rather unpleasant position. His entire collection of manuscripts, packed in suitcases along with their carbon copies, has been stolen. Only two of his manuscripts survive. At the time, Hemingway had been trading boxing lessons with Ezra Pound in exchange for Pound's writing advice. Pound countered Hemingway's grief from the theft with, "If the middle, i.e., *FORM*, of the story is right then one ought to be able to reassemble it from memory. . . . If the thing wobbles and won't reform . . . then it never *wd. have* been *right*."[1]

Perturbed by this elliptical advice, Hemingway authored "Out of Season," a short story launching his "iceberg theory." The tale recounts an expatriate couple's day fishing with a drunken Italian guide. Its layered narrative addresses themes of alienation and male frailty. Critical details were intentionally omitted from the account in a wildly experimental approach for the time. Likening the story to an iceberg and its written form to the iceberg's visible peak, Hemingway states, "The dignity of movement of an iceberg is due to only one-eighth of it being above water,"[2] anticipating the reader's ability to identify veiled truths from subtext.

Hemingway might seem a curious place to begin when thinking about the evolution of Vincent Valdez's practice. Innovators in their respective disciplines, both essentialize American life. The writer and the artist even share an affinity for boxing. Their similarity also lies in their use of ellipses as a storytelling strategy. This lexical device conventionally omits words and hints at unsaid fragments. Walt Whitman regularly employed this grammatical gesture to present pronounced pauses, a signal to slow down. His early work was scattered with ellipses of varying lengths, often four dots rather than the standard three. "Whitman's ellipses aren't marking something left out so much as indicating everything that could, in principle, be let in."[3]

Seemingly slight in measure yet robust in effect, Valdez's exhibition title introduces an ellipsis. *Just A Dream...* references his painting *Just a Dream (In America)* (2020–21), which depicts a fatigued boxer.[4] At the core of his practice, Valdez responds to our country's overlooked or politically motivated redactions—the ellipses of our society—which exemplify the duality between what is seen and unseen that is so elemental to the artist's work.

Valdez's elliptical form does not truncate truths; rather, he fills the space between his picture and the viewers' eyes with an invitation to look at the stories untold. In turn, we then can imagine the trajectory of his figures and, perhaps, society as a whole. As viewers we get to fill in the narrative gaps. While Valdez's work is laden with references revealed with attention and time, his ellipses are a physical extension of himself, imbuing his work with generosity built through the convergence of his life and his long-standing sociopolitical concerns. "The personal is political" reverberates throughout Valdez's decades-long practice.

Valdez's primary focus is on the principal subject of power: who receives it and to whom it is denied. The artist finds it challenging to celebrate the United States blindly, as its victories have often come at immense expense to others. Valdez's work regularly references the abuse of power, with persistent concerns around state sanctioned violence and racial profiling. Inhabiting philosopher Michel Foucault's musings on "fearless speech,"[5] or the moral duty to tell the truth despite resulting risk, Valdez's work serves as an antidote to looking past inequitable treatment. Akin to artist Mark Lombardi's webbed drawings of political networks, Valdez identifies connective tissues between constellations of power. Valdez states: "They choke people. We choke their budgets. See how quickly their loss of hearing and amnesia gets cured. Police unions and departments, mega churches, media networks, banks, developers, politicians, institutions and corporations. Connect the dots. Nothing but dominoes."[6]

Valdez embodies truth to power, urgently prompting us to seek veracity through his stylized scenes. Reminding us that "lying is our national hobby," the artist confronts distorted truths and the myths that undergird them. This destabilization causes discomfort, addressing the gap between a fantastical recounting of this country's history and its present condition. While exploring authoritarian power dynamics, his paintings recall lives brushed aside by the powers that be, which he then brings back to the fore with his brushstrokes. Valdez's work has a magnifying power, while appealing to public awareness by reminding viewers of their own power to act. That merging of political and personal is evident throughout this text, which unfurls the evolution of Valdez's practice not merely to chart his work through a biographical lens but instead to open portals of understanding, or invitational ellipses.

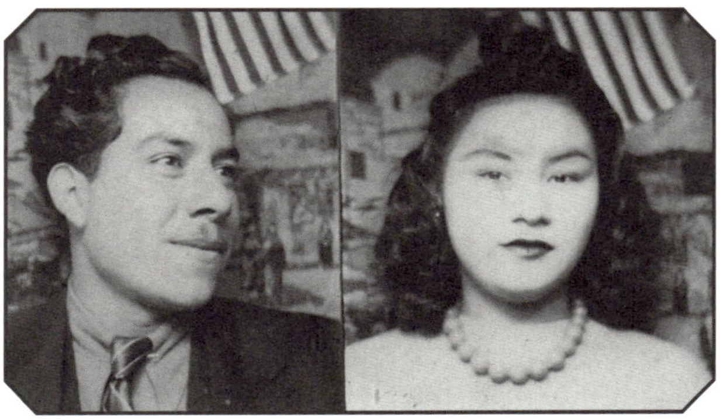

Valdez's grandparents, Carmen and Gabriel Santana, photobooth circa 1941
Photo: Izaac Costiniano, Courtesy of Art League Houston

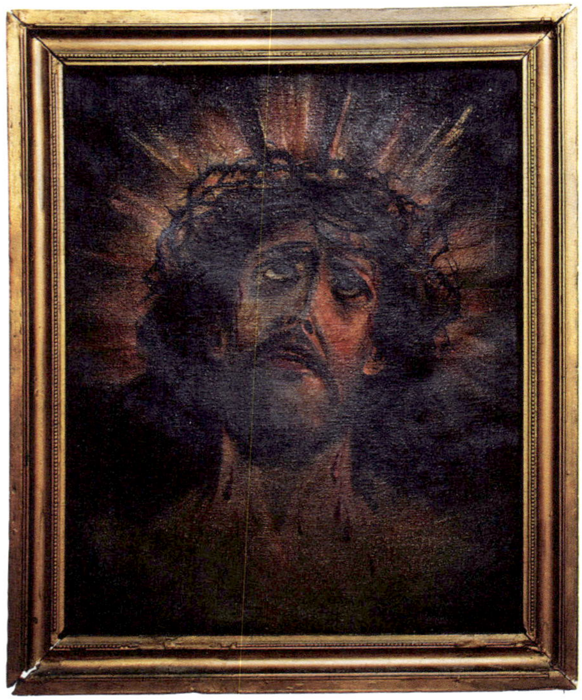

Jose Maria Valdez (great-grandfather), *Crucifixion*, 1898
Oil on canvas
Photo: Abdurrahman Danquah

Make Food, Not War **1987–93**

Valdez's artistic trajectory precedes his birth. The artist recalls his first "museum" experience at age four or five: staring at dozens of paintings by Jose Maria Valdez, his great-grandfather, proudly hanging in his grandparents' home. One particularly impactful piece was a classically rendered Christ, gazing up through his crown of thorns, painted in the late 1890s. The young Valdez was mesmerized by the imagery and its palpable power. His great-grandfather's work was so indelible that Valdez had the piece translated into a tattoo for his left forearm as a reminder of his beginnings.

Jose Maria Valdez had hoped his children would follow similar artistic pursuits, imprinting the importance of the Mexican Muralist tradition by taking his son, Arthur, to Palacio de Bellas Artes in Mexico City to see David Alfaro Siqueiros's monumental mural *Nueva Democracia* circa 1964. Although they never met, Valdez felt he knew his great-grandfather through the body of images he left behind. While his intergenerational family members did not come to be artists, they understood the significance of documenting histories.

It is thanks to the Valdez inclination to record and memorialize moments otherwise lost to time that we learn about Valdez's earliest artistic pursuits. He began drawing around three years old; an early first drawing was of the ugly duckling. Decades later, the artist identified this image as an apt self-portrait, one of an underdog or outcast. He learned to draw from books with photographic images, where he would trace figures prior to coloring them in, later turning to comic books and encyclopedias for source imagery. Yet Valdez would not hold a paintbrush until he learned to paint murals in 1987.

That year, Valdez found himself shoulder to shoulder, figuratively speaking, with politically minded Chicano artists in his hometown of San Antonio; Alex Rubio, nine years his senior, treated him as an equal and recognized his significant talent and insatiable desire to paint. Valdez was intrigued by Rubio, with his dangling cigarette and long hair held back by a bandana, and the two became close collaborators and friends, working together every Saturday on murals across the city for the Community Cultural Arts program. At the former site of the Esperanza Peace and Justice Center, Valdez and Rubio were joined by Valdez's fifth-grade peers on a month-long mural project about world peace. While his classmates painted stick figures, rainbows, and hearts, Valdez's scene depicted fighter jets dropping napalm over field workers with an emblazoned text in the sky reading "make food, not war."

Rubio taught Valdez the basic techniques of painting: "How to hold and clean brushes, how to scoop paint out of its can, how to blend color, how to hold a palette, how to consider composition, how to build light and shadow." Since Valdez was too young to climb high on the scaffolding, the two often divided the wall, with Valdez taking the lower portion. From 1987 through 1993, Rubio and Valdez produced murals across the city of San Antonio, drawing attention to the AIDS crisis, memorializing Vietnam war veterans, and paying homage to La Virgen de Guadalupe. In a more fantastical scene, they rendered a fictional soccer match between an Aztec warrior and a modern player, a tribute to the historic legacy of soccer in the Americas, on the gymnasium wall at Valdez's high school.

This labor-intensive, community-centered work was deeply impactful for Valdez, who also began to see himself as part of Chicano art traditions. Murals were a site where the young artist felt himself reflected, linking Valdez with the world around him. The artist was also empowered by his ability to recount narratives alternative to those found in his textbooks, focusing on cultural community warriors instead of addressing American figures such as Nelson Rockefeller and Davy Crockett. After all, muralism was a route to excavate histories that highlight communities of color and diverse socio-economic classes. Even at a young age, Valdez understood the power of counter-monuments, speaking to the masses with critical messages of resistance. He also learned to consider audiences, as he worked in the open with visitors frequently stopping to discuss the work or inquire about its progress. In many ways, this type of painting foreshadowed the arc of a career recognized for crafting an accessible art practice, centered on the immediacy of the image and clarity of his voice.

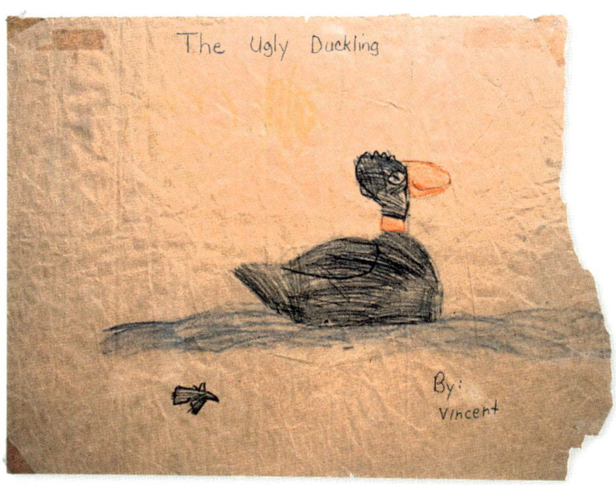

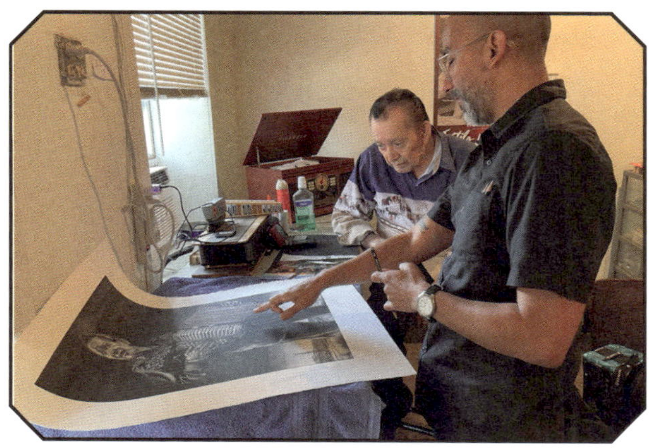

Valdez's drawing of the ugly duckling, 1981
Photo: Abdurrahman Danquah

Vincent Valdez with Flaco Jiménez, 2022
Photo: Adriana Corral

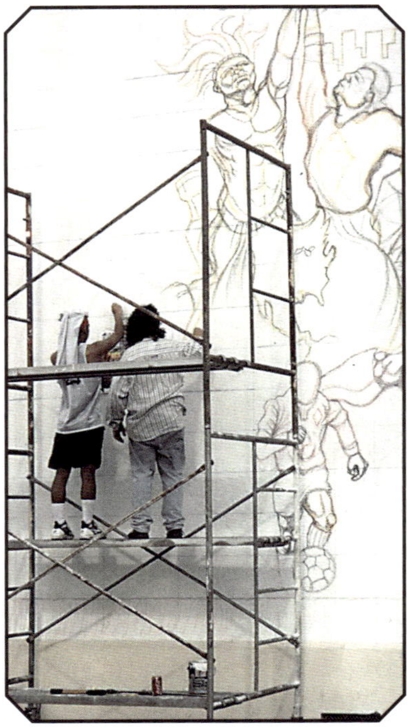

Alex Rubio and Valdez painting a mural, Burbank High School, San Antonio, TX, 1993

***Recuerdo (Remembering)*, 1999**
House paint on wood
Collection of Joe A. Diaz

Another place where Valdez found community through art was at one of the nation's oldest Chicano/a organizations, The Guadalupe Cultural Arts Center (GCAC) in San Antonio. GCAC provided Valdez with numerous resources, thanks to the mentorship of artists Alex Rubio and Kathy Vargas. Here, Valdez intensely studied the work of Chicano artists like Luis Jiménez, Jose Luis Rivera, and César Martínez. Valdez began to understand the legacy of political printmaking; many source images featured a black and red color palette, which became the artist's predominant choice for a number of years. Through GCAC, music and its cultural impact also assumed a vital role in the artist's life, harkening back to his weekly record store trips with Vargas. Valdez was introduced to his perennial favorites, including Leonard Cohen, Bob Dylan, The Doors, Jimi Hendrix, and important Tex-Mex/conjunto musicians like Flaco Jiménez—whom he would later render in his ongoing series *The Beginning is Near (An American Trilogy), Chapter Three: The New Americans, Veteranos #1 (Flaco)* (2024).

Alongside his experience with mural painting, Valdez was also bewitched by the spectacle of both television and movie screens. In 1988, he sat stunned watching Michael Jordan's famous televised slam dunk, its low camera angle allowing for seemingly impossible feats of human athleticism. In his youth, Valdez would pause movies on the VCR and copy the frozen image. Television became his teacher of human anatomy and expression, as well as composition. Valdez was also entranced by the collective experience of the cinema, where his attention shifted between the movie and the gaze of fellow viewers. He traces his desire to captivate audiences with images to his experience watching the film *Platoon* (1986) at age eight or nine. In the packed theater, while others sat watching the screen, Valdez focused on the audience's silence and concentration on the projected image.

Valdez also credits film with influencing his approach to portraiture, creating a cinematic feel in much of his work through dramatic lighting and palpable energy. Rendered with skillful chiaroscuro, many of Valdez's paintings contain a light source interior to the work, be it truck headlights, radiating suns, or camera flashes. The artist's signature elongated panoramic canvases also recall the widescreen format of the cinema. For as much as it offered to him, the screen simultaneously was a space that made Valdez feel unseen. At that time Latinos were even more rarely depicted in advertisements, television series, or the quotidian portrayals of "Americans." This lack of representation prompted Valdez to ask his mother about their own American identity. A lingering sensation of otherness would cause him to interrogate who he and his country are to this day.

Mosquito Weight 1997 & 2001-2

In 1997, Valdez left Texas after being awarded a full scholarship to the Rhode Island School of Design (RISD) in Providence. He began studying illustration, but was deterred by the constraints of client-based work. His junior year, unable to return home for Thanksgiving, Valdez stayed on campus. He found familial connection through painting. He recalls how, "stocked up on sandwiches and cereal, I was completely isolated in the studio. And so I listened to songs from home and thought about my family—my grandma's cooking and my grandpa in his backyard, after a long day of cutting lawns in the scorching Texas heat. I painted day and night, uninterrupted, for two weeks straight. These personal memories, along with a conjunto song lyric that sparked my imagination . . . I sat at a table and let out a sigh, and thought of how things used to be."

The resulting *Recuerdo (Remembering)* (1999) portrays his grandfather Gabriel, who sits in his backyard at dusk smoking, reminiscing, and playing his accordion after a hard day's work. The cigarette dangling out of his mouth comically and implausibly sags as if wet, yet its red embers claim otherwise. The sun sets as the protagonist reflects on his own setting life. Over twenty candles dot the background, while a central *veladora* (or prayer candle) casts dramatic shadows on the man's face and knotted knuckles. A breeze is palpable as the hanging laundry catches flight, one item impossibly ghostly, while others are recognizable as serapes and socks. Despite the work's revelrous potential with instruments and ceremonial lighting, there is a somber energy epitomized by a small cemetery marker.

By connecting with his family in *Recuerdo (Remembering)*, despite the thousands of miles separating them physically, Valdez found painting a tool for transcending space and time through the mining of memory. In this moment, Valdez tapped into his singular capacity for storytelling, stating, "This painting depicts an important moment for me—it was the moment that I fully realized what my voice and my vision was about to become as a painter."

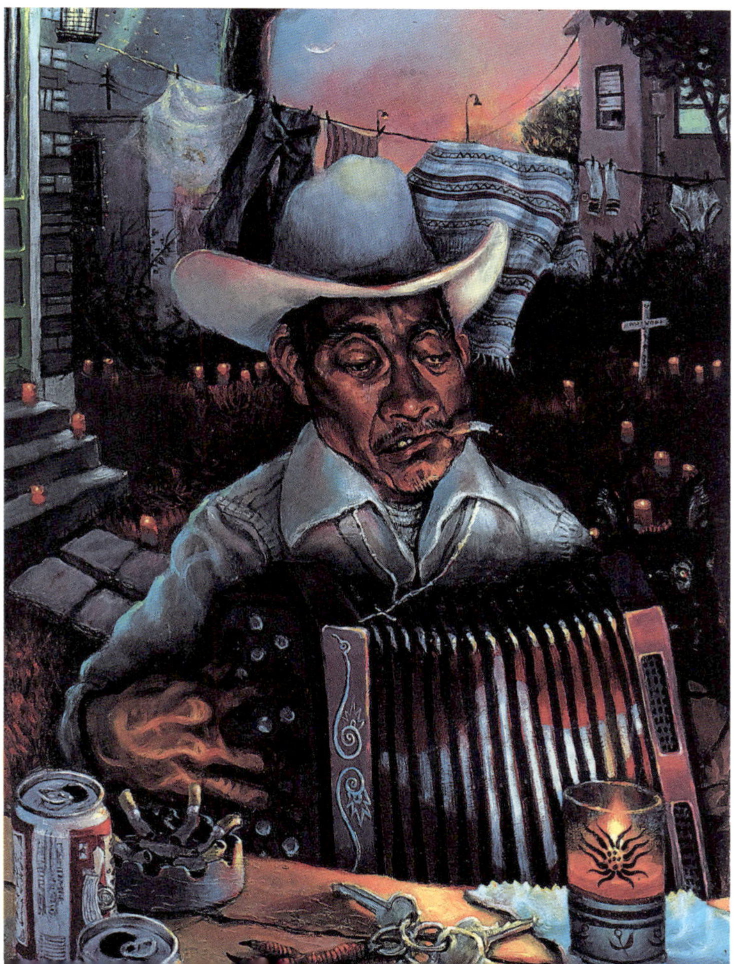

This work brings to mind a later painting also honoring Valdez's family, *People of the Sun (Grandma & Grandpa Santana)* (2019). The tender piece pays homage to the artist's grandparents, who spent over seventy years together: Gabriel, who is depicted in *Recuerdo (Remembering)*, and Carmen Santana. In the work, we encounter objects that speak to a life lived—a vintage AM radio, a spritely Southwestern cactus, a painted pot with Aztec codex iconography. This allusion to the Aztecs, who called themselves the people of the sun, honors the sun as a vital life force. We witness other signs of their sun-filled existence in the form of "their weathered hands, my grandpa's sunburned flesh from a lifetime of labor under the Texas sun, and my grandmother's levitated bed sheets that serve as shield and protector." The laundry shielding his grandparents, like a backdrop behind them, mirrors the laundry hanging in the foreground of *Recuerdo (Remembering)*. Valdez's familial lineage is held by these signifiers, wrapped in symbolic protection.

The stature and pride of Valdez's grandparents make them both a loving and formidable presence on the canvas and in the world beyond the picture. Valdez's *People of the Sun* recalls Edward Hopper's *People in the Sun* (1960), which presents a melancholic and isolated group of sunbathers. Yet for Valdez, more importantly, *People of the Sun* "serves as a visual testimony to the historic presence of Mexican Americans and the American Southwest, often unacknowledged within the canon of American history, both past and present. Our story is an undeniable part of the epic, unfolding American tale." In his quest to memorialize the personal, Valdez increasingly depicts family and friends in an inward turn, eschewing the cool reserve of the Hopper painting.

While at RISD, Valdez became interested in boxing, a common theme within much of his work to the present. During his senior year, he joined a gym, joking to himself that he might be crowned a "mosquito weight" champ. He ultimately gave life to these dreams on paper, rendering

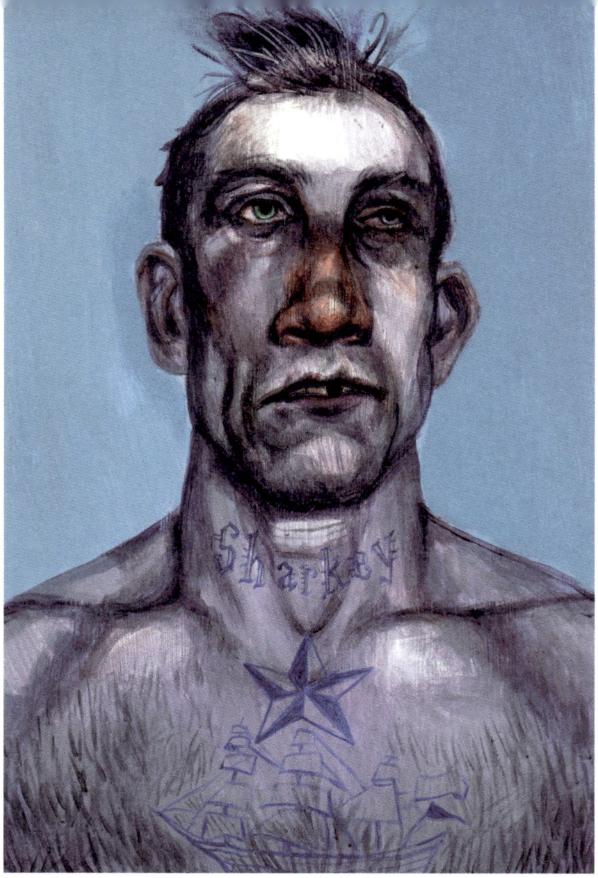

Sharkey, 2000
House paint on board
Photo: Holland Photo Imaging, Courtesy of Art League Houston

Yo Soy-ee Blaxican (I Am Blaxican), 2003
Pastel on paper

a boxer for the first time that same year. Down a front tooth, and likely his bout, this battered green-eyed fighter re-collects himself inside the ring.

Valdez's boxers contradict customary representations as powerful and invulnerable. Instead, they are often scarred, physically and emotionally. In conflict, not with fearsome foes, but with themselves, the fighters cause self-inflicted psychological wounds perhaps exceeding their physical injuries. These athletes are nearing collapse, struggling to stand in the ring and carry on. They symbolize the fight for survival. Valdez links these figures to Mary Shelley's *Frankenstein* (1818)— invented, created, and used by a society, only to be turned on and discarded. Valdez's images of boxers exceed their literal connotation; they are an analogue for our daily attempts to persist despite everyday pressures, speaking to the internal emotional, physical, and mental challenges we face in our respective rings.

The boxers, then and now, ultimately represent the struggles and joys of humanity, which takes many forms in Valdez's work and life. For example, Valdez experienced culture shock studying at RISD, a landscape and environment far removed from Texas. The artist simultaneously encountered a lack of representation in his art history textbooks and began to consider approaches and methods to counter these concerning patterns. During his final year at RISD, he began digging online for source material about the Zoot Suit Riots, an important yet overlooked chapter of American history. During a five-day period in 1943, Pachucos, or Mexican American youths, were beaten publicly by American armed servicemen and civilians for donning Zoot Suits. These flamboyant suits, popular amongst African American, Latino, and Filipino youth throughout America, were demonized as anti-patriotic because of their excessive use of fabric, which during the war was frowned upon due to rationing. Yet Valdez reminds us that "the violence was more about racial tension than fashion."

The resulting painting, *Kill the Pachuco Bastard!* (2001), premiered in his senior exhibition at RISD. Valdez visualizes a stylized version of the conflict: a gruesome bar brawl between the servicemen and Pachucos. A card game has been interrupted as bottles fly into the air, faces are smashed, clothing is ripped, a rabid dog wrestles with a sailor's uniform, while drunken servicemen urinate and leave a wake of destruction in the background. The red-tiled floor camouflages spilled blood. The complex scene is marked by Valdez's deft handling of contorted bodies and mastery over nuances of light play and sources of illumination, including barely visible police lights. The scene is chilling, made even more so by the fact that Valdez was the physical model for all of the depicted figures, embodying a multiplicity of identities and stances. *Kill the Pachuco Bastard!* was met with resistance when several of Valdez's professors critiqued this type of work as not palatable and miscalculated that he would have a short career. Actor and collector Cheech Marin, however, saw the work and purchased it the following year. Here Valdez began to truly understand his own fight and launched a decades-long commitment to confronting overlooked violence in his paintings through the use of arresting details and technical mastery that would hold a viewer's attention. While this particular work depicts a bloody and violent mid-fight freeze, later Valdez evolves from overt representation to more allusory and haunting traces, like ellipses bookending violence's culmination: unseen yet insidious.

I'm Blaxican 2000-3

After graduating from RISD in 2000, Valdez returned to Texas where he began developing a palette of colors, one that reflected the light found in the physical, historical, and political landscapes of the American Southwest. He was reminded of a midsummer day, dominated by deep violets, blood oranges, and fire reds, when the sun hung in its purgatory state separating night and day. Valdez's background details have not received sufficient recognition in prior analysis of his work, which has frequently focused on the body. Yet when looking across Valdez's oeuvre, it is clear that the setting becomes the psychological and symbolic state of his depicted subjects, making them inseparable from one another.

This keen focus on the landscape translates to the intensity of color evident in *Yo Soy-ee Blaxican (I Am Blaxican)* (2003). In the center of the composition, we exchange glances with a young man, head cocked with a backwards cap and posturing with his chin up. The figure's confident pose assures us that his presence is undeniable. The sun electrifyingly reddens the space behind him. A symbol of resistance, the painting's red and black palette pays homage to political graphics, particularly those from the civil rights movement that Valdez had studied in his youth. The stylistic approach of *Yo Soy-ee Blaxican (I Am Blaxican)* also nods to Chicano artists from Texas whom Valdez admired, such as César Martínez, who is celebrated for his portraits of Mexican Americans set against vibrant color-field backgrounds.

In *Yo Soy-ee Blaxican (I Am Blaxican)*, Valdez represents a hybrid American identity central to the twenty-first century. Upon returning to Texas, Valdez had a formative conversation with his younger brother Daniel,[7] then in high school; the artist asked which race category he identified with when filling out official academic testing and ID forms. His brother quipped that he had "never been to Mexico, did not know what a Chicano was, shrugged at the term Latino, and does not speak Spanish." Instead, he kissed two of his fingers, threw them up in the air for the recently deceased rapper Tupac Shakur, and exclaimed, "I'm Blaxican." Valdez realized Daniel's merging of cultures invited a new approach to identity formation. "Blaxican" was his brother's way of making space and forming a place in his world, reflecting his own complex environment as America is "forever regurgitating its own identity, mutating itself, evolving and adapting."[8]

In the early 2000s, Valdez expanded his archetype of the boxer, fusing a character's fight for survival with the underlying tension of something on the verge of happening.[9] This led to the four-panel work, *Made Men*, (2002). To create this series, Valdez functioned as a film director, staging live models in his studio. Produced in five

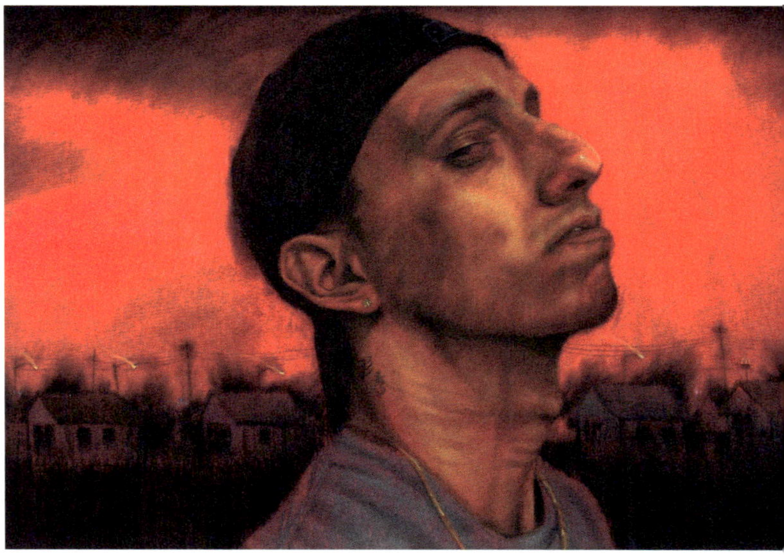

tones of pastel, a medium Valdez calls his "oldest friend," the four fatigued figures are rendered individually. They each look off the paper, statuesque, yet glimpsing their destinies of defeat. Despite the feeling that their matches are fixed, that their game is rigged, they stand defiant. The figures in this series are not just boxers; they are based on heroic masculine archetypes found in western mythology and history: warriors, martyrs, gladiators, contemporary homeboys. They remain the anti-heroes in their fighting rings, war zones, and in the contemporary American streets.

Study for *El Chavez Ravine*, 2005
Pencil on paper

Valdez working on *El Chavez Ravine*, Los Angeles, 2006
Photo: Ray Santisteban

The small bright bursts of light that encase the figures' upper heads are symbolic. The boxer with one eye nearly shuttered from injury sees the proverbial stars before collapsing. He is followed by a figure resembling Christ, who witnesses falling stars as the light preceding his death or end-time prophecies. The soldier sporting his dog tags might be reliving wartime flares. The fourth is Valdez's brother, Daniel. In this image, urban street lamps barely illuminate an obscure path as he reflects back across the preceding portraits, perhaps pondering the few options and paths available to him.

The *Made Men* series also includes the diptych *Expulsion from the Great City* (2002), Valdez's largest work at that time. Standing fourteen feet tall, the scale of the pastel drawings echoes his past as a muralist. The male and female figures are naked and cropped from their nostrils to their toes, arguing across their respective canvases. Strewn around their feet are discarded cigarette butts, fast food containers, and crumpled newspapers. There is tension in their body posture, finger pointing, and mouths formed in disgust, all of which speak to an inability to find common ground. As they stand on a sidewalk that abruptly ends, seemingly leading them to the edge of the earth, the foundation beneath their feet is unstable. Their toes precariously hang off. Left with another ellipsis, we decide their fate.

Find Their Way Home 2004 & 13

In 2004, iconic American musician Ry Cooder called Valdez with a genre-defying opportunity to render power anew. Cooder was searching for an artist to tackle a novel dream: painting a 1953 ice cream truck with an allegorical rendering of the story of the Chavez Ravine. Cooder was convinced Valdez was just the right artist when he saw *Kill The Pachuco Bastard*! in Cheech Marin's *Chicano Visions: American Painters on the Verge* (2002) exhibition catalogue.

In order to untangle this regionally centered history, Valdez moved to Los Angeles for two years to complete the mammoth undertaking of *El Chavez Ravine* (2005-7). Although the work is centered on a place beyond Valdez's birthplace, its undercurrents of government run amok, erasure of historic communities of color, and the people's resistance to those forces were already throughlines in his work. Of the city, Norman Klein says, "Los Angeles is a city which has long thrived on the continual re-creation of [its] own myth,"[10] which Valdez sees as a parallel statement to the whole of the United States.

Across the truck's surface, Valdez depicts the evolution of the Chavez Ravine neighborhood during the 1950s. Here, he merges two traditional Mexican American art forms: murals and car customization. The expansive panorama is rendered in colors reflecting the California sunset. There are visual references to the land grab saga that eliminated the historic Latine neighborhood, including eminent

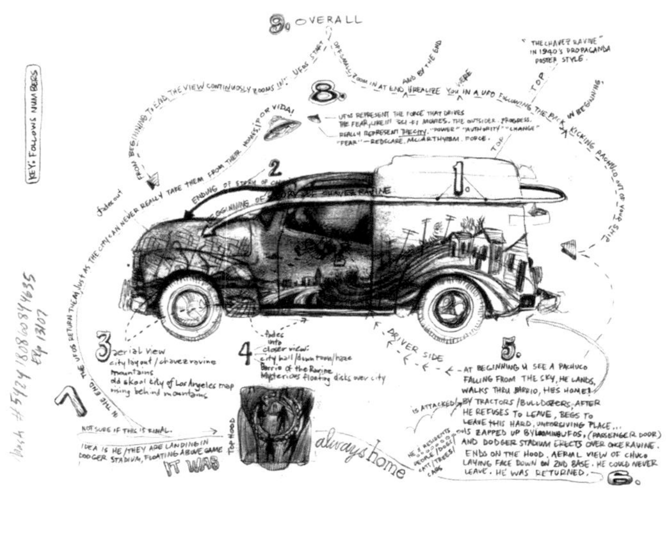

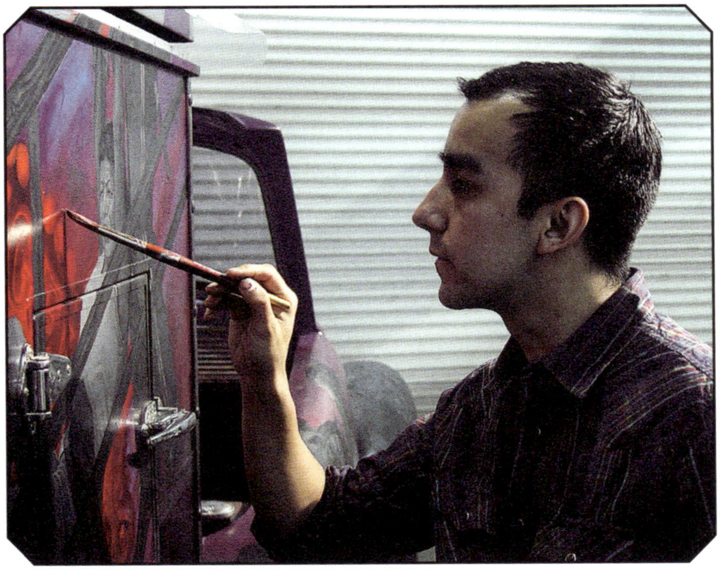

domain acquisition by the city to make way for proposed public housing, the forced eviction of the long-standing residents, and the construction of Dodger Stadium on top of the rubble of the razed homes. Also imaged are the neighborhood's original homes, alongside scheming politicians whose skin is eerily red, recalling the anti-communist hysteria of the McCarthy, or Red Scare, era.

This collaboration with Cooder on *El Chavez Ravine* cemented Valdez's use of painting as *homage* to undertold histories and also an attempt to write new futures. While hope is oriented toward the future, the fertile territory for the production of hope requires remembrance. Valdez brought this concept close to home in *Excerpts for John* (2012). The artist's lifelong friend, 2nd Lt. John R. Holt Jr., a combat medic who served in Iraq, passed away in 2009. John did not die in a combat zone, but rather upon his return to the United States, where he became a statistic of post-traumatic stress disorder. Valdez voices that "*Excerpts for John* is a eulogy for those who can't find their way home."[11] Across six panels, the hazy and monochromatic unfolding of the military funeral procession is stirring. As Susan Sontag articulated, "Remembering is an ethical act, has ethical value in and of itself. Memory is, achingly, the only relation we can have with the dead."[12] The video *Home* (2012), which accompanies the paintings, follows John's flag-draped coffin floating without any visible support, cruising like a lowrider, low and slow, through San Antonio to arrive at its final resting place. The casket's centrality addresses the elliptical erasure in American awareness of this crisis for veterans given an eighteen-year ban on photographing flag-draped coffins returning to the United States, which was only overturned in 2009.

In 2012, thinking about other histories condemned to erasure and the associated lives ungrieved, Valdez began researching the lynchings of Mexican Americans in Texas from the late 1880s through 1930s. In the last two decades of the nineteenth century, the number of lynchings surpassed the number of lawful executions.[13] And yet, the country's history of lynching Mexicans and Mexican Americans remains little known. Lynching, a "distinctively American institution," makes clear Judith Butler's writings on "grievability," or the pernicious valuing of some lives above others. She states, "One way of posing the question of who 'we' are in these times of war is by asking whose lives are considered valuable, whose lives are mourned, and whose lives are considered ungrievable."[14]

Valdez bristles at the notion of history as a faithful record, instead seeing the opportunity to reverse erasure by claiming agency over the past. To that end, he completed *The Strangest Fruit* (2013) as an antidote to our country's motivated forgetting of state-ignored violence. The series images nine contemporary Mexican American men, contorted and suspended from invisible nooses. Their bodies collectively rotate around a central axis. We recognize that they are our contemporaries primarily through their clothing—blue jeans, a Houston Rockets basketball jersey, hoodies, and Nike tennis shoes.

These figures are removed from their surroundings and instead float in space, the void symbolizing forgotten narratives of racialized violence. While anchored in specific histories, Valdez's images also speak to our present moment. The artist states of the series: "Presenting this historical subject in a contemporary context enables me to present the noose as both a metaphor and to suggest that the threat of it still looms."[15] Therefore, Valdez recognizes that our country was founded on violence, leaving racism embedded in our national DNA. Systemic injustice manifests itself in less obvious forms—economic violence, urban planning, predatory corporate policies, mass incarceration, racial profiling, inequitable justice and educational systems, and immigration politics.

Valdez made *The Strangest Fruit* deeply personal by working with friends and family members as the portrait sitters (his brother Daniel is recognizable again). While

Sketch for *The Beginning is Near (An American Trilogy), Chapter One: The City The City I*, 2015–16
Ink on paper
Photo: Brad Trone

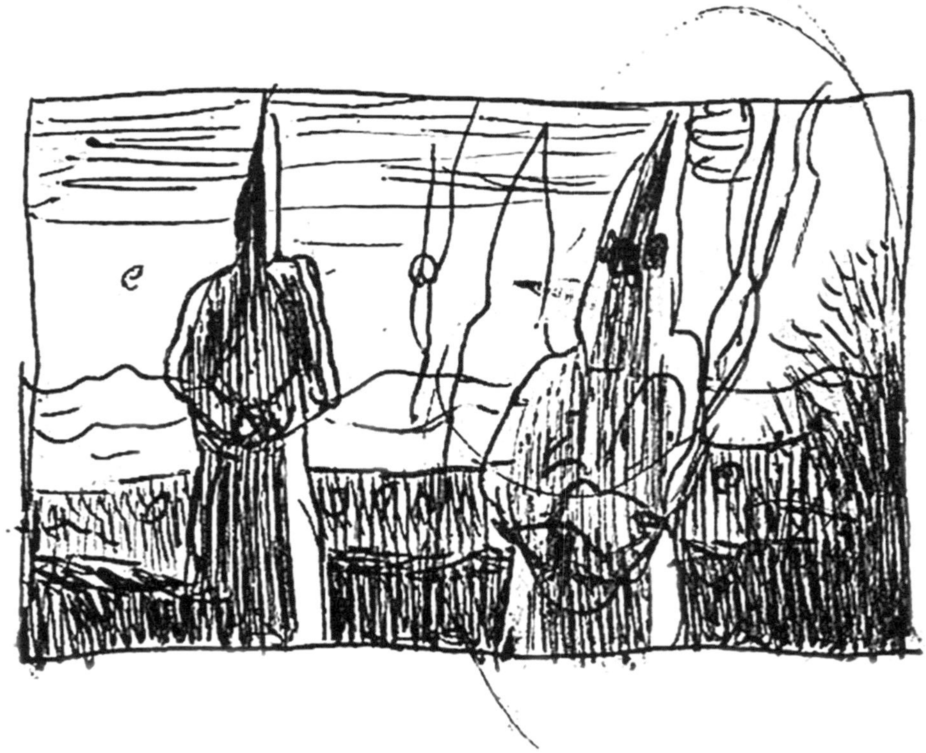

this series omits graphic violence, it instead looks at residual violence. The figures are caught in an ambiguous limbo; we as viewers determine whether they are ascending peacefully or sinking into oblivion.

Belong Here **1993** & **2015-16**

Valdez often felt that discrimination kept him outside of American life, yet he had a strong desire to understand politics as a way to have agency in this country. This became all too evident when, as a sixteen years old, he was leaving his shift at the AMC cinema next door to the Alamo in downtown San Antonio. Valdez unknowingly stumbled into a white nationalist rally and came face-to-face with a circling group of Klan members. Valdez recalls a hooded figure holding an American flag over his shoulder who made eye contact with him, leaned forward, and whispered, "You don't belong here."

Years later, in 2015, Valdez saw Philip Guston's painting *City Limits* (1969) in the exhibition *Witness: Art and Civil Rights in the Sixties* at the Blanton Museum of Art in Austin, Texas. Guston's painting depicts a cartoonish car with three hooded Ku Klux Klan members stuffed inside, all before the backdrop of a cityscape. *City Limits* sparked Valdez's motivation to address a vision that he had been harboring for several years, one based on his memory of encountering the white power rally as a teenager. Valdez drove straight to his studio to sketch what would become his epic painting *The Beginning is Near (An American Trilogy), Chapter One: The City* (2016). This two-part work truly merges life experience and art historical reference. Valdez charted its progress as, "First, a sense. Then, a vision. Next, an idea. Then, a reality."

Fourteen hooded members of the Ku Klux Klan meet our uncomfortable gaze in the first thirty-foot-long panel, *The City I*. We have interrupted their gathering as the uninvited guest. The group contains not only adults, but also a toddler, whose pointing finger eerily references the World War I Uncle Sam recruitment advertisement, which was depicted as a poster inside the bar of *Kill the Pachuco Bastard!* over a decade earlier. Valdez debated including the child, recognizing it might be a flashpoint for controversy. Yet, he contends that racism and its persistent ideologies are taught, passed down from generation to generation.

The Klanspeople have convened on a bluff overlooking a nocturnal metropolis in *The City I*. Valdez refers to the surrounding cityscape as "the foundation that ties the entire image together."[16] Sidestepping the viewers' tendency to focus only on the figures, Valdez pairs *The City I* with a companion panel: *The City II*. Here again, the landscape begs for our attention. Devoid of the human figure, it depicts a pile of mattresses accompanied by refuse in a symbolic representation of *The City I*.

Blurring the distinction between past and present with a black and white palette, Valdez reminds us that racism is persistent; the present is always pregnant with potential for violence. Such everyday racism recalls Hannah Arendt's writings on evil, dividing the evil nature of crimes and the ordinary persons responsible.[17] Her term "banality" parallels Valdez's visual cues, be it the Budweiser beer can or glowing iPhone. These details disrupt traditional representations of evil as exceptional or demonic and instead make them commonplace and routine. As James Baldwin articulated, "It has always been much easier (because it has always seemed much safer) to give a name to the evil without than to locate the terror within."[18] Valdez's work seems to warn us that bigotry should not be historicized or externalized; rather, the potential for hate is encountered in all of us. Guston similarly claimed that his hooded figures were self-portraits, thereby acknowledging his complicity in social ills.

A key aspect of *The City I* is the fact that the hooded figures' eye levels meet those of the viewers. Of this decision, the artist states: "Presenting them caught in ordinary mundane acts was my way of stripping them of their power." How do these works recalling trauma function in our present moment, which is flooded with images of violence? Valdez contends they perform a necessary function—he invites his images to leave a psychological residue, as viewers grapple with banality's juxtaposition with evil. Valdez's images linger, as ghosts. Of this phenomena, writer Andrew Gallix observes: "When you come to think of it, all forms of representation are ghostly. Works of art are haunted, not only by the ideal forms of which they are imperfect instantiations, but also by what escapes representation."[19] What escapes representation is also the submerged part of the iceberg.

The City was prescient in its foreshadowing of the normalization of bigoted speech during the 2016 election, and since. As Valdez feared, his art and the external political situation merged. While America billed itself as a post-racial society after Barack Obama's presidency, Valdez felt an oppressive backlash forming and warned that we had become too complacent in our denial.

The City became the first chapter in the three-part series, followed by *The Beginning is Near (An American Trilogy), Chapter Two: Dream Baby Dream* (2018). As Valdez completed the final panel of *The City I*, revered boxer Muhammad Ali died on June 3, 2016. The artist watched television coverage of Ali's funeral service from his studio and was moved by the diversity and the unity of the invited speakers, a portrayal of the real twenty-first century America of which the artist dreamed. *Dream Baby Dream* consists of twelve monochrome panels depicting mourners standing before a pair of microphones and a backdrop of funerary wreaths. We see the face of Ali's widow obscured by a large-brimmed hat, a trio of Native Americans, a Jewish rabbi, a politician, and a Muslim poet. We encounter another elliptical moment: the eulogists are poised to speak yet remain silent. One image within the series even appears as an empty podium.

The funerary rituals of *Dream Baby Dream* marked a rare occasion upon which the United States grieved for a defiant protestor, a devout Muslim, an anti-war activist, and black American. Across numerous languages and from an array of cultural backgrounds, the eulogists celebrated an individual committed to advancing often unpopular political opinions in the movement toward progress. Not pictured like Hemingway's iceberg, Ali is rendered through those mourning him, a portrait of the extraordinary fighter through those reconciling "Ali's life and legacy with the dawning apprehension, anxiety, division and disillusionment that echoed across the country from screen to shining screen."[20] The final work in this series, and the only vertical painting, shows Ali's funeral wreath, across which the inscribed banner reads: "Keep them dreams burnin' forever....," quoting Suicide's 1979 song *Dream Baby Dream*. Valdez's lyrical reference allows viewers to imagine new potential endings to this bifurcated time in our nation's history. Is this the loss or rebirth of an American dream?

Waiting to Be Determined **2018-19**

In several works from 2018–19, Valdez experimented with fragmentation as a visual strategy to render political decline. These works were created in a period marked by Brett Kavanaugh's Supreme Court confirmation battle, migrant family separation at the US-Mexico border, and widespread attempts at voter suppression. *Eaten* (2018–19) is an allegory of greed's destructive path with an

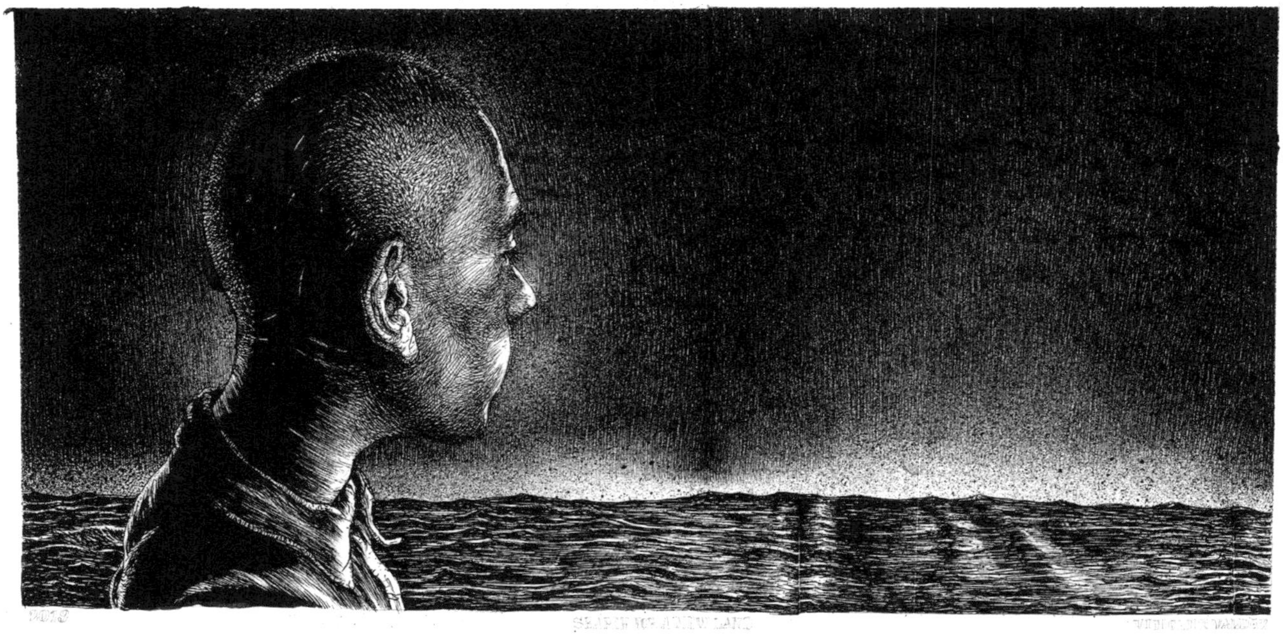

***Search for a New Land*, 2018** Ink on paper. Photo: Paul Salveson

unlikely central protagonist. A gluttonous pig sits gorged amidst a post-apocalyptic environment, calling to mind the wasteland of *The City II*. Daily detritus—eyeglasses, crumpled dollar bills, a watch, a smoldering cigarette, a dead bug, a half-eaten book—litters the canvas. A human hand and foot stick out from under the pig's bloated body, recalling Théodore Géricault's paintings of severed limbs in which the male body has been broken into pieces and then re-conjoined. The pig's physical features are pulled from familiar American faces who have shaped our country's foreign and domestic policy, politics, and daily life—the ears of Robert McNamara, former United States Secretary of Defense and architect of the military strategy for the Vietnam War; the eyes of J. Edgar Hoover, leader of the FBI for nearly a half century; and the skin of Steve Bannon, founder of Breitbart News. Gazing directly at us, the pig has devoured everyone and everything in its path, with no end in sight.

Since 1977 (2019), from the same period as *Eaten*, contains the mere suggestions of the physical features of American politicians. Across eight drawings, Valdez renders portraits of the seven presidents who have taken office since his birth year as referenced in the work's title. This series offers unconventional political portraits, as well as an unconventional self-portrait. The images are freeze frames of the American figureheads of power that Valdez has observed throughout his life. As "the face is the place of politics,"[21] these prominent figures are reduced to their upper heads, notably their iconic hairstyles, eyes, and emotive foreheads. Their basic human emotions, including shame, pride, greed, and anxiety—as well as insolence—are palpable. We encounter them as almost mere men, stripped of their power through orchestrated framing. This series complements the earlier *Expulsion from the Great City*, where we encounter the figures' full bodies, save for their eyes and upper faces.

Art historian Linda Nochlin equated such cropping of the figure as a modernist grief over the loss of a utopian wholeness. She argues that the artistic portrayal of a fragmented human body emerged during the late nineteenth century from "that sense of social, psychological, even metaphysical fragmentation that so seems to mark modern experience—a loss of wholeness, a shattering of connection, a destruction or disintegration."[22] The fragmented heads of executive seats of power in *Since 1977* gradually shift lower and lower, insinuating a steady decline as time marches on. Valdez proposes as the work's conclusion "an abyss-like void, waiting to be determined by you, the American people."

Shine Bright 2020-24

In 2020, Valdez moved to New Haven, Connecticut to begin a studio residency. Coinciding with the outbreak of COVID-19, Valdez's yearlong residency was stretched to two. This period, marked by isolation and uncertainty for most, was no different for the artist, who found himself in a new environment far from family and friends. A body of highly personal work followed, including regimented daily drawings of "my immediate surroundings" to mark each day. Valdez started his *Amnesia* series imaging fellow residents, followed by young amateur boxers training in the community center next door. He experimented with more immediate expression and compressed time constraints, evidenced by gestural mark making. These rendered pillars of support hung in his studio as an optimistic presence during an increasingly precarious period. The figures' quiet resolve grounds the anxiety and unease palpable in his earlier works, confidently addressing the forlorn faces of the *Made Men* boxers.

The specificity of portraiture seen in the *Amnesia* drawings continues with Valdez's most recent works, cementing his belief in individuals first and foremost. The artist initially intended to conclude *The Beginning is Near* with *Dream Baby Dream*, but instead felt it urgent to conclude on a personal and powerful note with *The Beginning is Near (An American Trilogy) Chapter Three: The New Americans* (2021-ongoing). Here, the panoramic format of the first two chapters is flipped vertically and in full color, as Valdez focuses on a single individual per panel. In 2021, Valdez committed to paint twenty-one Americans in the twenty-first century who are still fighting "the good fight" within their communities. These monuments portray individual anchors for Valdez, including fellow artists Teresita Fernández and Adriana Corral, as well as activists Mr. Checkpoint (#AFTP) and Juan Cartegena (founder of Latino Justice PRLDEF). "*The New Americans*, for me, are a simple reminder that the future, even in its darkest, most uncertain hour, can still shine bright," says Valdez.

This suite also becomes Valdez's self-portrait of sorts, a personal chronicling of the individuals who have inspired and encouraged him to continue pushing forward. In celebration of the sitters' differing yet noble aims, motivated beyond profit or fame, these works are monumental in scale at nearly eight feet tall, rendering the subjects larger than life. They stand defiant, in full color, "a stubborn pulse in a dying heartbeat."[23] Each sitter chose their respective background as an active participant in their portrayal. For example, Fernández is seen in her verdant backyard in Brooklyn, a significant nod to her artistic practice that looks at histories embedded in the landscape. Valdez's portrait of Mr. Checkpoint looks on from the intersection across from the Santa Monica police department, where he was wrongfully arrested and detained in 2012. Earlier chapters in the trilogy that challenged injustice and political inefficacy are turned on their head in *The New Americans*, transforming into portraits of love and strength. These testimonies affirm that we are connected through collective action. As Valdez reminds us: "Even when the odds are stacked and the game is rigged—justice, truth and humanity must prevail. Hold your heads high."

The Beginning is Near series addresses duality—turmoil and contemplation, tension and peace—in order to ignite both our empathy and apprehension. This dichotomy is evident in *Rise* (2019). In this work, Valdez foregrounds a hulking pile of stones as the sun breaks on the horizon. Are these building blocks, or remnants of collapse? The heap is illuminated by a glistening sun, ambiguously referencing both sunrise and sunset, a sky in transition. In this disorienting environment, time is suspended and unclear, and haze sets in. The beginning seems near, as does the end.

This work, a signal of hope emerging from despair, recalls Ry Cooder's *There's a Bright Side Somewhere* lyrics:

> Well there's a bright side somewhere
> There's a bright side somewhere
> Now I ain't gonna rest until I find it
> There's a bright side somewhere
> And there's more love somewhere
> And there's more peace somewhere
> I ain't gonna rest until I find it
> There's a bright side somewhere[24]

In contrast with the "bright side," Valdez's work may seem somber. Perhaps an alternate definition of elliptical is better: obscure. Obscurity can signify the unseen, unknown, and undiscovered, opening possible futures rather than insinuating gloom. Valdez's practice similarly should not be flattened to a one-dimensional connotation of darkness, for over the last twenty-five years he has offered visual testimony, rejecting the seduction to ignore the past. Identifying hope in the face of uncertainty is what Valdez does best; we see it again and again: the void of the last panel of *Since 1977*, or the sun shining in *Rise*. Valdez reminds us there are still plenty of things worth fighting to protect. This dare to imagine an alternative is not born out of naïveté but rooted in critical evaluation.

Valdez has built an emancipatory legacy, disorienting us to reveal a new horizon in which no lodestar of order readily presents itself. Consider his self-portrait *Search for a New Land* (2018), where he depicts himself scanning across a barren land, an America unbuilt or sunken, which of the two we cannot tell. Yet, he still searches. Through this image, Valdez invites us to join him in finding new figures to celebrate: your neighbor, the fighter still standing, your sense of self, and, just maybe, a new land . . .

---

[1] Paul Smith, "1924: Hemingway's Luggage and the Miraculous Year," in *The Cambridge Companion to Ernest Hemingway*, ed. Scott Donaldson (Cambridge: Cambridge University Press, 1966), p. 41.

[2] Charles M. Oliver, *Ernest Hemingway A to Z: The Essential Reference to the Life and Work* (New York: Facts on File, 1999), p. 322.

[3] Seamus Perry, *America is a poem in our eyes* (Times Literary Supplement, Issue 6127, September 2020), p. 4.

[4] Valdez's title is derived from the 1958 song by Jimmy Clanton and His Rockets.

[5] Michel Foucault, *Fearless Speech*, ed. Joseph Pearson (Los Angeles, Semiotext(e), 2001).

[6] All quotes from the artist are from a series of interviews with the author during 2023 and 2024, unless otherwise noted.

[7] Daniel shows up repeatedly in Valdez's work, also seen in *Made Men: I Swear I See My Reflection* (2003), and as the central boxer in *Stations* (2002–4).

[8] *Vincent Valdez: In Conversation*, Museum of Fine Arts Boston, May 7, 2022, 24:54.

[9] Oral history interview with artist and educator Vincent Valdez, interviewed by Brookes Ebetsch, University of Notre Dame, IN, 2005, 28:00.

[10] Norman Klein, *A History of Forgetting* (London: Verso Books, 1997), cover copy.

[11] *Vincent Valdez: Excerpts for John* by Walley Films, 2012.

[12] Susan Sontag, *Regarding the Pain of Others* (New York: Farrar, Straus and Giroux, 2003), p. 115.

[13] Richard Hofstadter, "Reflections on Violence in the United States," *The Baffler Magazine*, no. 28, 2015, p. 28.

[14] Judith Butler, *Frames of War: When Is Life Grievable?* (London and New York: Verso Books, 2010), p. 38.

[15] Juan Cartagena, "The Noose, the Hoodie, and the State," in *Vincent Valdez: The Strangest Fruit* (Waynesboro, VA: McClung Companies, 2015), p. 39.

[16] Andrea Lepage, *Interview with Vincent Valdez, The Beginning is Near*, pamphlet, 2016, p. 3.

[17] Hannah Arendt, *Eichmann in Jerusalem: A report of the banality of evil* (New York: Penguin Books, 1992), p. 287.

[18] James Baldwin and Richard Avedon, *Nothing Personal* (Cologne: Taschen, 2017), p. 17.

[19] Andrew Gallix, "Hauntology: A Not-So-New Critical Manifestation: The New Vogue in Literary Theory Is Shot Through with Earlier Ideas," *The Guardian*, June 17, 2011.

[20] Ian Alden Russell, *Dream Baby Dream*, pamphlet for David Shelton Gallery, Houston, TX, 2018.

[21] Giorgio Agamben, *When the House Burns Down: From the Dialect of Thought* (Chicago: University of Chicago Press, 2022), p. 8.

[22] Linda Nochlin, *The Body in Pieces: The Fragment as a Metaphor of Modernity* (London: Thames & Hudson, 2001), p. 56.

[23] *Vincent Valdez—Tuesday Evenings with the Modern Lecture Series*, Modern Art Museum of Fort Worth, March 8, 2022, 54:04.

[24] Ry Cooder, *My Name Is Buddy*, Nonesuch Records, 2007.

Till then, when all the world will be free

Till then, lets dream of what there will be

Till then, we'll call on each memory

—**THE MILLS BROTHERS** excerpt from "Till Then" (1948)

THE FIGHT

***Just a Dream* *(In America)*, 2020–21**
Oil on canvas, audio component, and bricks
Photos: Chris Gardner

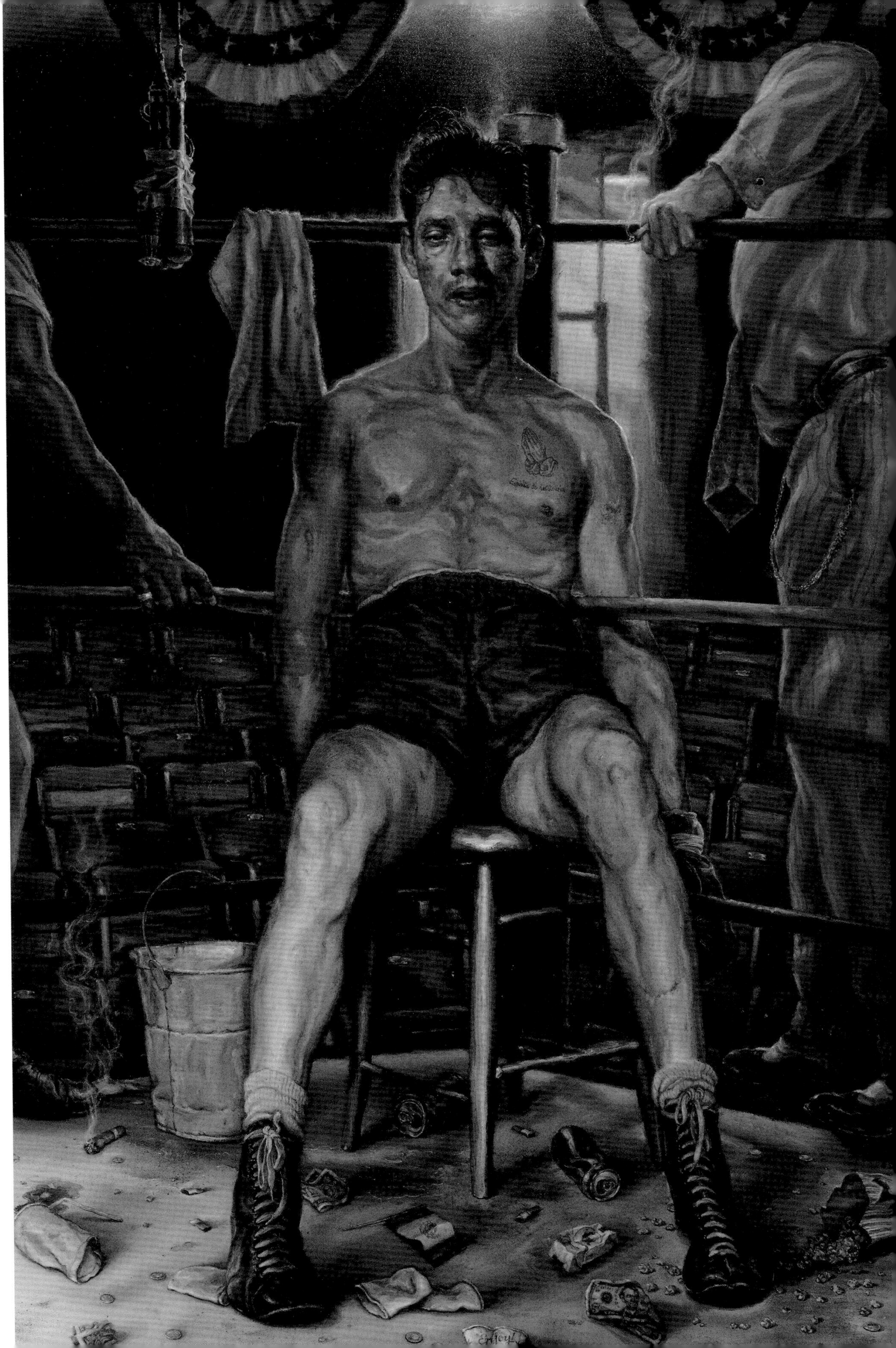

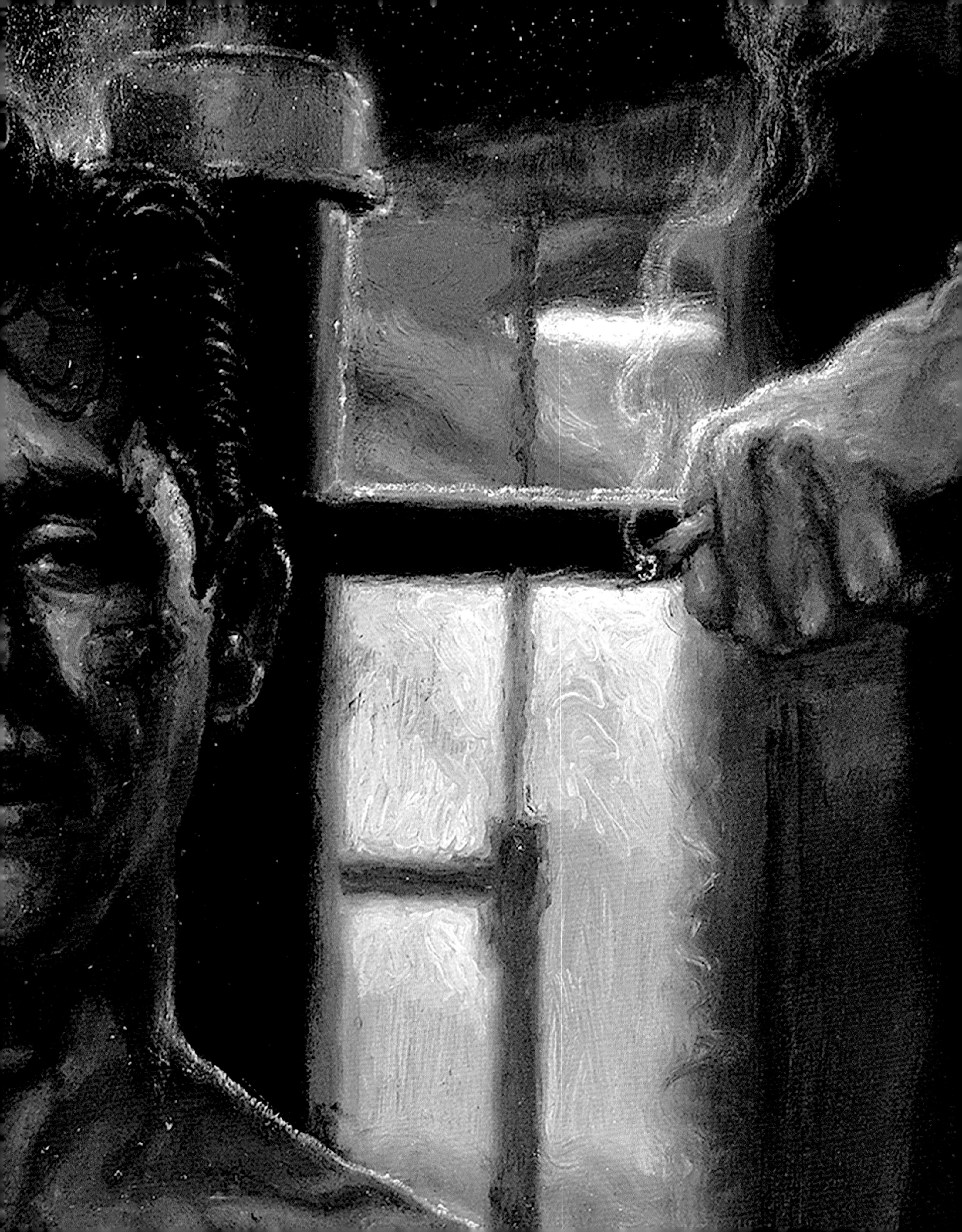

***So Long, Mary Ann*, 2019**
Oil on canvas
Photos: Paul Salveson

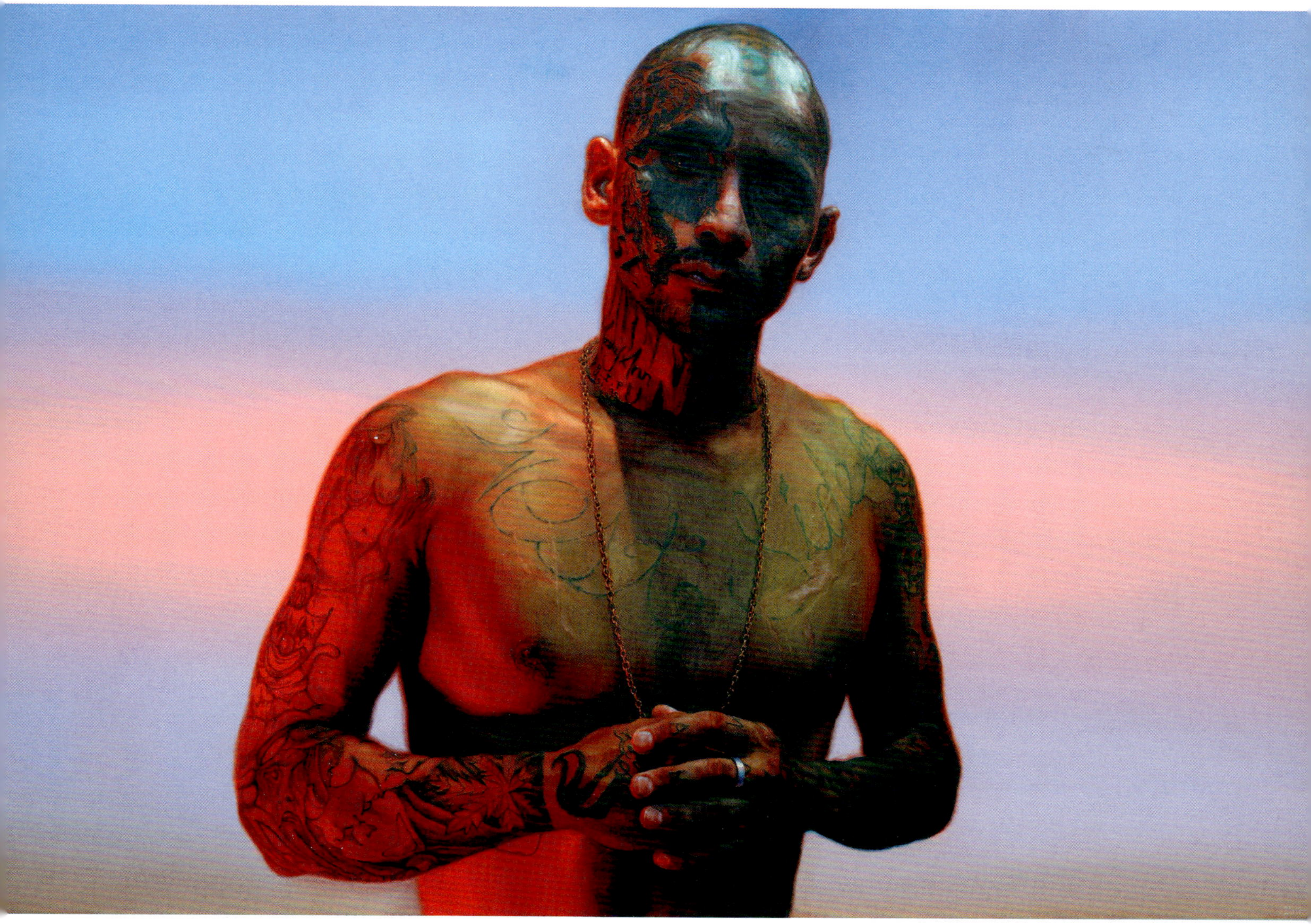

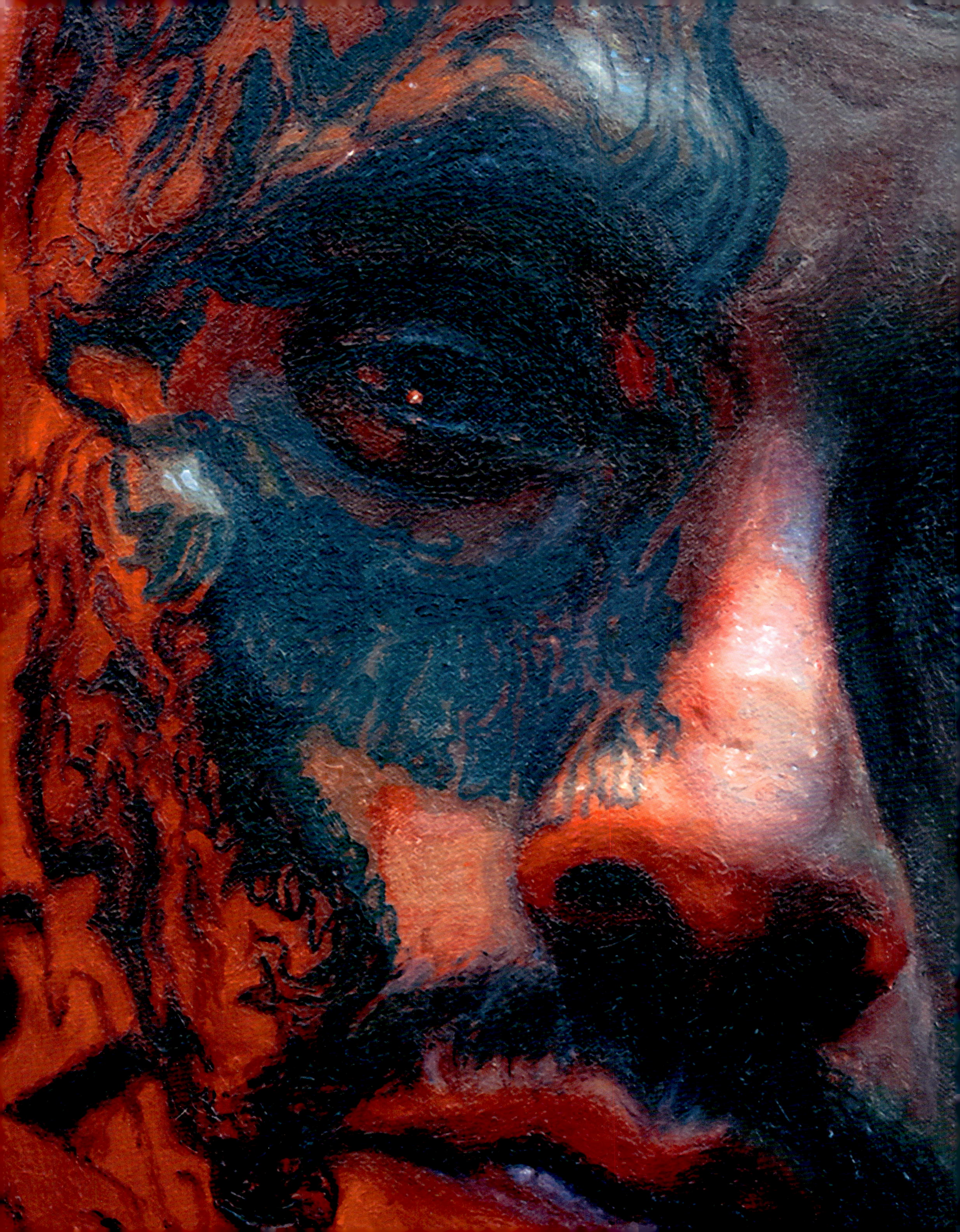

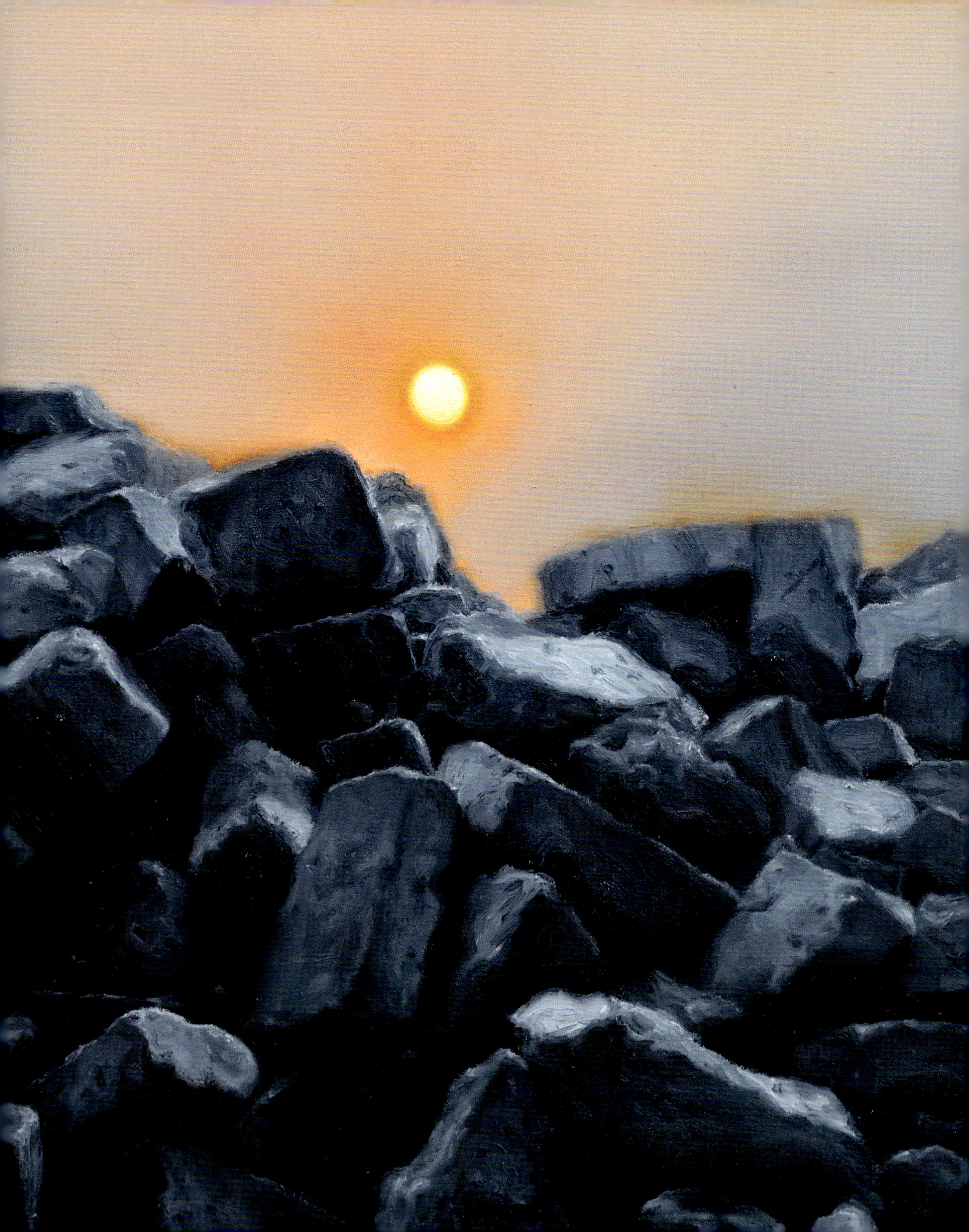

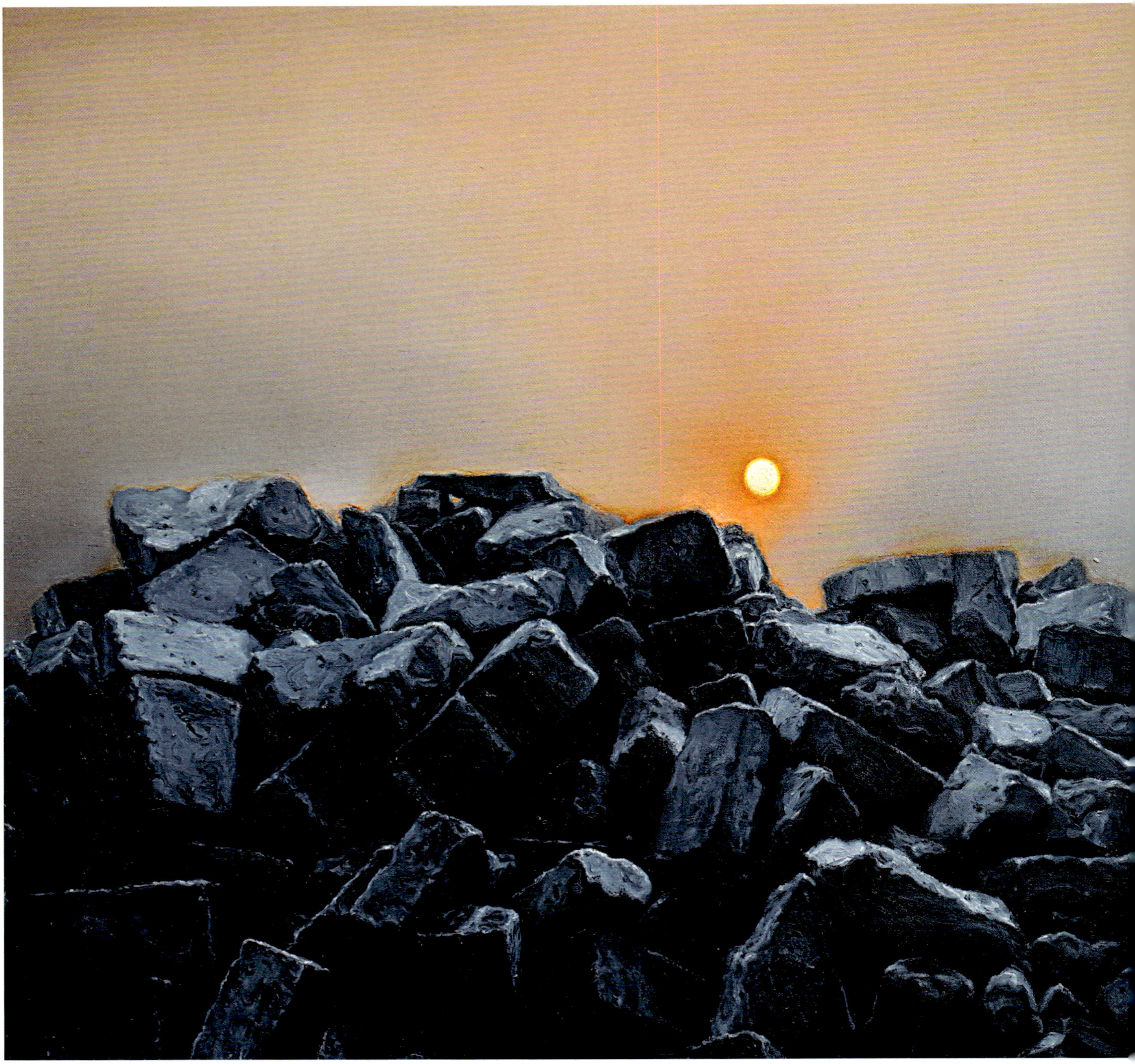

***Rise*, 2019**
Oil on canvas
Photos: Paul Salveson

On Boxing

JOYCE CAROL OATES

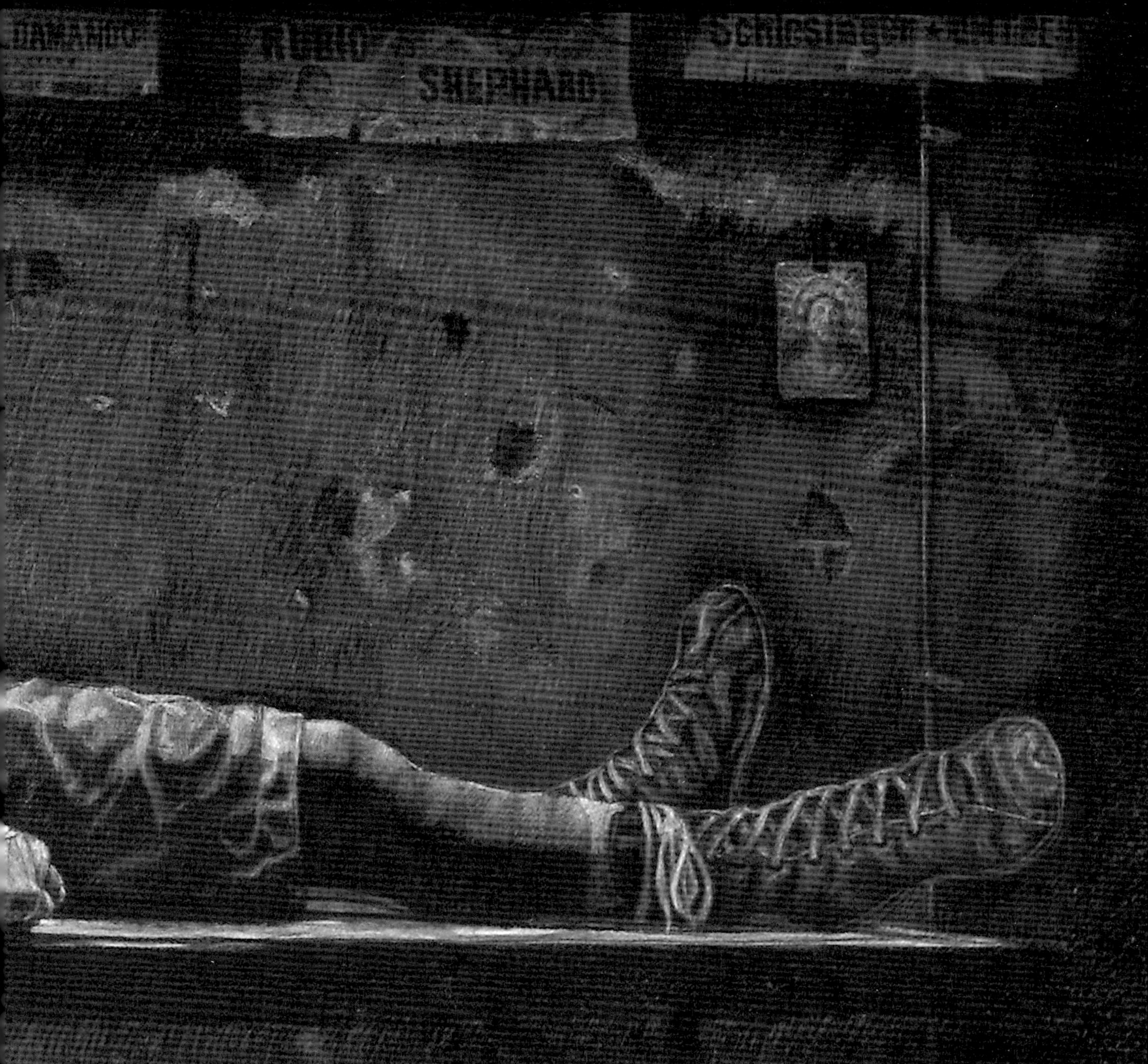

Stations IX: Laid Out, 2001–4
Charcoal on wove paper
Photo: Museum of Fine Arts, Houston

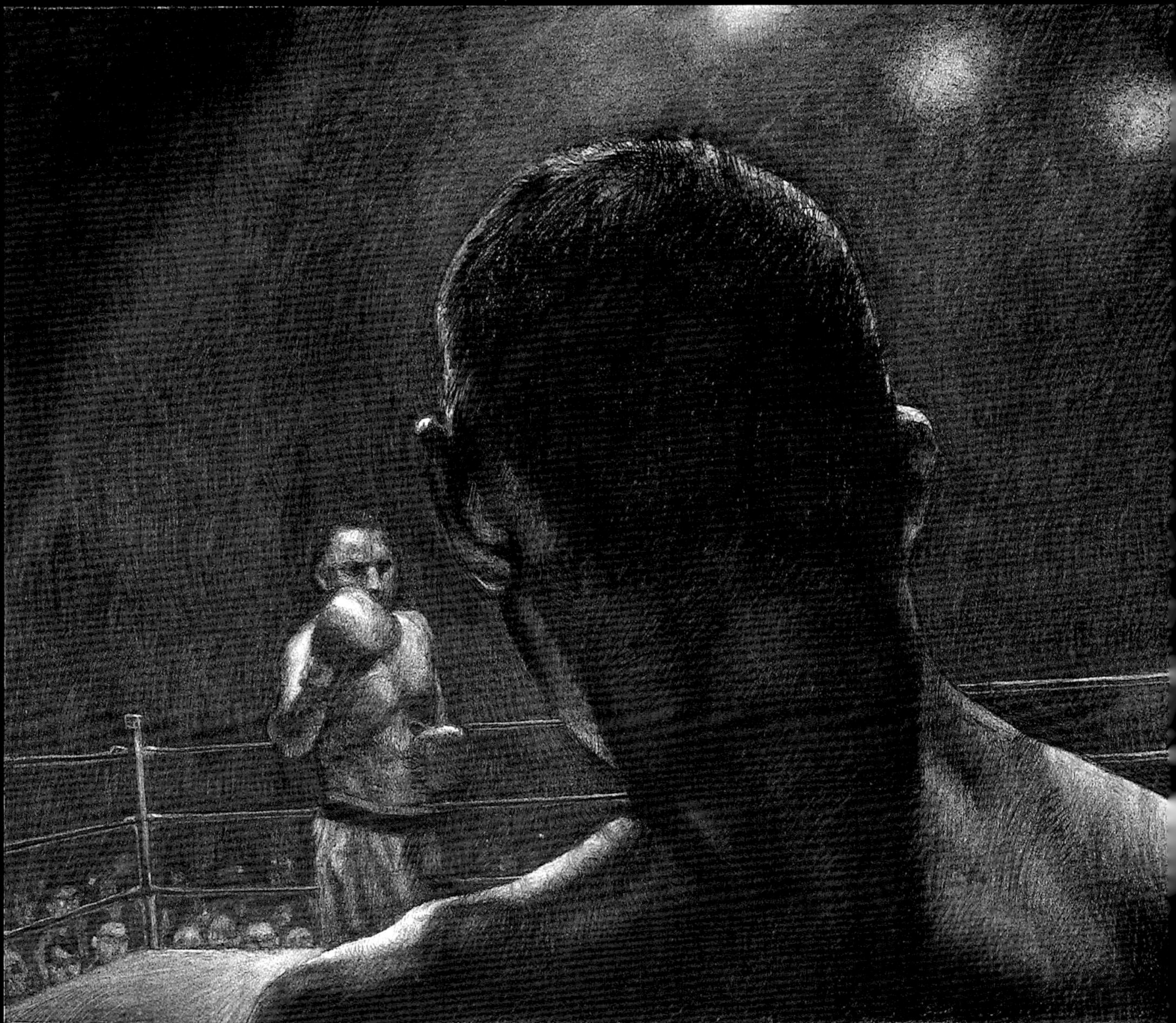

Stations: Get Outta There!
(III Part, No Mercy), Final Bell, 2001–4
Charcoal on paper
Photo: Peter Molick

Why are you a boxer, Irish featherweight champion Barry McGuigan was asked. He said: "I can't be a poet. I can't tell stories..."

Each boxing match is a story—a unique and highly condensed drama without words. Even when nothing sensational happens: then the drama is "merely" psychological. Boxers are there to establish an absolute experience, a public accounting of the outermost limits of their beings; they will know, as few of us can know of ourselves, what physical and psychic power they possess of how much, or how little, they are capable. To enter the ring near-naked and to risk one's life is to make of one's audience voyeurs of a kind: boxing is so intimate. It is to ease out of sanity's consciousness and into another, difficult to name. It is to risk, and sometimes to realize, the agony of which *agon* (Greek, "contest") is the root.

In the boxing ring there are two principal players, overseen by a shadowy third. The ceremonial ringing of the bell is a summoning to full wakefulness for both boxers and spectators. It sets into motion, too, the authority of Time.

The boxers will bring to the fight everything that is themselves, and everything will be exposed—including secrets about themselves they cannot fully realize. The physical self, the maleness, one might say, underlying the "self." There are boxers possessed of such remarkable intuition, such uncanny prescience, one would think they were somehow recalling their fights, not fighting them as we watch. There are boxers who perform skillfully, but mechanically, who cannot improvise in response to another's alteration of strategy; there are boxers performing at the peak of their talent who come to realize, mid-fight, that it will not be enough; there are boxers—including great champions—whose careers end abruptly, and irrevocably, as we watch. There has been at least one boxer possessed of an extraordinary and disquieting awareness not only of his opponent's every move and anticipated move but of the audience's keenest shifts in mood as well, for which he seems to have felt personally responsible—Cassius Clay / Muhammad Ali, of course. "The Sweet Science of Bruising" celebrates the physicality of men even as it dramatizes the limitations, sometimes tragic, more often poignant, of the physical. Though male spectators identify with boxers no boxer behaves like a "normal" man when he is in the ring and no combination of blows is "natural." All is style.

Every talent must unfold itself in fighting. So Nietzsche speaks of the Hellenic past, the history of the "contest"—athletic, and otherwise—by which Greek youths were educated into Greek citizenry. Without the ferocity of competition, without, even, "envy, jealousy, and ambition" in the contest, the Hellenic city, like the Hellenic man, degenerated. If death is a risk, death is also the prize—for the winning athlete.

In the boxing ring, even in our greatly humanized times, death is always a possibility—which is why some of us prefer to watch films or tapes of fights already past, already defined as history. Or, in some instances, art. (Though to prepare for writing this mosaic-like essay I saw tapes of two infamous "death" fights of recent times: the Lupe Pintor–Johnny Owen bantamweight match of 1982, and the Ray Mancini–Duk Koo-Kim lightweight match of the same year. In both instances the boxers died as a consequence of their astonishing resilience and apparent indefatigability—their "heart," as it's known in boxing circles.) Most of the time, however, death in the ring is extremely unlikely; a statistically rare possibility like your possible death tomorrow morning in an automobile accident or in next month's headlined airline disaster or in a freak accident involving a fall on the stairs or in the bathtub, a skull fracture, subarachnoid hemorrhage. Spectators at "death" fights often claim afterward that what happened simply seemed to happen—unpredictably, in a sense accidentally. Only in retrospect does death appear to have been inevitable.

If a boxing match is a story it is an always wayward story, one in which anything can happen. And in a matter of seconds. Split seconds! (Muhammad Ali boasted that he could throw a punch faster than the eye could follow, and he may have been right.) In no other sport can so much take place in so brief a period of time, and so irrevocably.

Because a boxing match is a story without words, this doesn't mean that it has no text or no language, that it is somehow "brute," "primitive," "inarticulate," only that the text is improvised in action; the language a dialogue between the boxers of the most refined sort (one might say, as much neurological as psychological: a dialogue of split-second reflexes) in a joint response to the mysterious will of the audience which is always that the fight be a worthy one so that the crude paraphernalia of the setting—ring, lights, ropes, stained canvas, the staring onlookers themselves—be erased, forgotten. (As in the theater or the church, settings are erased by way, ideally, of transcendent action.) Ringside announcers give to the wordless spectacle a narrative unity, yet boxing as performance is more clearly akin to dance or music than narrative.

To turn from an ordinary preliminary match to a "Fight of the Century" like those between Joe Louis and Billy Conn, Joe Frazier and Muhammad Ali, Marvin Hagler and Thomas Hearns is to turn from listening or half-listening to a guitar being idly plucked to hearing Bach's *Well-Tempered Clavier* perfectly executed, and that too is part of the story's mystery: so much happens so swiftly and with such heart-stopping subtlety you cannot absorb it except to know that something profound is happening and it is happening in a place beyond words.

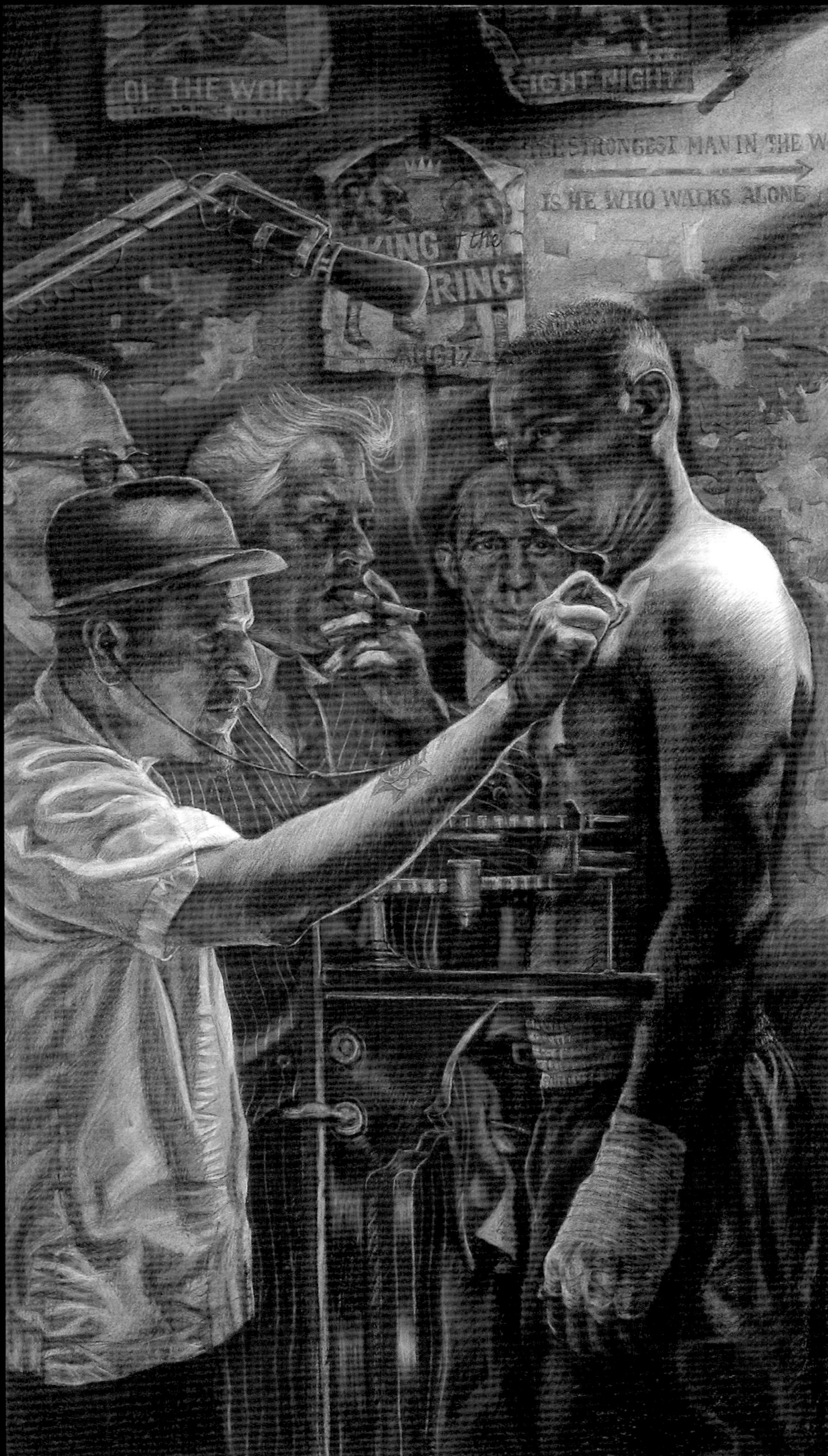

Stations: Weigh In: Coming in at 140 lbs 8 oz,
2001–4
Charcoal on paper
Photo: Peter Mellick

I try to catch my opponent on the tip of his nose because I try to punch the bone into his brain. —MIKE TYSON

Boxing's claim is that it is superior to life in that it is, ideally, superior to all accident. It contains nothing that is not fully willed.

The boxer meets an opponent who is a dream-distortion of himself in the sense that his weaknesses, his capacity to fail and to be seriously hurt, his intellectual miscalculations—all can be interpreted as strengths belonging to the Other; the parameters of his private being are nothing less than boundless assertions of the Other's self. This is dream, or nightmare: my strengths are not fully my own, but my opponent's weaknesses; my failure is not fully my own, but my opponent's triumph. He is my shadow-self, not my (mere) shadow. The boxing match as "serious, complete, and of a certain magnitude"—to refer to Aristotle's definition of tragedy—is an event that necessarily subsumes both boxers, as any ceremony subsumes its participants. (Which is why one can say, for instance, that the greatest fight of Muhammad Ali's career was one of the few fights Ali lost—the first heroic match with Frazier.)

The old boxing adage—a truism surely untrue—that you cannot be knocked out if you see the blow coming, and if you *will* yourself not to be knocked out, has its subtler, more daunting significance: nothing that happens to the boxer in the ring, including death—"his" death—is not of his own will or failure of will. The suggestion is of a world-model in which we are humanly responsible not only for our own acts but for those performed against us.

Which is why, though springing from life, boxing is not a metaphor for life but a unique, closed, self-referential world, obliquely akin to those severe religions in which the individual is both "free" and "determined"—in one sense possessed of a will tantamount to God's, in another totally helpless. The Puritan sensibility would have understood a mouth filling with blood, an eye popped out of its socket—fit punishment for an instant's negligence.

A boxing trainer's most difficult task is said to be to persuade a young boxer to get up and continue fighting after he has been knocked down. And if the boxer has been knocked down by a blow he hadn't seen coming—which is usually the case—how can he hope to protect himself from being knocked down again? and again? The invisible blow is after all—invisible.

Stations: *Keep Your Guard Up Son, Now Get Back Out There and Fight*, 2001–4
Charcoal on paper
Photo: Peter Molick

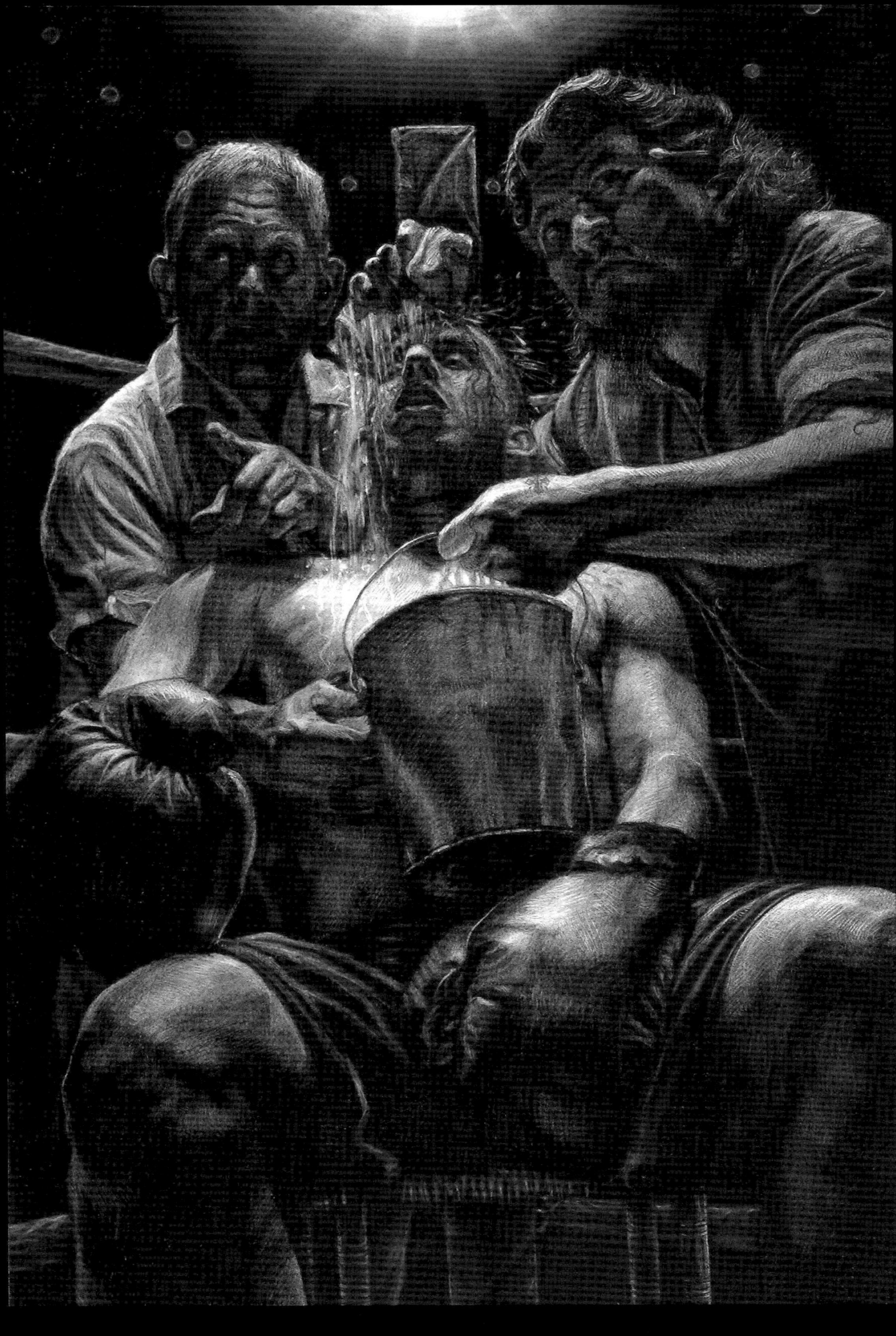

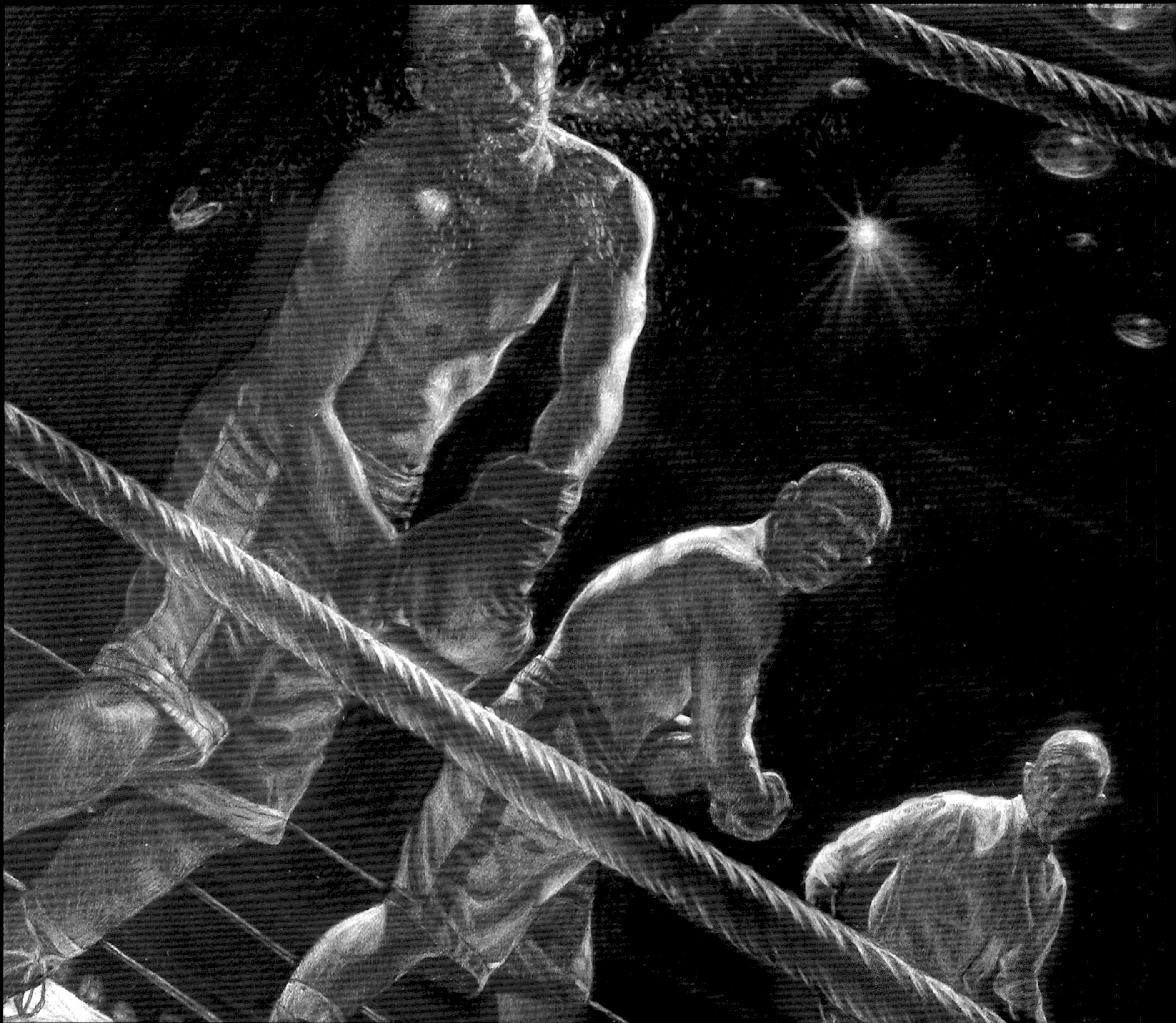

Stations: Get Outta There!, Kill 'Im!, No Mercy!, Finish Him!, 2001–4
Charcoal on paper
Photo: Peter Molick

"Normal" behavior in the ring would be unbearable to watch, deeply shameful: for "normal" beings share with all living creatures the instinct to persevere, as Spinoza said, in their own being. The boxer must somehow learn, by what effort of will non-boxers surely cannot guess, to inhibit his own instinct for survival; he must learn to exert his "will" over his merely human and animal impulses, not only to flee pain but to flee the unknown. In psychic terms this sounds like magic. Levitation. Sanity turned inside out, "madness" revealed as a higher and more pragmatic form of sanity.

The fighters in the ring are time-bound—surely nothing is so excruciatingly long as a fiercely contested three-minute round—but the fight itself is timeless. In a sense it becomes all fights, as the boxers are all boxers. By way of films, tapes, and photographs it quickly becomes history for us, even, at times, art. Time, like the possibility of death, is the invisible adversary of which the boxers—and the referee, the seconds, the spectators—are keenly aware. When a boxer is "knocked out" it does not mean, as it's commonly thought, that he has been knocked unconscious, or even incapacitated; it means rather more poetically that he has been knocked out of Time. (The referee's dramatic count of ten constitutes a metaphysical parenthesis of a kind through which the fallen boxer must penetrate if he hopes to continue in Time.) There are in a sense two dimensions of Time abruptly operant: while the standing boxer is *in time* the fallen boxer is *out of time*. Counted out, he is counted "dead"—in symbolic mimicry of the sport's ancient tradition in which he would very likely be dead. (Though, as we may recall, the canny Romans reserved for themselves as spectators the death blow itself: the triumphant gladiator was obliged to wait for a directive from outside the arena before he finished off his opponent.)

If boxing is a sport it is the most tragic of all sports because more than any human activity it consumes the very excellence it displays—its drama is this very consumption. To expend oneself in fighting the greatest fight of one's life is to begin by necessity the downward turn that next time may be a plunge, an abrupt fall into the abyss. *I am the greatest* says Muhammad Ali. *I am the greatest* says Marvelous Marvin Hagler. You always think you're going to win, Jack Dempsey wryly observed in his old age, otherwise you couldn't fight at all. The punishment—to the body, the brain, the spirit—a man must endure to become even a moderately good boxer is inconceivable to most of us whose idea of personal risk is largely ego-related or emotional. But the punishment as it begins to show in even a young and vigorous boxer is closely gauged by his rivals, who are waiting for him to slip. (After junior-welterweight champion Aaron Pryor won a lackluster fight last year a younger boxer in his weight division, interviewed at ringside, said with a smile: "My mouth is watering." And there was twenty-nine-year-old Billy Costello's bold statement—"If I can't beat an old man [of thirty-three] then I should retire"—shortly before his bout with Alexis Arguello, in which he was knocked out in an early round.)

When I see blood, I become a bull.
—MARVIN HAGLER

In the ring, boxers inhabit a curious sort of "slow" time—amateurs never box beyond three rounds, and for most amateurs those nine minutes are exhausting—while outside the ring they inhabit an alarmingly accelerated time. A twenty-three-year-old boxer is no longer young in the sense in which a twenty-three-year-old man is young; a thirty-five-year-old is frankly old. (Which is why Muhammad Ali made a tragic mistake in continuing his career after he had lost his title for the second time—to come out of retirement, aged thirty-eight, to fight Larry Holmes; and why Holmes made a similar mistake, years later, in needlessly exposing himself to injury, as well as professional embarrassment, by meeting with the light-heavyweight champion Michael Spinks. The victory of the thirty-seven-year-old Jersey Joe Walcott over the thirty-year-old Ezzard Charles, for the heavyweight title in 1951, is *sui generis*. And Archie Moore is *sui generis*.) All athletes age rapidly but none so rapidly and so visibly as the boxer.

So it is, the experience of watching great fighters of the past is radically different from having seen them perform when they were reigning champions. Jack Johnson, Jack Dempsey, Joe Louis, Sugar Ray Robinson, Rocky Marciano, Muhammad Ali, Joe Frazier—as spectators we know not only how a fight but how a career ends. The trajectory not merely of ten or fifteen rounds but that of an entire life...

Everything that man esteems

Endures a moment or a day.

Love's pleasure drives his love away,

The painter's brush consumes his dreams;

The herald's cry, the soldier's tread

Exhaust his glory and his might:

Whatever flames upon the night

Man's own resinous heart has fed.

—WILLIAM BUTLER YEATS
from "The Resurrection"

Stations: He Then Fell Once More, 2001–4
Charcoal on paper
Photo: Peter Molick

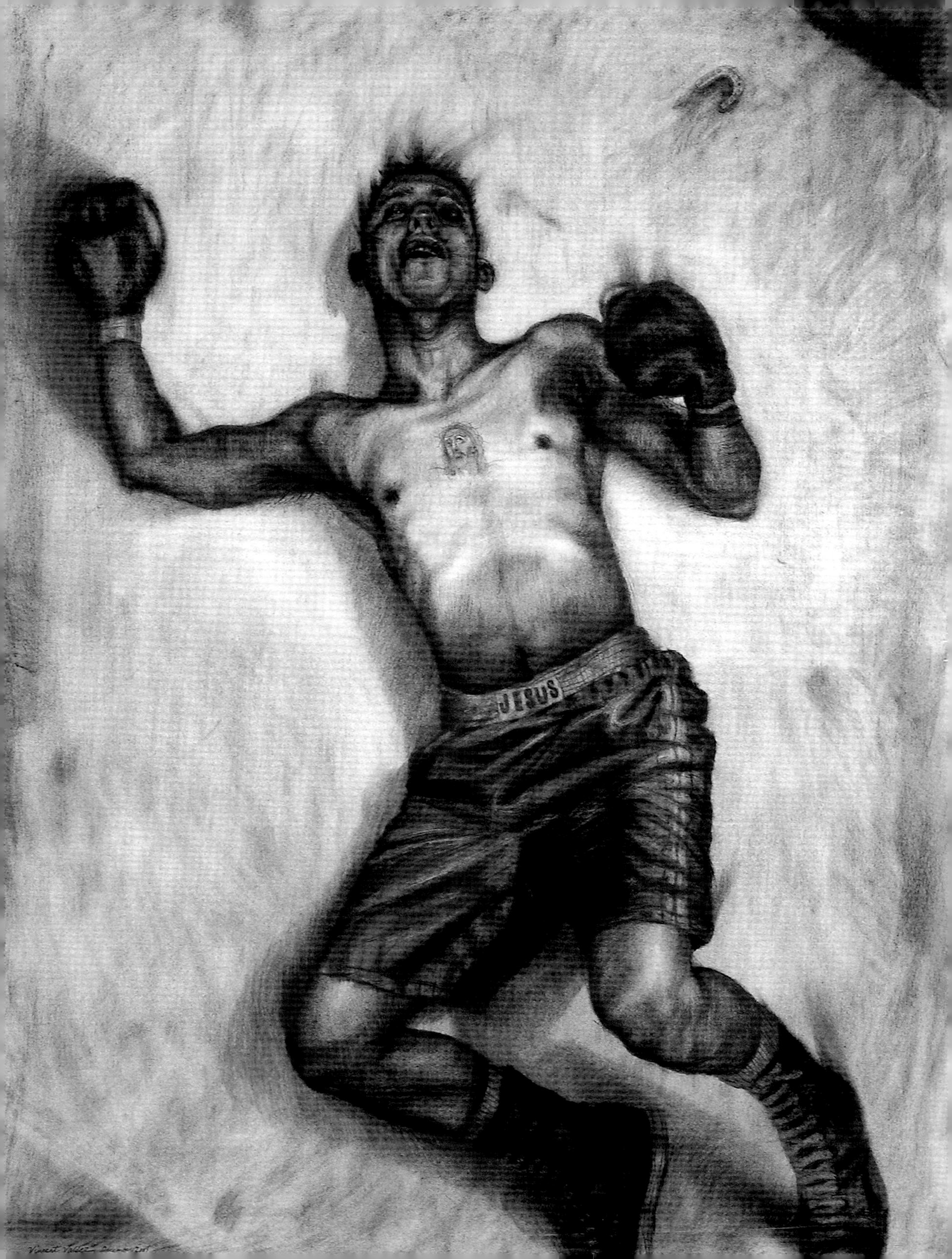
JESUS

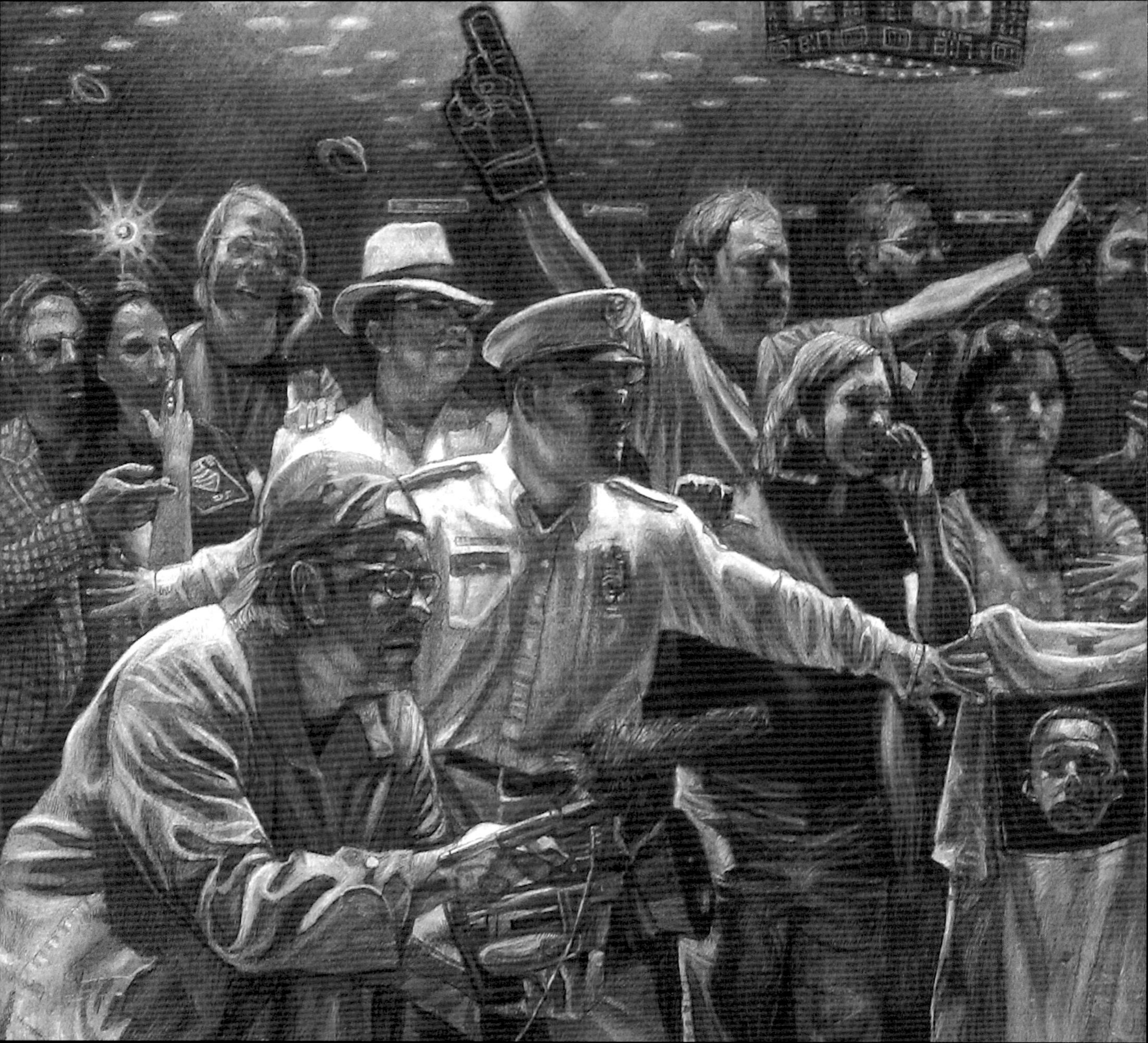

I hate to say it, but it's true—I only like it b

—FRANK "THE ANIMAL" FLETCHER, former mid

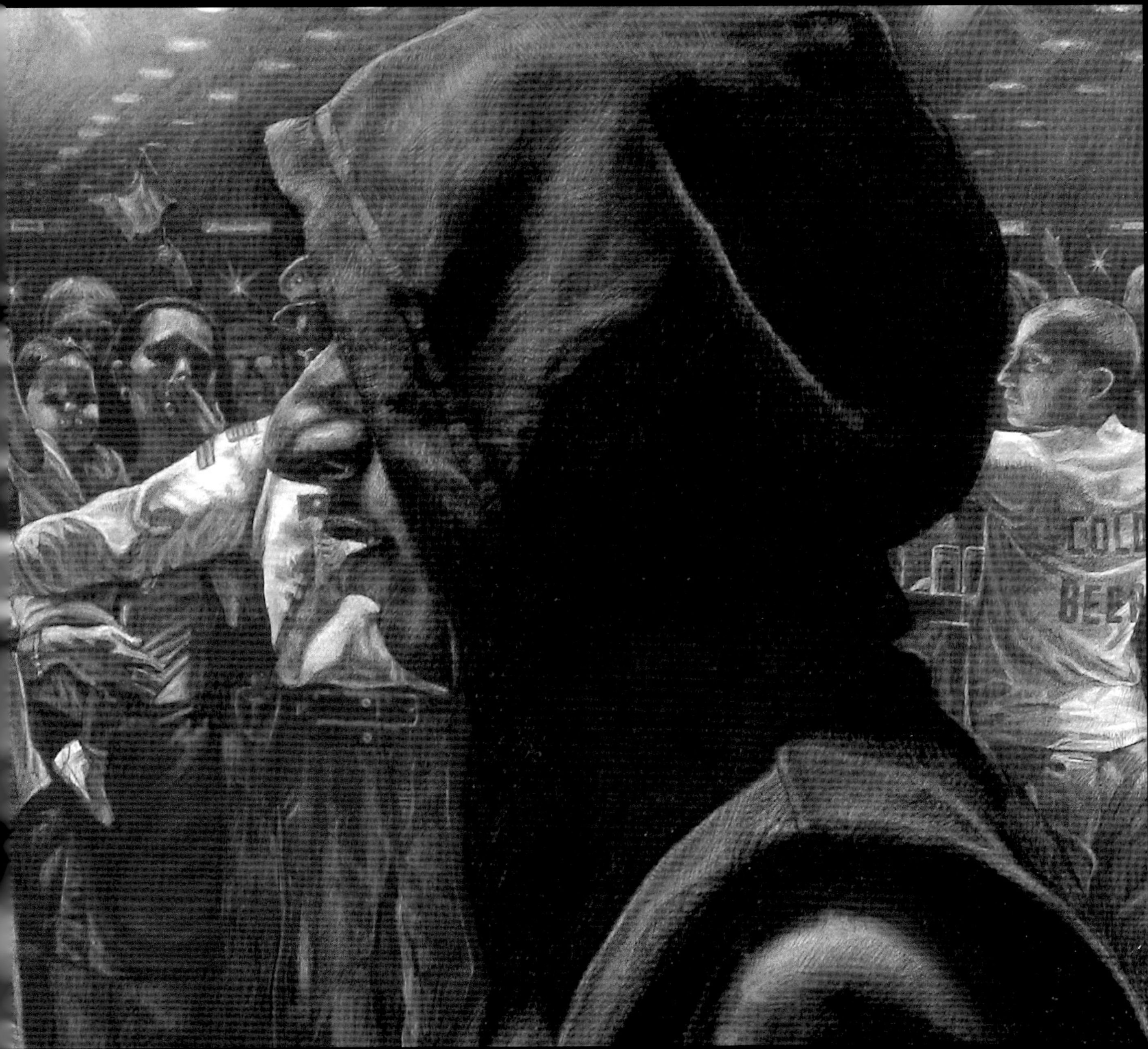

ter when pain comes.

eweight contender

Stations: The Strongest Man in the World is He Who Walks Alone, 2001–4
Charcoal on paper
Photo: Peter [illegible]

have no difficulty justifying boxing as a sport because I have never thought of it as a sport.

There is nothing fundamentally playful about t; nothing that seems to belong to daylight, to pleasure. At its moments of greatest ntensity it seems to contain so complete and so powerful an image of life—life's beauty, vulnerability, despair, incalculable and often self-destructive courage—that boxing s life, and hardly a mere game. During a superior boxing match (Ali–Frazier I, for nstance) we are deeply moved by the body's communion with itself by way of another's ntransigent flesh. The body's dialogue with ts shadow-self—or Death. Baseball, football, basketball—these quintessentially American pastimes are recognizably sports because they involve *play*: they are games. One *plays* football, one doesn't play boxing.

Observing team sports, teams of adult men, one sees how men are children in the most felicitous sense of the word. But boxing in ts elemental ferocity cannot be assimilated nto childhood. (Though very young men box, even professionally, and many world champions began boxing in their early or mid-teens. By the time he was sixteen Jack Dempsey, rootless and adrift in the West, was fighting for small sums of money in unrefereed saloon fights in which—in the natural course of things—he might have been killed.) Spectators at public games derive much of their pleasure from reliving the communal emotions of childhood but spectators at boxing matches relive the murderous infancy of the race. Hence the occasional savagery of boxing crowds—

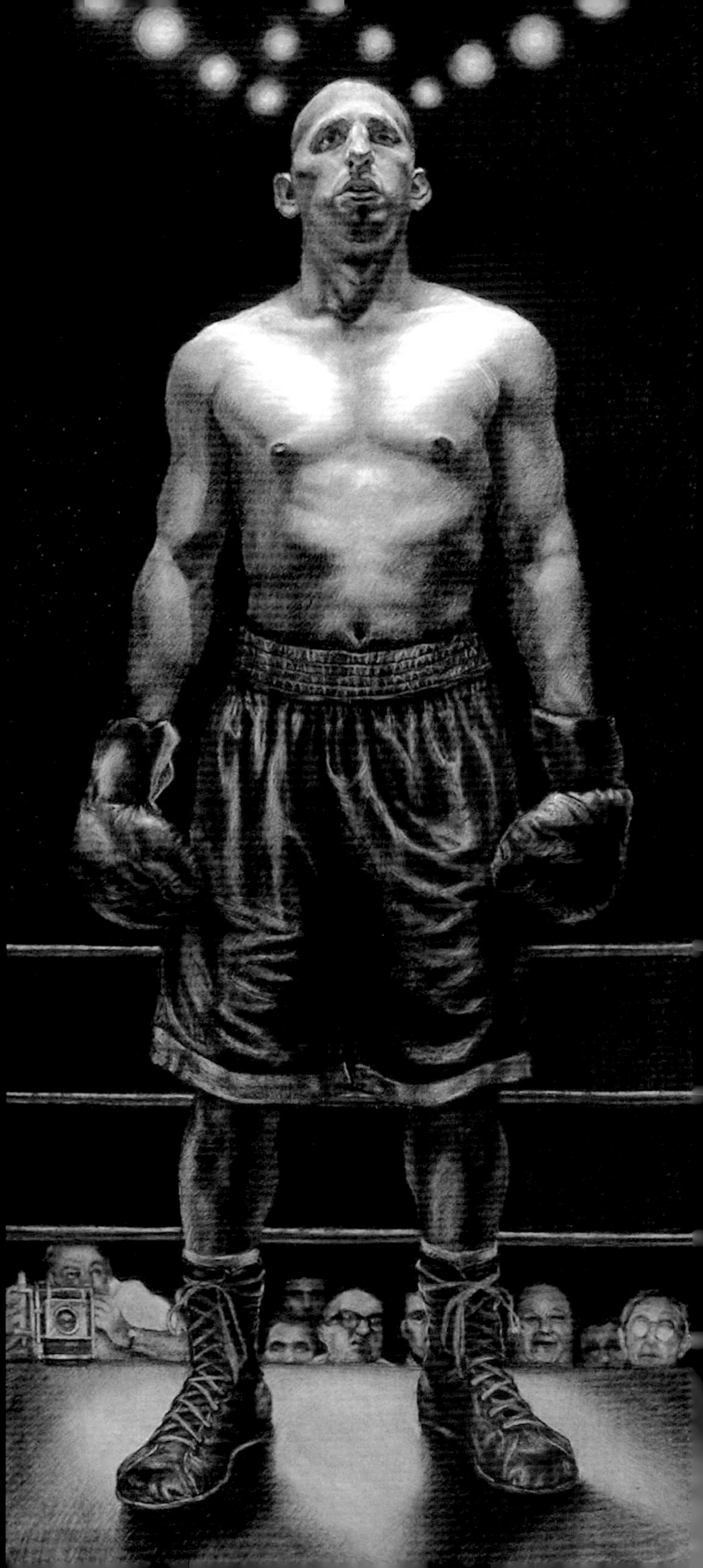

the crowd, largely Hispanic, that cheered as the Welshman Johnny Owen was pounded into insensibility by the Mexican bantamweight champion Lupe Pintor, for instance—and the excitement when a man begins to seriously bleed.

Marvelous Marvin Hagler, speaking of blood, is speaking, of course, of his own.

Considered in the abstract the boxing ring is an altar of sorts, one of those legendary spaces where the laws of a nation are suspended: inside the ropes, during an officially regulated three-minute round, a man may be killed at his opponent's hands but he cannot be legally murdered. Boxing inhabits a sacred space predating civilization; or, to use D. H. Lawrence's phrase, before God was love. If it suggests a savage ceremony or a rite of atonement it also suggests the futility of such gestures. For what possible atonement is the fight waged if it must shortly be waged again . . . and again? The boxing match is the very image, the more terrifying for being so stylized, of mankind's collective aggression; its ongoing historical madness.

Years ago in the early 1950s when my father first took me to a Golden Gloves boxing tournament in Buffalo, New York, I asked him why the boys wanted to fight one another, why they were willing to get hurt. As if it were an explanation my father said, "Boxers don't feel pain quite the way we do."

Pain, in the proper context, is something other than pain.

Stations: Main Event, 2001–4
Charcoal on paper
Photo: Peter Molick

Consider: Gene Tunney's single defeat in a thirteen-year career of great distinction was to a notorious fighter named Harry Greb who seems to have been, judging from boxing lore, the dirtiest fighter in history. Greb was infamous for his fouls—low blows, butting, "holding and hitting," rubbing his laces against an opponent's eyes, routine thumbing—as well as for a frenzied boxing style in which blows were thrown from all directions. (Hence, "The Human Windmill.") Greb, who died young, was a world middleweight champion for three years but a flamboyant presence in boxing circles for a long time. After the first of his several fights with Greb the twenty-two-year-old Tunney was so badly hurt he had to spend a week in bed; he'd lost an astonishing two quarts of blood during the fifteen-round fight. Yet, as Tunney said some years later:

> *Greb gave me a terrible whipping. He broke my nose, maybe with a butt. He cut my eyes and ears, perhaps with his laces . . . My jaw was swollen from the right temple down the cheek, along under the chin and partway up the other side. The referee, the ring itself, was full of blood . . . But it was in that first fight, in which I lost my American light-heavyweight title, that I knew I had found a way to beat Harry eventually. I was fortunate, really. If boxing in those days had been afflicted with the Commission doctors we have today—who are always poking their noses into the ring and examining superficial wounds—the first fight with Greb would have been stopped before I learned how to beat him. It's possible, even probable, that if this had happened I would never have been heard of again.*

Tunney's career, in other words, was built upon pain. Without it he would never have moved up into Dempsey's class.

Tommy Loughran, light-heavyweight champion in the years 1927–29, was a master boxer greatly admired by other boxers. He approached boxing literally as a science—as Tunney did—studying his opponents' styles and mapping out ring strategy for each fight, as boxers and their trainers commonly do today. Loughran rigged up mirrors in his basement so that he could watch himself as he worked out, for, as he said, no boxer ever sees himself quite as he appears to his opponent. He sees the opponent but not himself as an opponent. The secret of Loughran's career was that his right hand broke easily so that he was forced to use it only once each fight: for the knockout punch or nothing. "I'd get one shot then the agony of the thing would hurt me if the guy got up," Loughran said. "Anybody I ever hit with a left hook I knocked flat on his face, but I would never take a chance for fear if my [left hand] goes, I'm done for."

Both Tunney and Loughran, it is instructive to note, retired from boxing well before they were forced to retire. Tunney became a highly successful businessman, and Loughran a highly successful sugar broker on the Wall Street commodities market. (Just to suggest that boxers are not invariably stupid, illiterate, or punch-drunk.)

Then there was Carmen Basilio!—much loved for his audacious ring style, his hit-and-be-hit approach. Basilio was world middle- and welterweight champion 1953–57, stoic, determined, a slugger willing to get hit in order to deal powerful counter-punches of his own. Onlookers marveled at the punishment Basilio seemed to absorb though Basilio insisted that he didn't get hit the way people believed. And when he was hit, and hit hard—

> *People don't realize how you're affected by a knockout punch when you're hit on the chin. It's nerves is all it is. There's no real concussion as far as the brain is concerned. I got hit on the point of the chin [in a match with Tony DeMarco in 1955]. It was a left hook that hit the right point of my chin. What happens is it pulls your jawbone out of your socket from the right side and jams it into the left side and the nerve there paralyzed the whole left side of my body, especially my legs. My left knee buckled and I almost went down, but when I got back to my corner the bottom of my foot felt like it had needles about six inches high and I just kept stamping my foot on the floor, trying to bring it back. And by the time the bell rang it was all right.*

Basilio belongs to the rough-and-tumble era of LaMotta, Graziano, Zale, Pep, Saddler; Gene Fullmer, Dick Tiger, Kid Gavilan. An era when, if two boxers wanted to fight dirty, the referee was likely to give them license, or at least not to interfere.

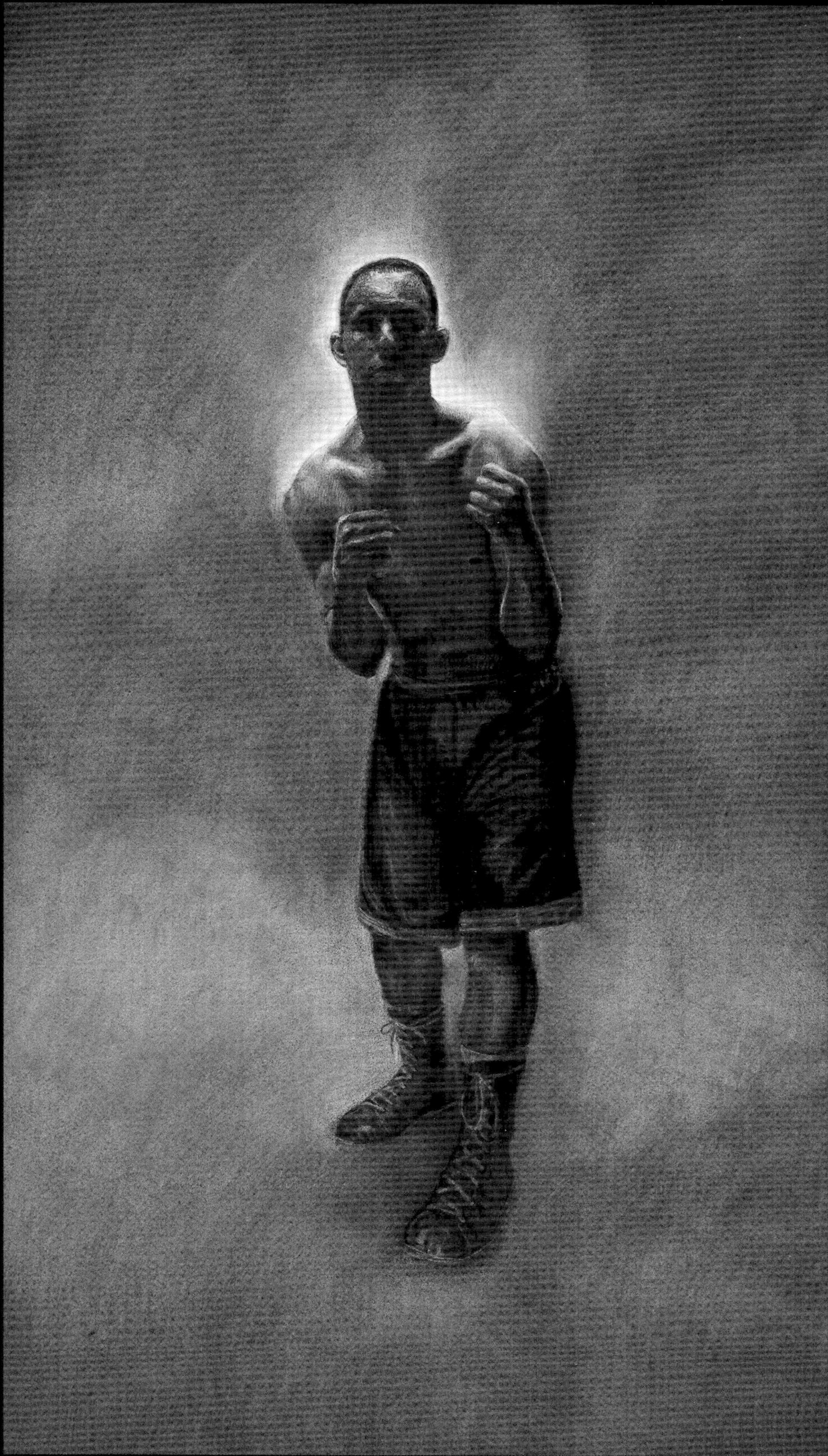

Stations: Collect 'Em All, 2001–4
Charcoal on paper
Photo: Peter Mollick

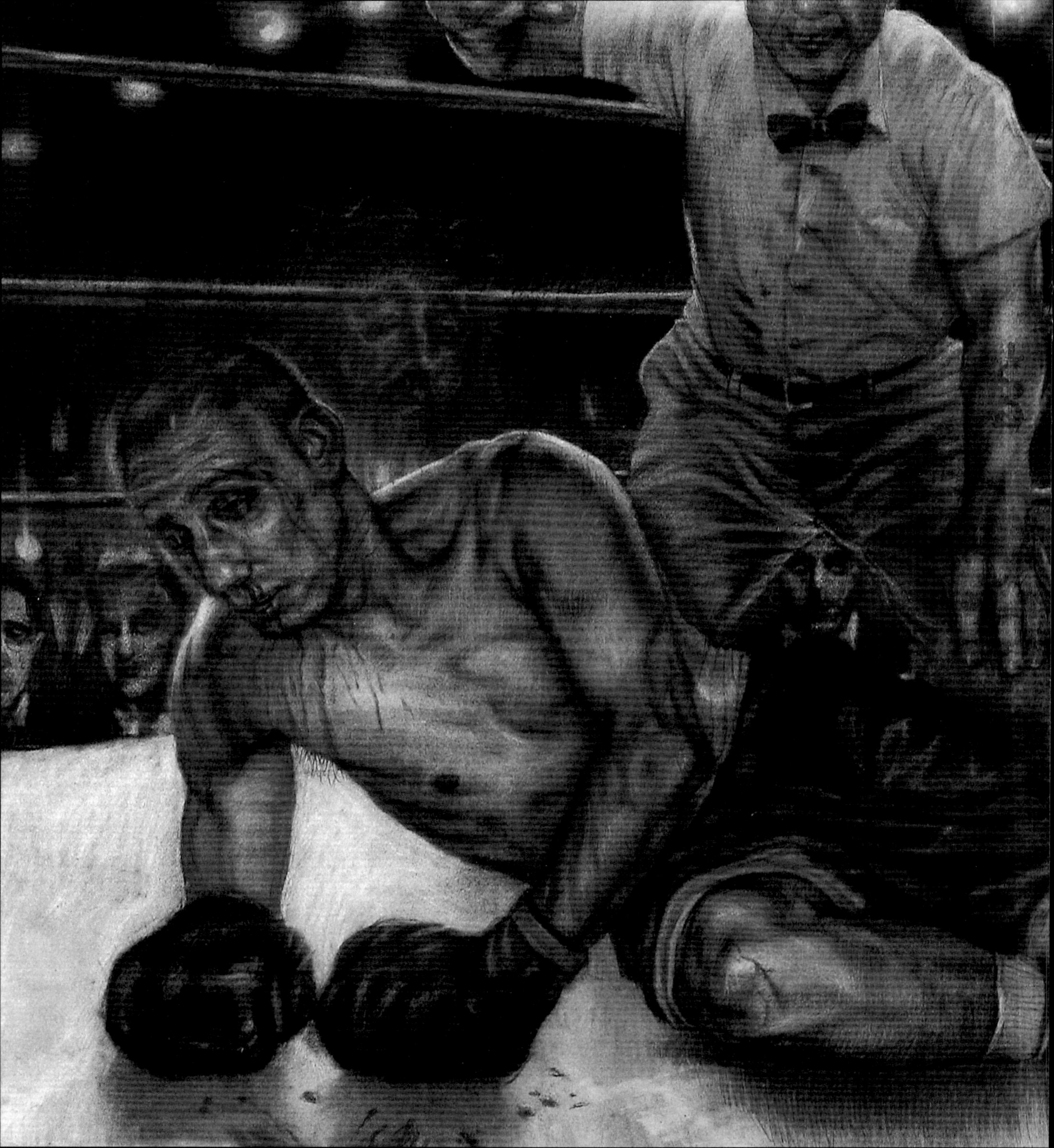

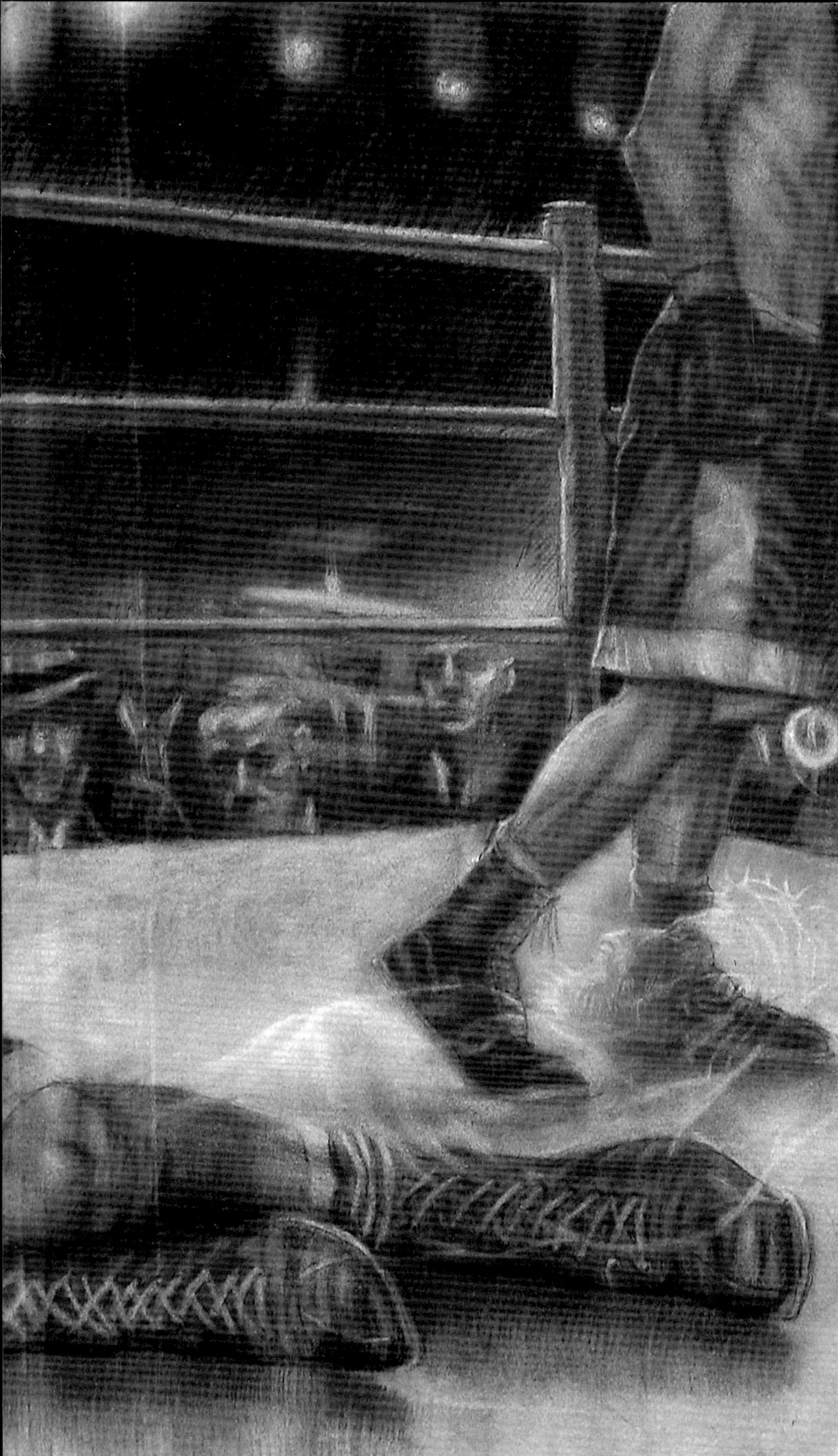

Stations: They Say
Every Man Must Fa
2001–4
Charcoal on paper
Photo: Peter Moore

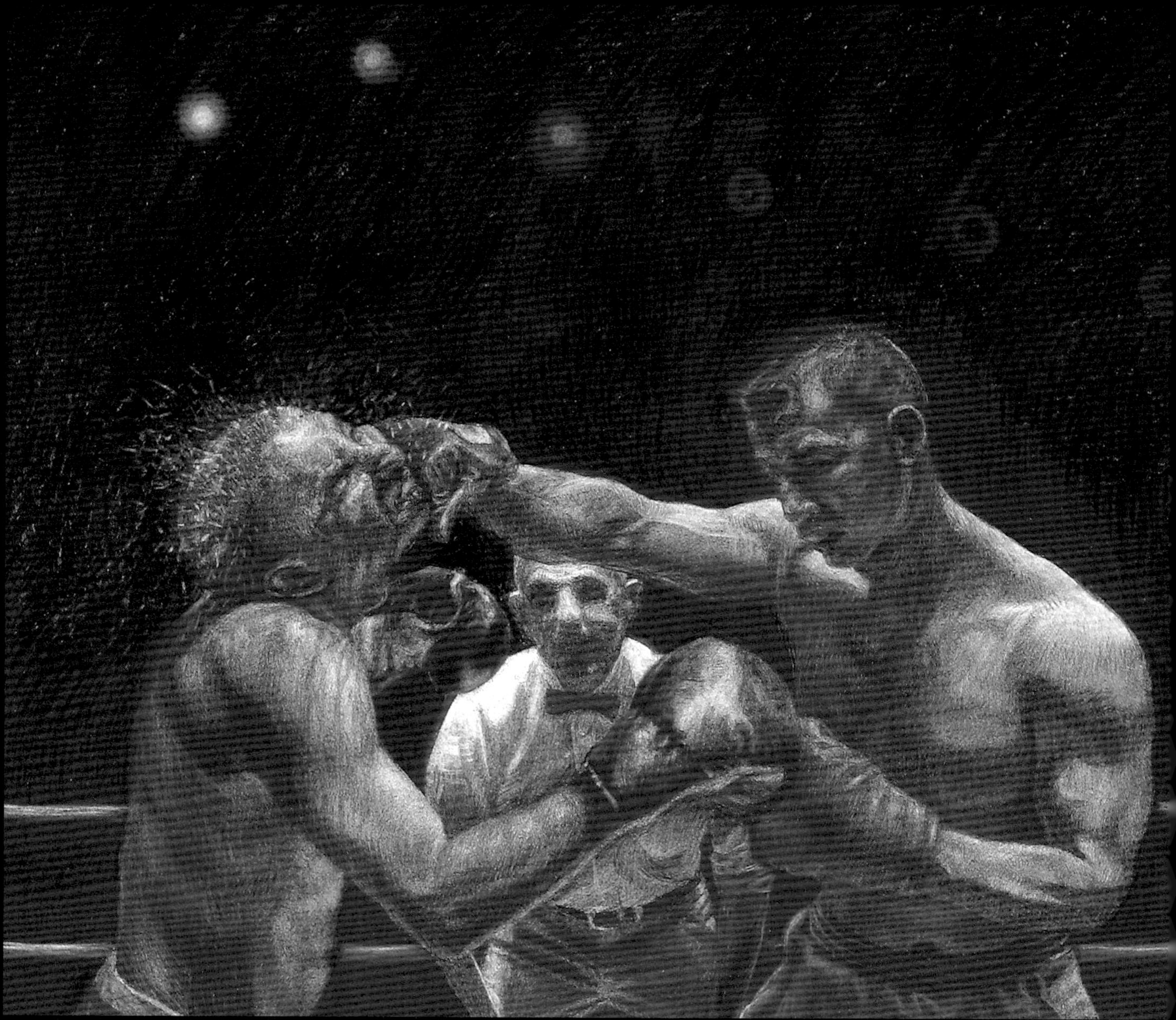

Stations: Get Outta There! Kill 'im!, No Mercy!, Finish Him! 2001–4
Charcoal on paper
[illegible]

Of Muhammad Ali in his prime Norman Mailer observed, "He worked apparently on the premise that there was something obscene about being hit." But in fights in his later career, as with George Foreman in Zaire, even Muhammad Ali was willing to be hit, and to be hurt, in order to wear down an opponent. Brawling fighters—those with "heart" like Jake LaMotta, Rocky Graziano, Ray Mancini—have little choice but to absorb terrible punishment in exchange for some advantage (which does not in any case always come). And surely it is true that some boxers (see Jake LaMotta's autobiographical *Raging Bull*) invite injury as a means of assuaging guilt, in a Dostoyevskian exchange of physical well-being for peace of mind. Boxing is about being hit rather more than it is about hitting, just as it is about feeling pain, if not devastating psychological paralysis, more than it is about winning. One sees clearly from the "tragic" careers of any number of boxers that the boxer prefers physical pain in the ring to the absence of pain that is ideally the condition of ordinary life. If one cannot hit, one can yet be hit, and know that one is still alive.

It might be said that boxing is primarily about maintaining a body capable of entering combat against other well-conditioned bodies. Not the public spectacle, the fight itself, but the rigorous training period leading up to it demands the most discipline, and is believed to be the chief cause of the boxer's physical and mental infirmities. (As a boxer ages his sparring partners get younger, the game itself gets more desperate.)

The artist senses some kinship, however oblique and one-sided, with the professional boxer in this matter of training. This fanatic subordination of the self in terms of a wished-for destiny. One might compare the time-bound public spectacle of the boxing match (which could be as brief as an ignominious forty-five seconds—the record for a title fight!) with the publication of a writer's book. That which is "public" is but the final stage in a protracted, arduous, grueling, and frequently despairing period of preparation. Indeed, one of the reasons for the habitual attraction of serious writers to boxing (from Swift, Pope, Johnson to Hazlitt, Lord Byron, Hemingway, and our own Norman Mailer, George Plimpton, Ted Hoagland, Wilfrid Sheed, Daniel Halpern, et al.) is the sport's systematic cultivation of pain in the interests of a project, a life-goal: the willed transposing of the sensation we know as pain (physical, psychological, emotional) into its polar opposite. If this is masochism—and I doubt that it is, or that it is simply—it is also intelligence, cunning, strategy. It is an act of consummate self-determination—the constant reestablishment of the parameters of one's being. To not only accept but to actively invite what most sane creatures avoid—pain, humiliation, loss, chaos—is to experience the present moment as already, in a sense, past. *Here* and *now* are but part of the design of *there* and *then*: pain now but control, and therefore triumph, later. And pain itself is miraculously transposed by dint of its context. Indeed, it might be said that "context" is all.

The novelist George Garrett, an amateur boxer of some decades ago, reminisces about his training period:

> *I learned something . . . about the brotherhood of boxers. People went into this brutal and often self-destructive activity for a rich variety of motivations, most of them bitterly antisocial and verging on the psychotic. Most of the fighters I knew of were wounded people who felt a deep, powerful urge to wound others at real risk to themselves. In the beginning. What happened was that in almost every case, there was so much self-discipline required and craft involved, so much else besides one's original motivations to concentrate on, that these motivations became at least cloudy and vague and were often forgotten, lost completely. Many good and experienced fighters (as has often been noted) become gentle and kind people . . . They have the habit of leaving all their fight in the ring. And even there, in the ring, it is dangerous to invoke too much anger. It can be a stimulant, but is very expensive of energy. It is impractical to get mad most of the time.*

Of all boxers it seems to have been Rocky Marciano (still our only undefeated heavyweight champion) who trained with the most monastic devotion; his training methods have become legendary. In contrast to reckless fighters like Harry "The Human Windmill" Greb, who kept in condition by boxing all the time, Marciano was willing to seclude himself from the world, including his wife and family, for as long as three months before a fight. Apart from the grueling physical ordeal of this period and the obsessive preoccupation with diet and weight and muscle tone, Marciano concentrated on one thing: the upcoming fight. Every minute of his life was defined in terms of the opening second of the fight. In his training camp the opponent's name was never mentioned in Marciano's hearing, nor was boxing as a subject discussed. In the final month Marciano would not write a letter since a letter related to the outside world. During the last ten days before a fight he would see no mail, take no telephone calls, meet no new acquaintances. During the week before the fight he would not shake hands. Or go for a ride in a car, however brief. No new foods! No dreaming of the morning after the fight! For all that was not *the fight* had to be excluded from consciousness. When Marciano worked out with a punching bag he saw his opponent before him, when he jogged he saw his opponent close beside him, no doubt when he slept he "saw" his opponent constantly—as the cloistered monk or nun chooses by an act of fanatical will to "see" only God.

Madness?—or merely discipline?—this absolute subordination of the self. In any case, for Marciano, it worked.

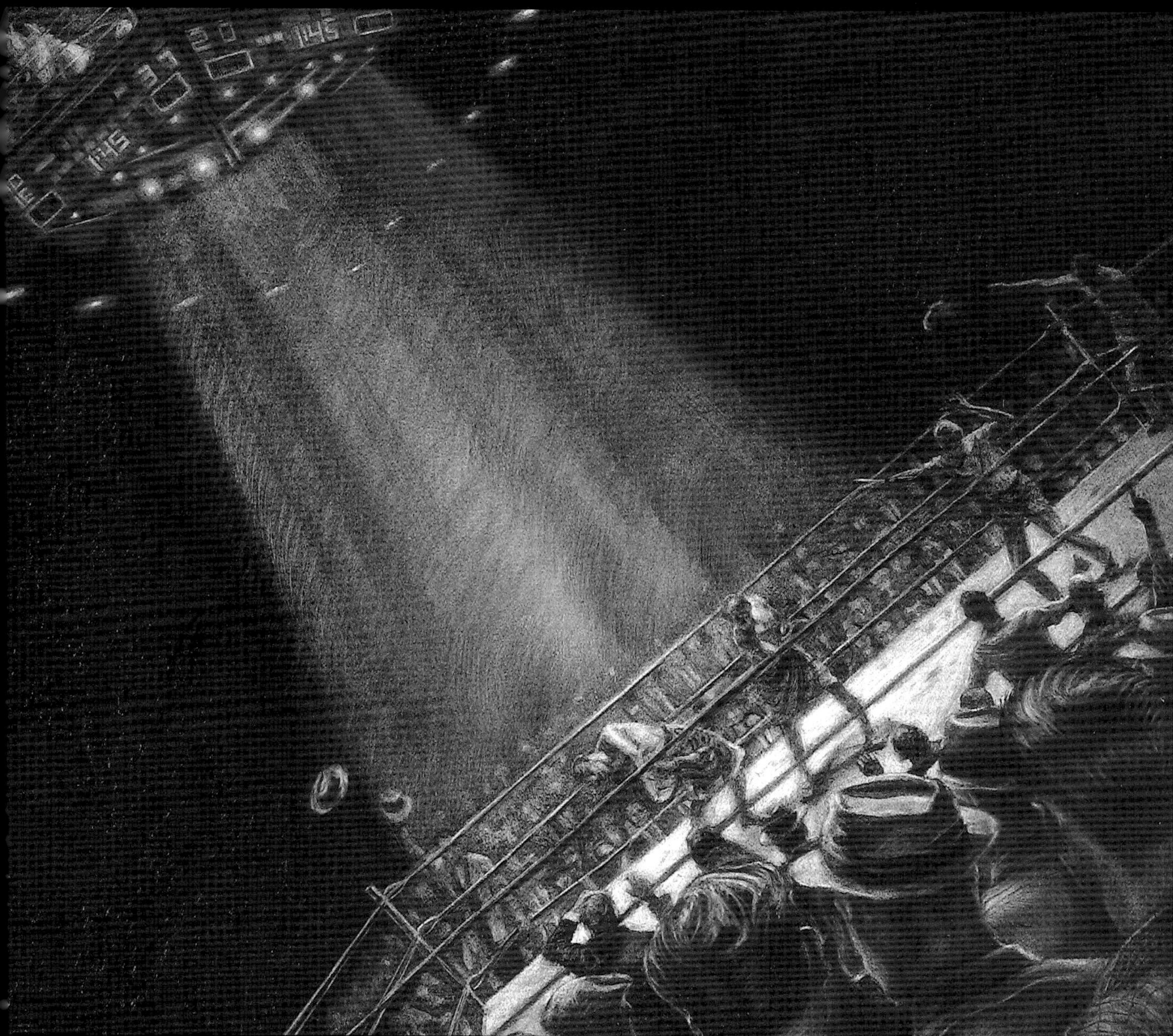

Stations: Get Outta There!, Kill 'Im!, No Mercy!, Finish Him!, 2001–4
Charcoal on paper
Photo: Peter Mallet

(following page)
Stations: A Fine Performance by Our Winning Fighter Tonight, 2001–4
Charcoal on paper
Photo: Peter Mallet

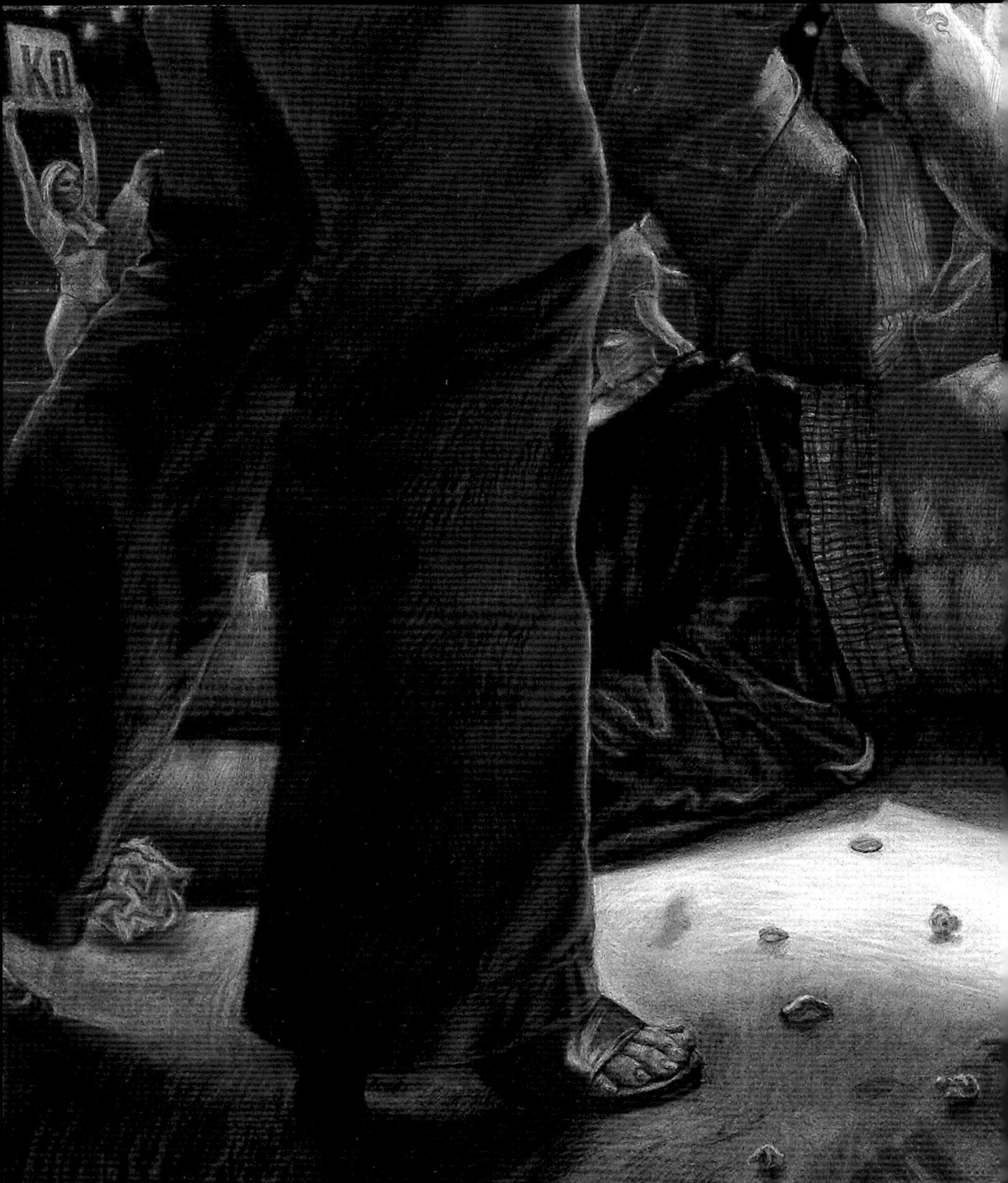
KO

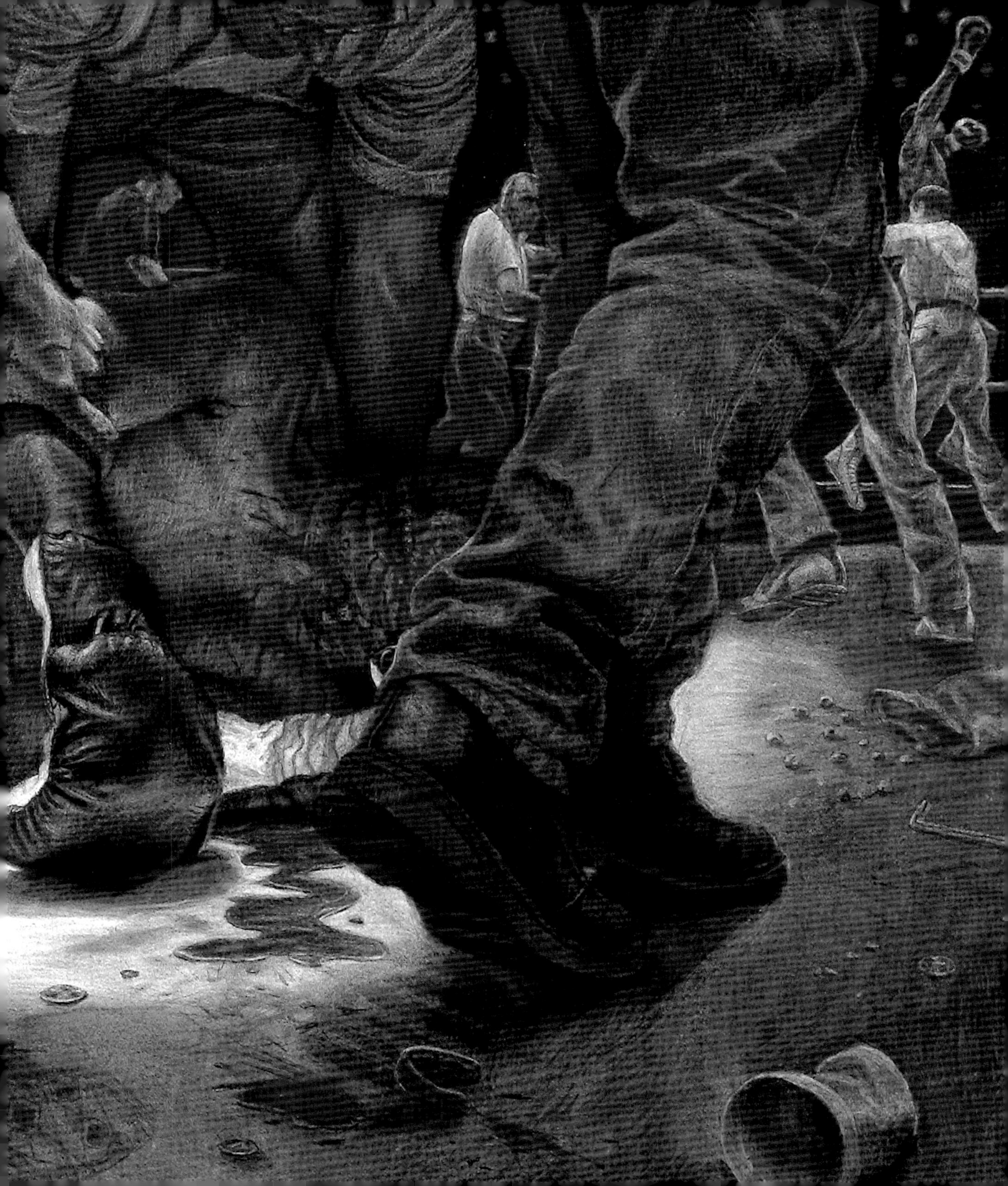

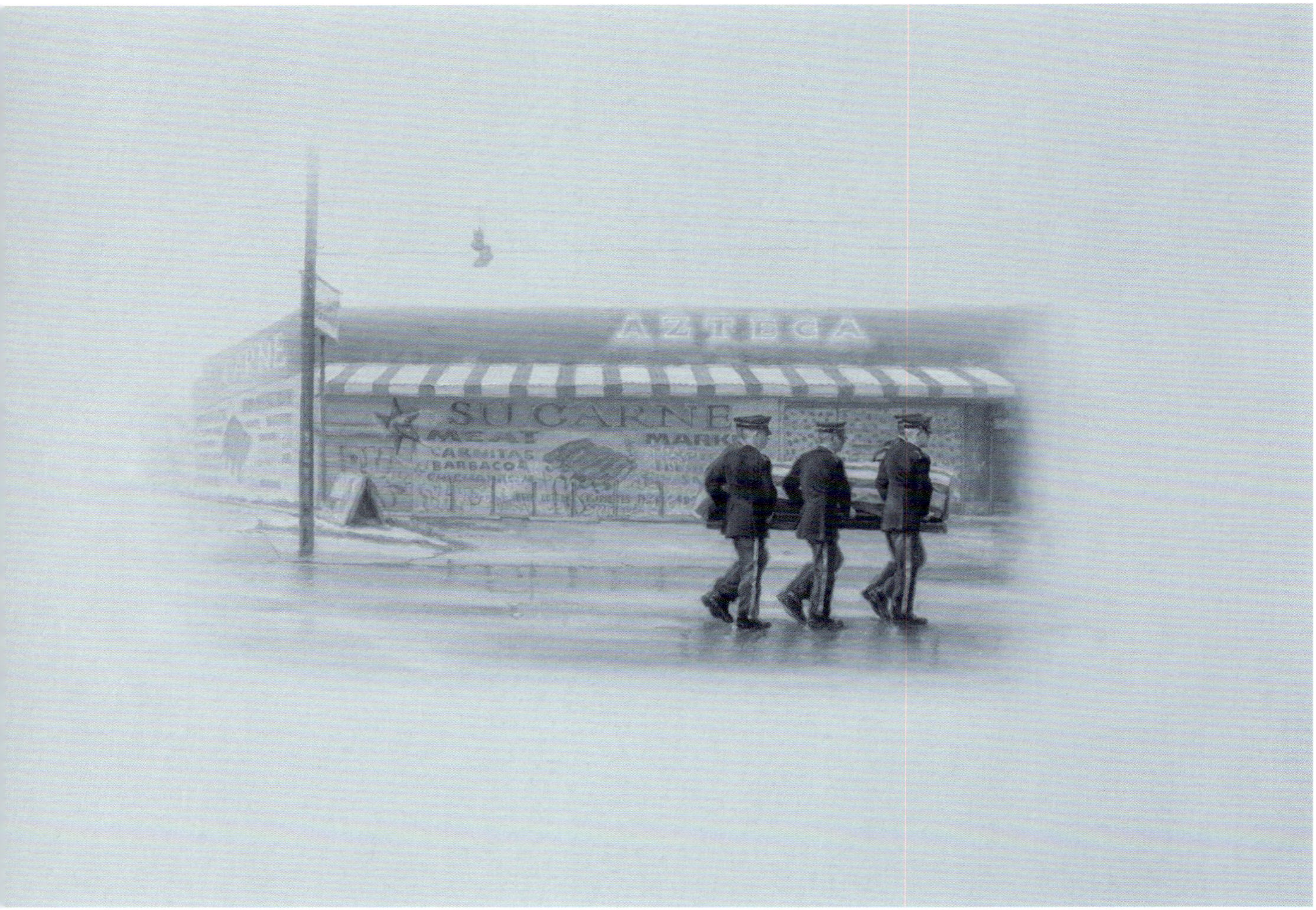

Excerpts for John
(detail from 6 panels), 2012
Oil on canvas
Photos: Peter Molick

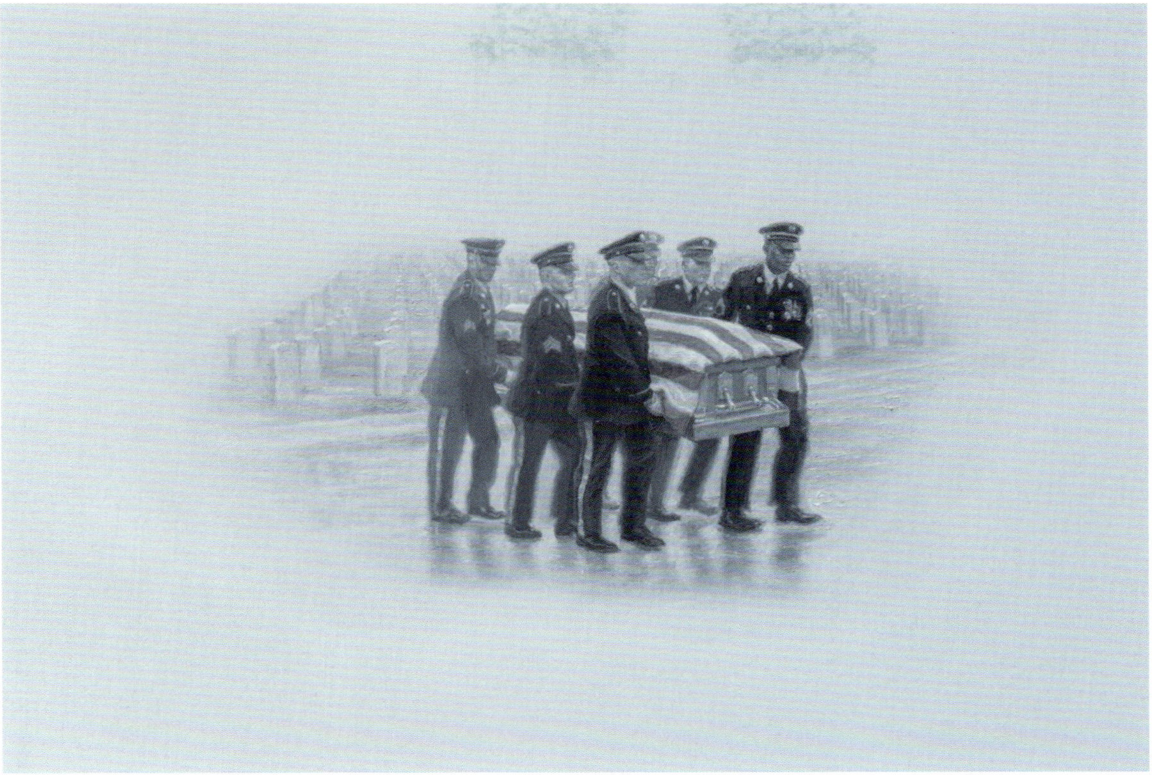

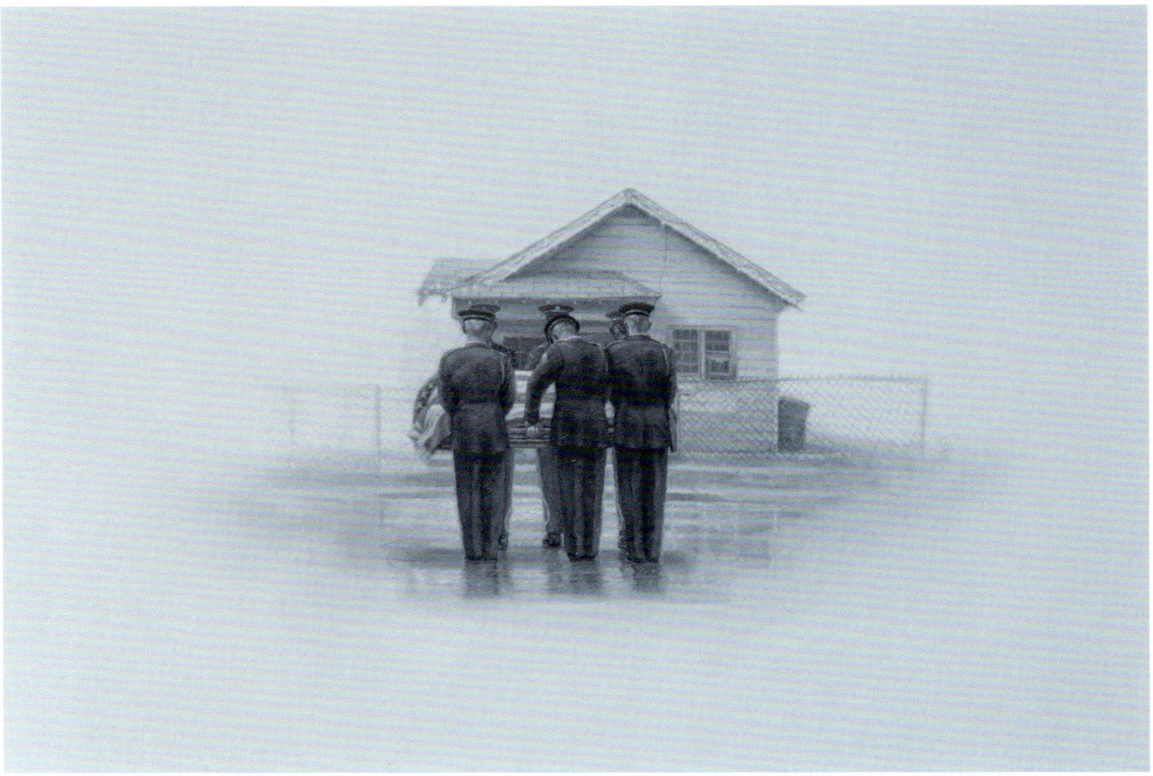

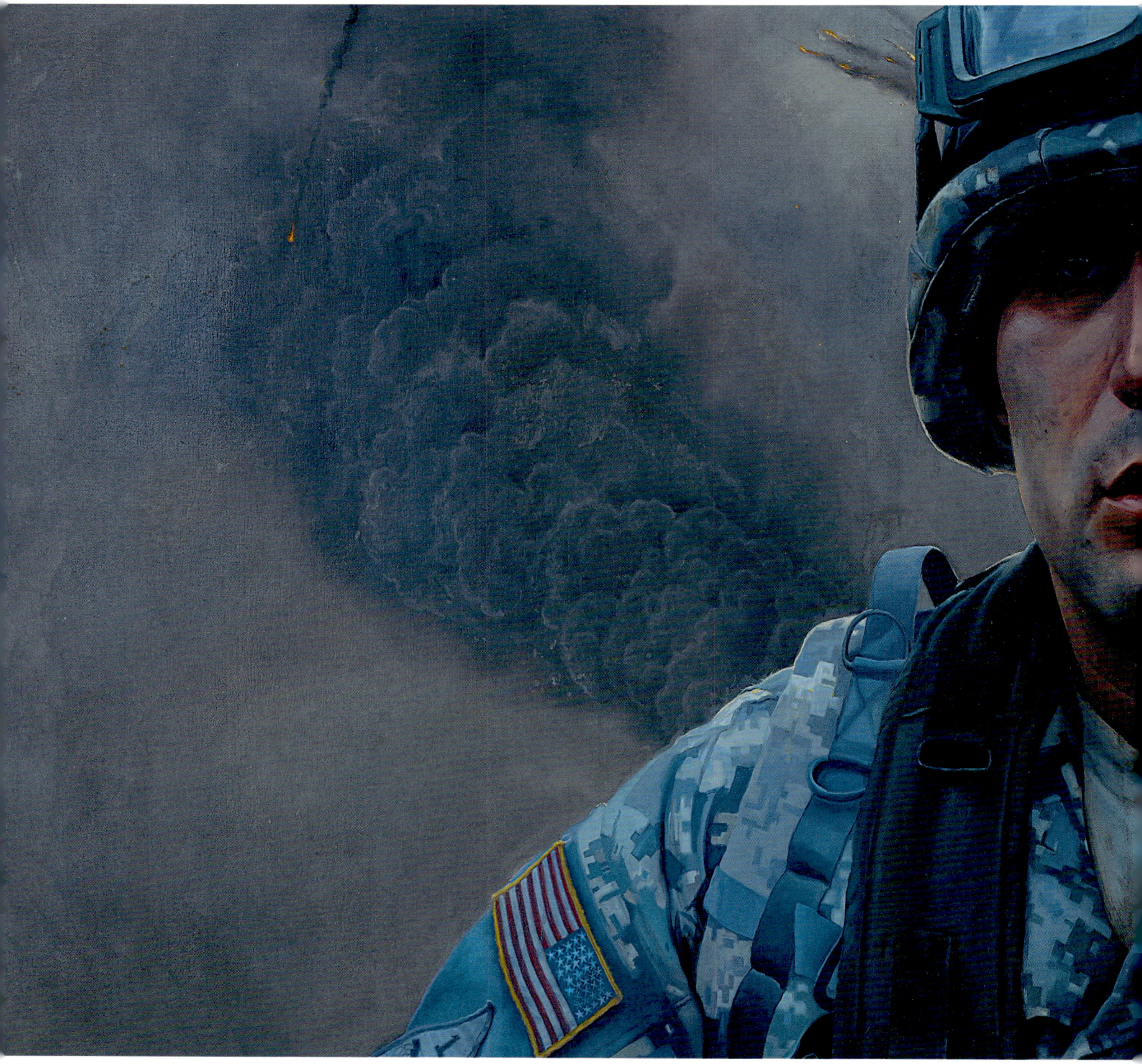

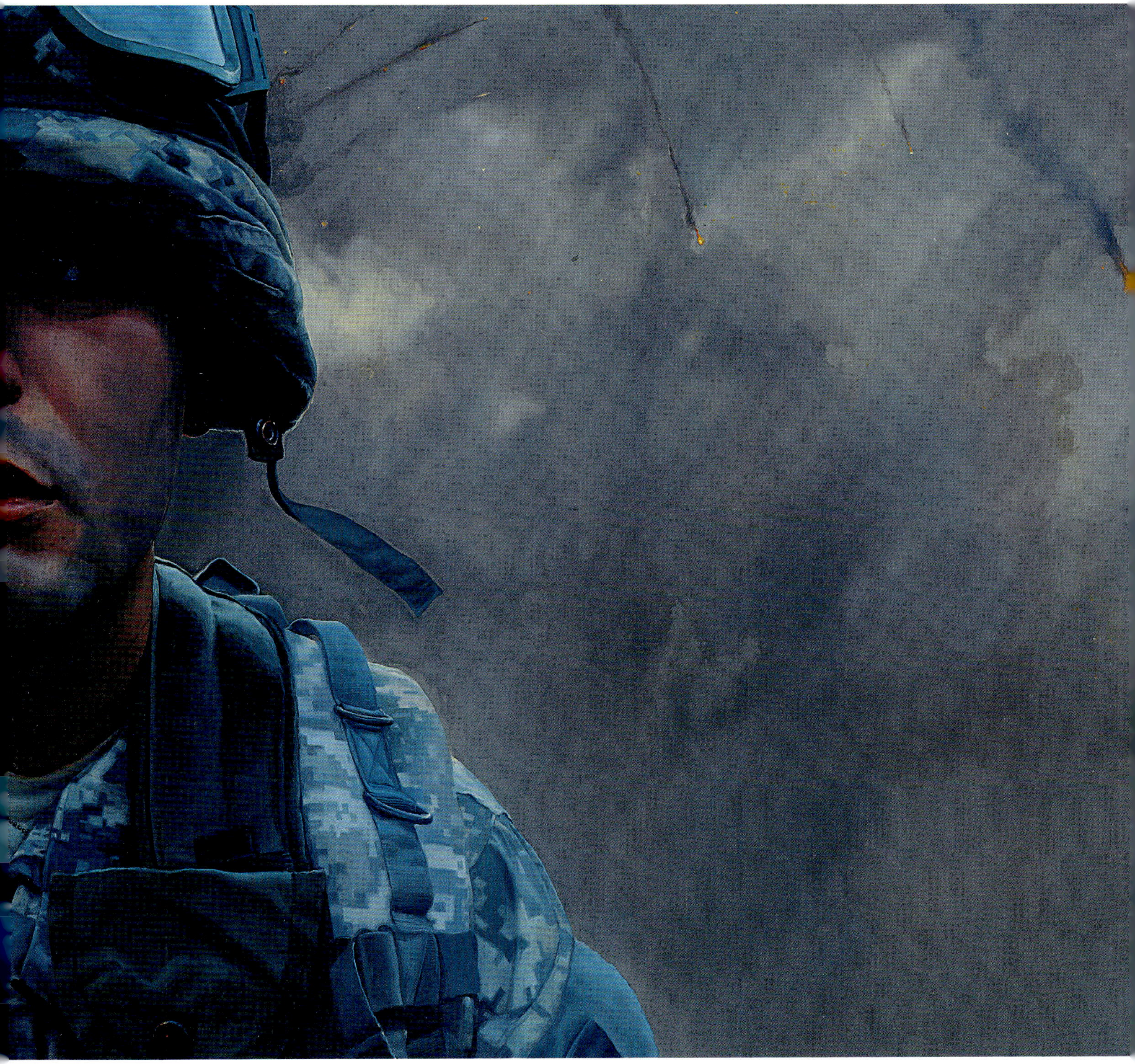

John, 2010–12
Oil on canvas
Smithsonian American Art Museum, gift of the artist.
Photo: Lucia RM Martino

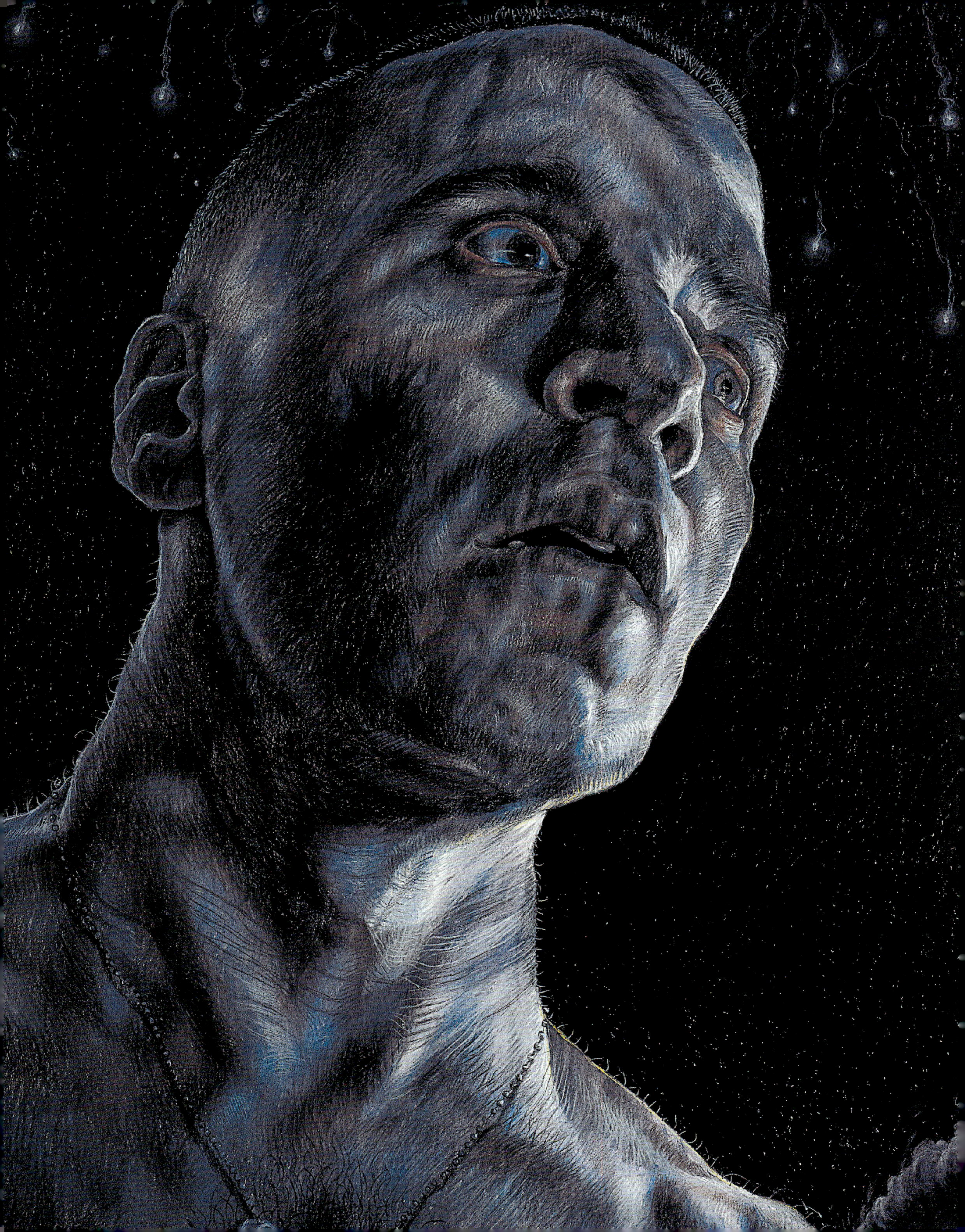

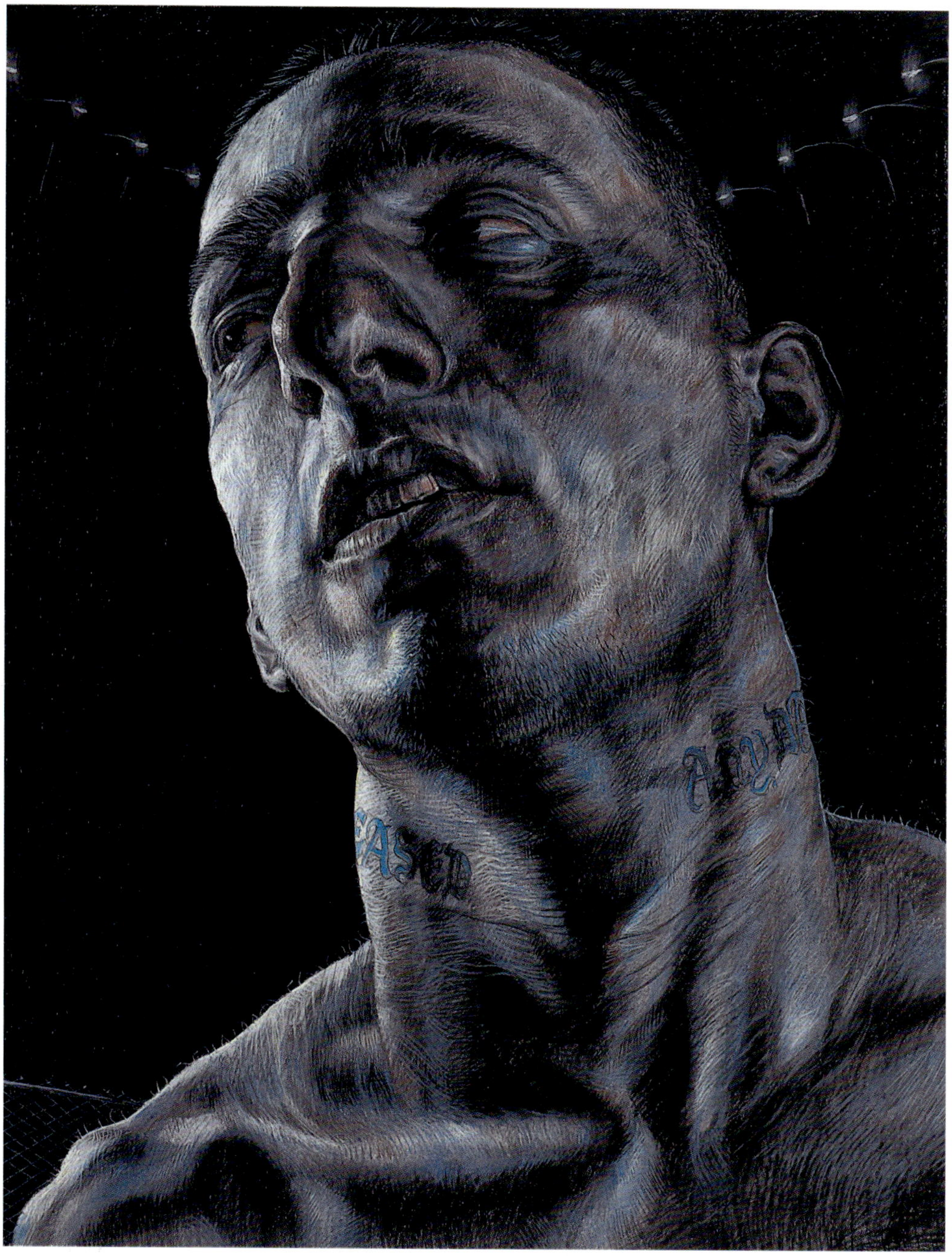

***Made Men: They Say Every Man Must Need Protection*, 2002**
Pastel on paper
Collection of the Modern Art Museum of Fort Worth, Gift of the Estate of Edmund W. Schenecker II in Memory of Anne Marion

***Made Men: They Say Every Man Must Fall*, 2002**
Pastel on paper
Collection of the Modern Art Museum of Fort Worth, Gift of the Estate of Edmund W. Schenecker II in Memory of Anne Marion

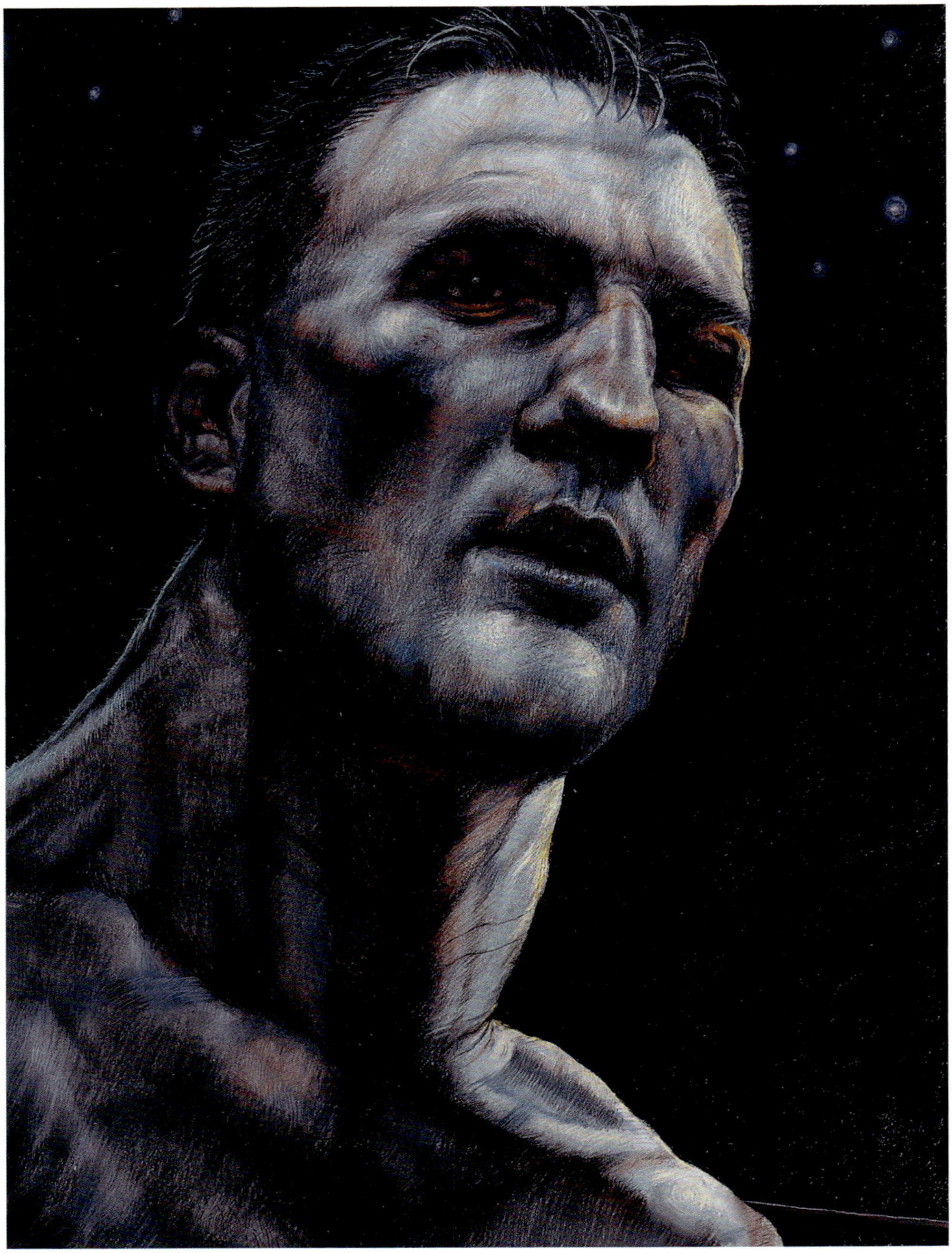

***Made Men: Yet I Swear I See My Reflection*, 2002**
Pastel on paper
Collection of the Modern Art Museum of Fort Worth, Gift of the Estate of Edmund W. Schenecker II in Memory of Anne Marion

***Made Men: Any Day Now, I Shall Be Released*, 2002**
Pastel on paper
Collection of the Modern Art Museum of Fort Worth, Gift of the Estate of Edmund W. Schenecker II in Memory of Anne Marion

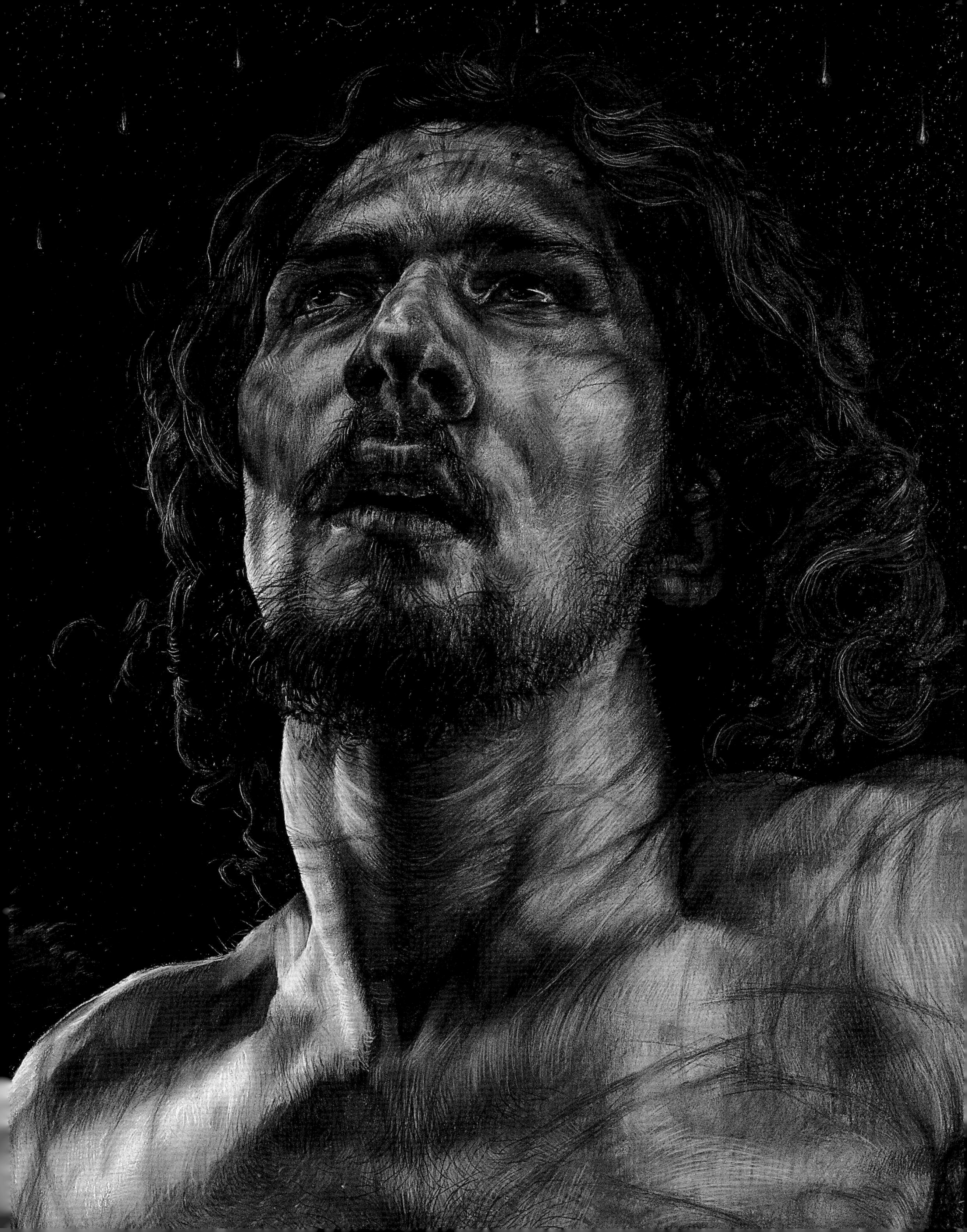

THE REMEMBERING

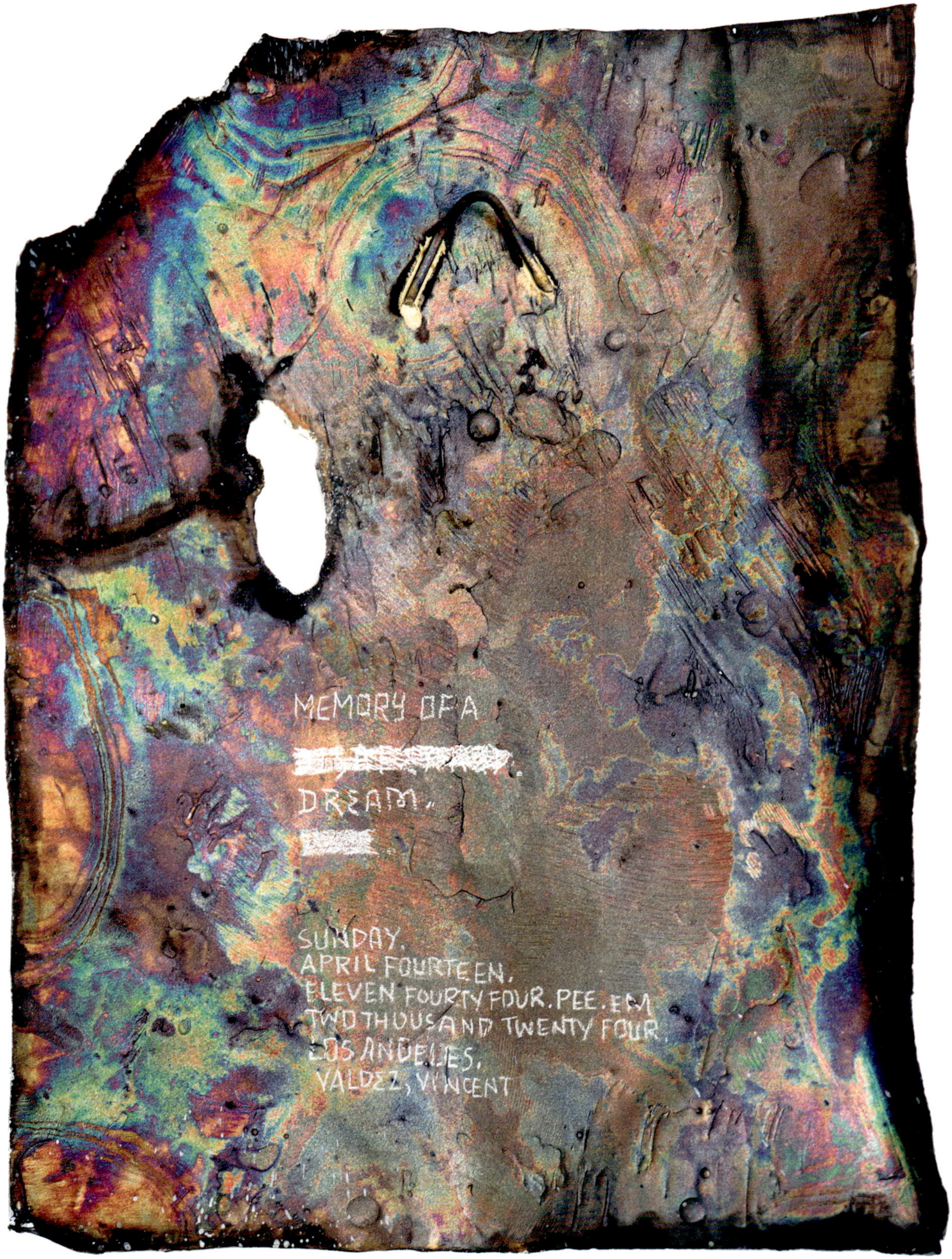
MEMORY OF A
DREAM.
SUNDAY.
APRIL FOURTEEN.
ELEVEN FOURTY FOUR. PEE. EM
TWO THOUSAND TWENTY FOUR.
LOS ANGELES.
VALDEZ, VINCENT

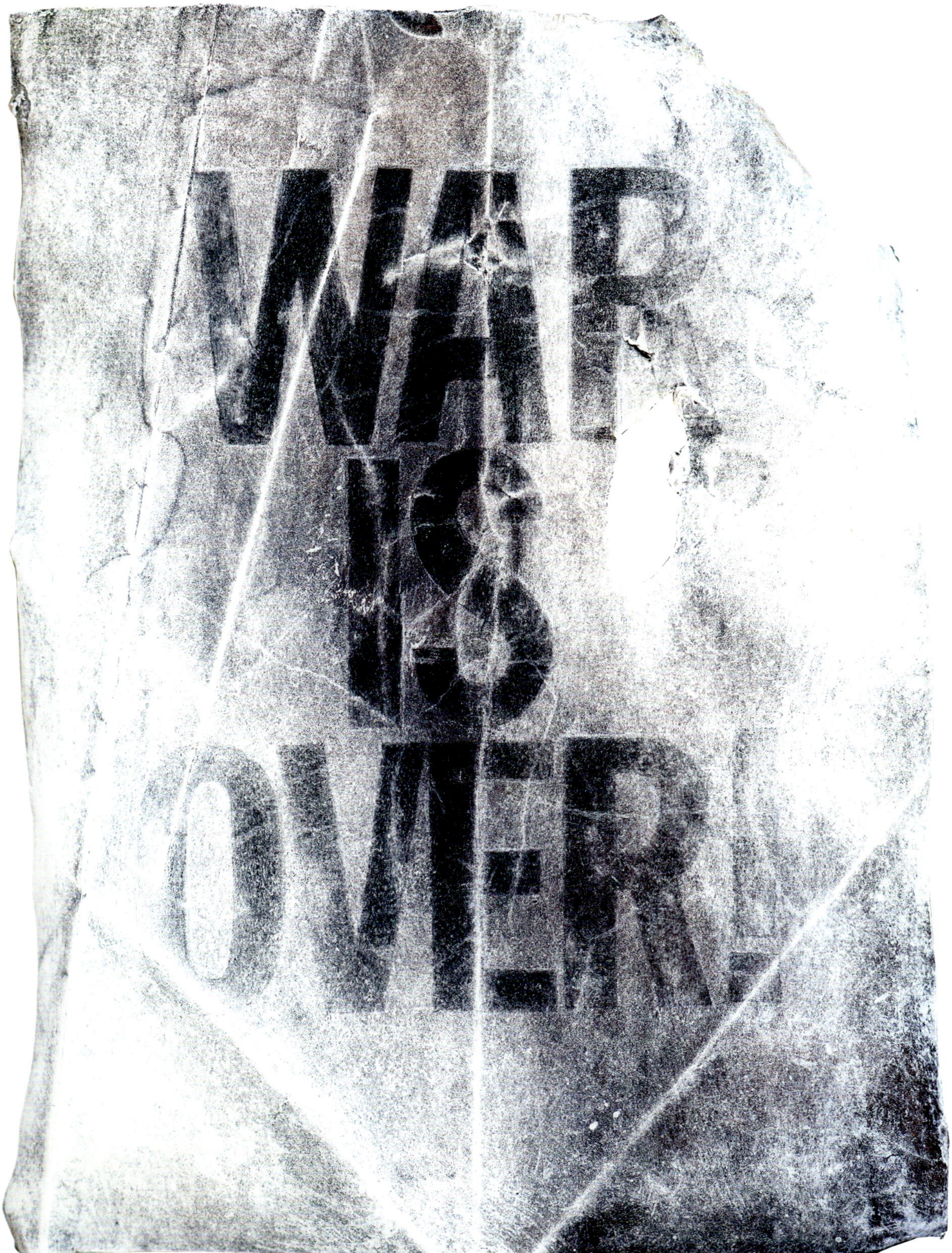
WAR
IS
OVER!

***Kill the Pachuco Bastard!*, 2001**
Oil on canvas
Photo: Elon Schoenholz

(Previous spread)
***Untitled (# 2)*, 2024**
from the series
Notes for a Future
Pencil on bronze
Photos: Robert LeBlanc

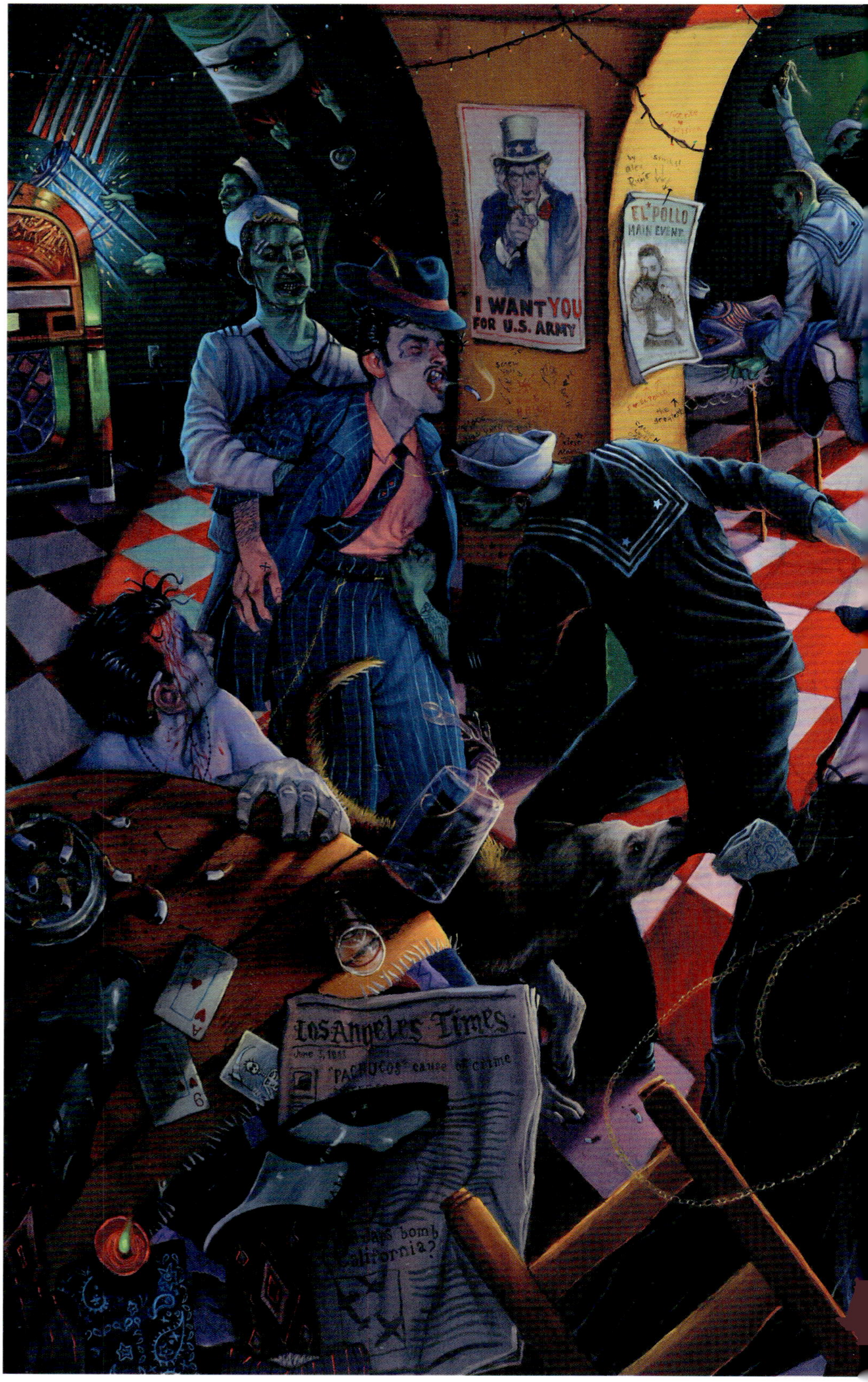

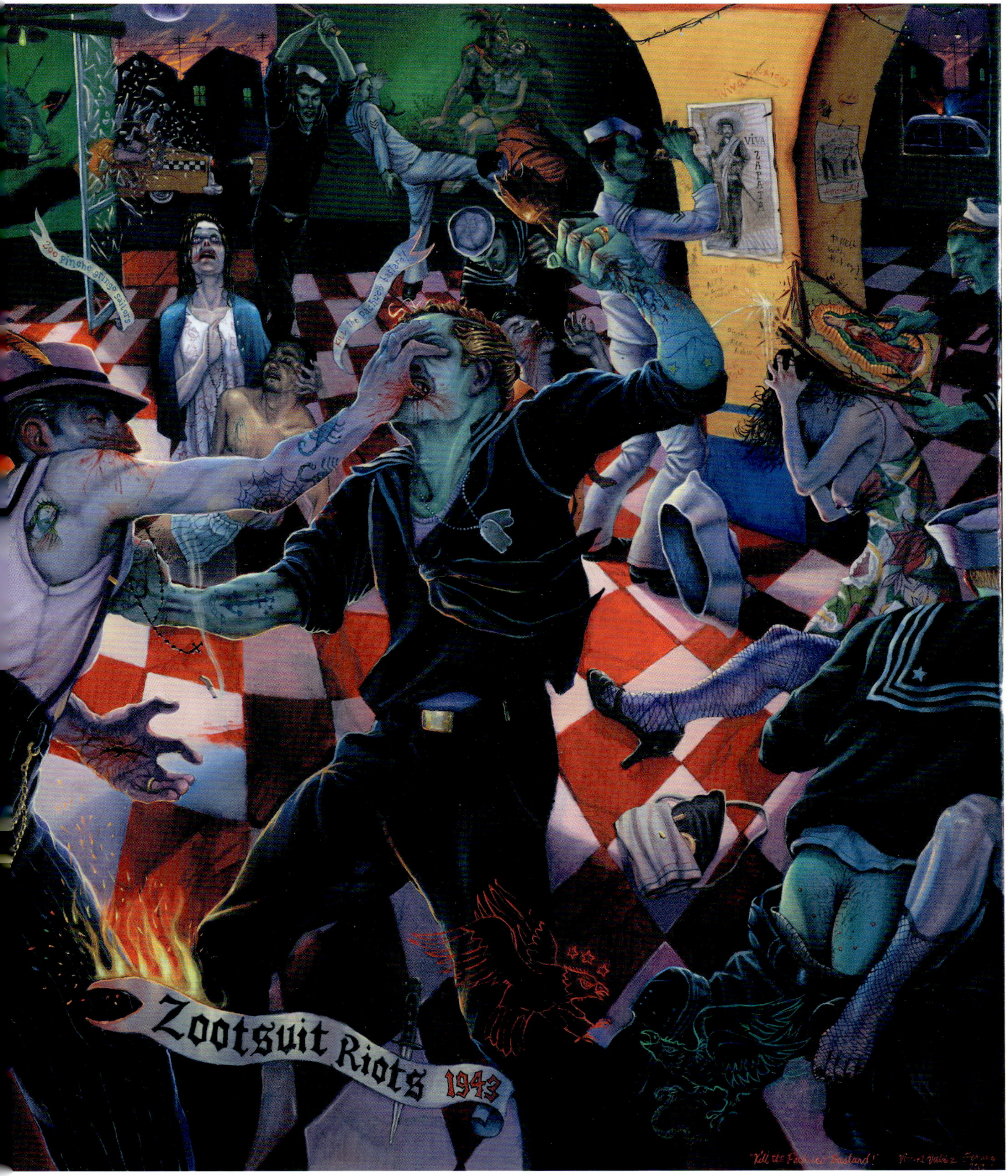
Zoo pinche gringo sailors
Kill the Pachuco bastard!
VIVA ZAPATA
Zootsuit Riots 1943

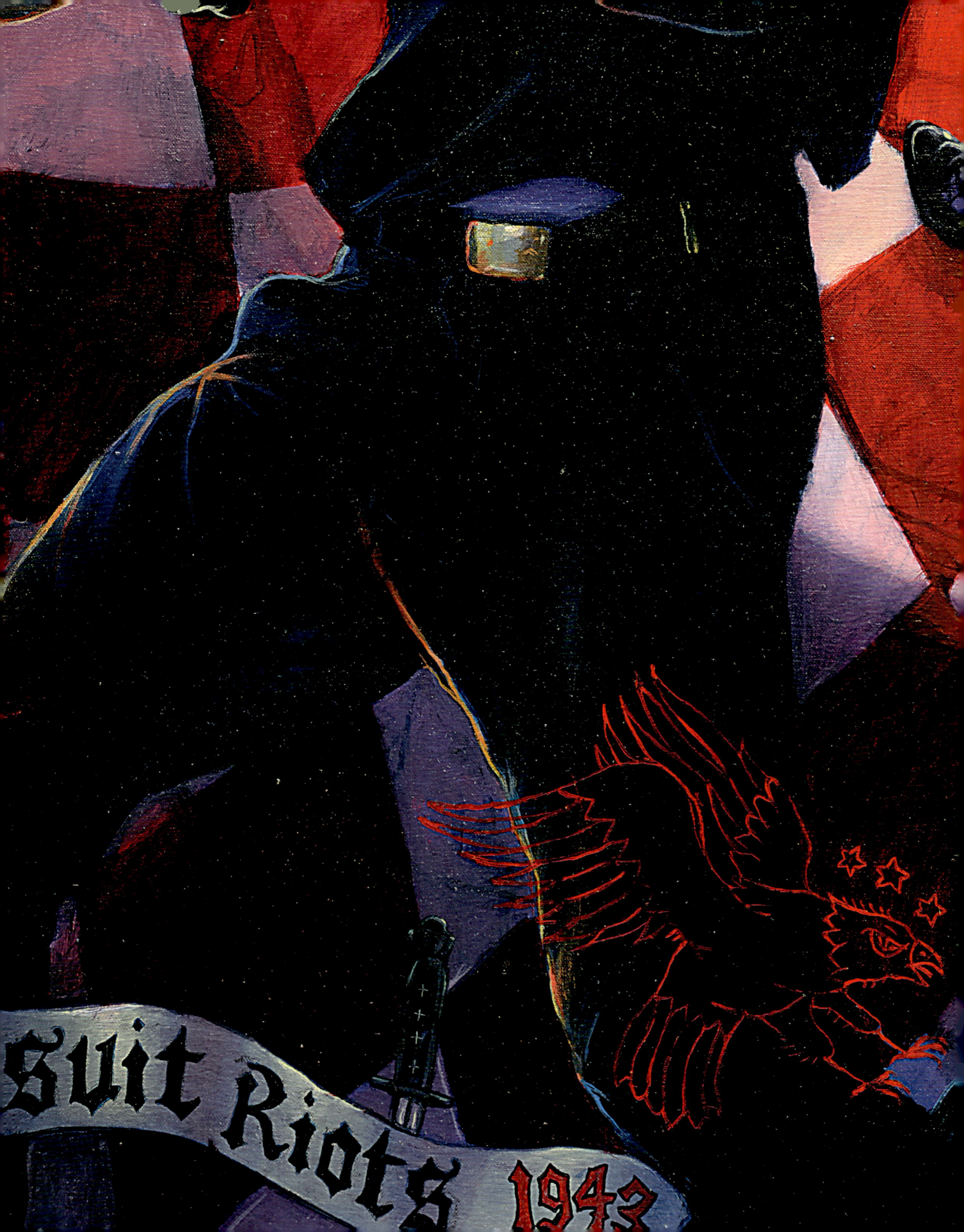
Suit Riots 1943

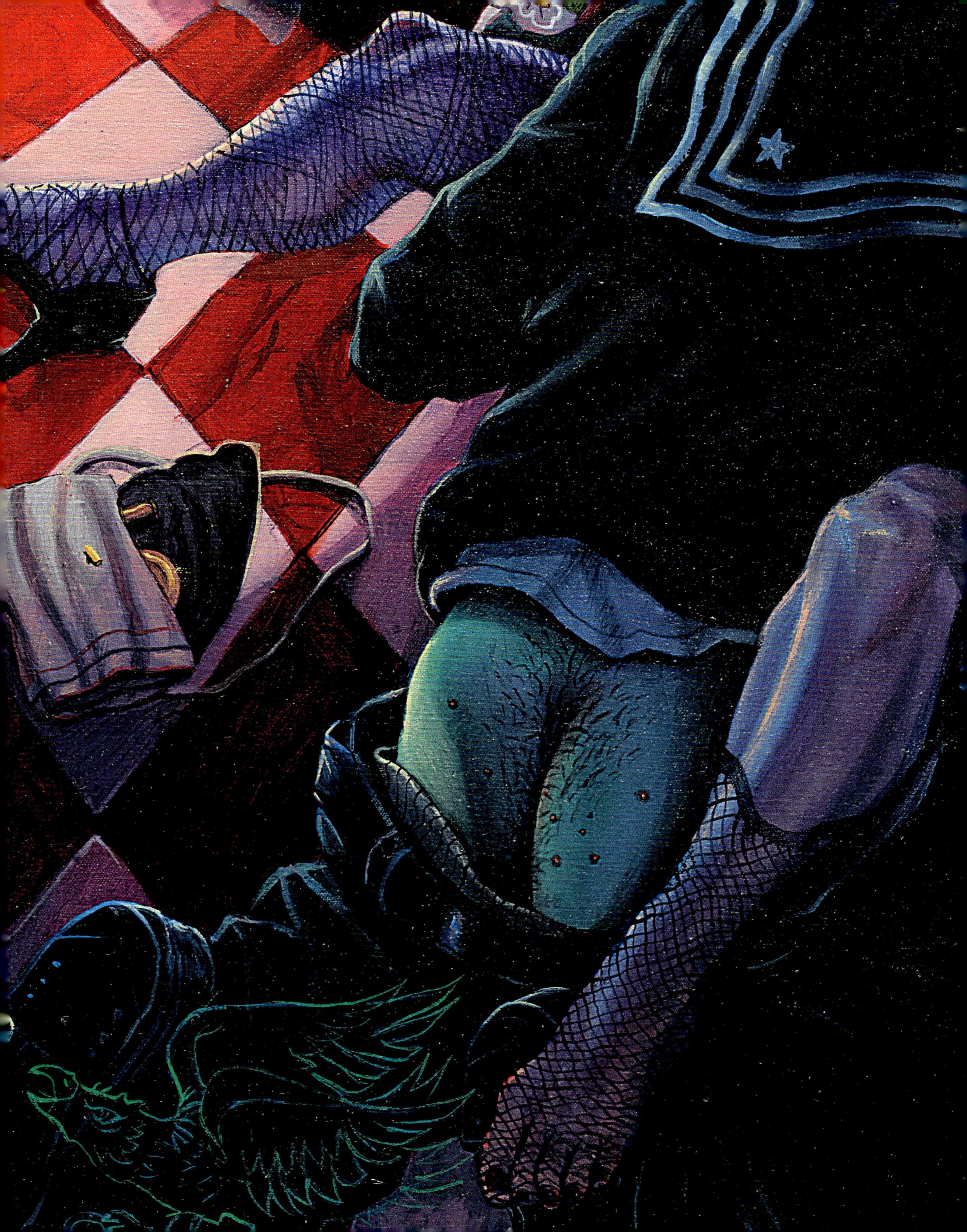

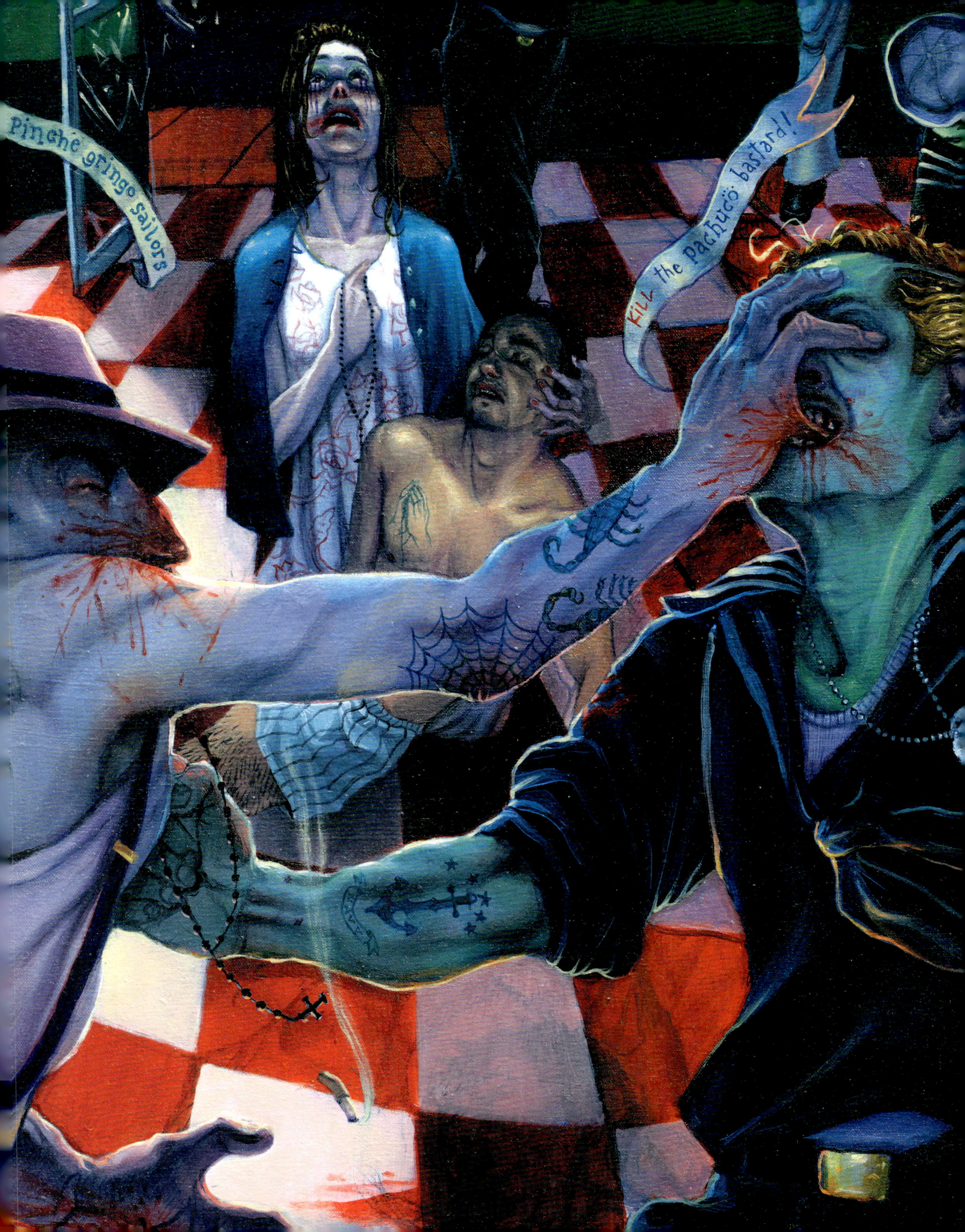
pinche gringo sailors
KILL the pachucö bastard!

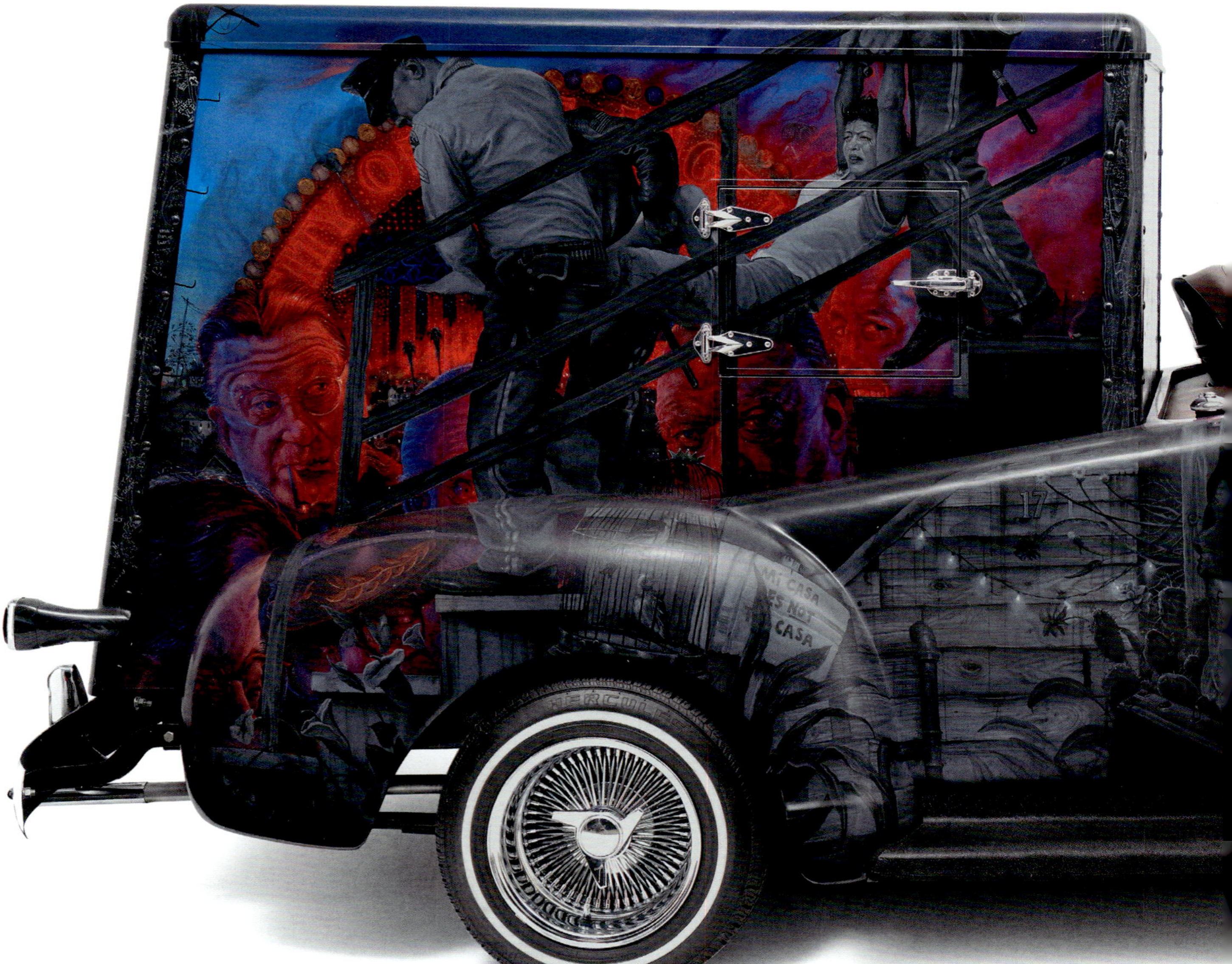

Vincent Valdez and Ry Cooder, *El Chavez Ravine*, 2005–7

Oil on 1953 Chevy Good Humor ice cream truck

Photo: Elon Schoenholz (details); LACMA (full truck) © Museum Associates/LACMA

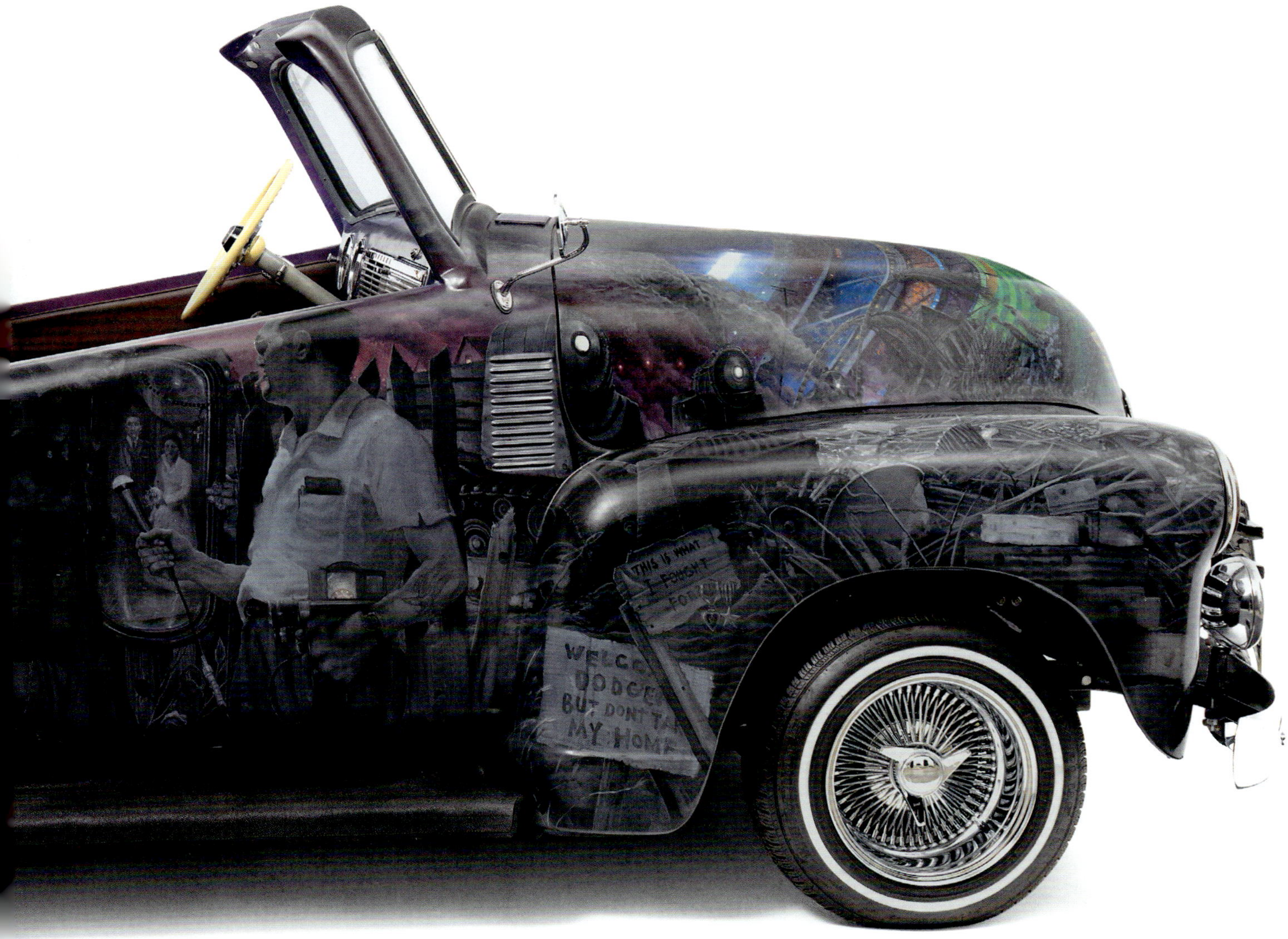

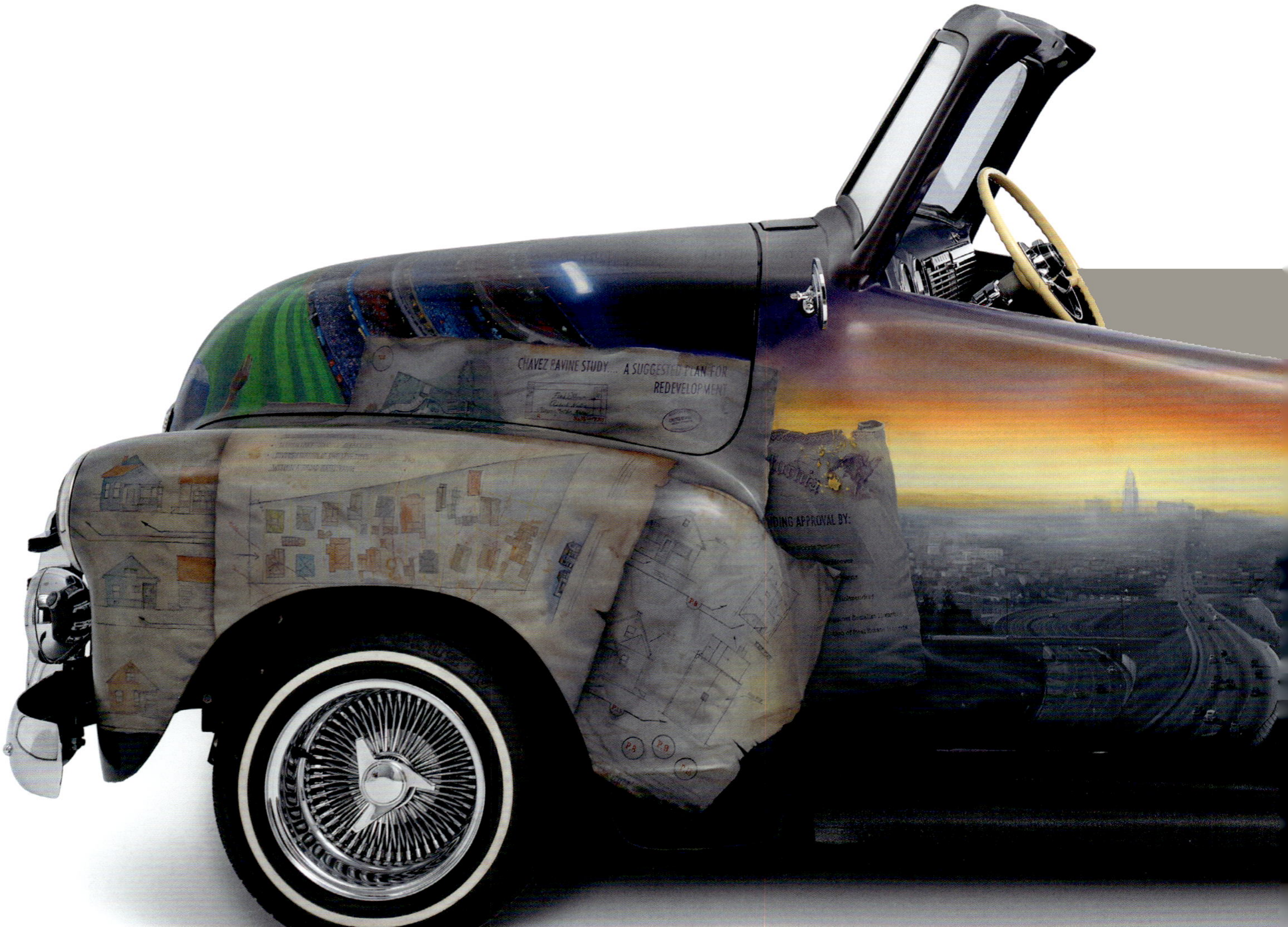
CHAVEZ RAVINE STUDY... A SUGGESTED PLAN FOR
REDEVELOPMENT
APPROVAL BY:

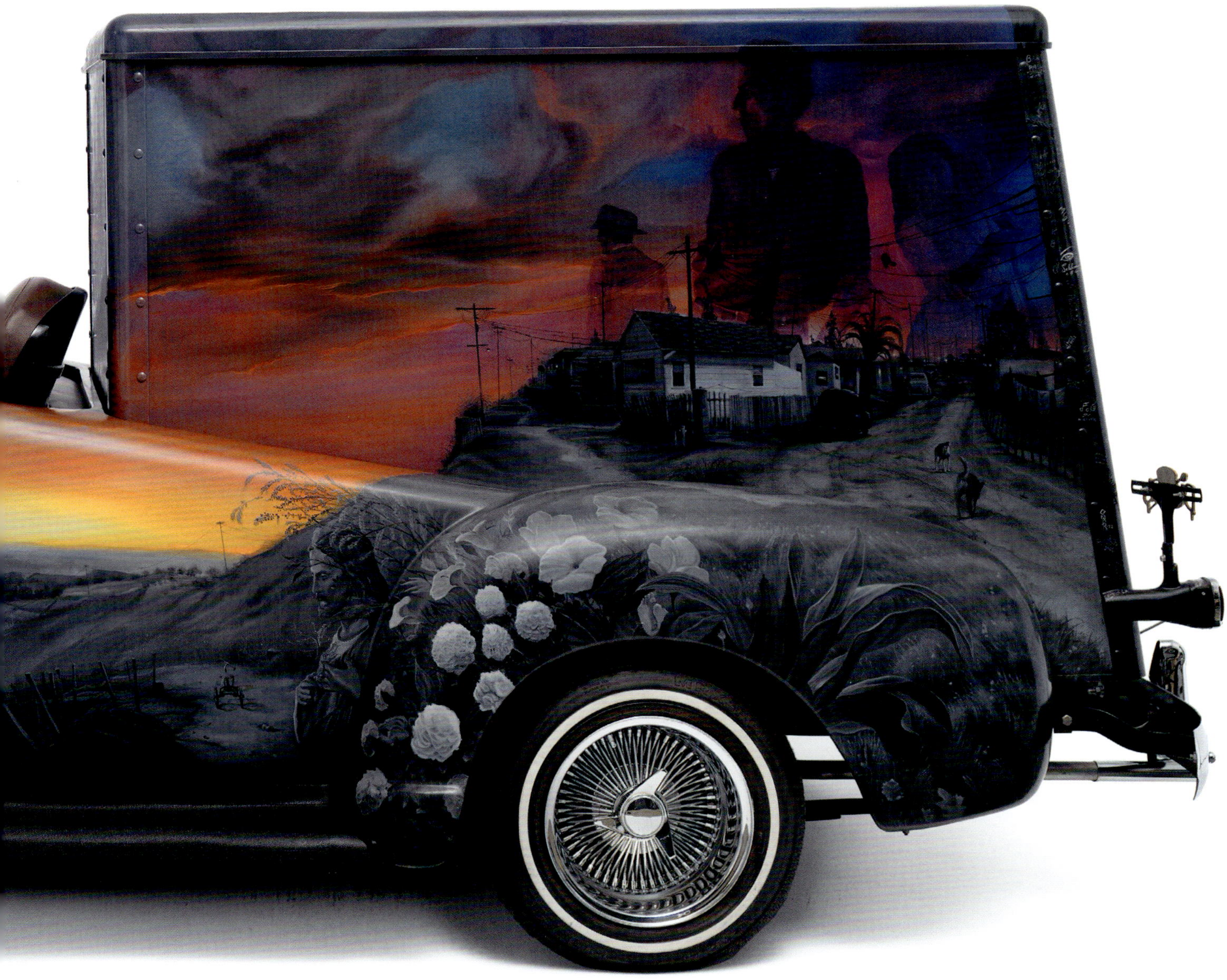

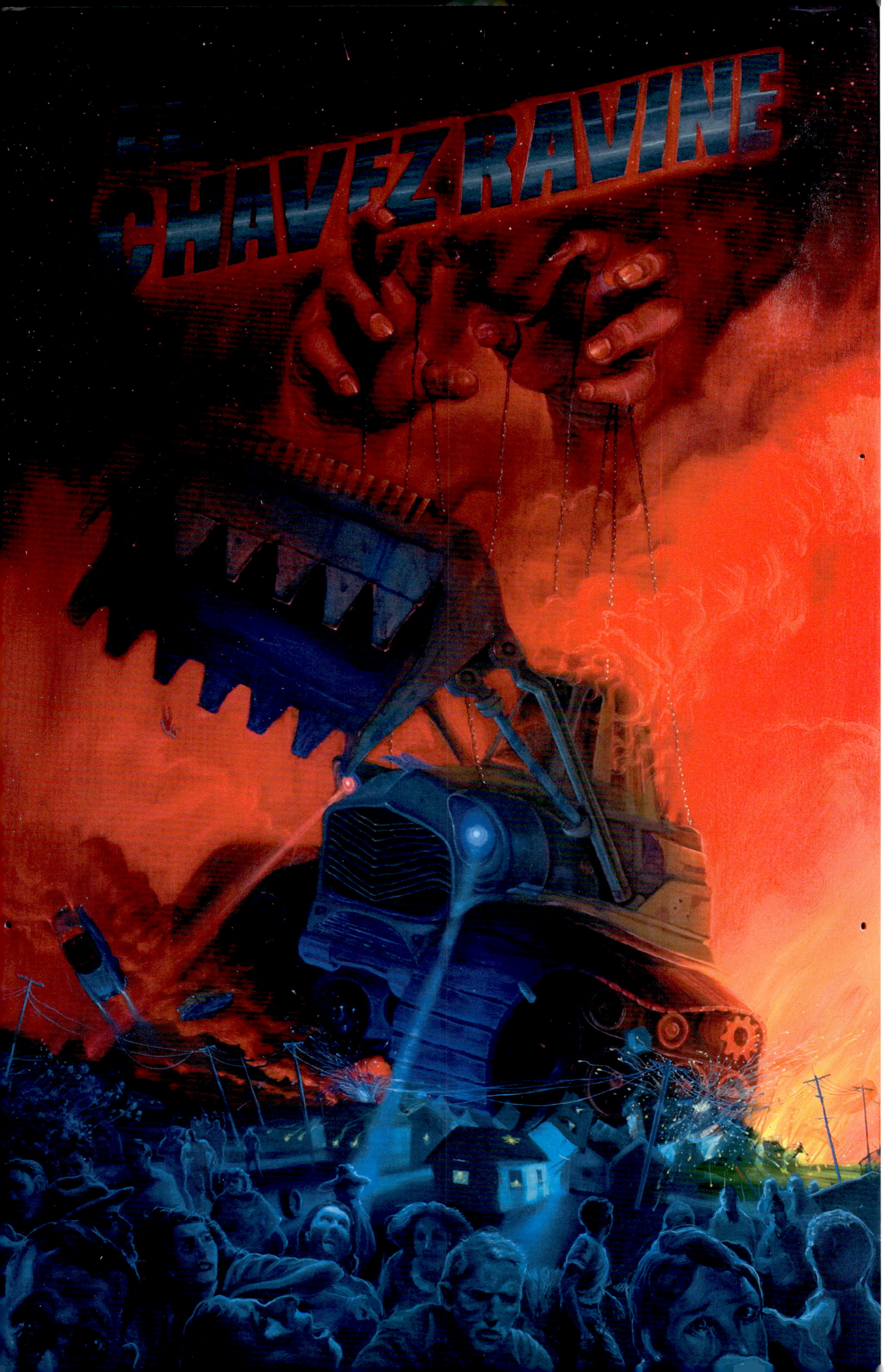
CHAVEZ RAVINE

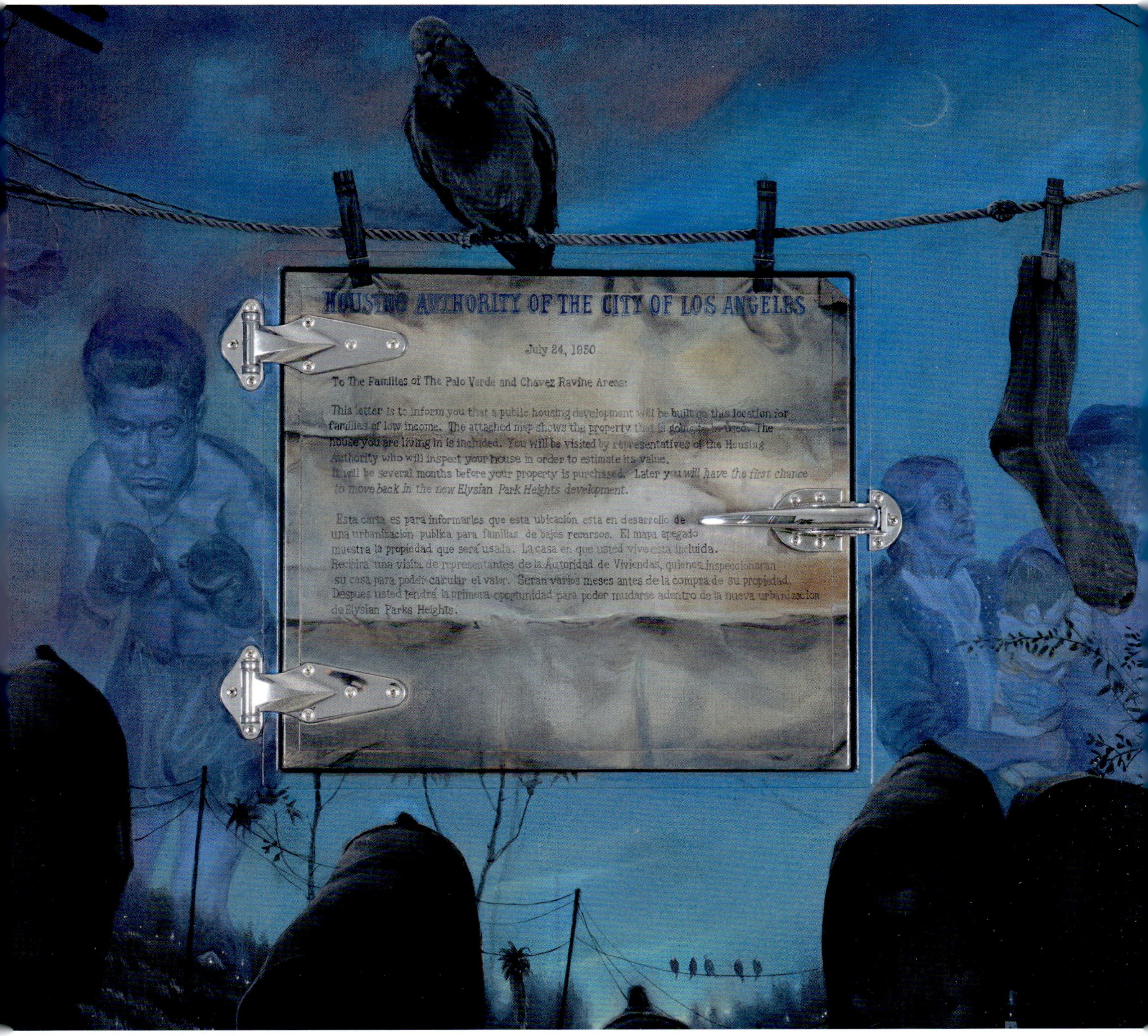
HOUSING AUTHORITY OF THE CITY OF LOS ANGELES
July 24, 1950
To The Families of The Palo Verde and Chavez Ravine Areas:
This letter is to inform you that a public housing development will be built on this location for families of low income. The attached map shows the property that is going to be used. The house you are living in is included. You will be visited by representatives of the Housing Authority who will inspect your house in order to estimate its value.
It will be several months before your property is purchased. Later you will have the first chance to move back in the new Elysian Park Heights development.
Esta carta es para informarles que esta ubicación esta en desarrollo de una urbanización publica para familias de bajos recursos. El mapa apegado muestra la propiedad que será usada. La casa en que usted vive esta incluida.
Recibira una visita de representantes de la Autoridad de Viviendas, quienes inspeccionaran su casa para poder calcular el valor. Seran varios meses antes de la compra de su propiedad.
Despues usted tendrá la primera oportunidad para poder mudarse adentro de la nueva urbanizacion de Elysian Parks Heights.

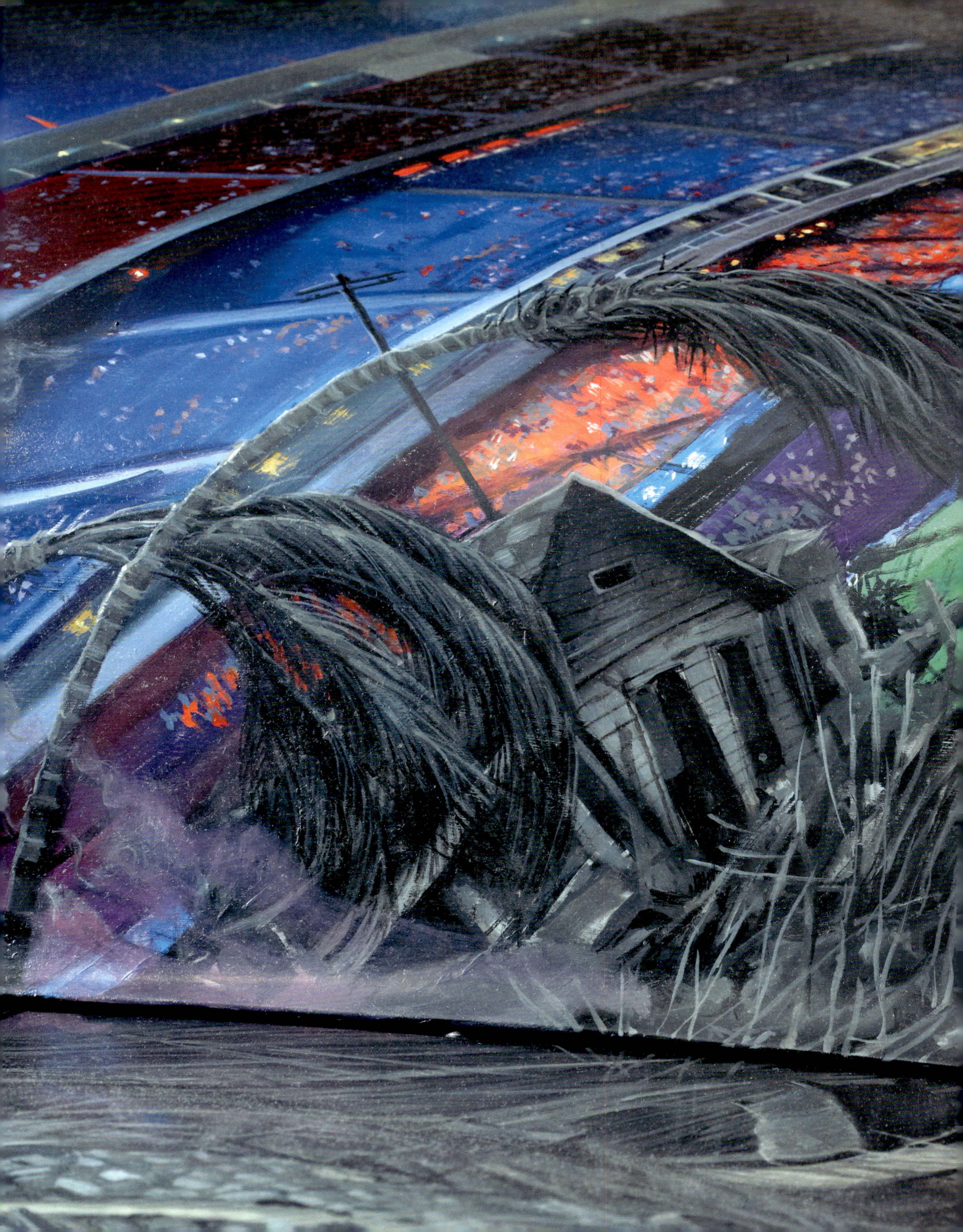

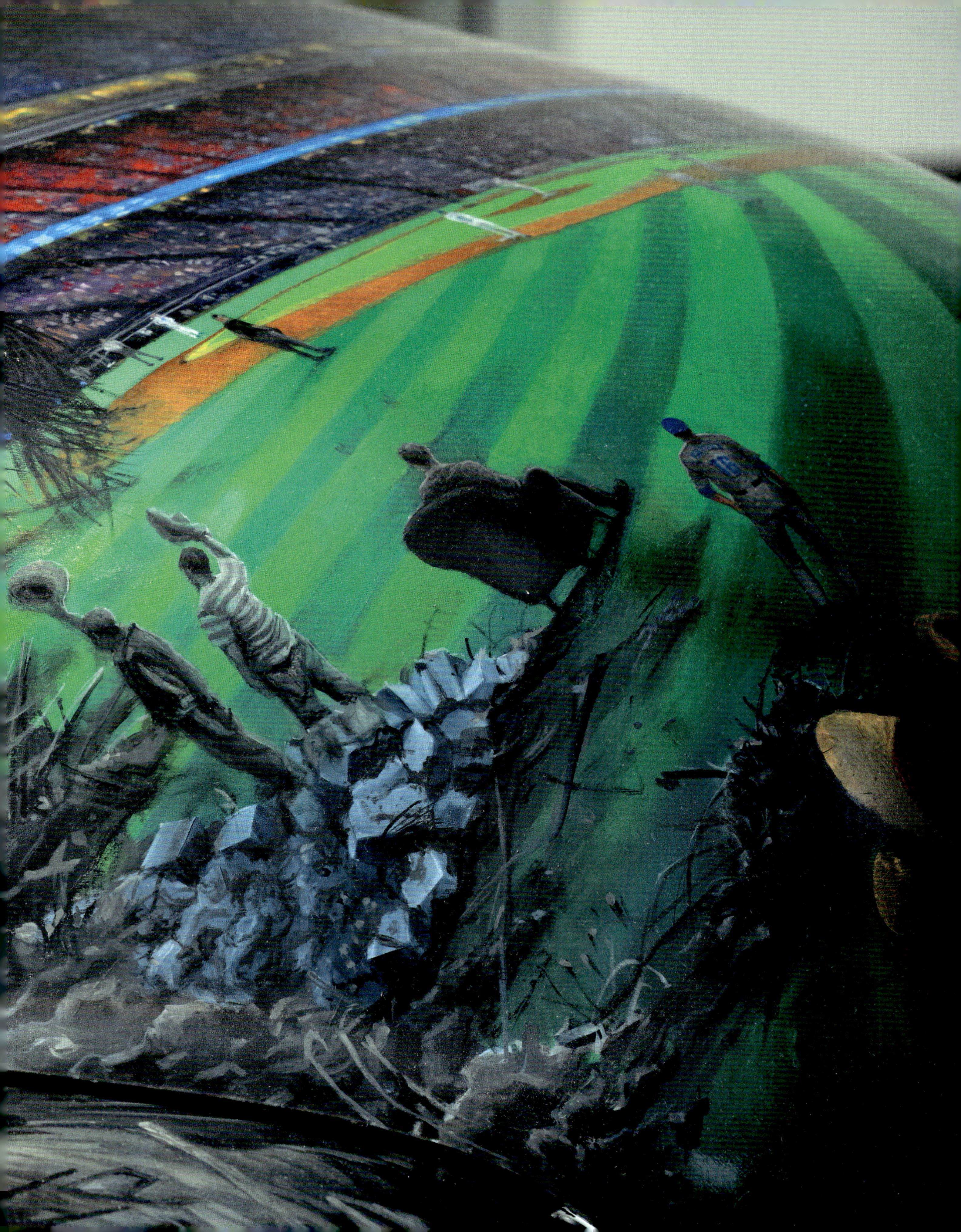

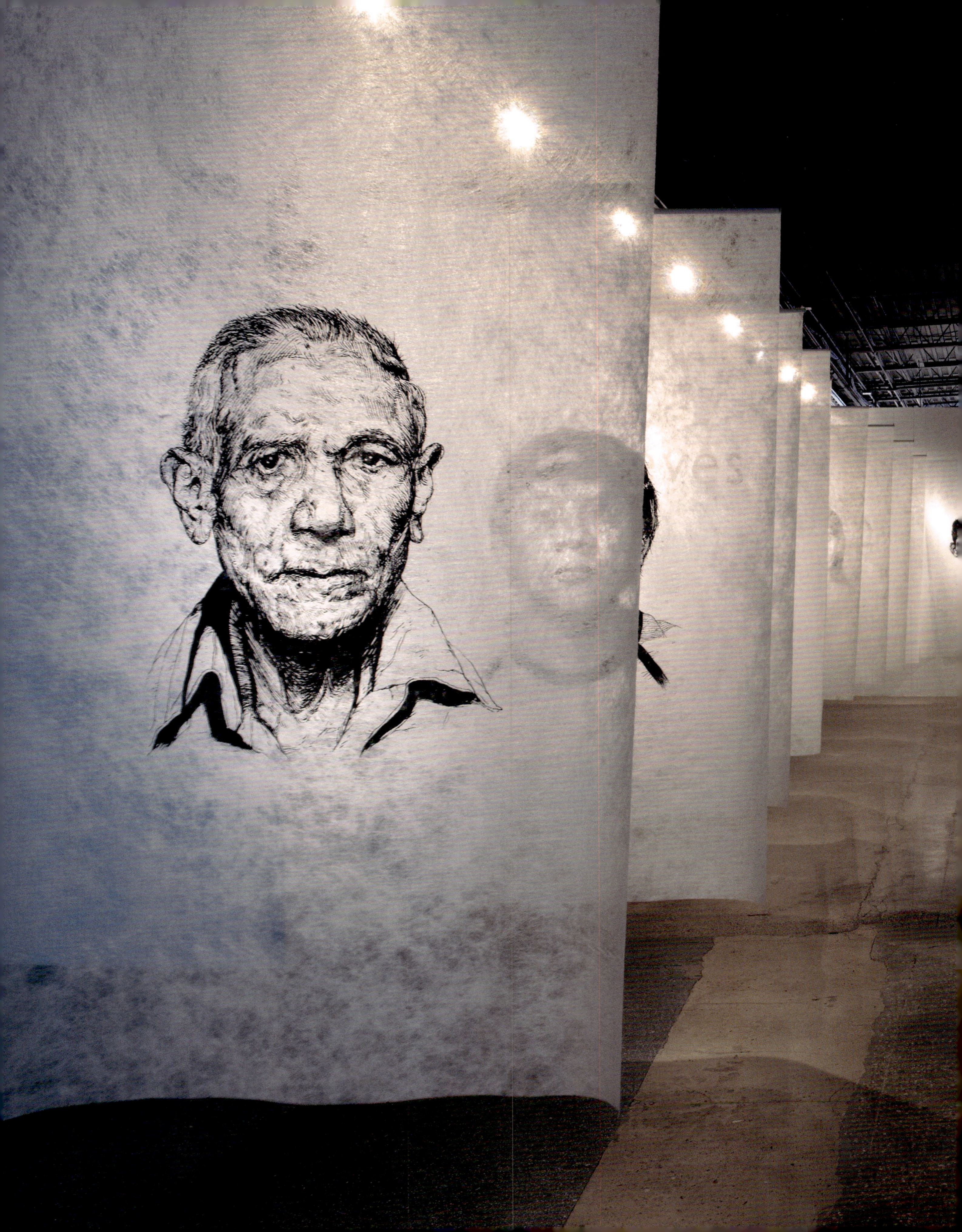

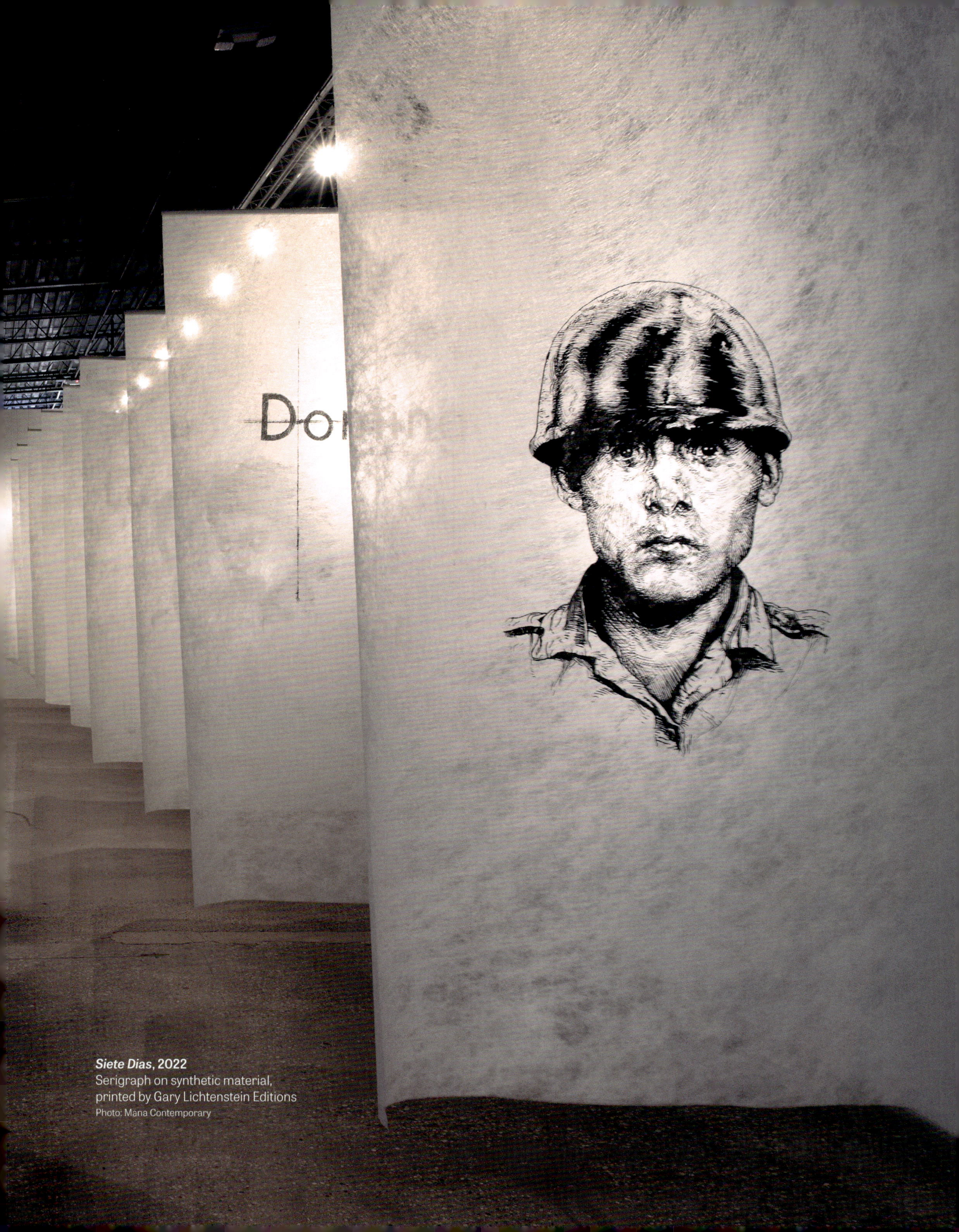

***Siete Dias*, 2022**
Serigraph on synthetic material,
printed by Gary Lichtenstein Editions
Photo: Mana Contemporary

***People of the Sun (Grandma & Grandpa Santana)*, 2019**
Oil on canvas
Photo: Peter Molick

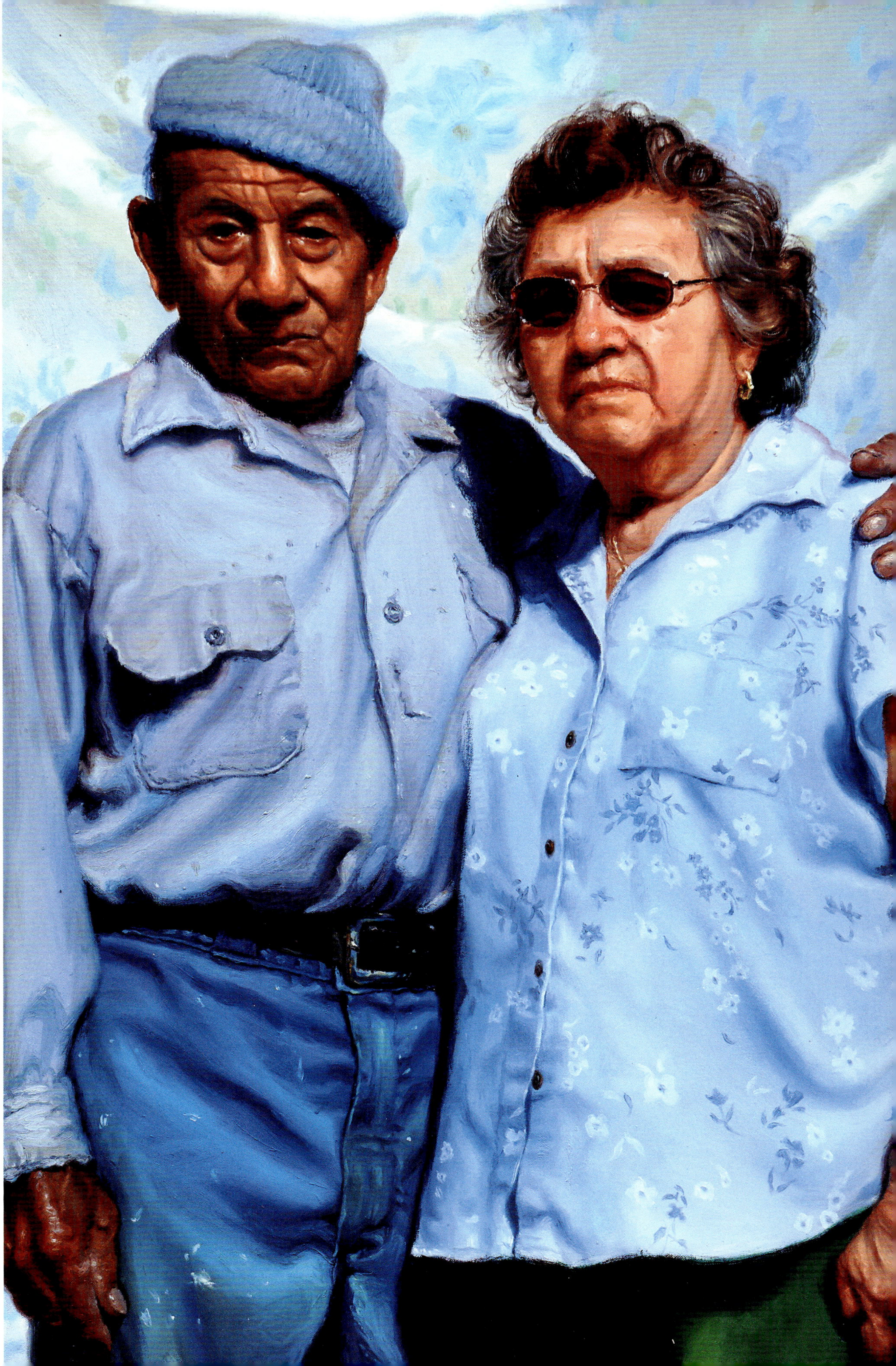

THE UNITED STATES OF AMNESIA

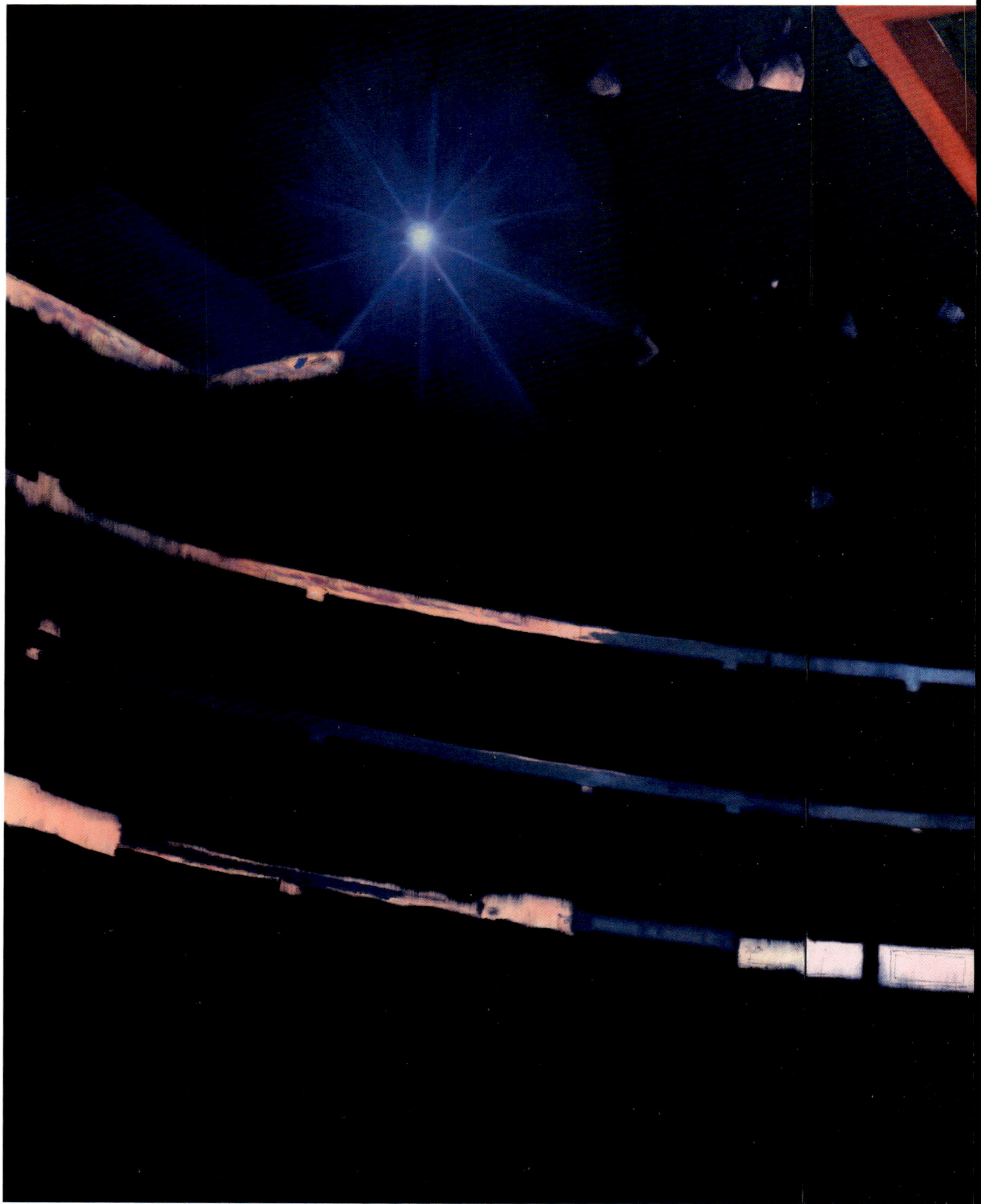

***It Was a Very Good Year (Nineteen Eighty Eight*, 2004**
(work-in-progress),
Valdez studio, 2024
Oil on canvas
Photo: Elon Schoenholz

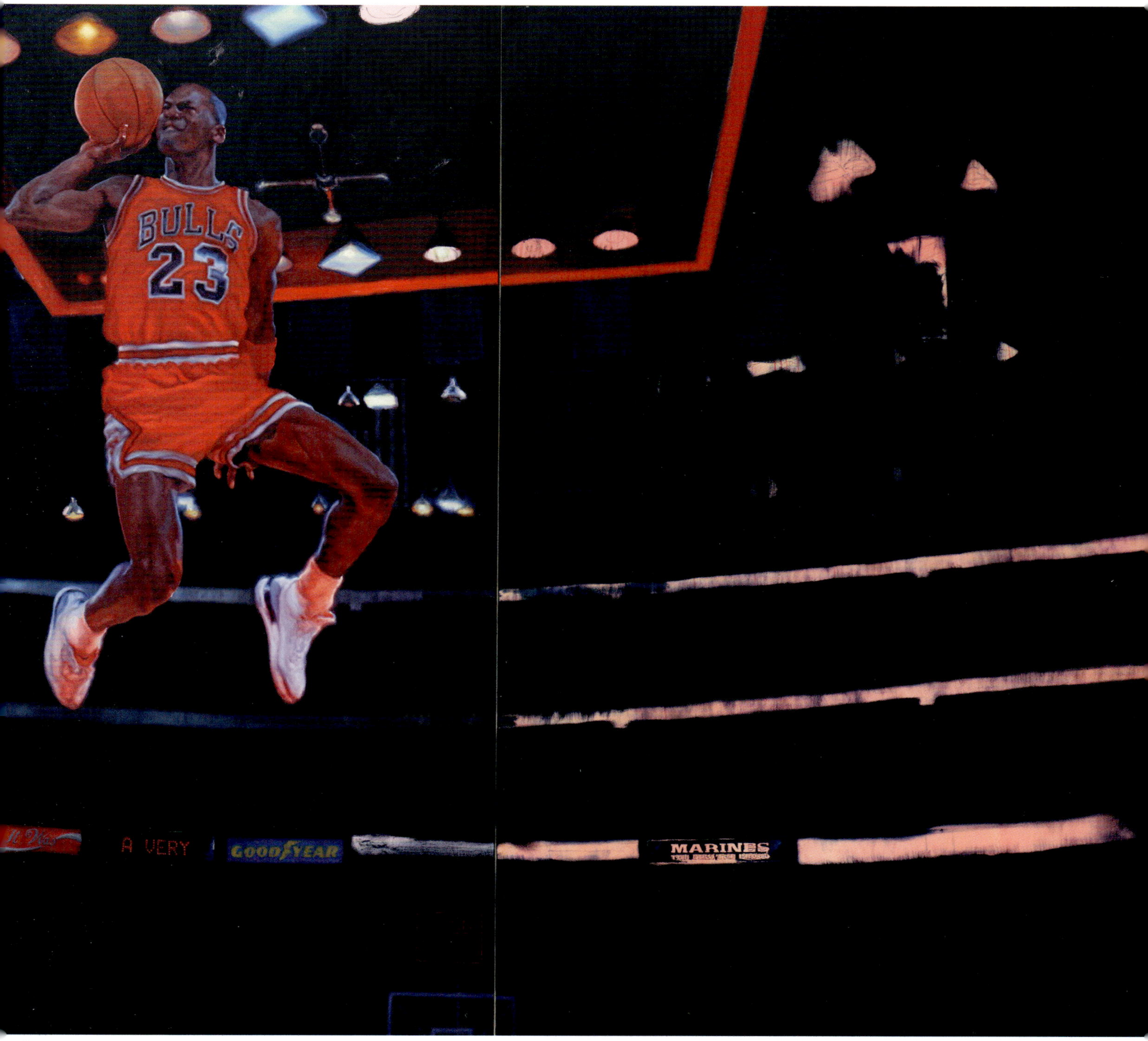
BULLS
23
A VERY
GOODYEAR
MARINES

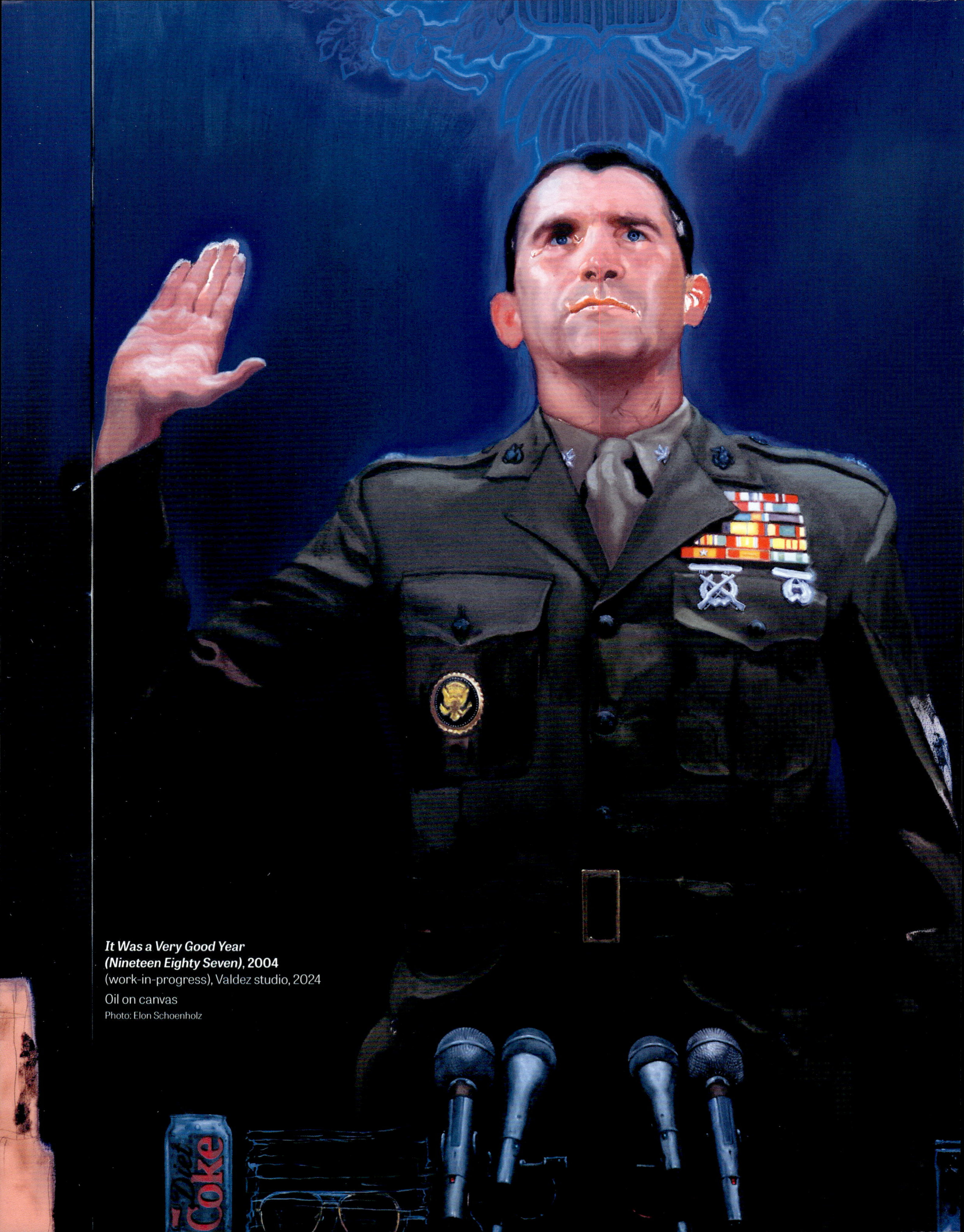

***It Was a Very Good Year* *(Nineteen Eighty Seven)*, 2004**
(work-in-progress), Valdez studio, 2024
Oil on canvas
Photo: Elon Schoenholz

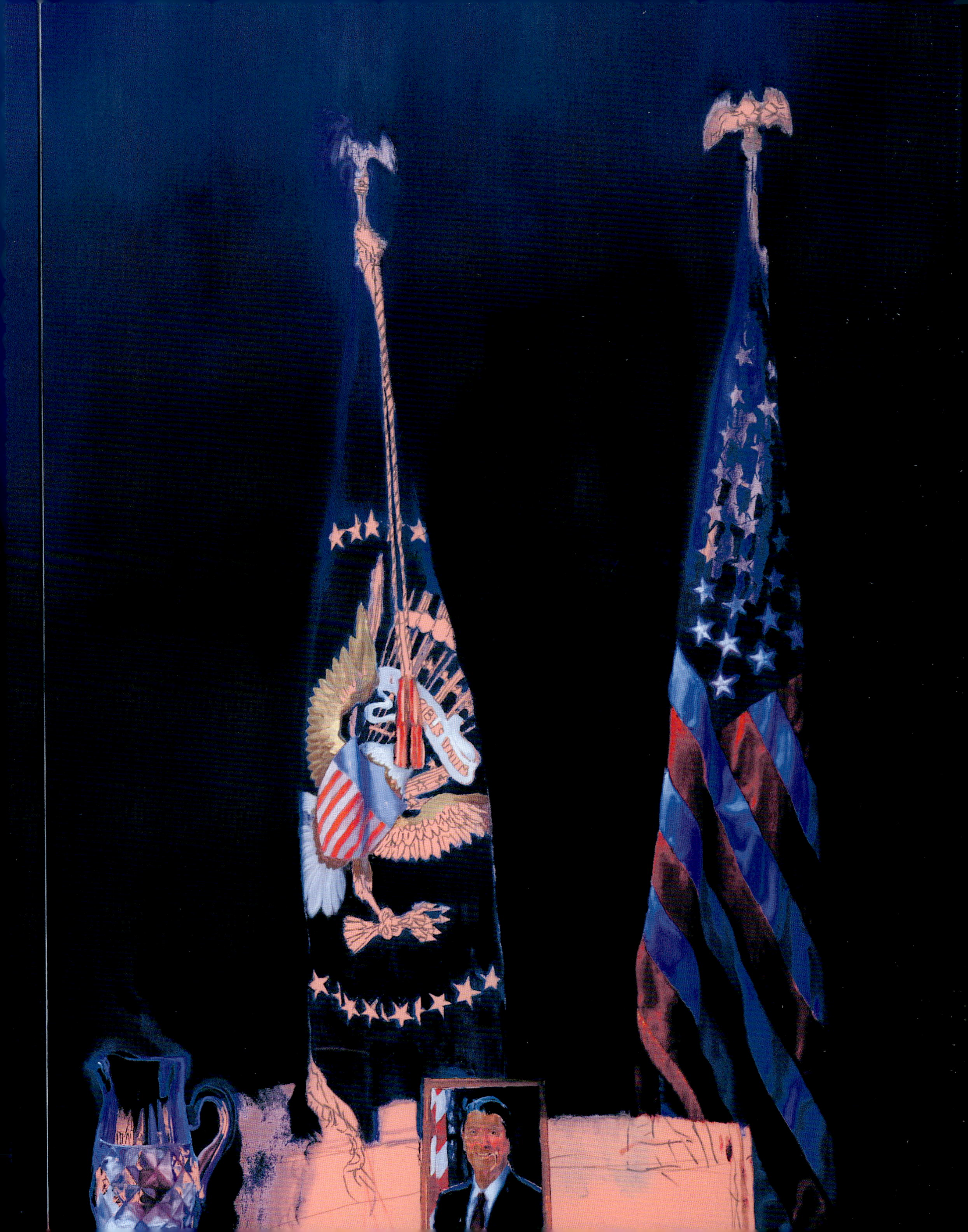

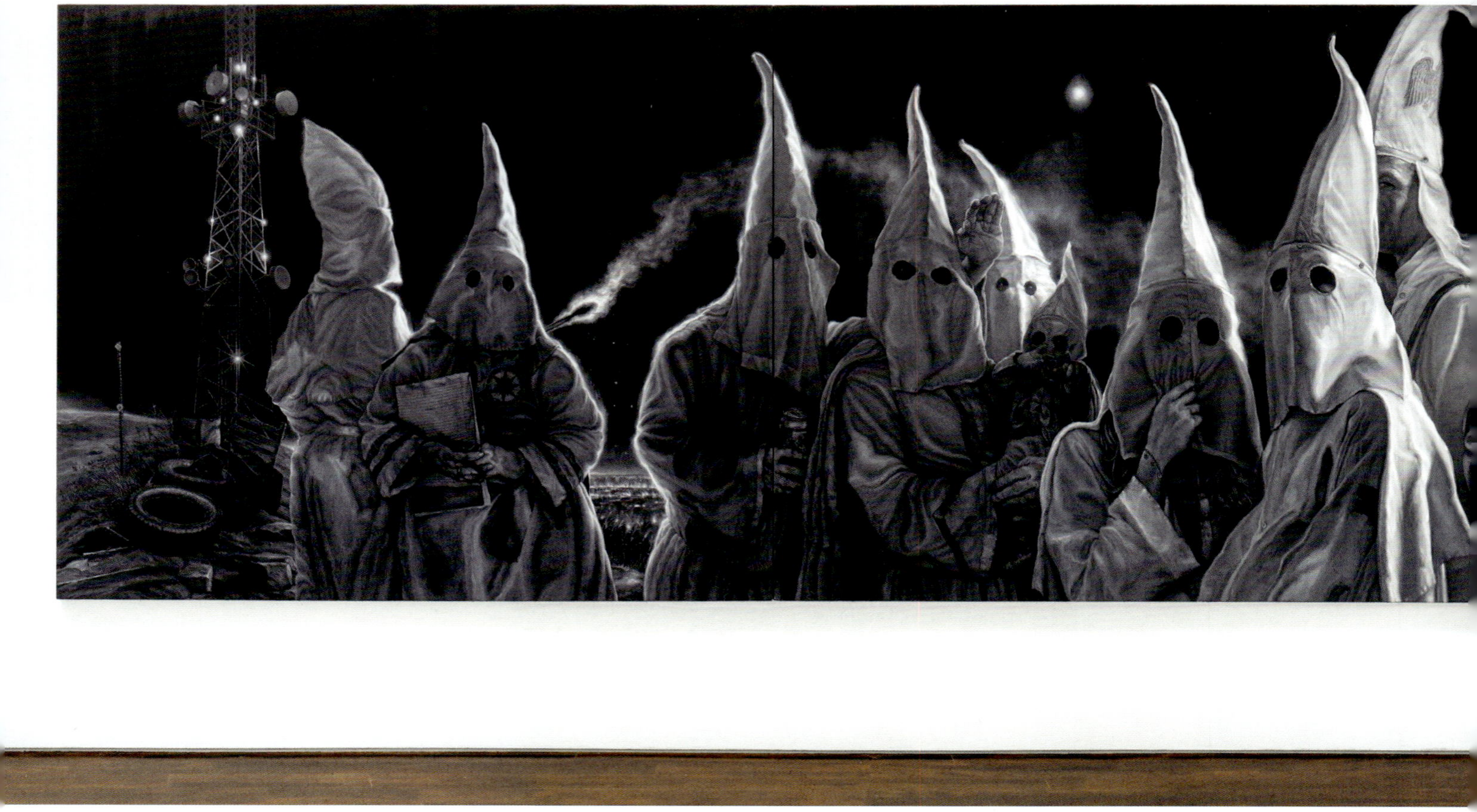

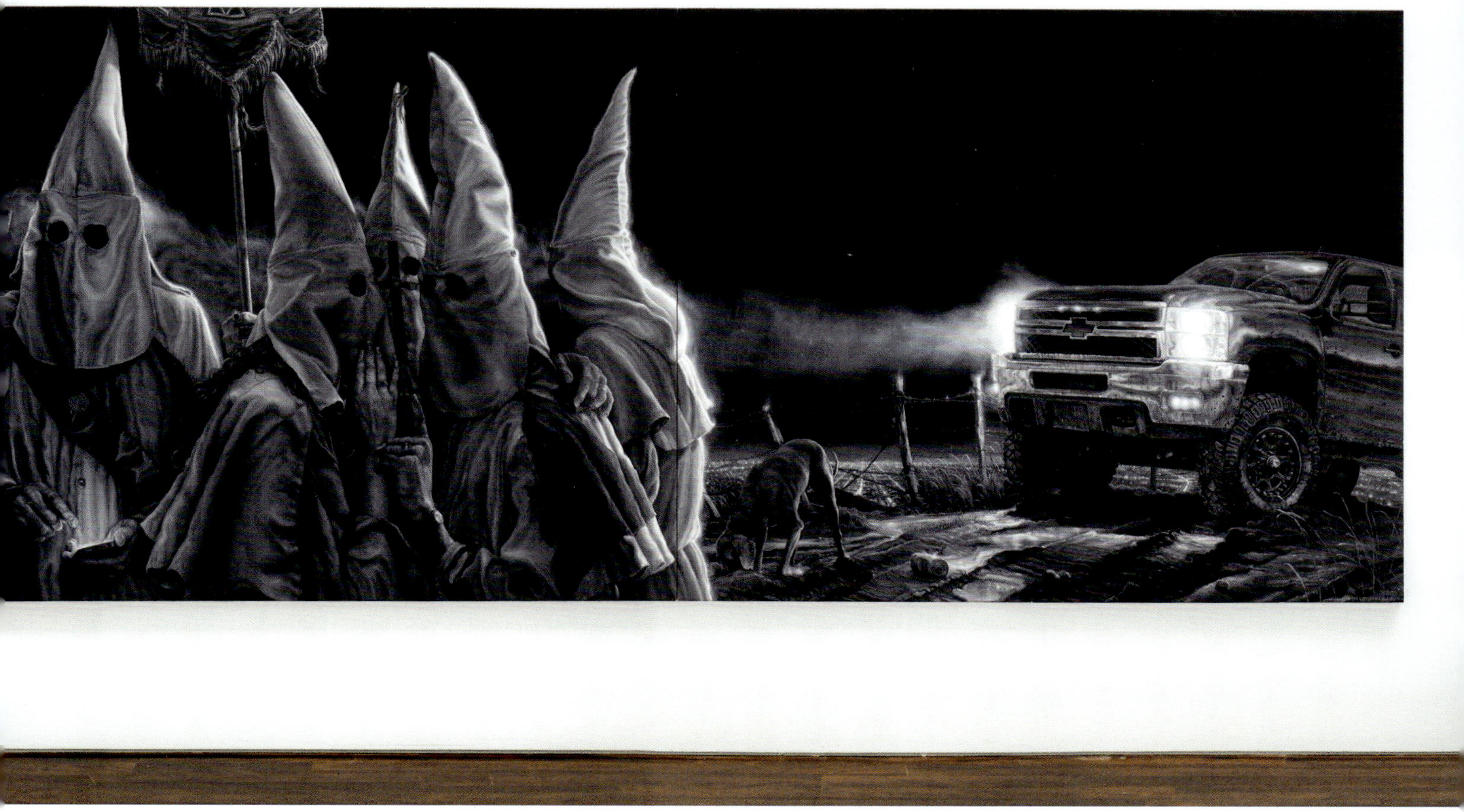

***The Beginning is Near (An American Trilogy), Chapter One: The City, The City I and The City II*, 2015–16**
Oil on canvas
Photos: Peter Molick

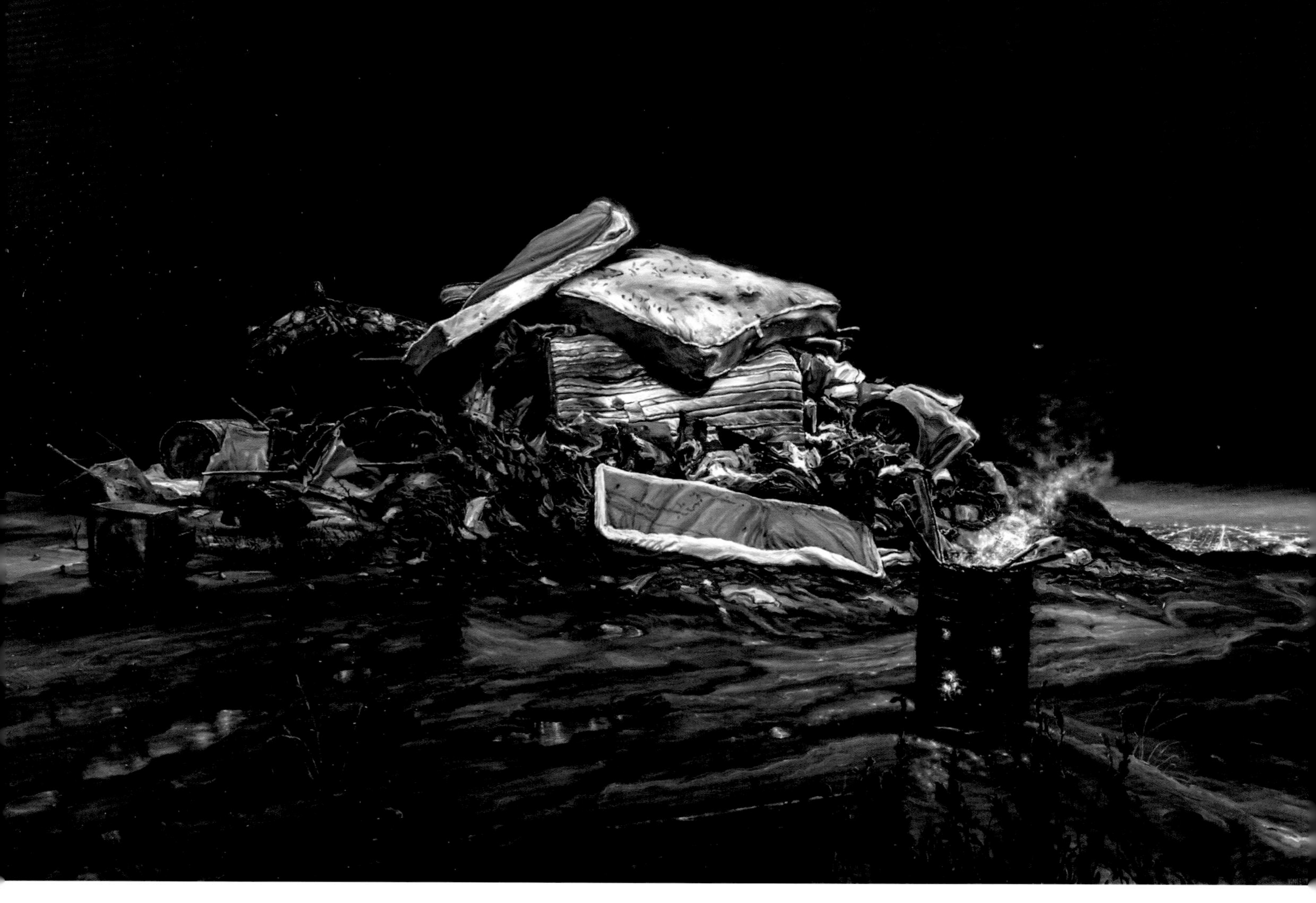

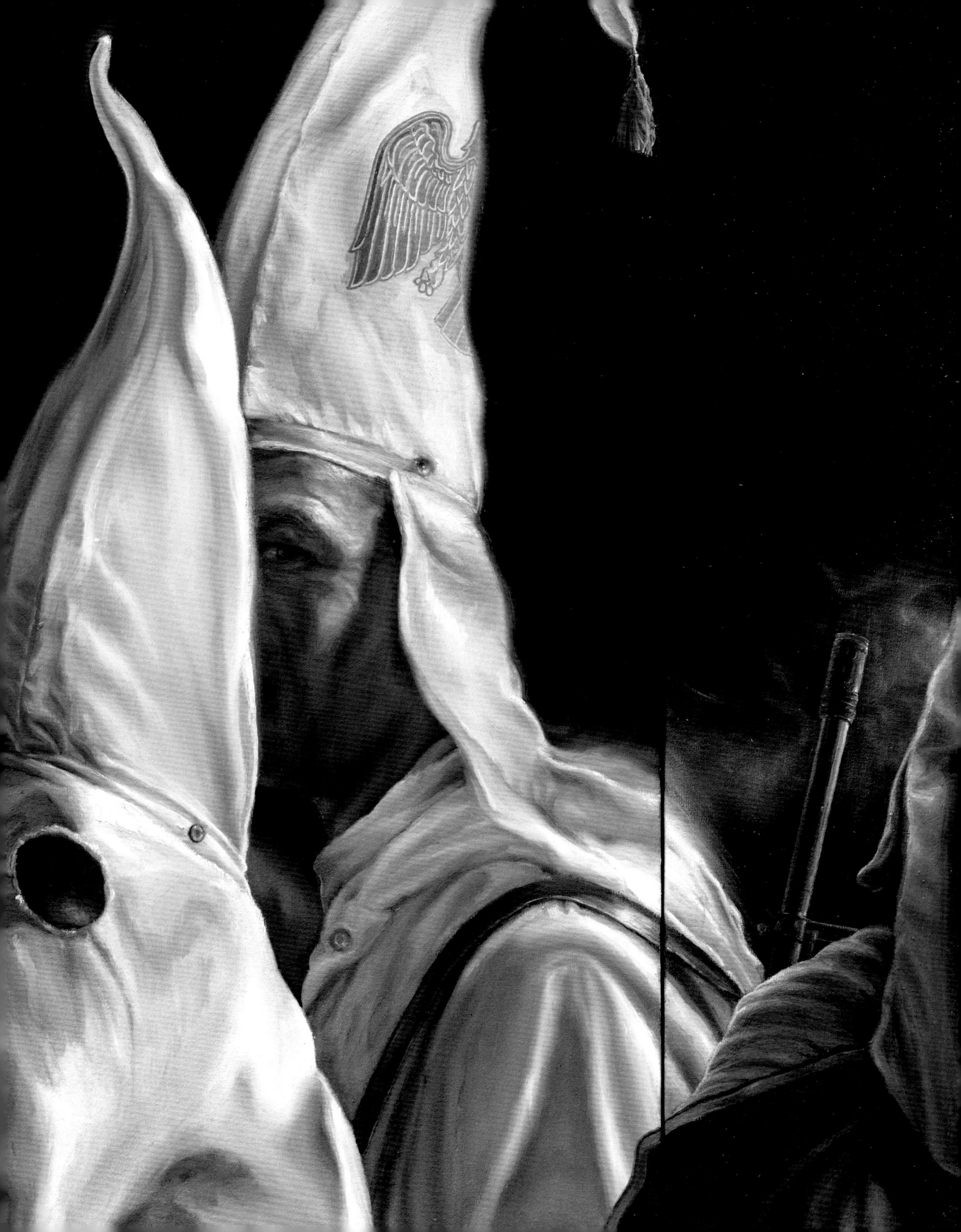

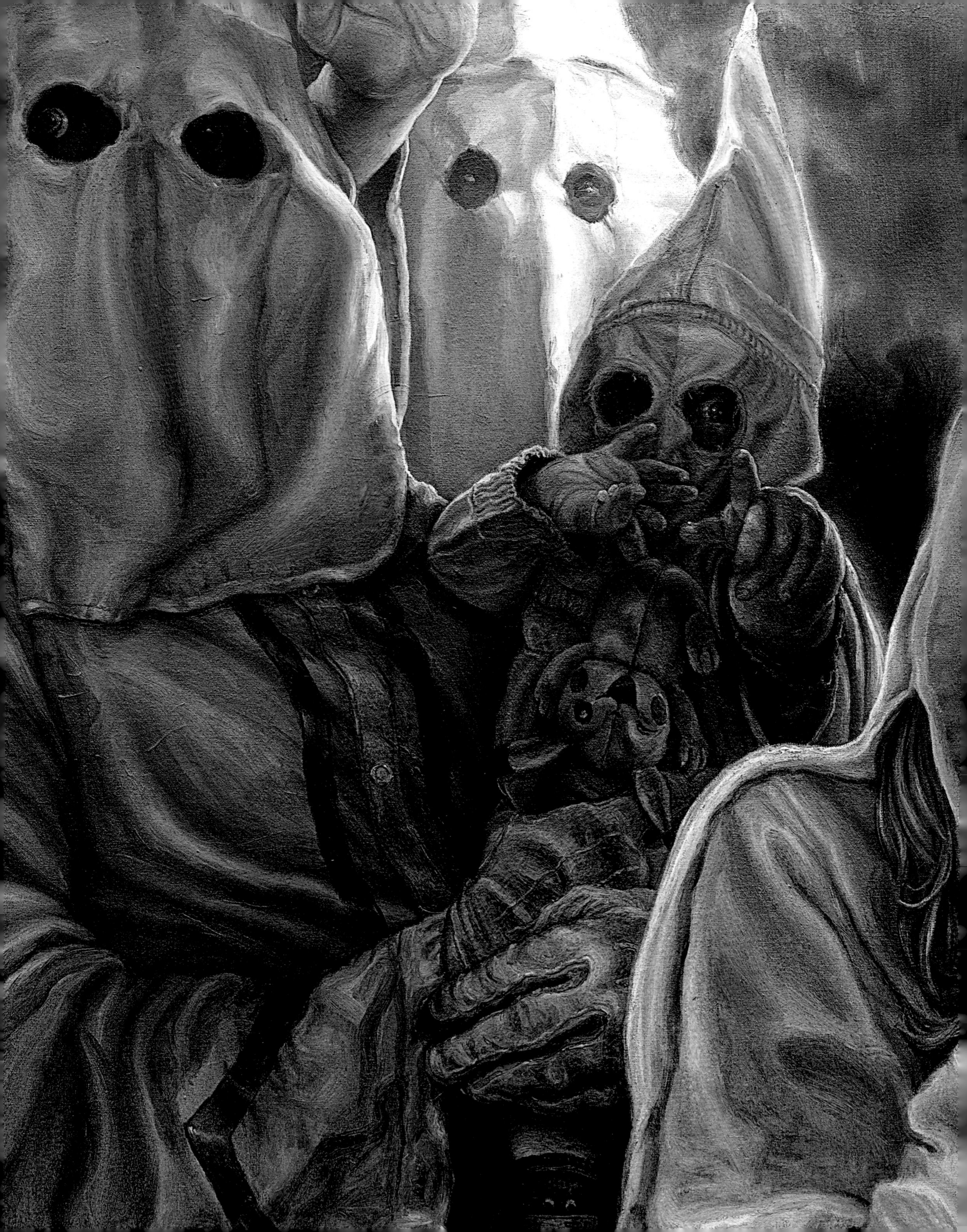

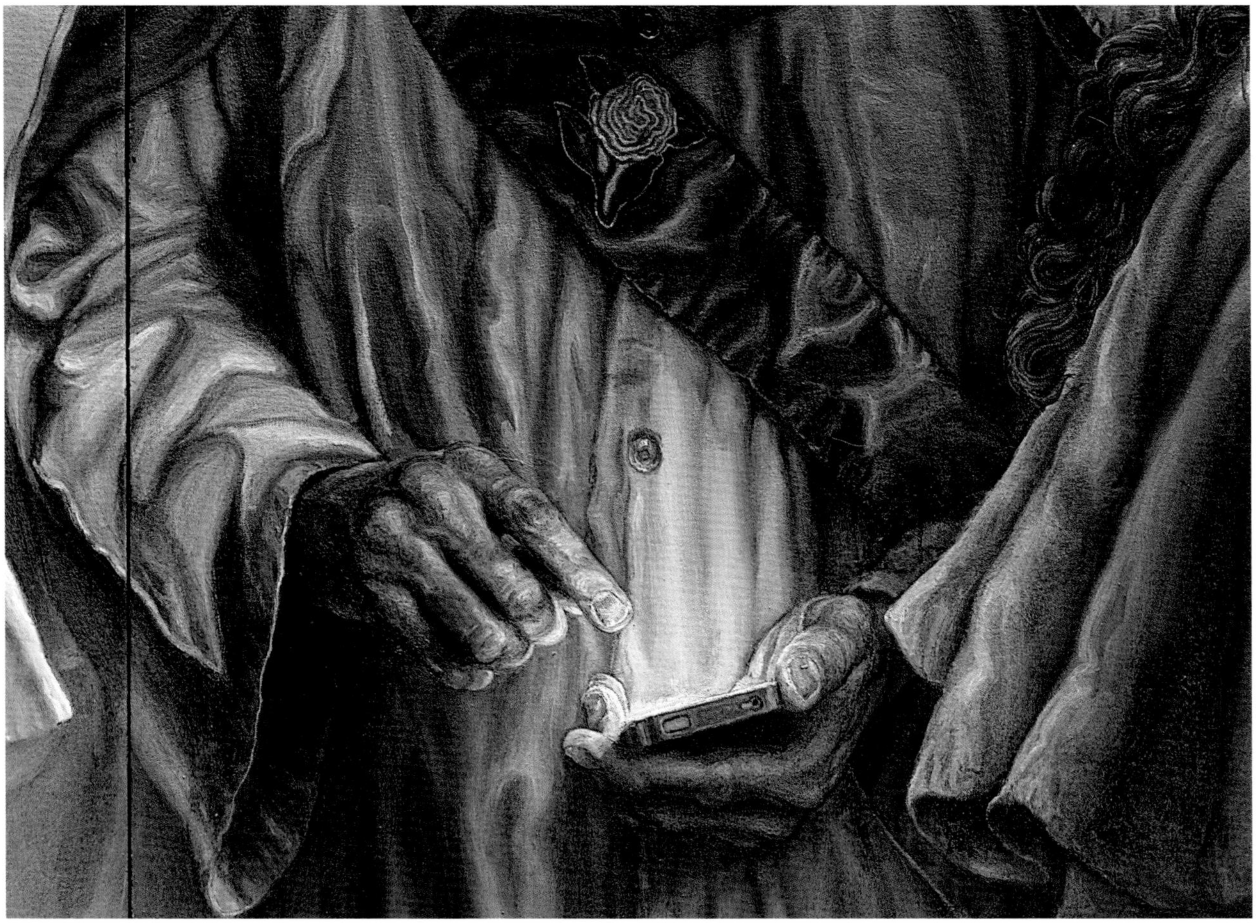

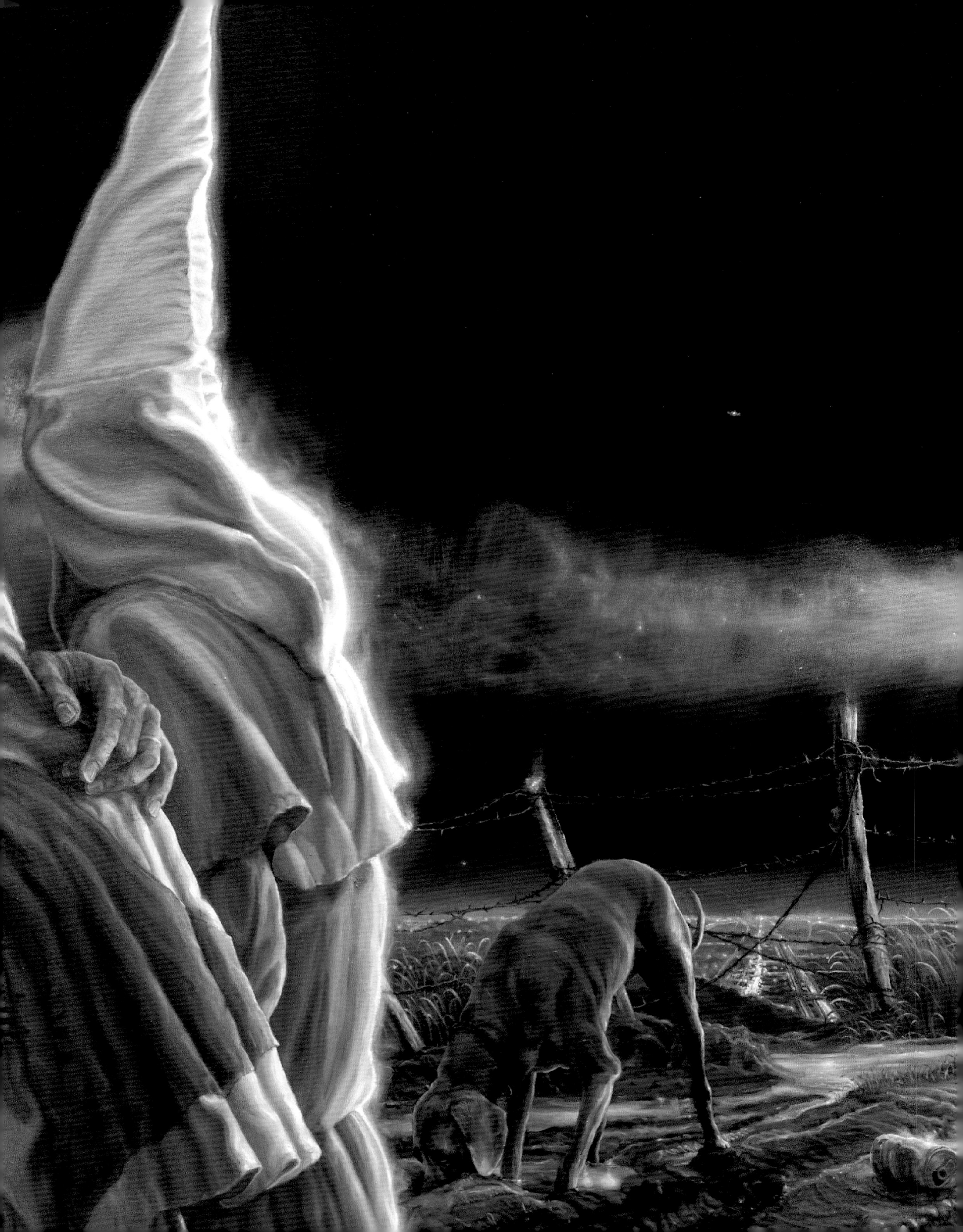

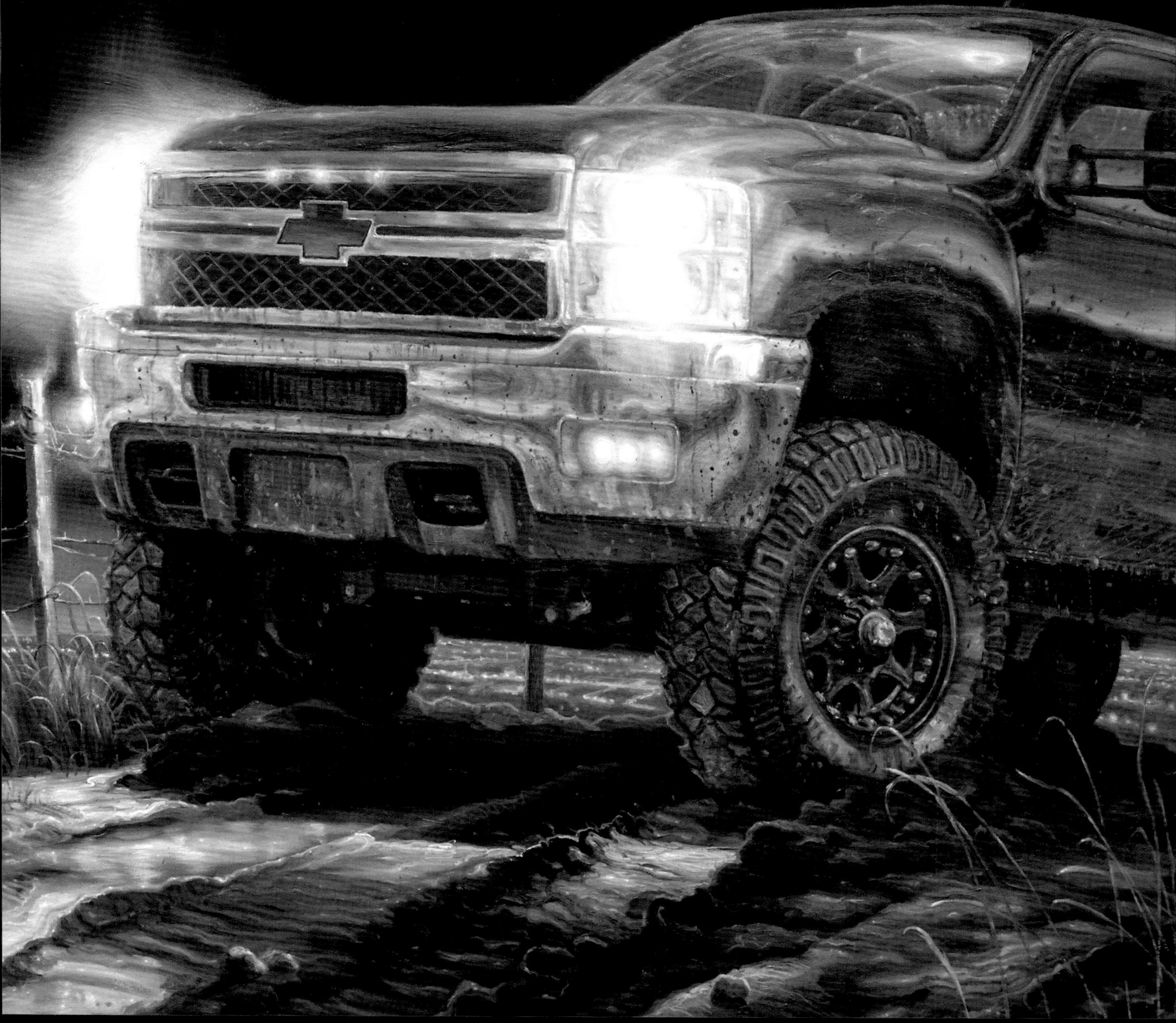

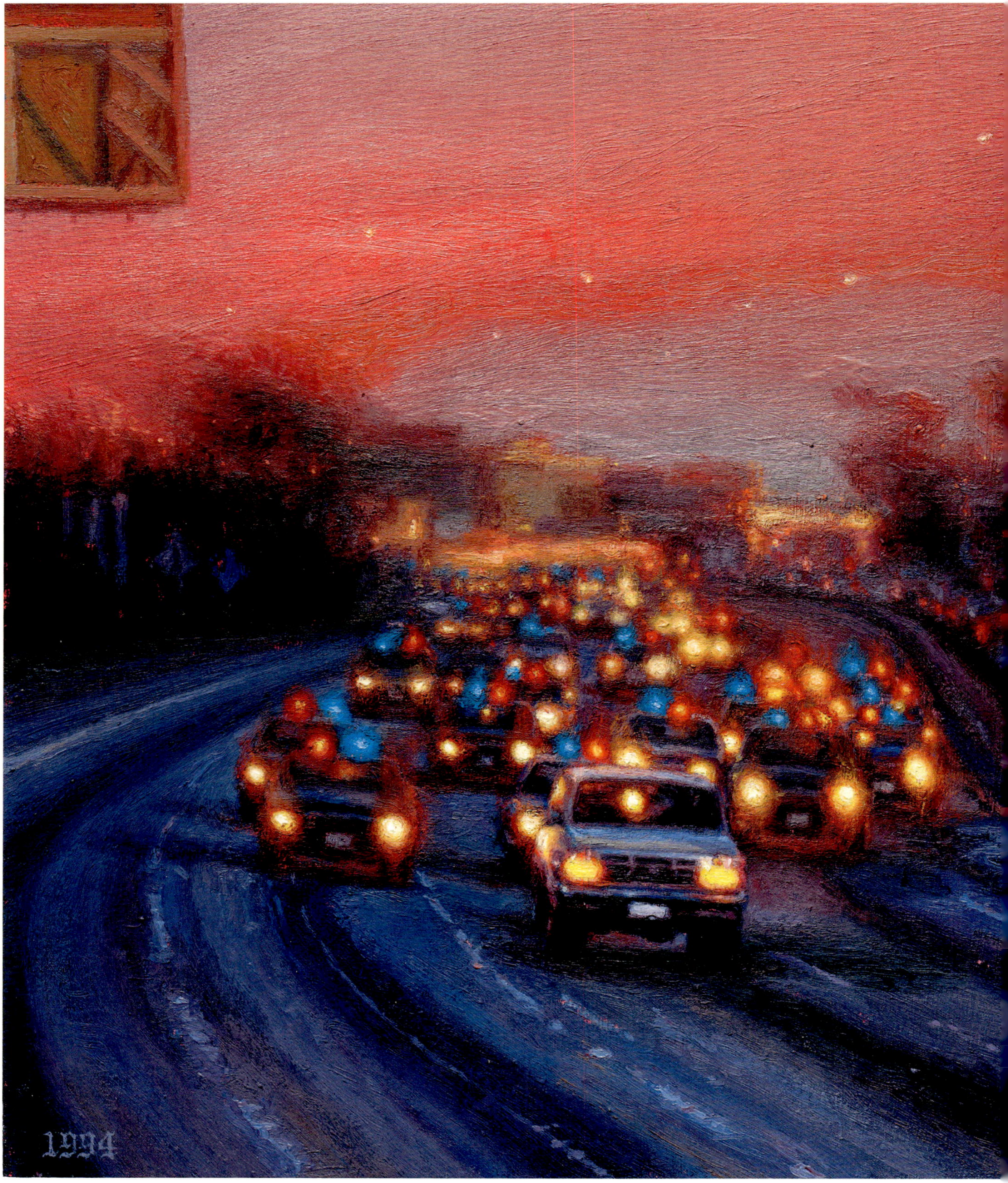
1994

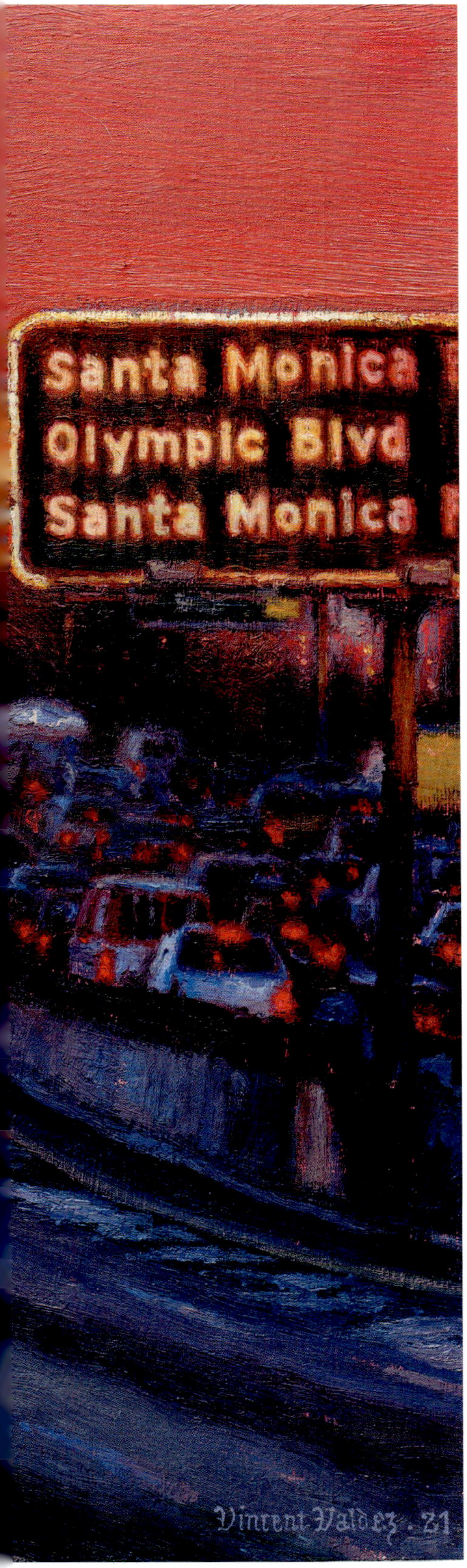

***Study for American Procession #1*, 2021**
Oil on wood
Photo: Paul Salveson

THE BEGINNING OF

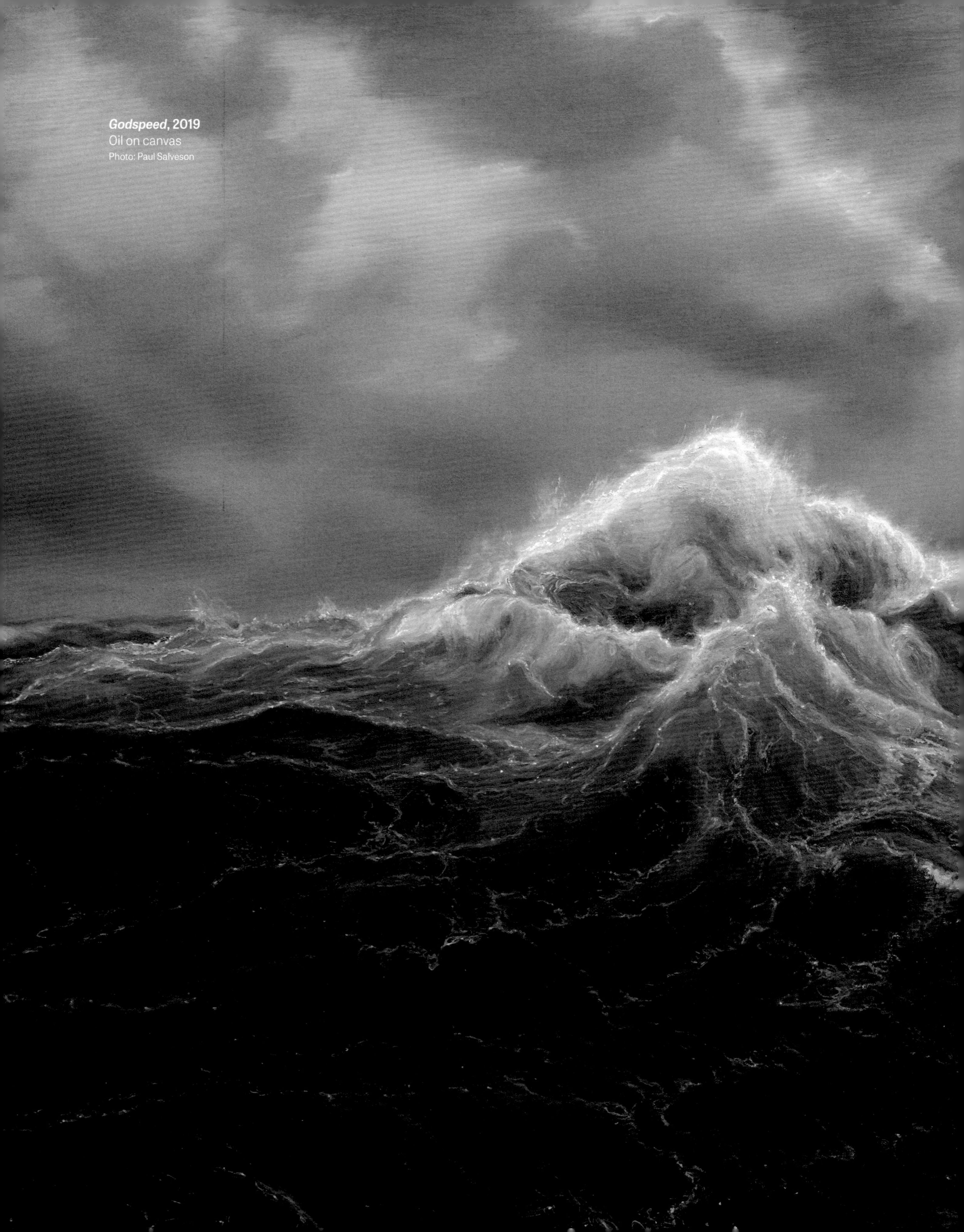

***Godspeed*, 2019**
Oil on canvas
Photo: Paul Salveson

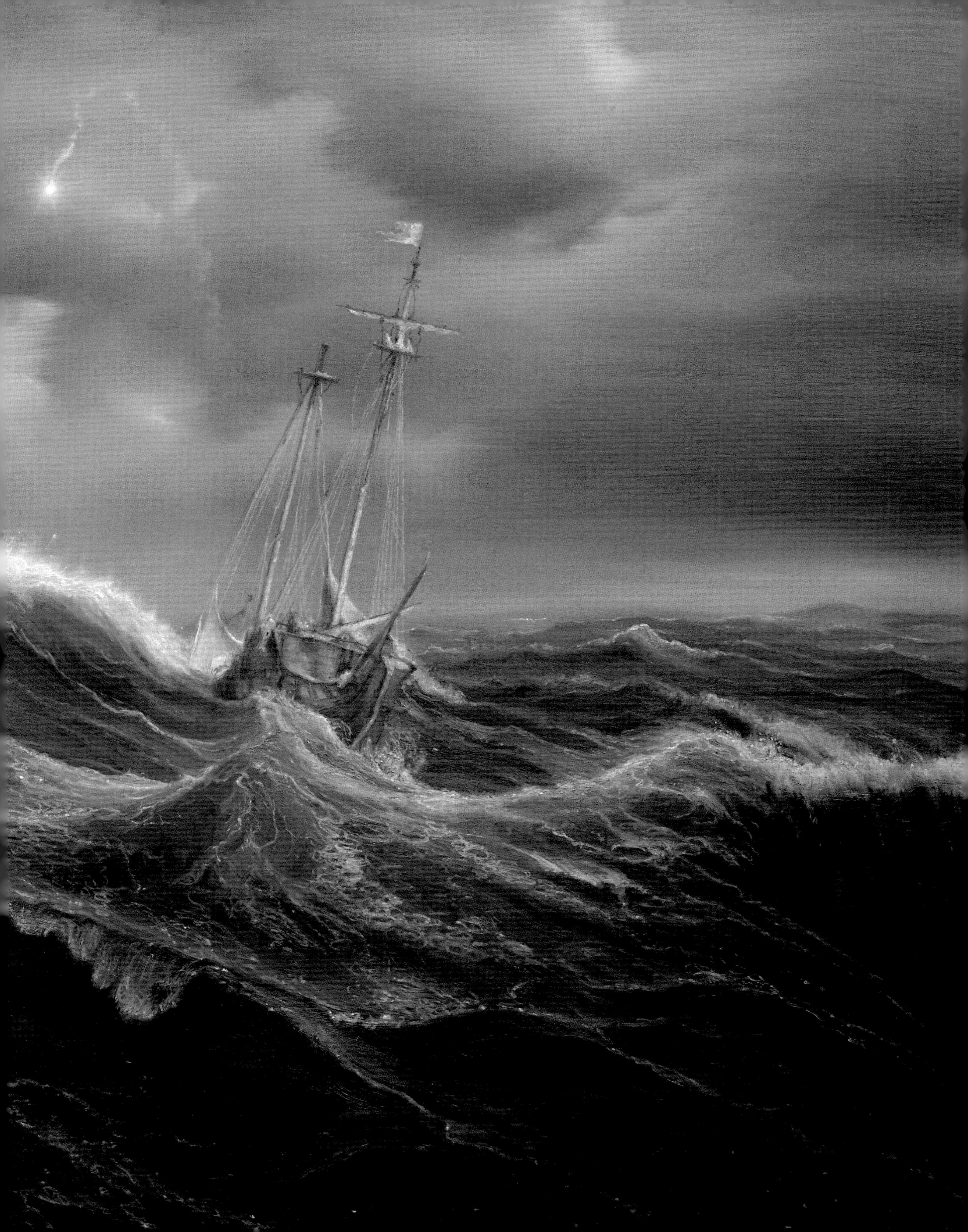

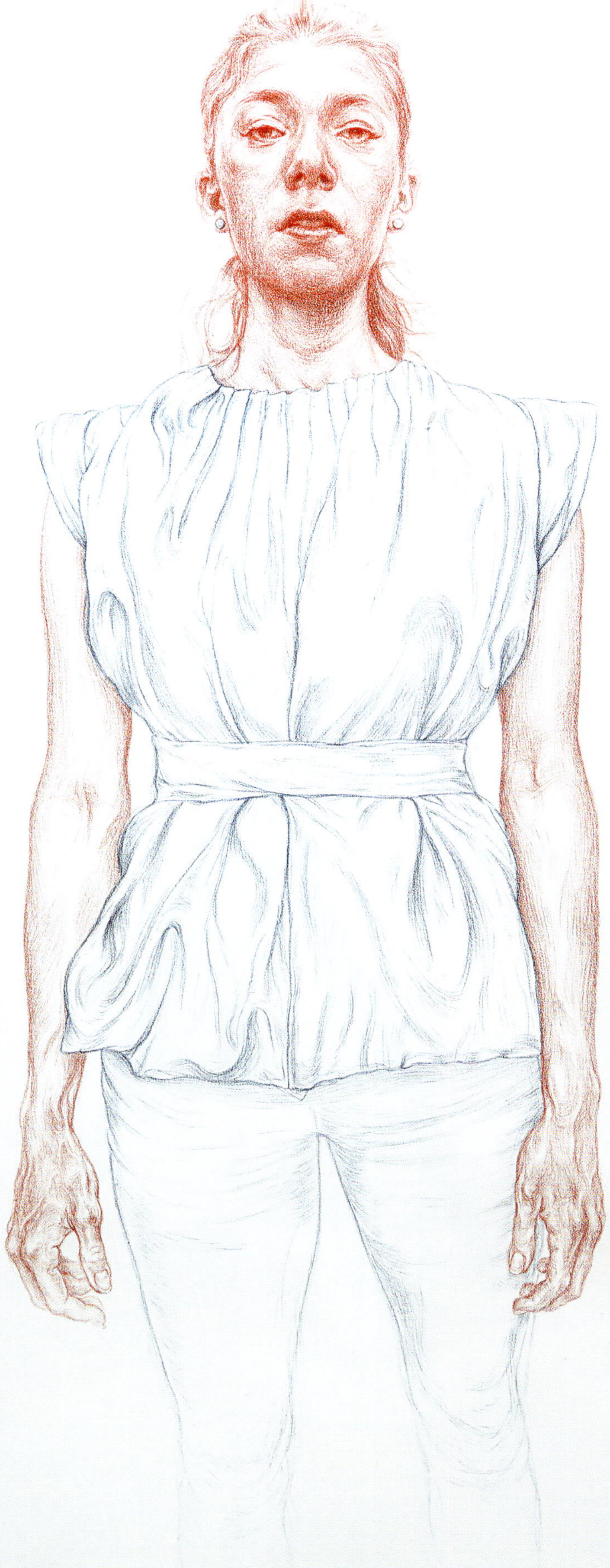

***Study for The New Americans (Adriana)*, 2021**
Pencil on paper
Photo: Peter Molick

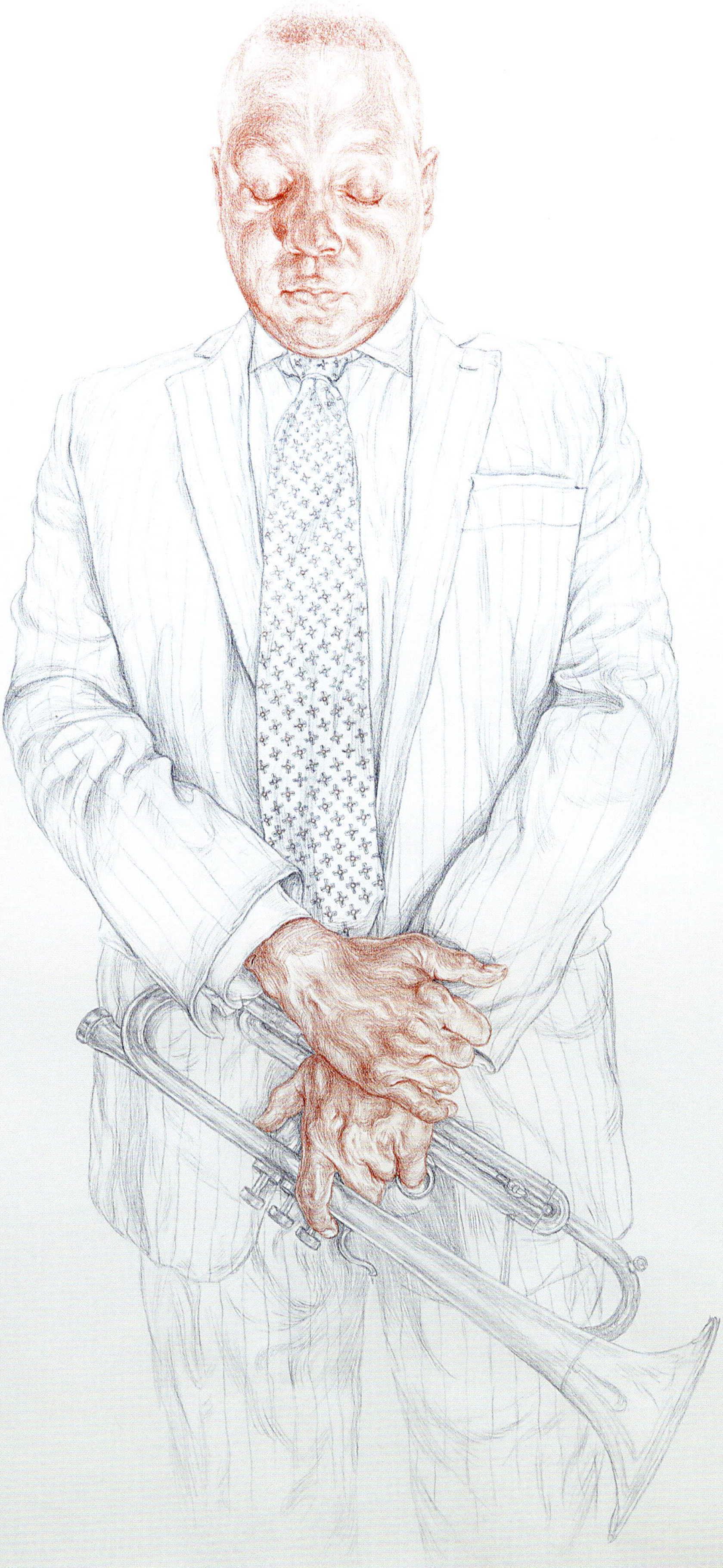

***Study for The New Americans (Wynton)*, 2021**
Pencil on paper
Photo: Peter Molick

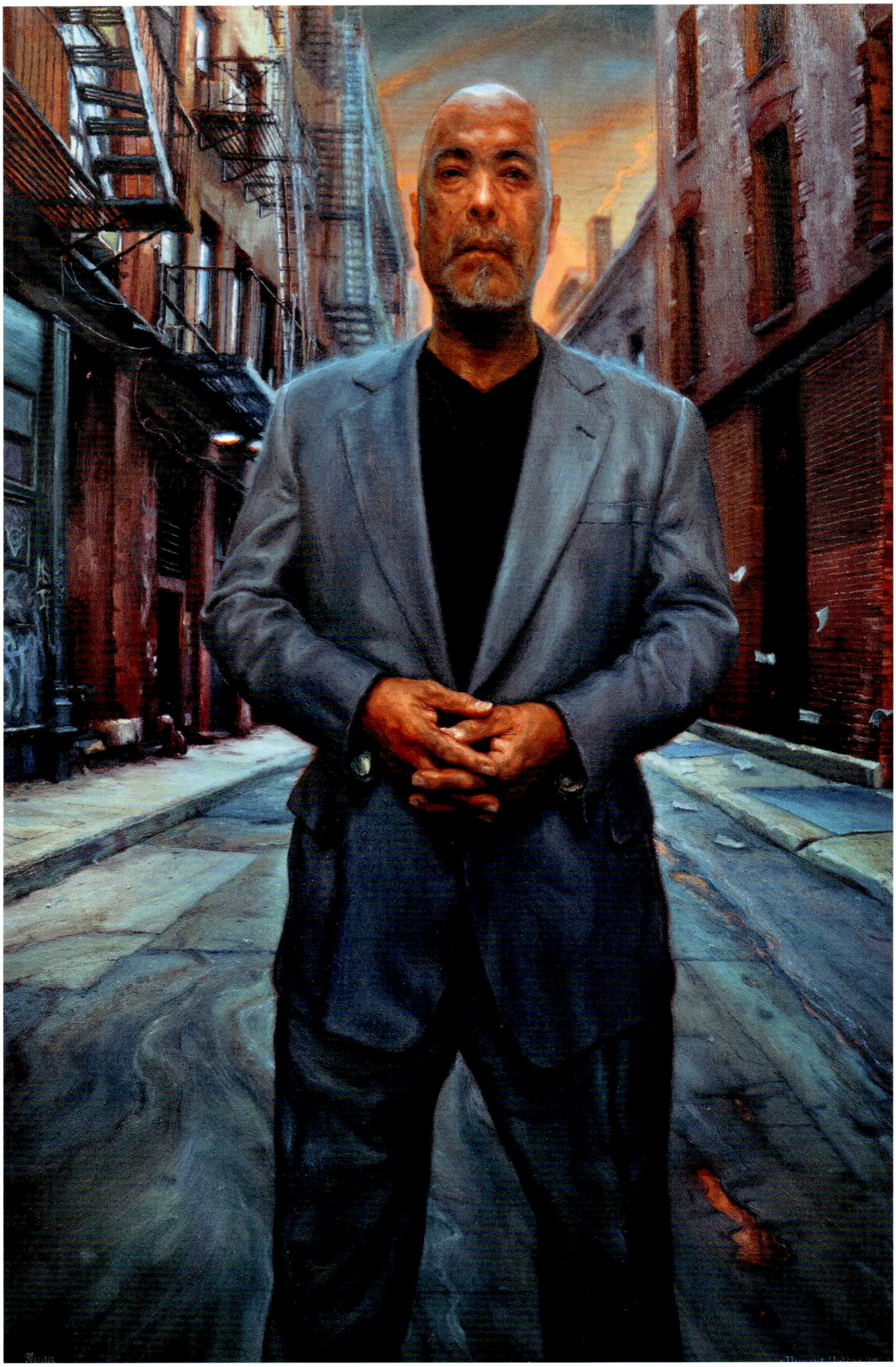

The Beginning is Near (An American Trilogy), Chapter Three: The New Americans, The New Americans #3 (Juan), **2021**
Oil on canvas
Photo: Peter Molick

The Beginning is Near (An American Trilogy), Chapter Three: The New Americans, The New Americans #4 (Teresita), **2021**
Oil on canvas
Photo: Peter Molick

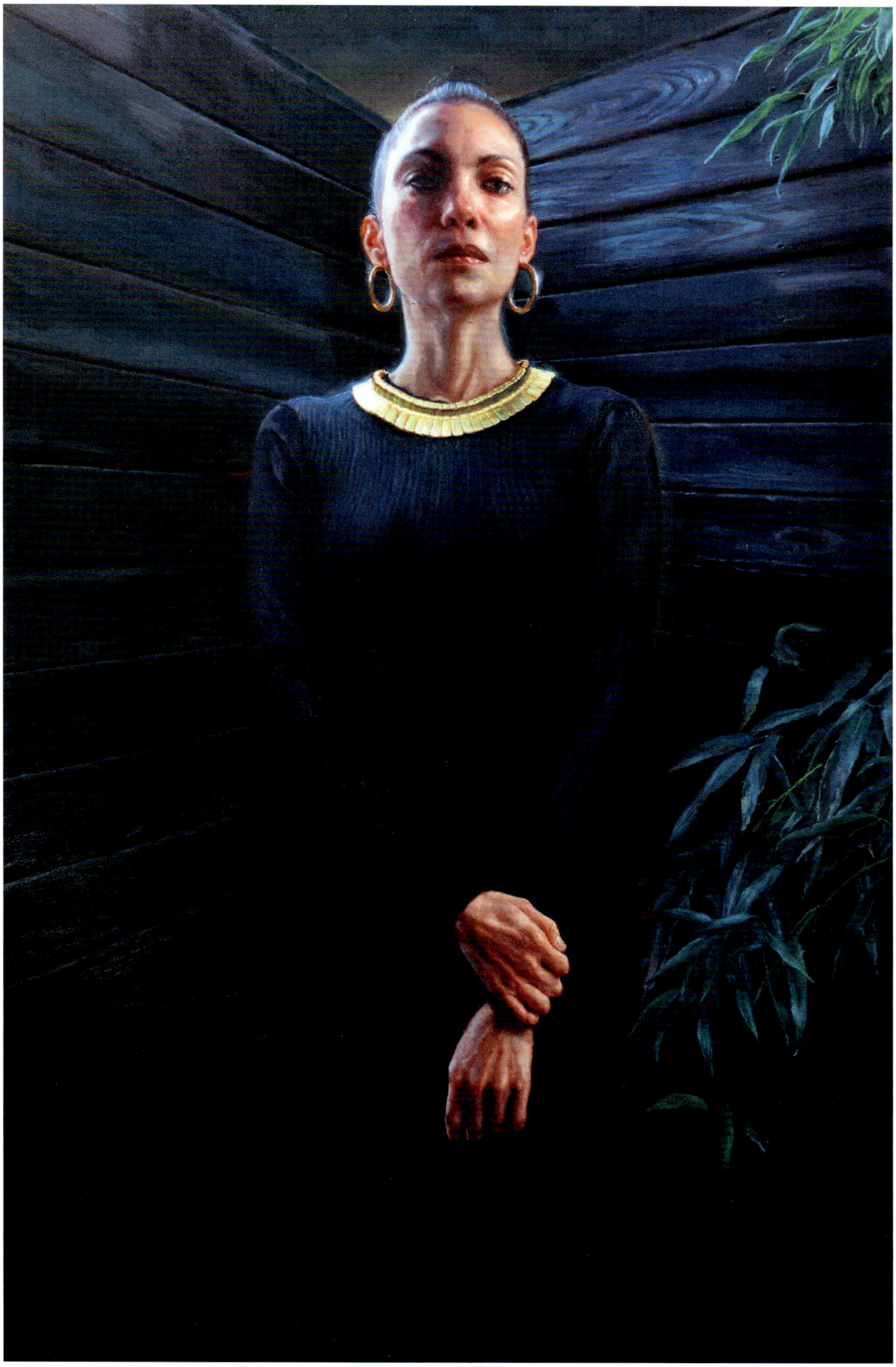

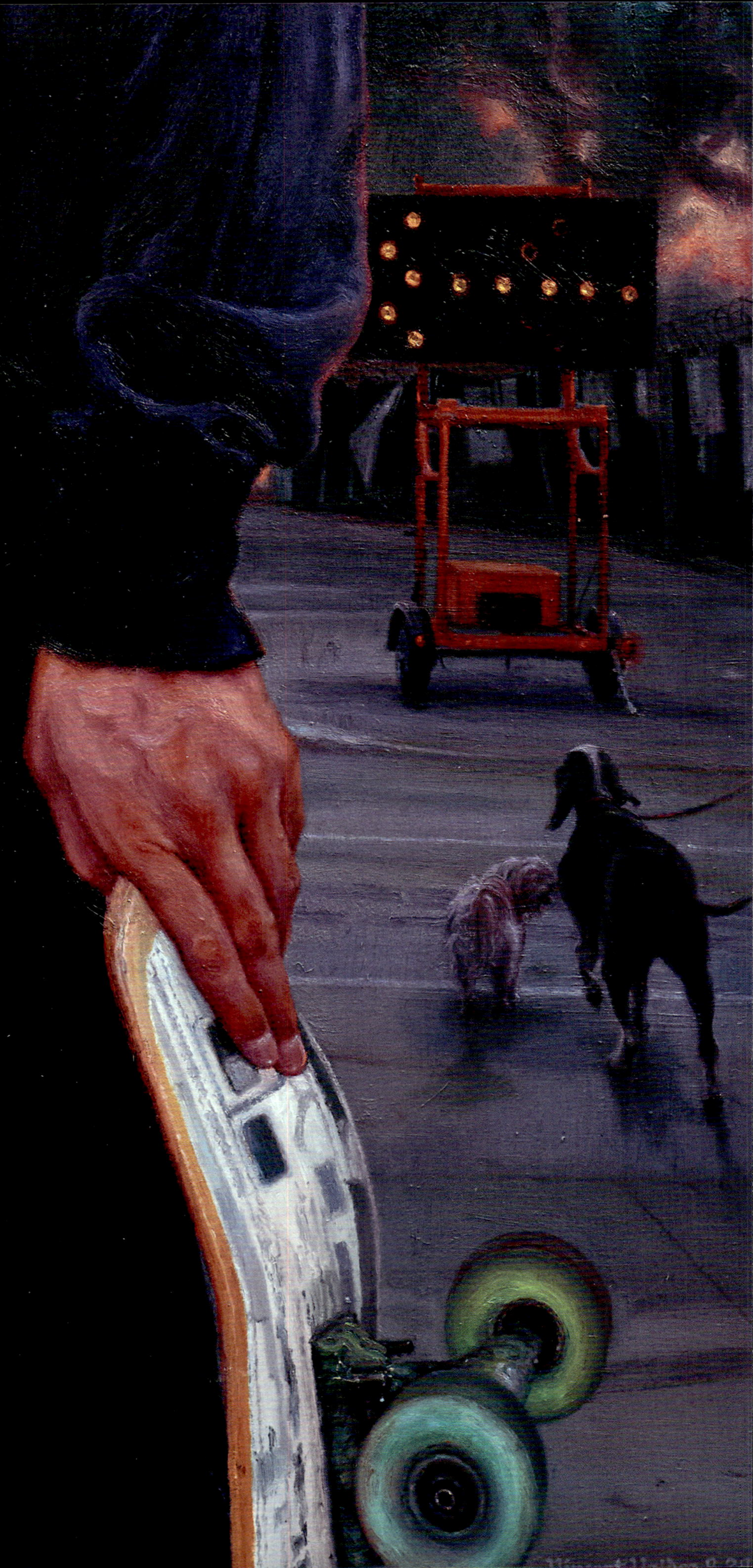

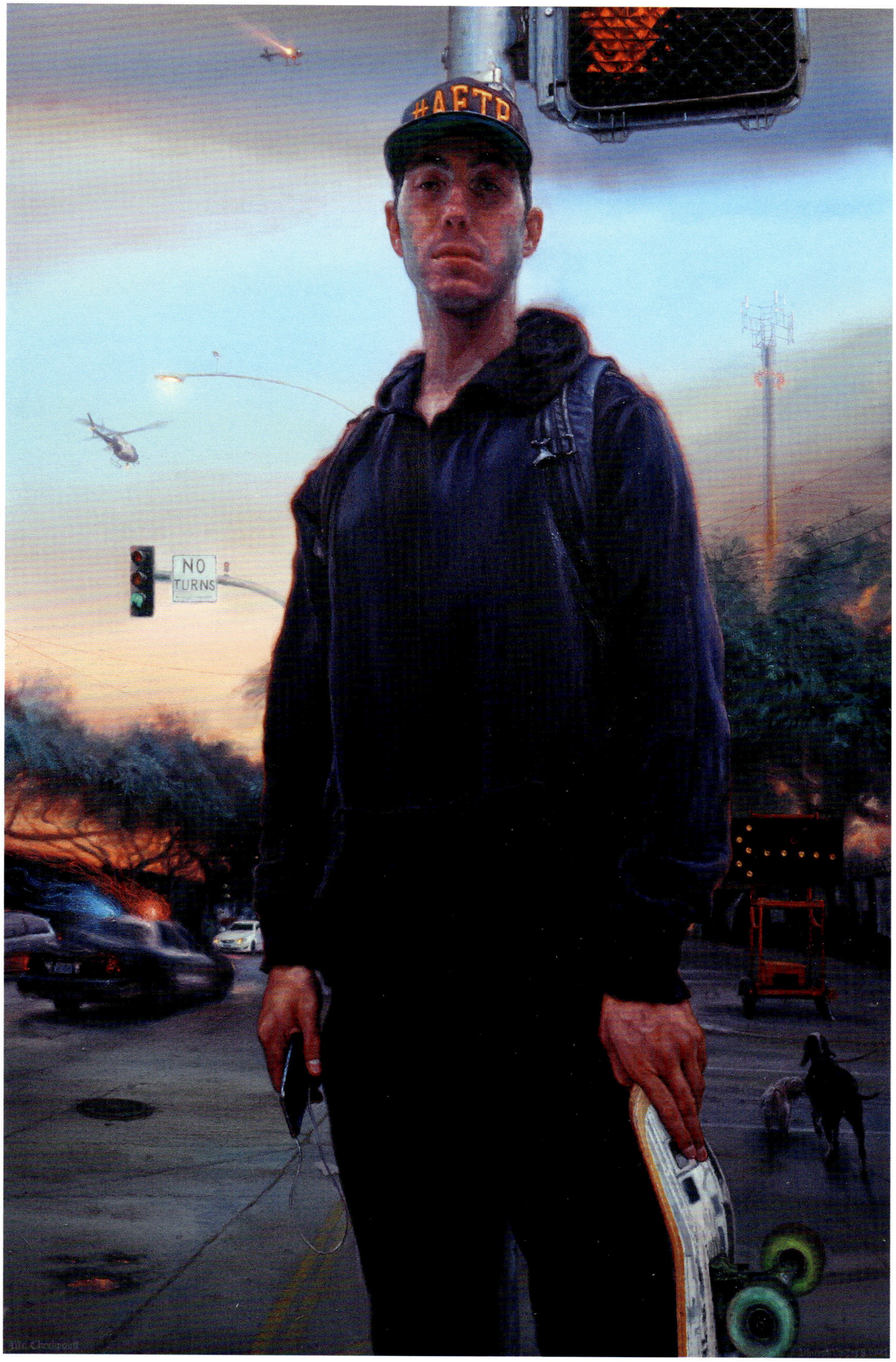
#AFTR
NO
TURNS

THE END

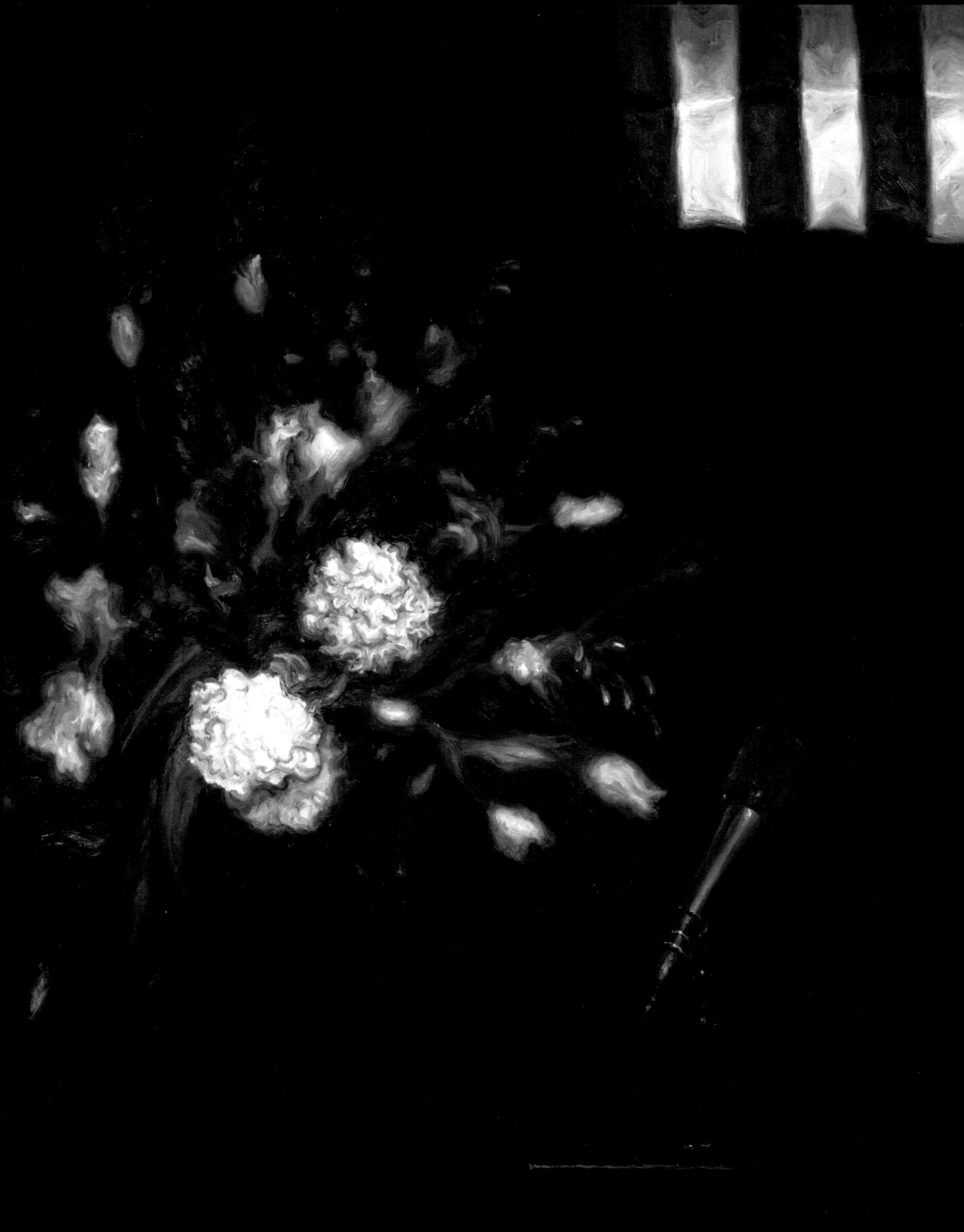

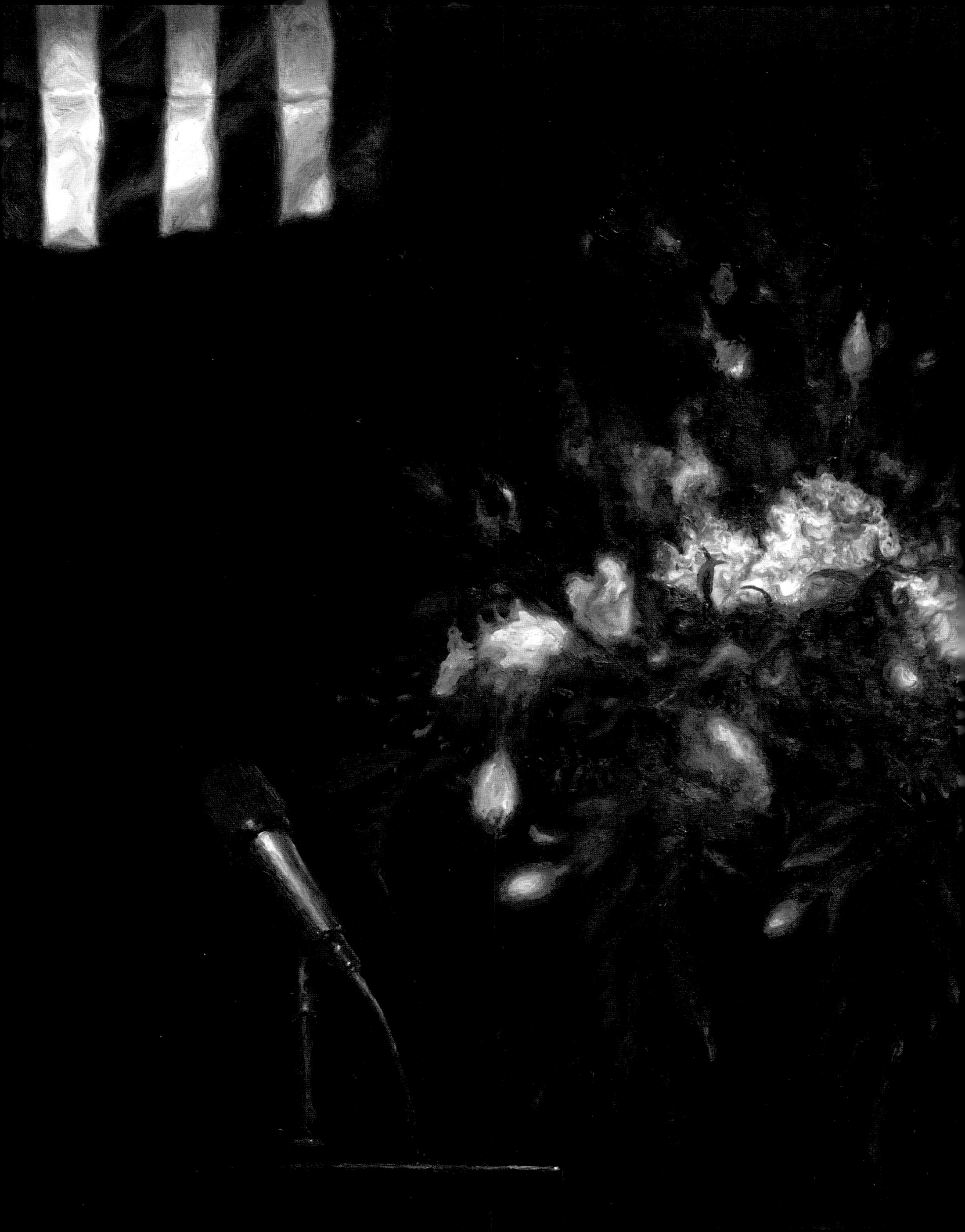

***The Beginning is Near (An American Trilogy), Chapter Two: Dream Baby Dream*, 2018**
Oil on canvas
Photos: Peter Molick

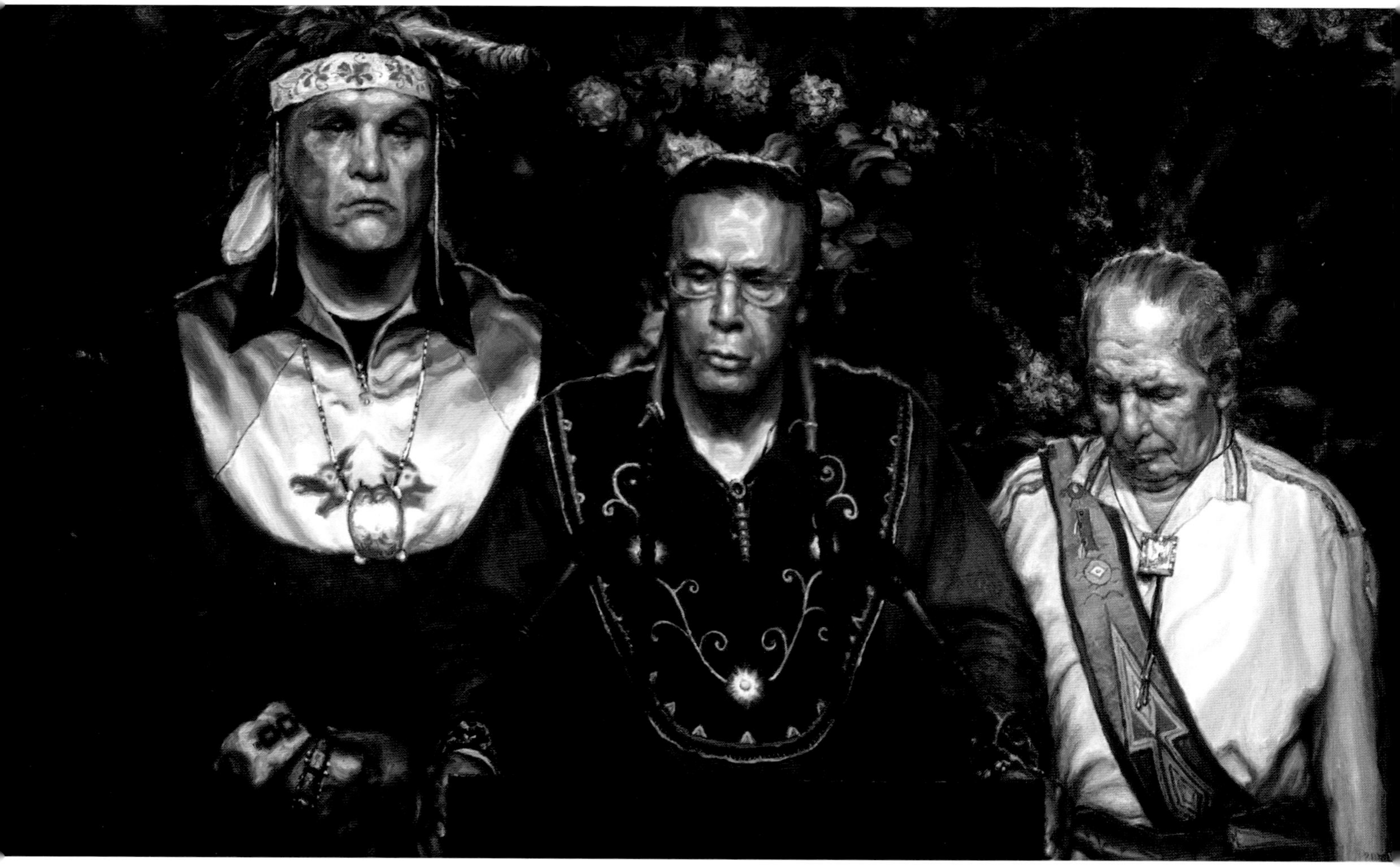

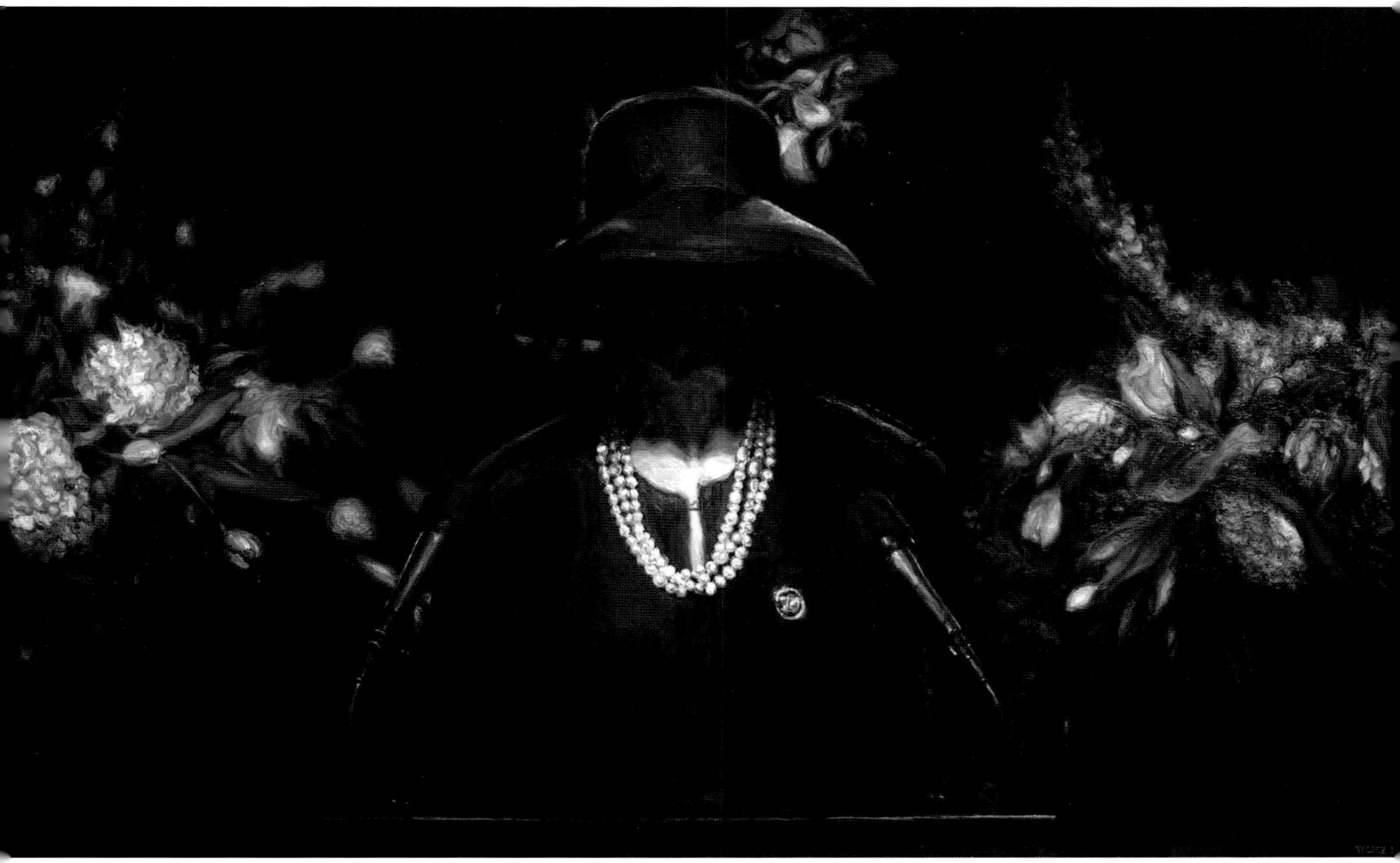

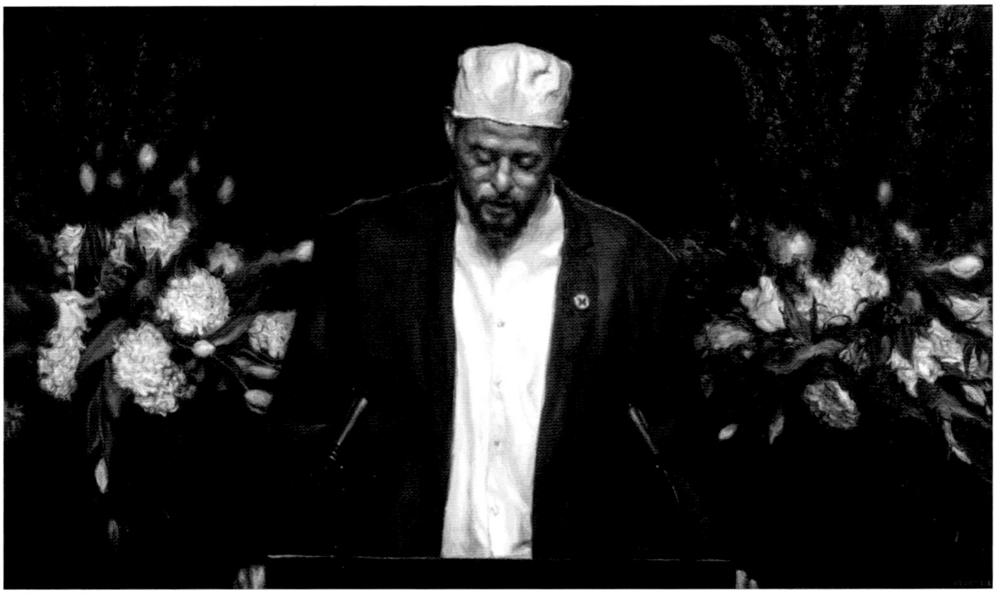

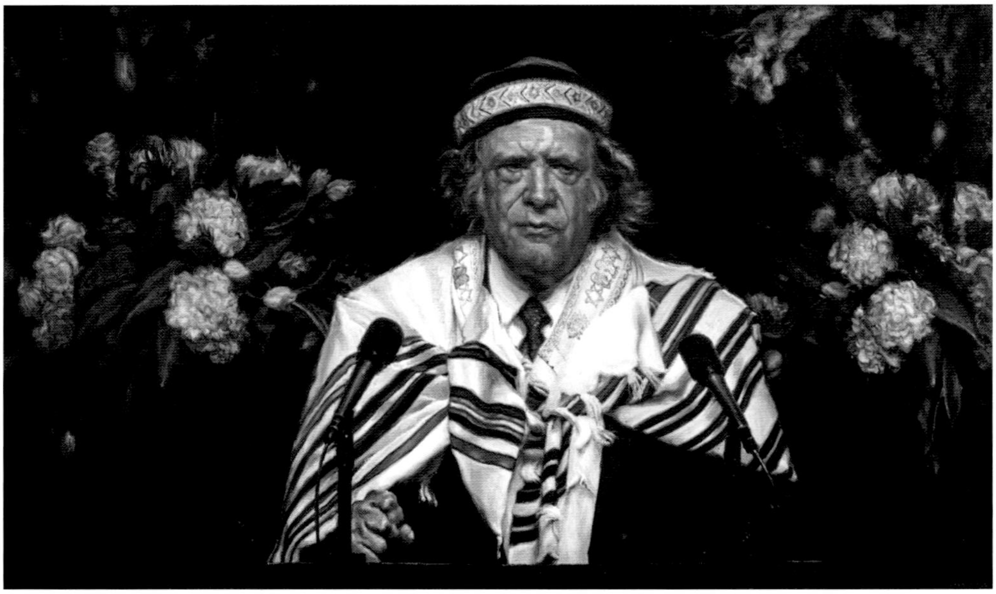

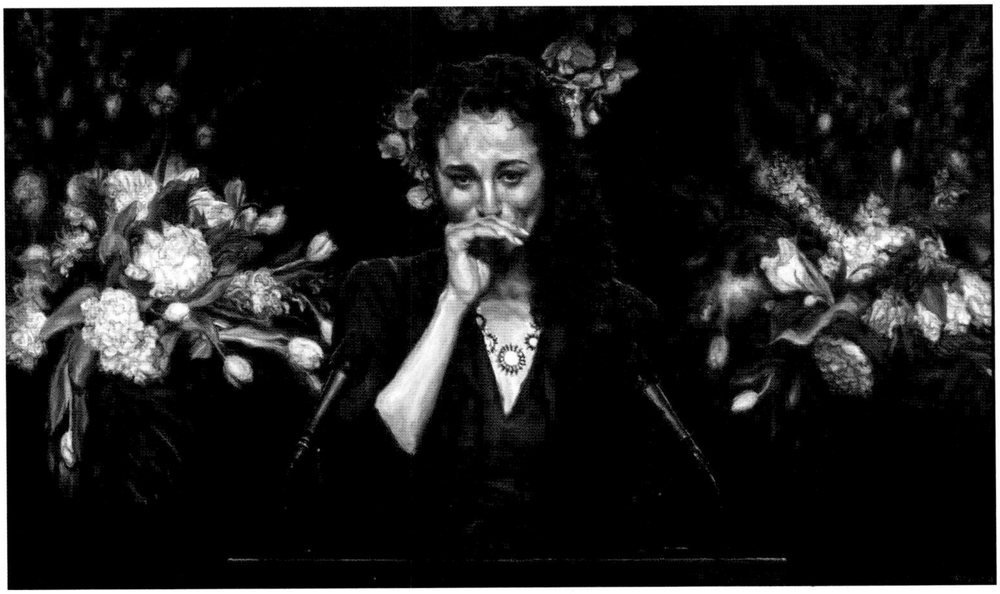

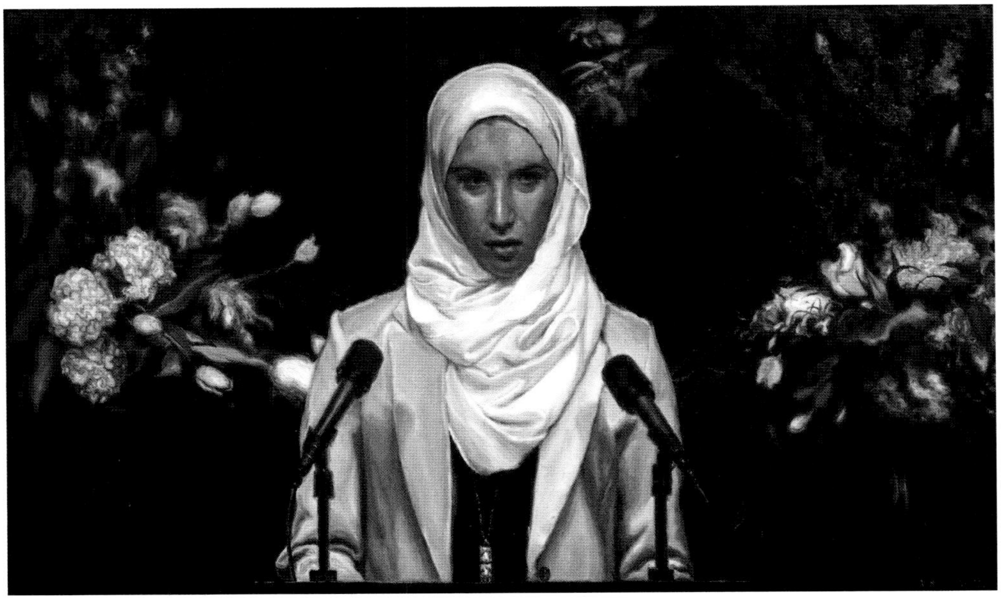

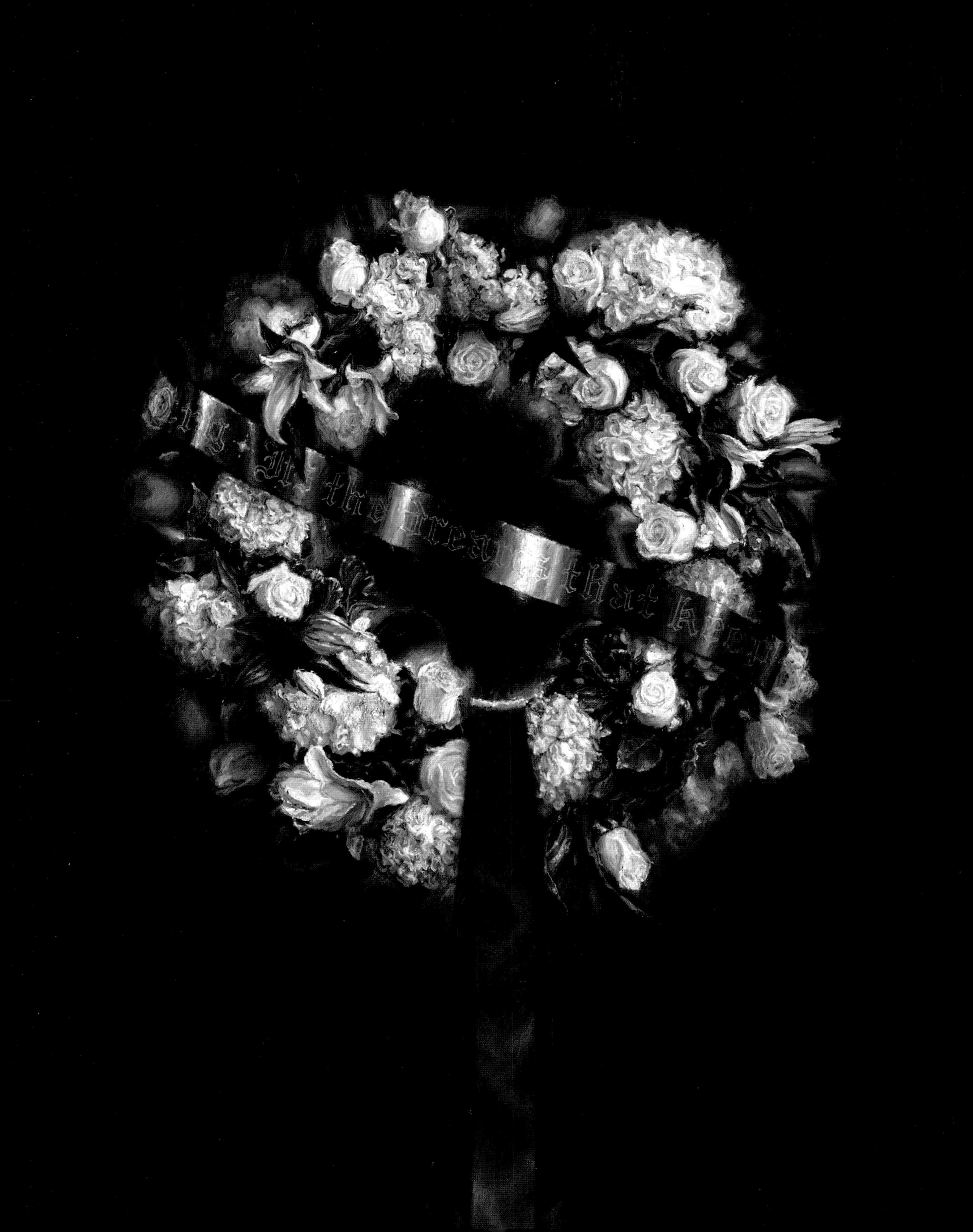
the
that

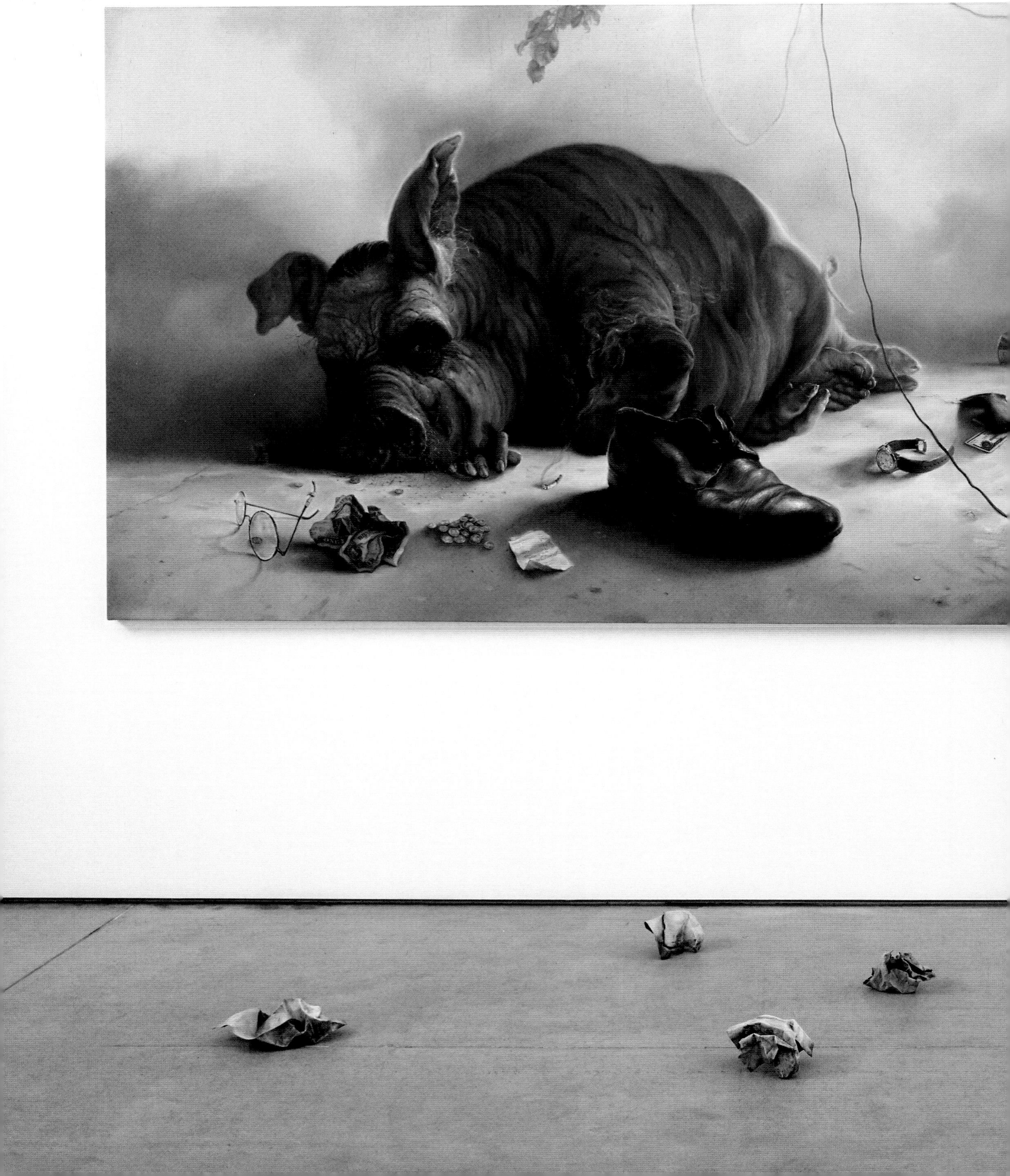

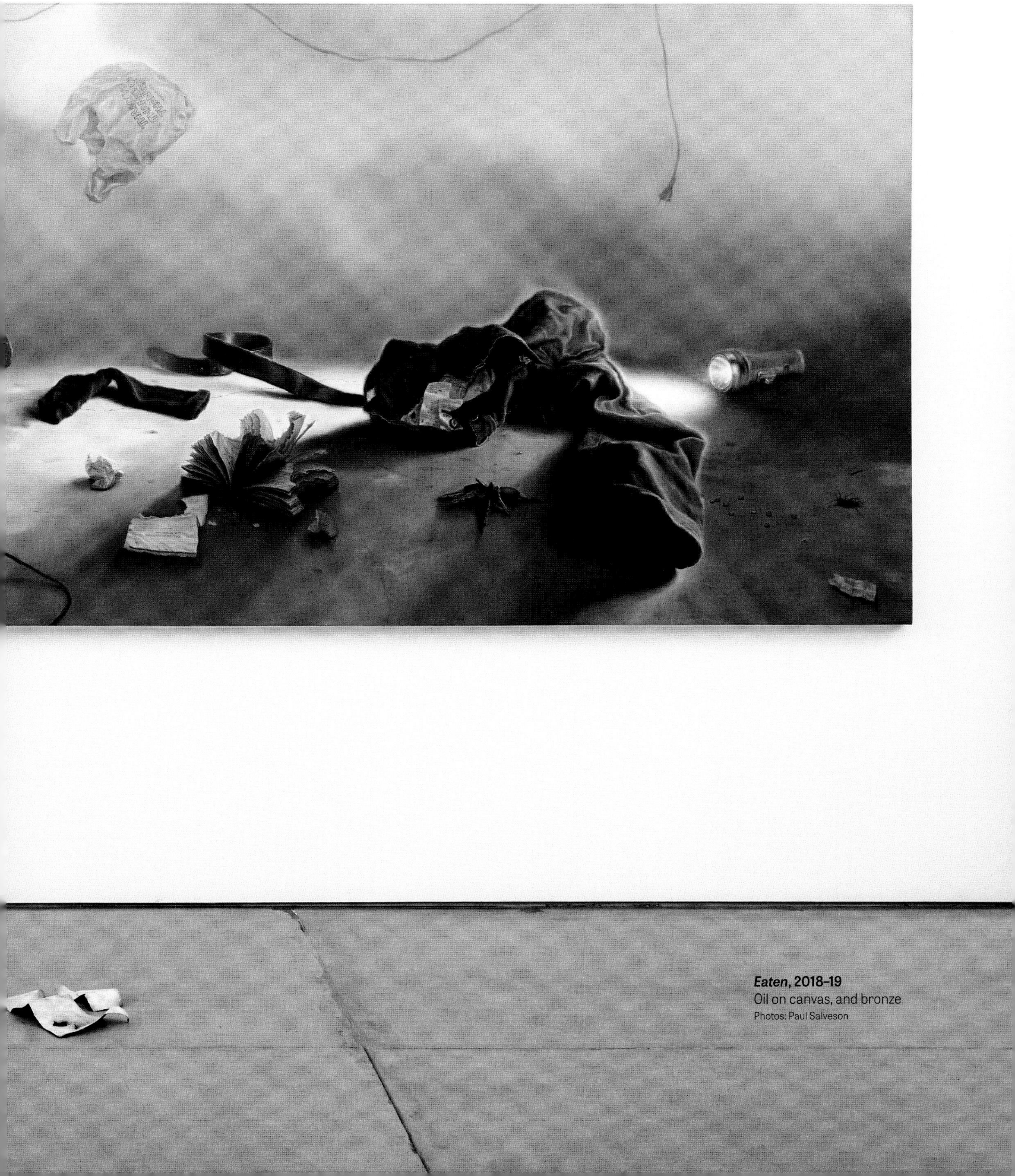

***Eaten*, 2018–19**
Oil on canvas, and bronze
Photos: Paul Salveson

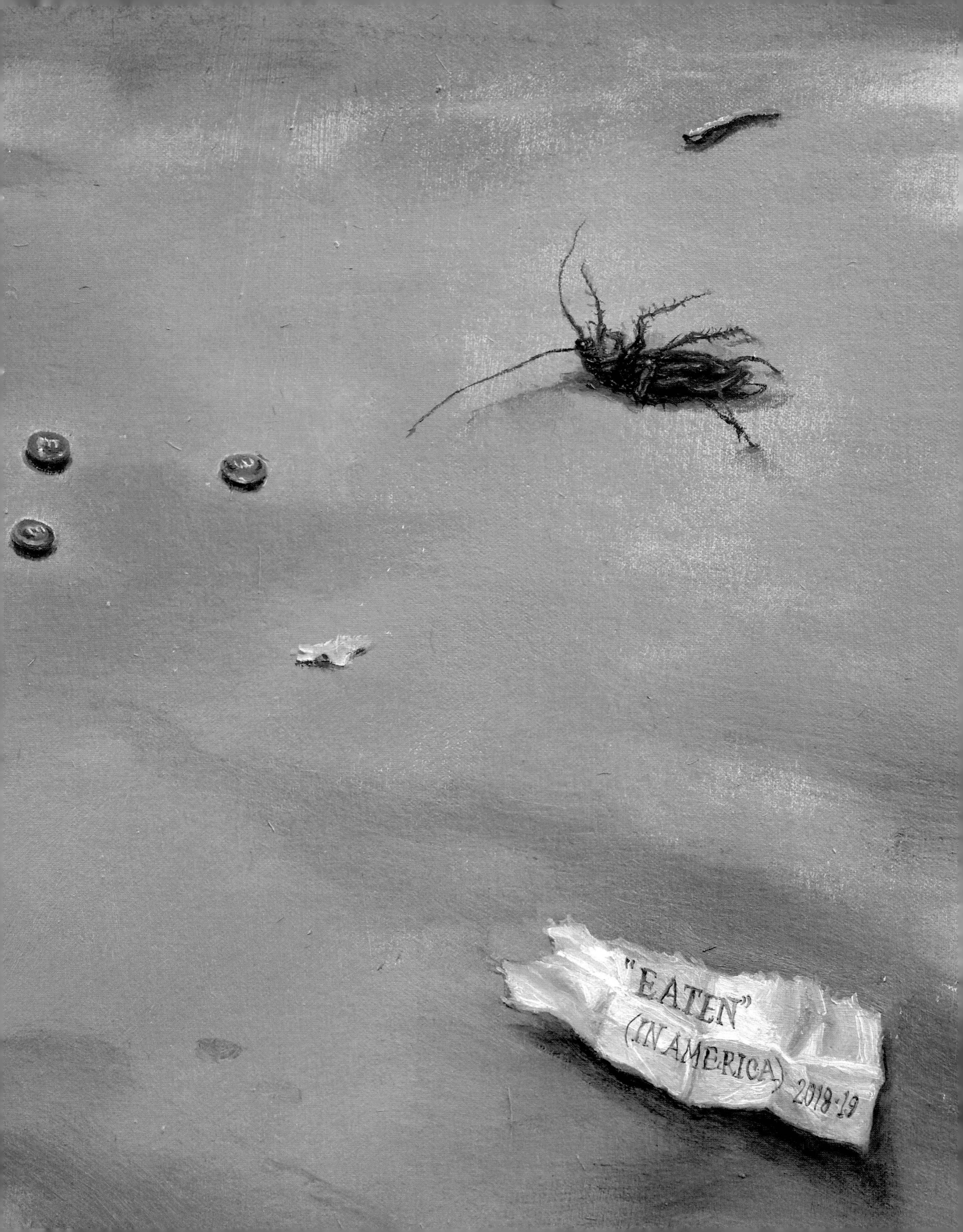
"EATEN"
(IN AMERICA)
2018-19

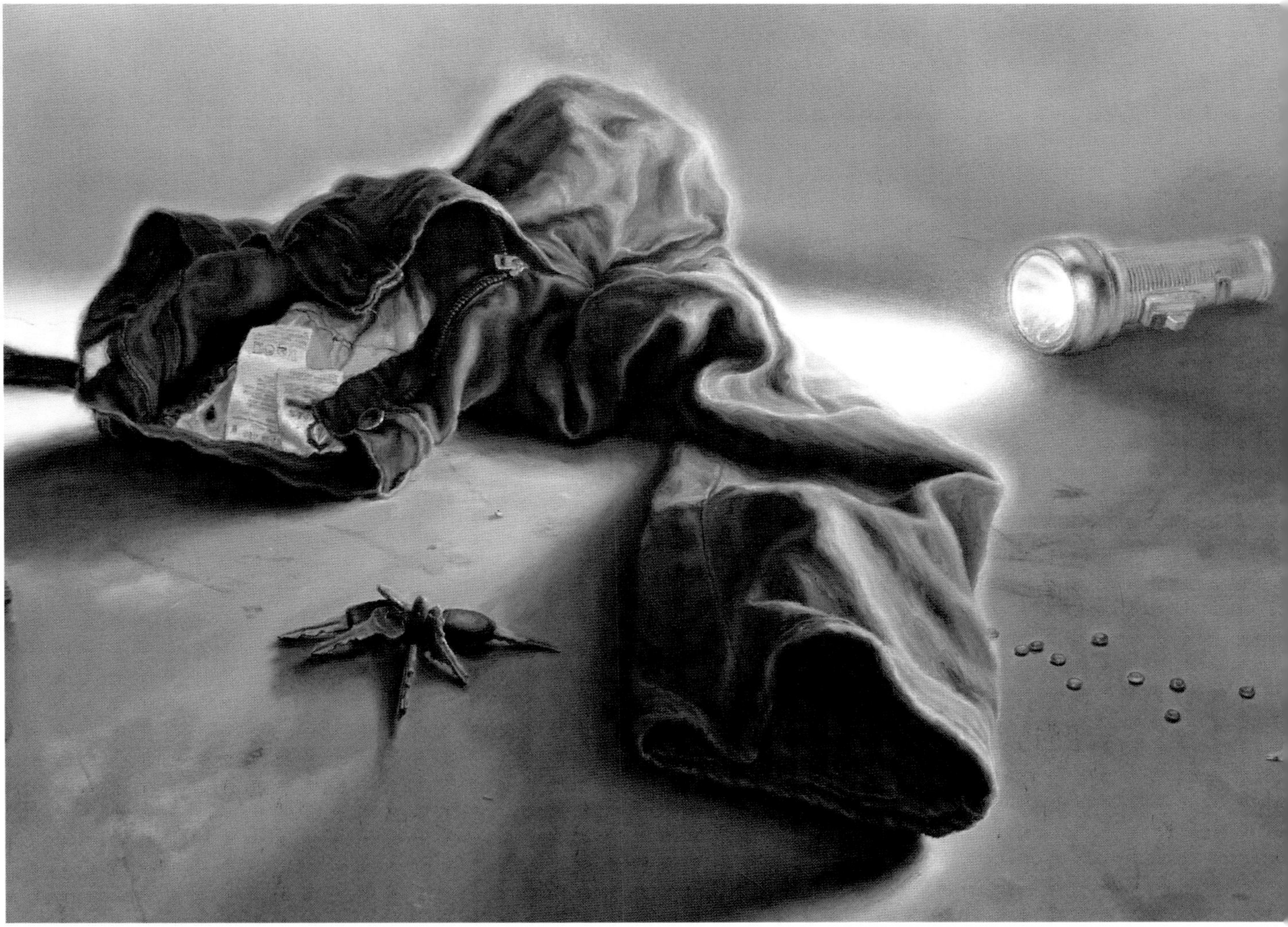

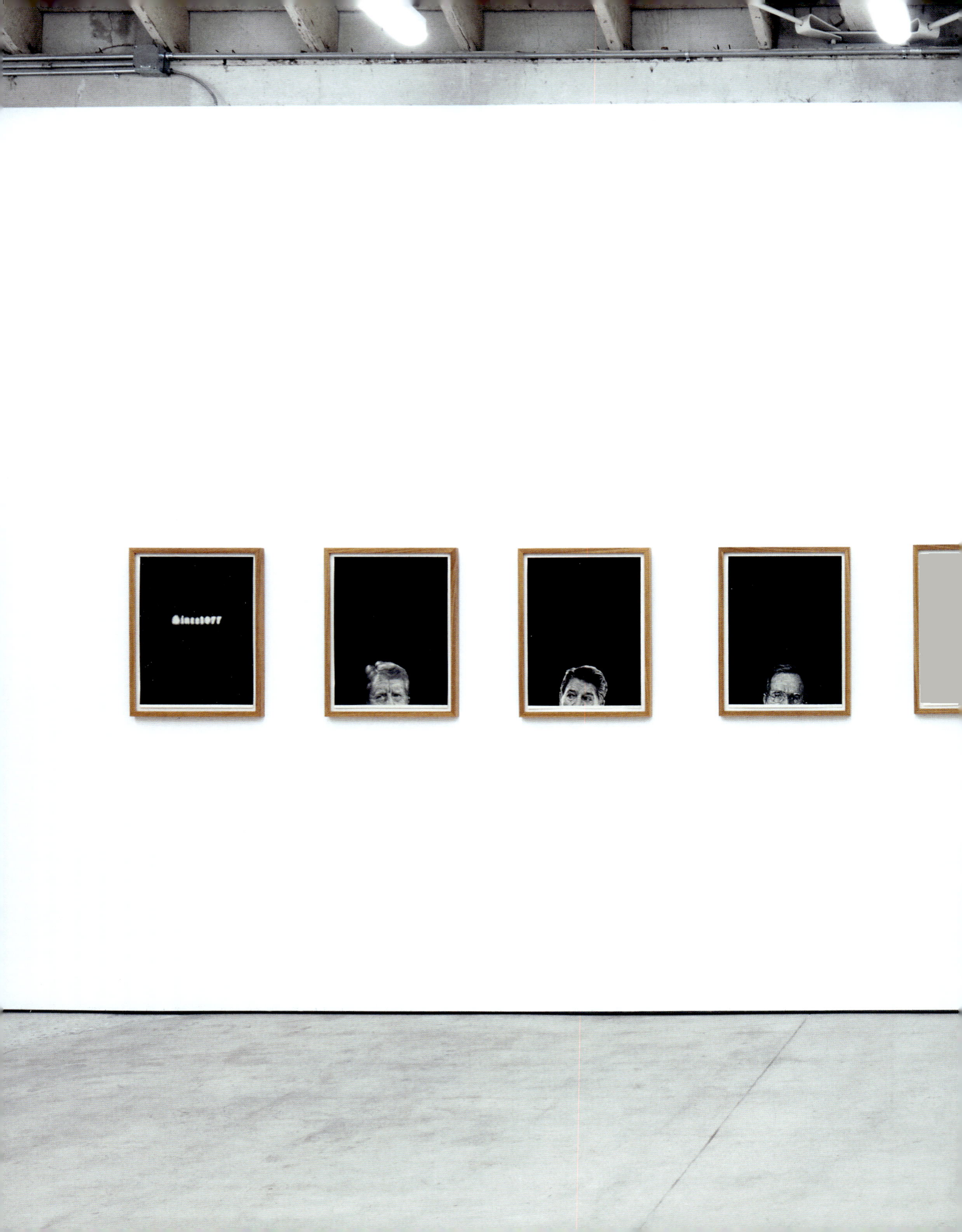

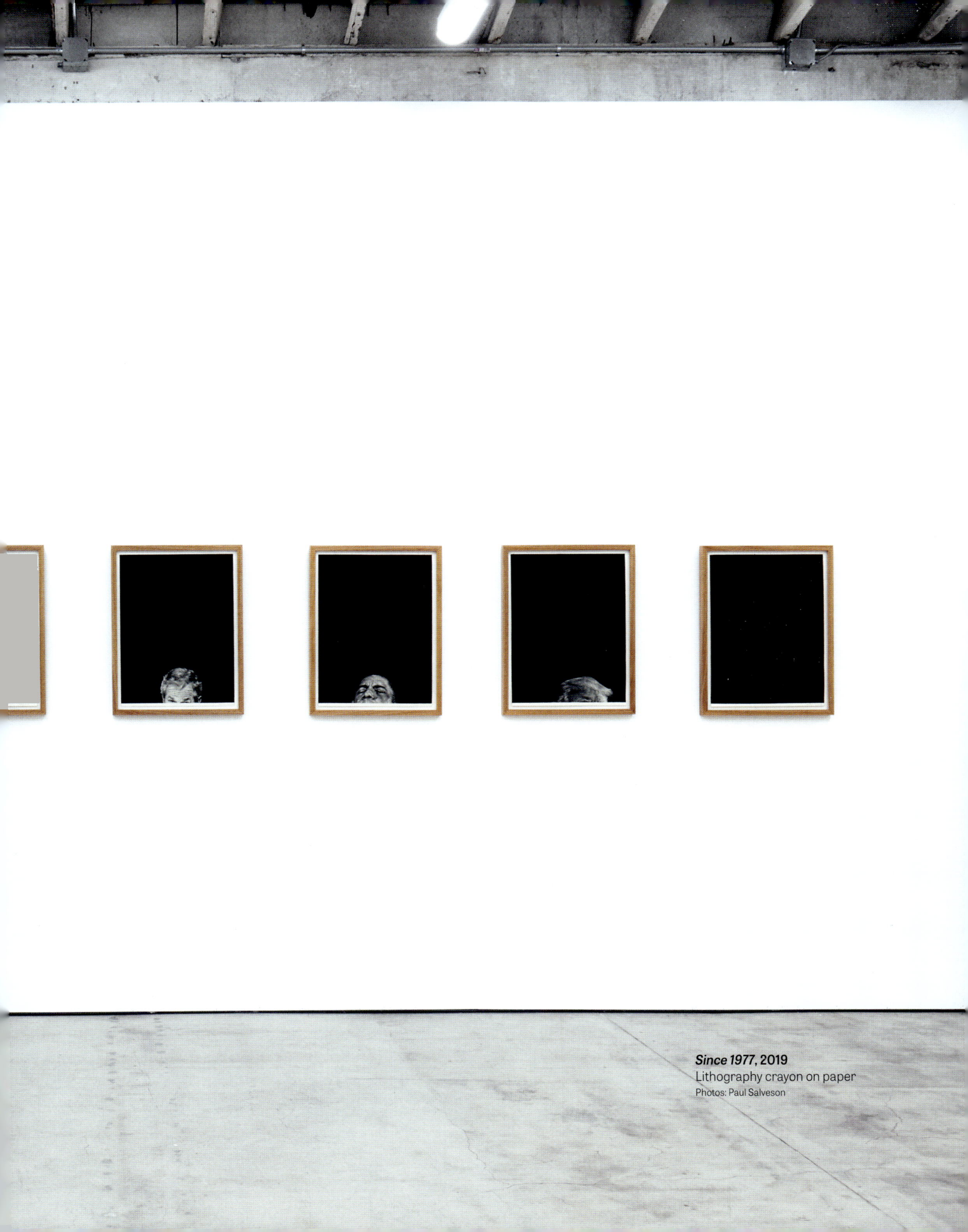

***Since 1977*, 2019**
Lithography crayon on paper
Photos: Paul Salveson

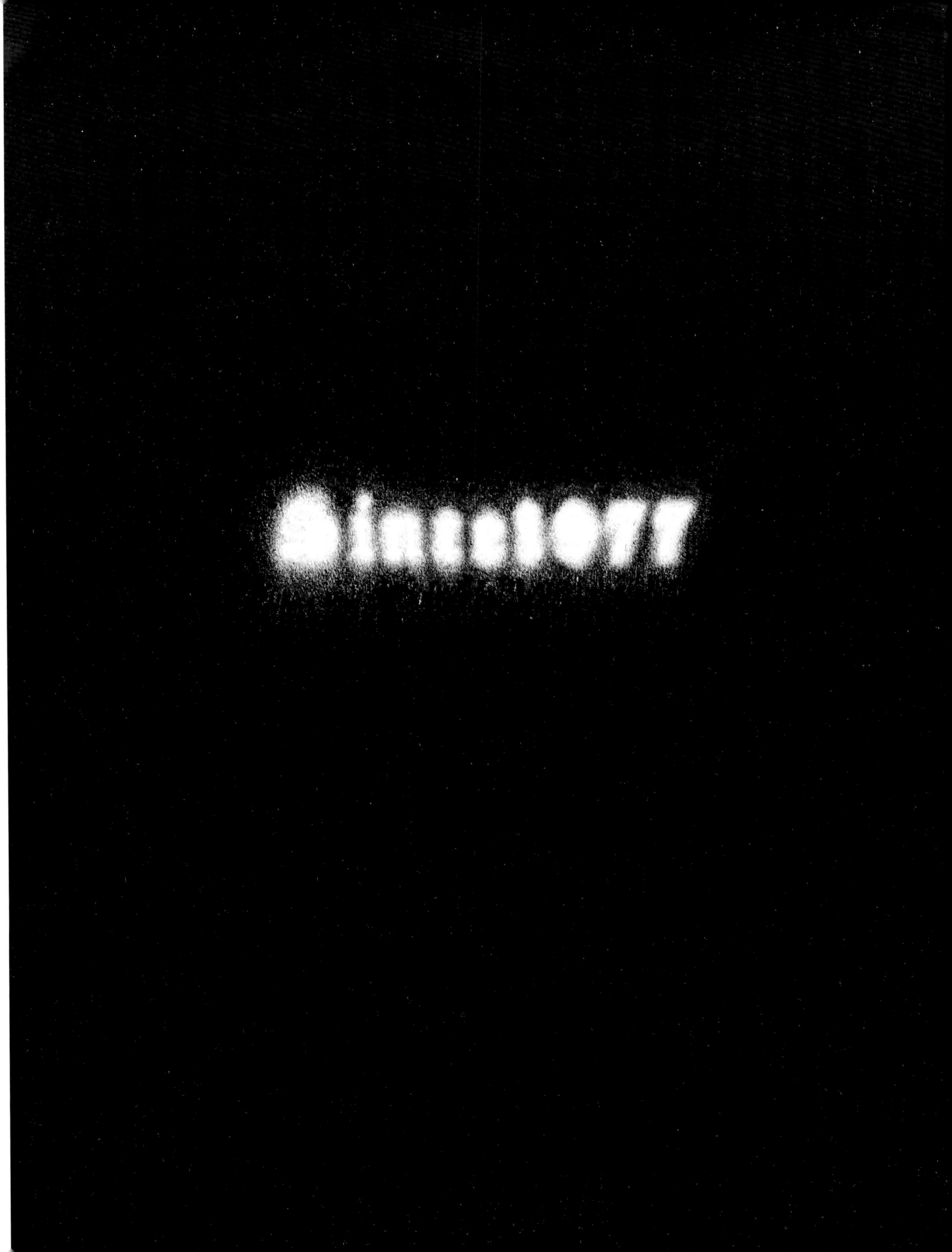

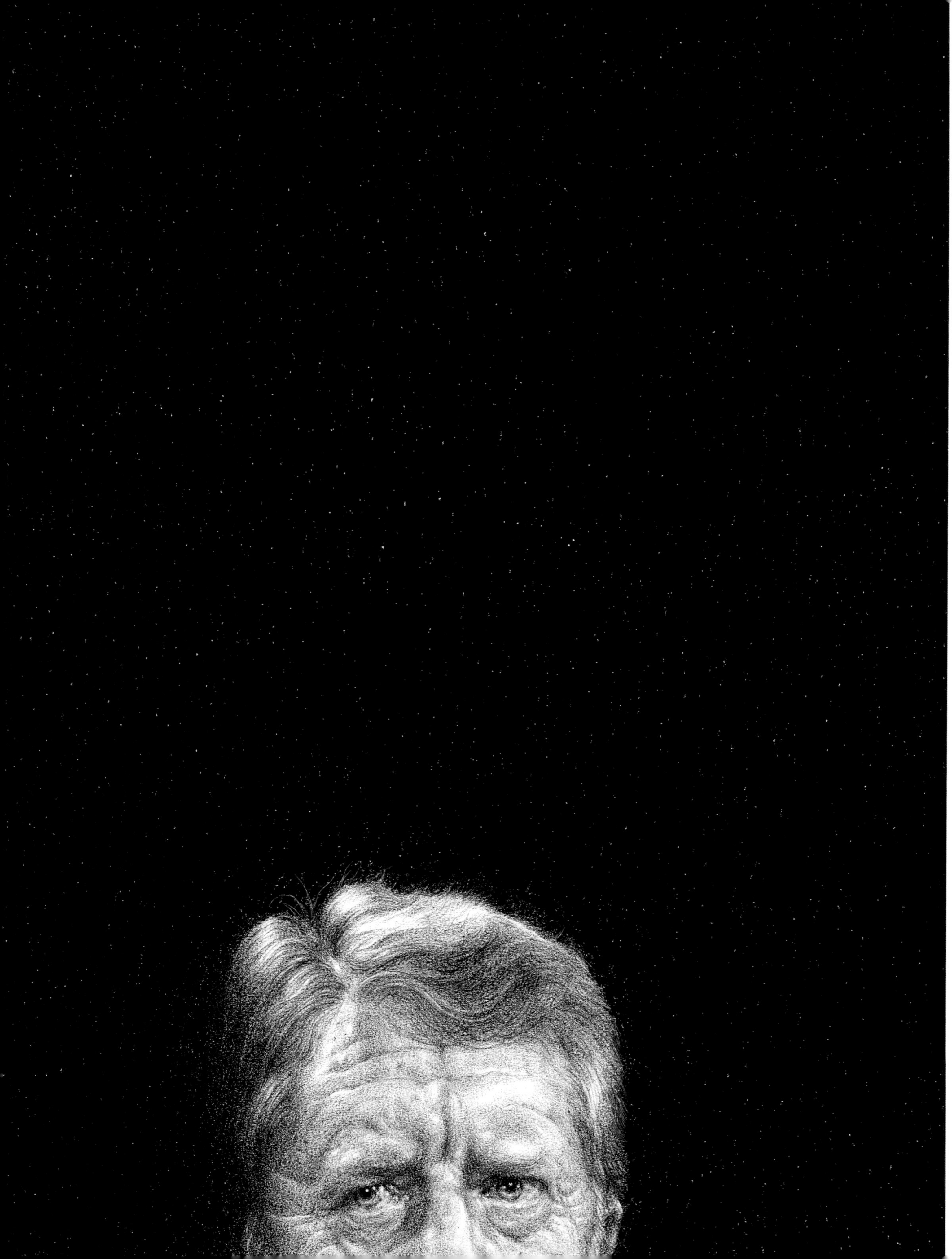

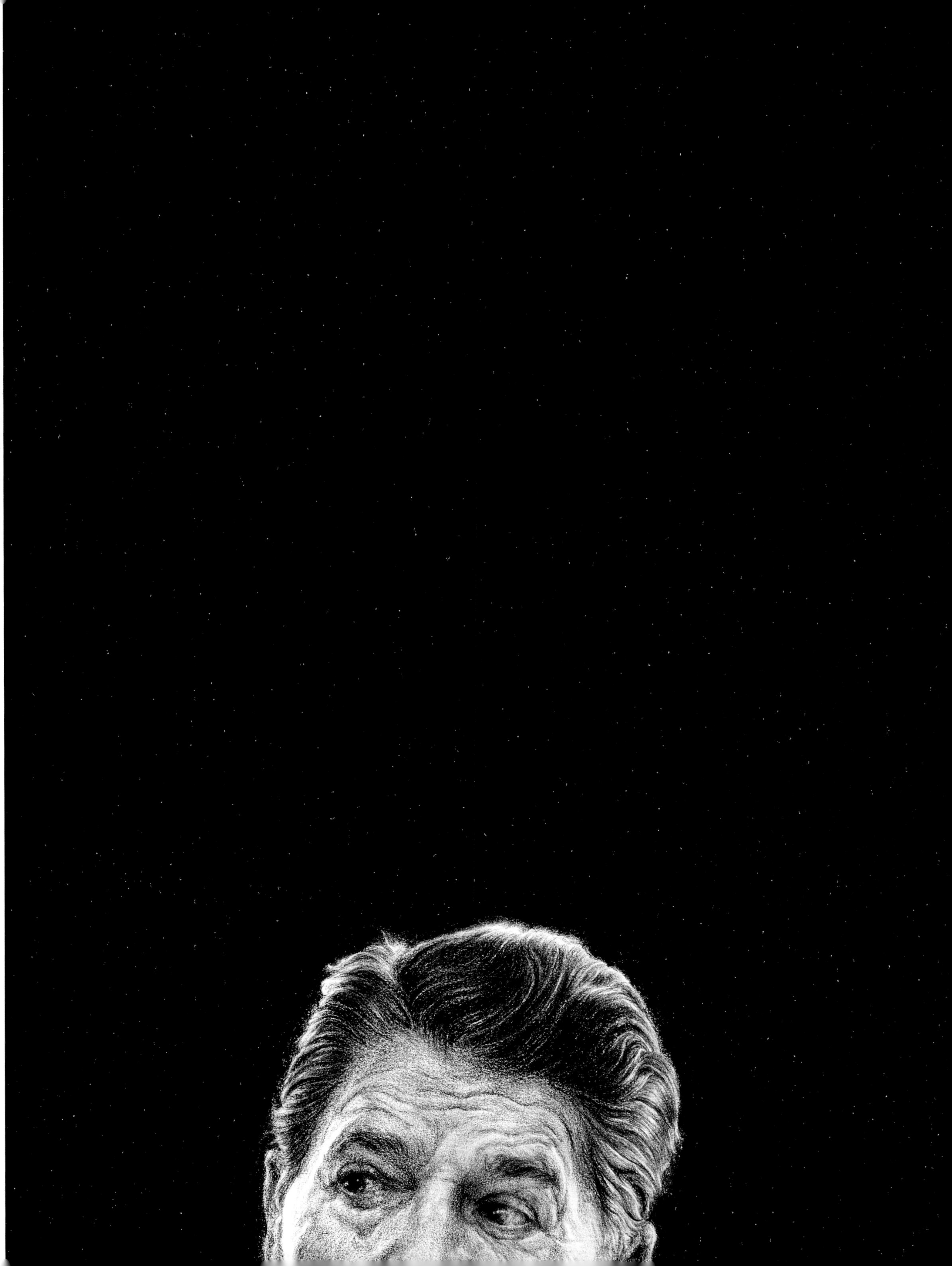

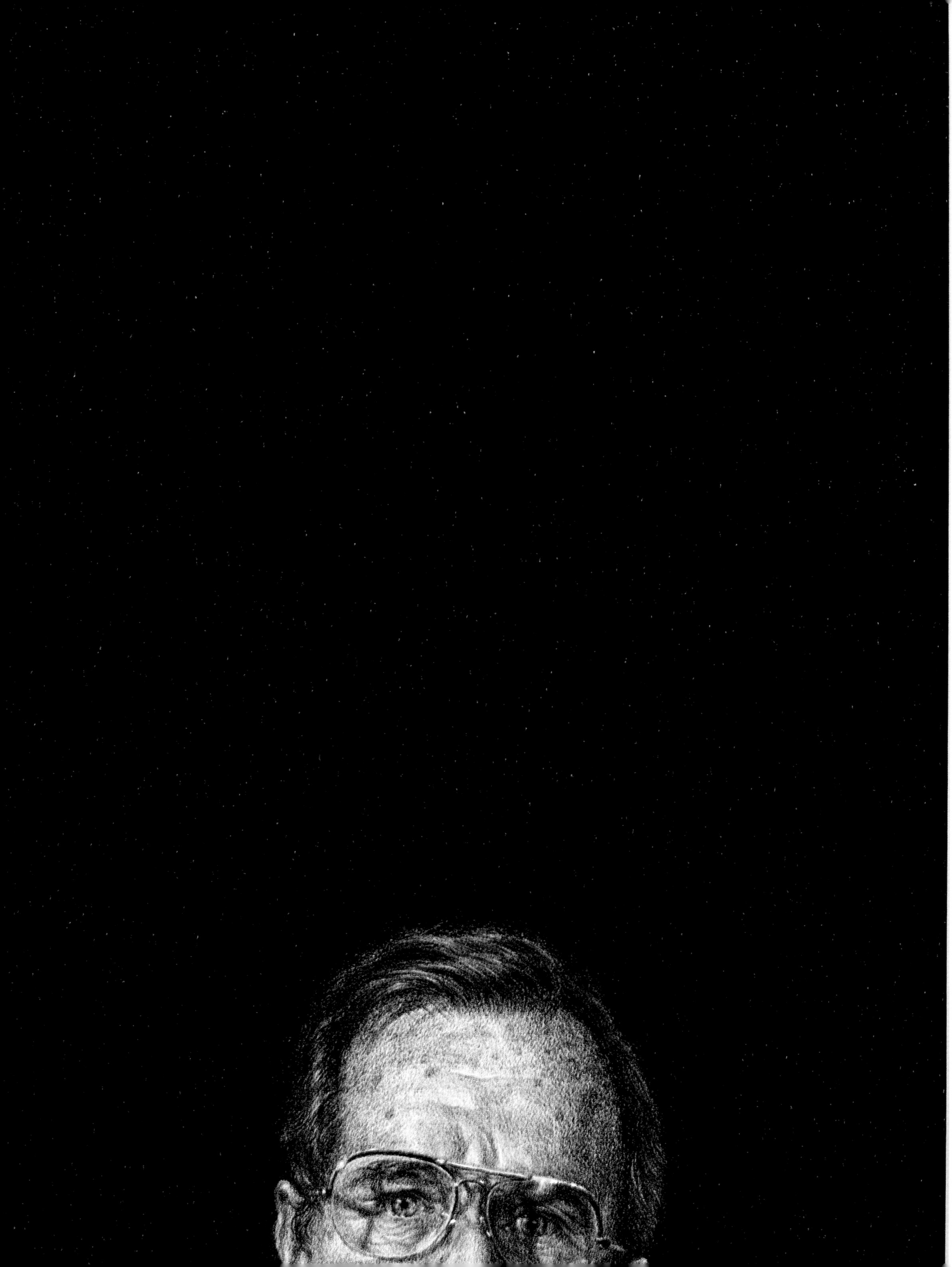

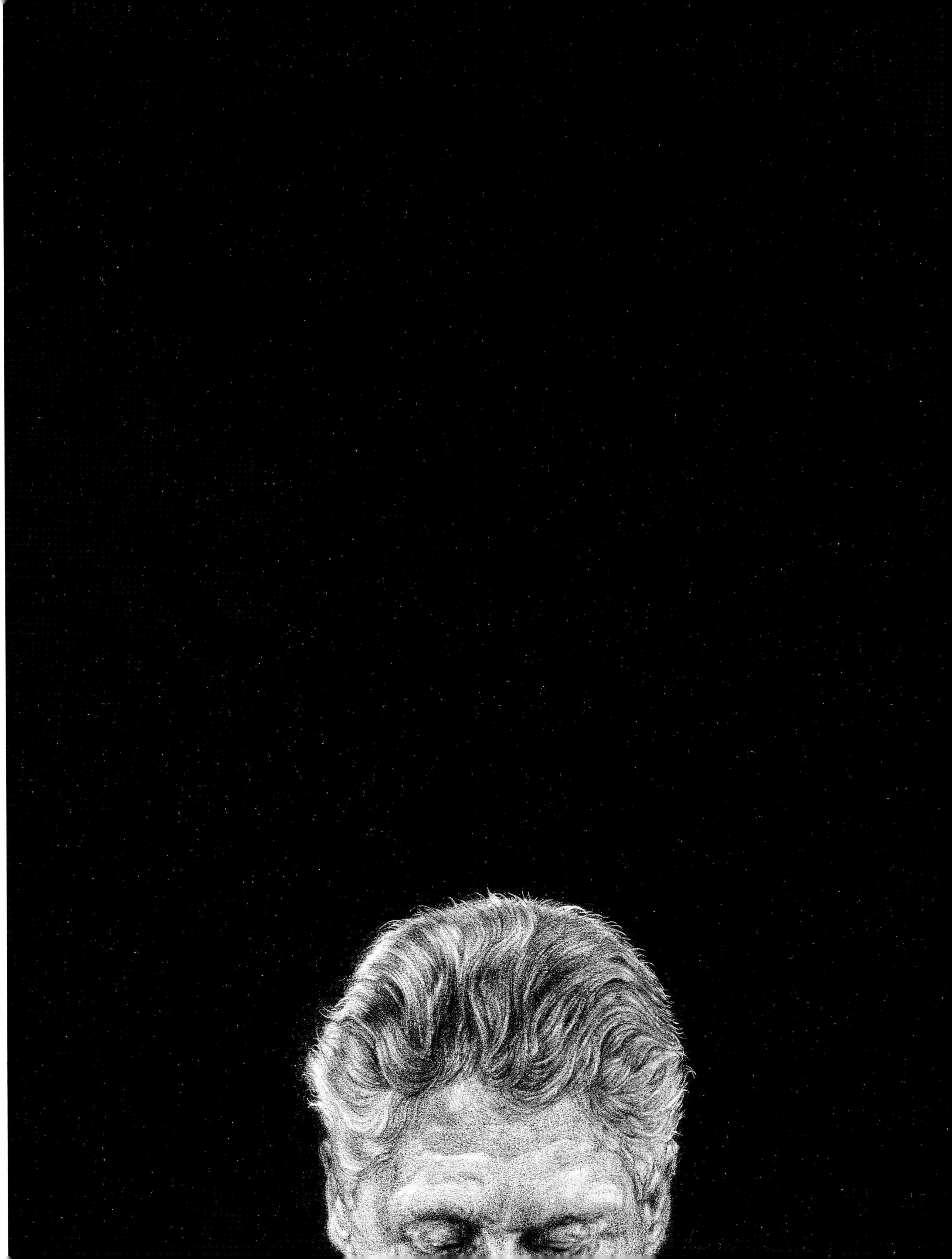

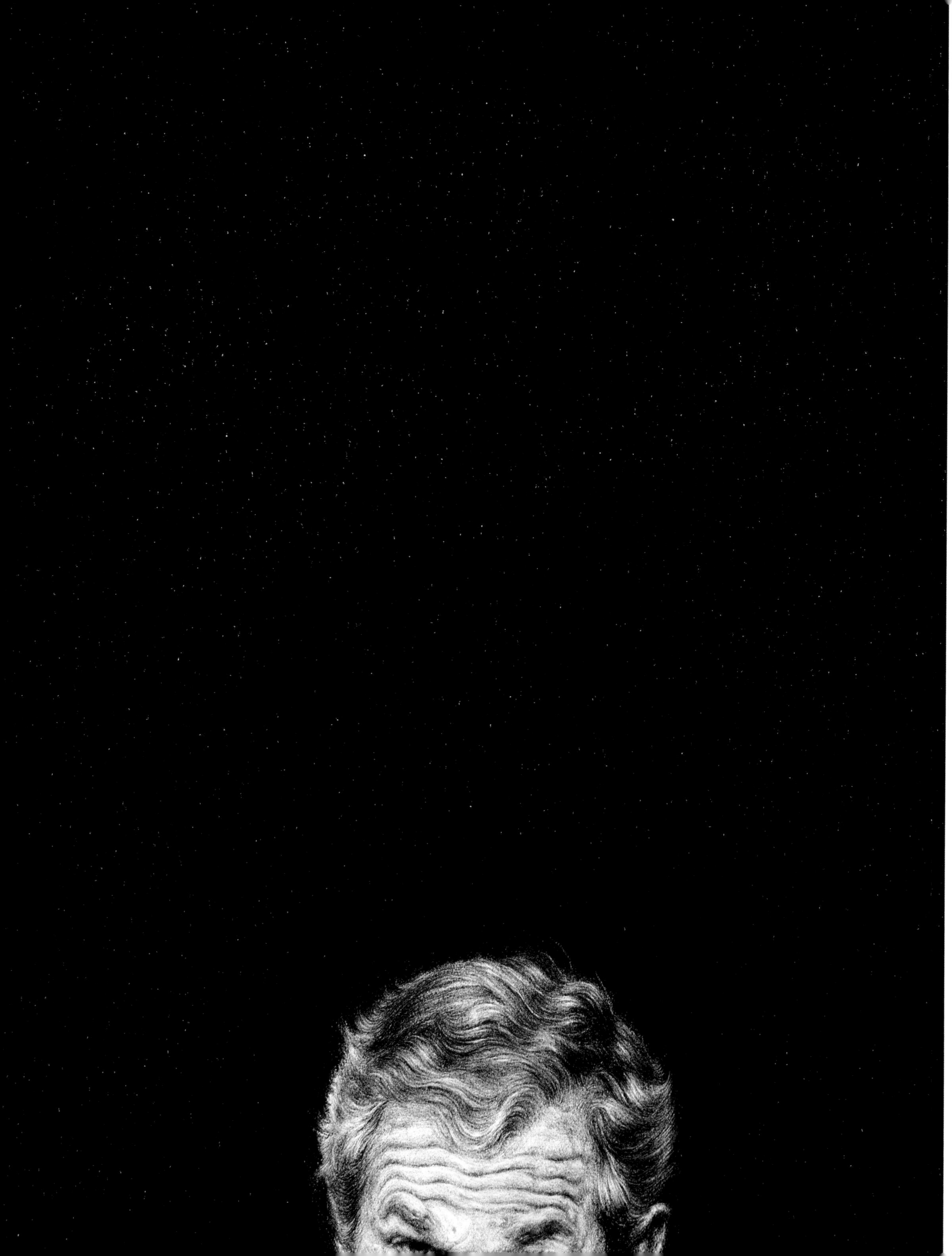

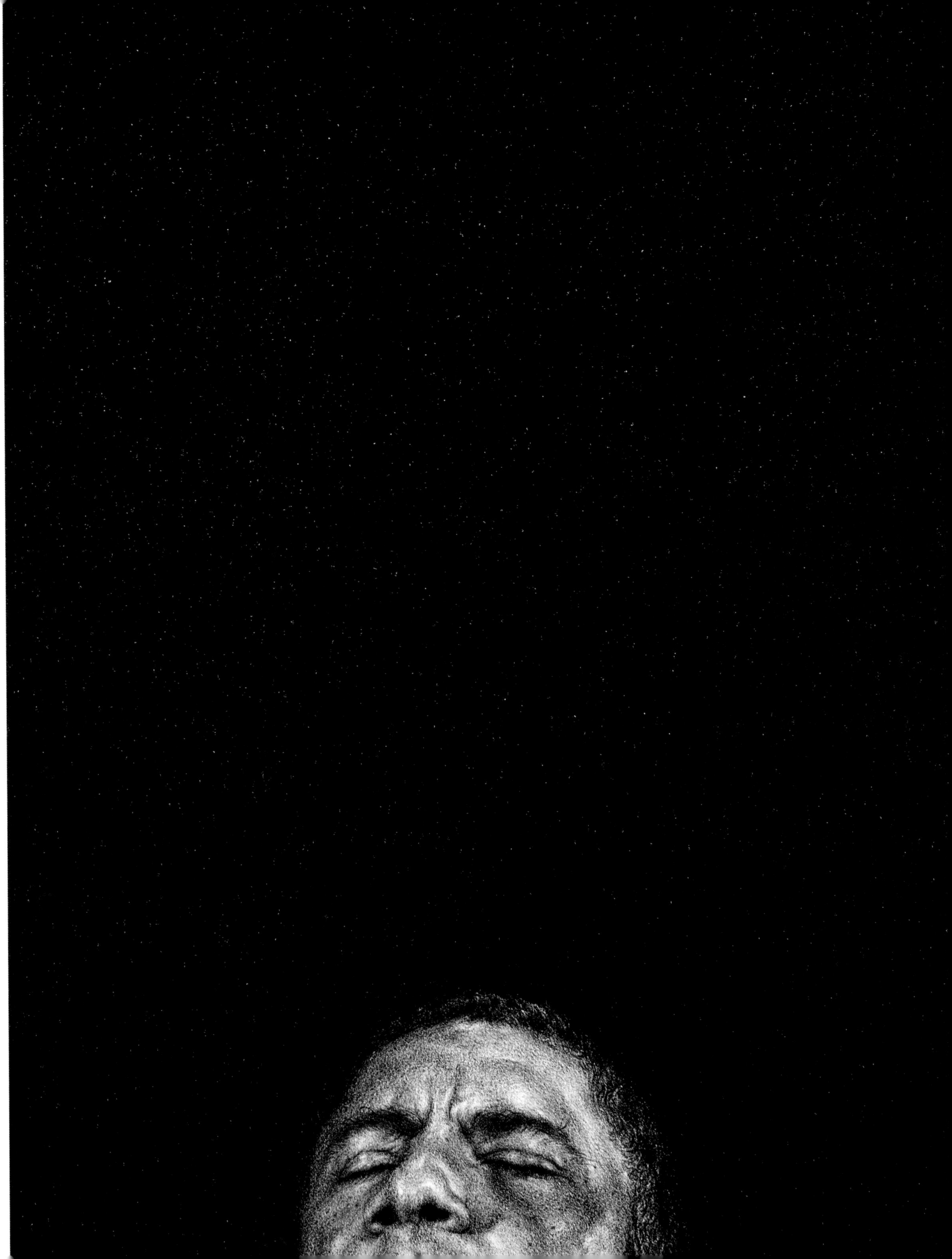

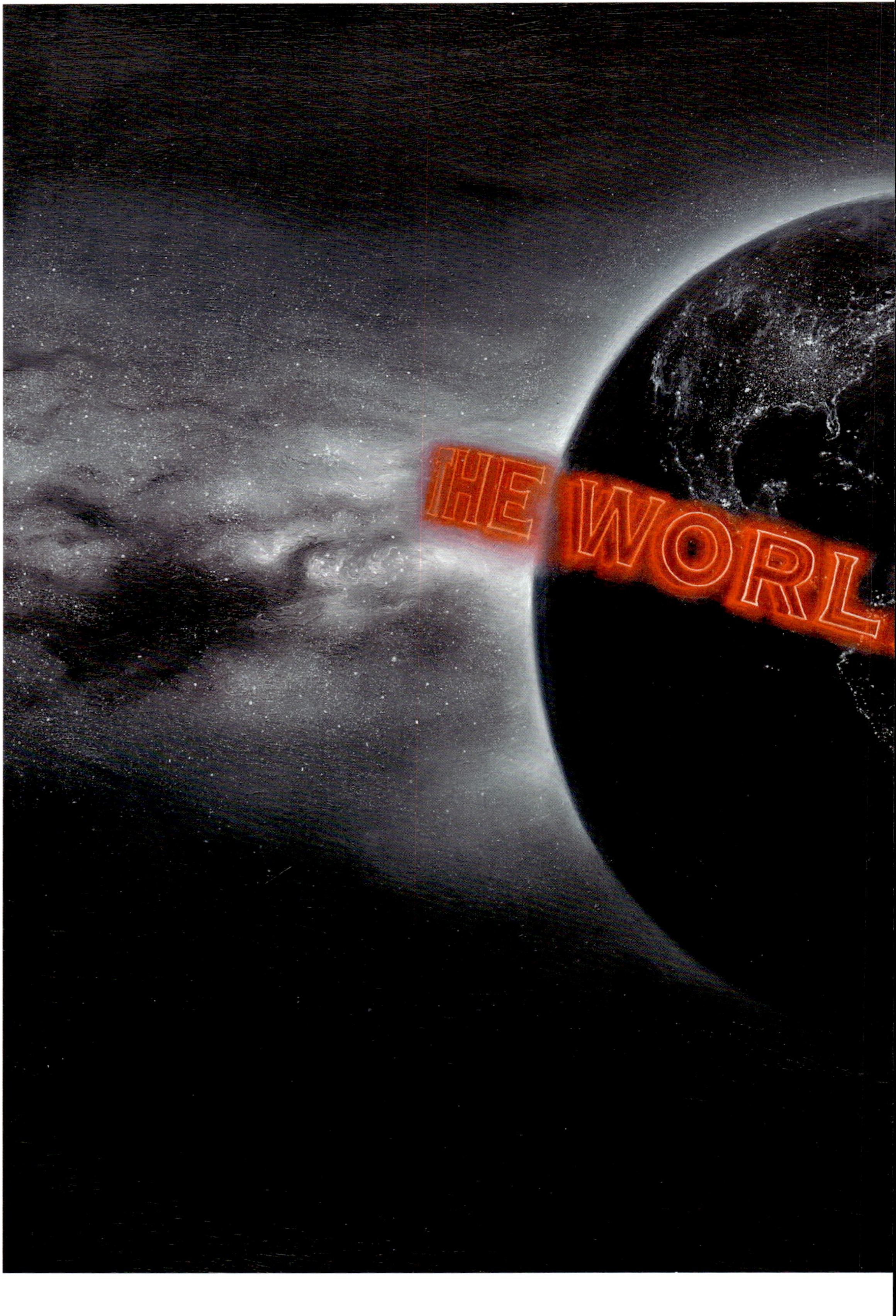
THE WORL

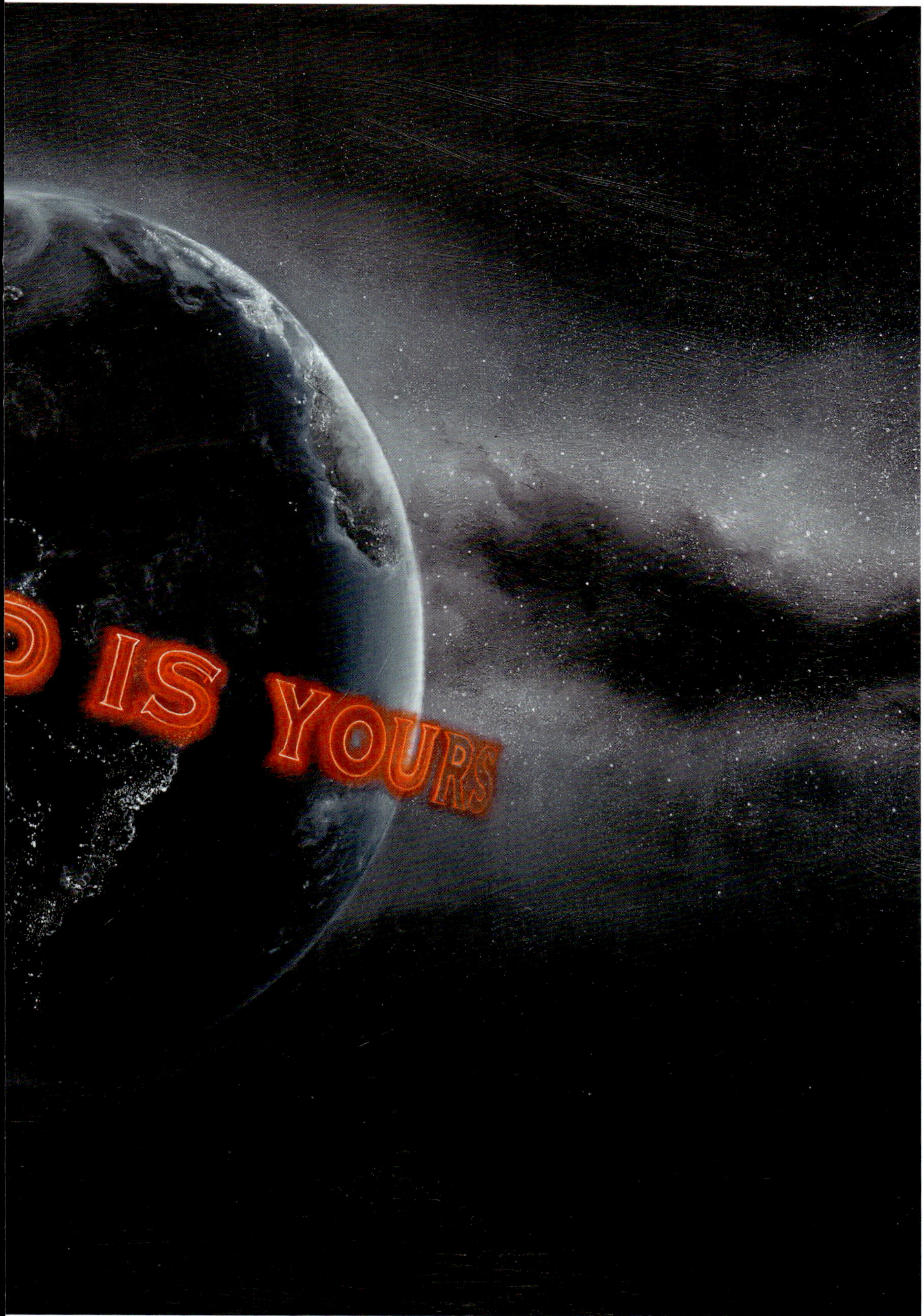

It Was Never Yours, 2019
Oil on paper
Photo: Paul Salveson

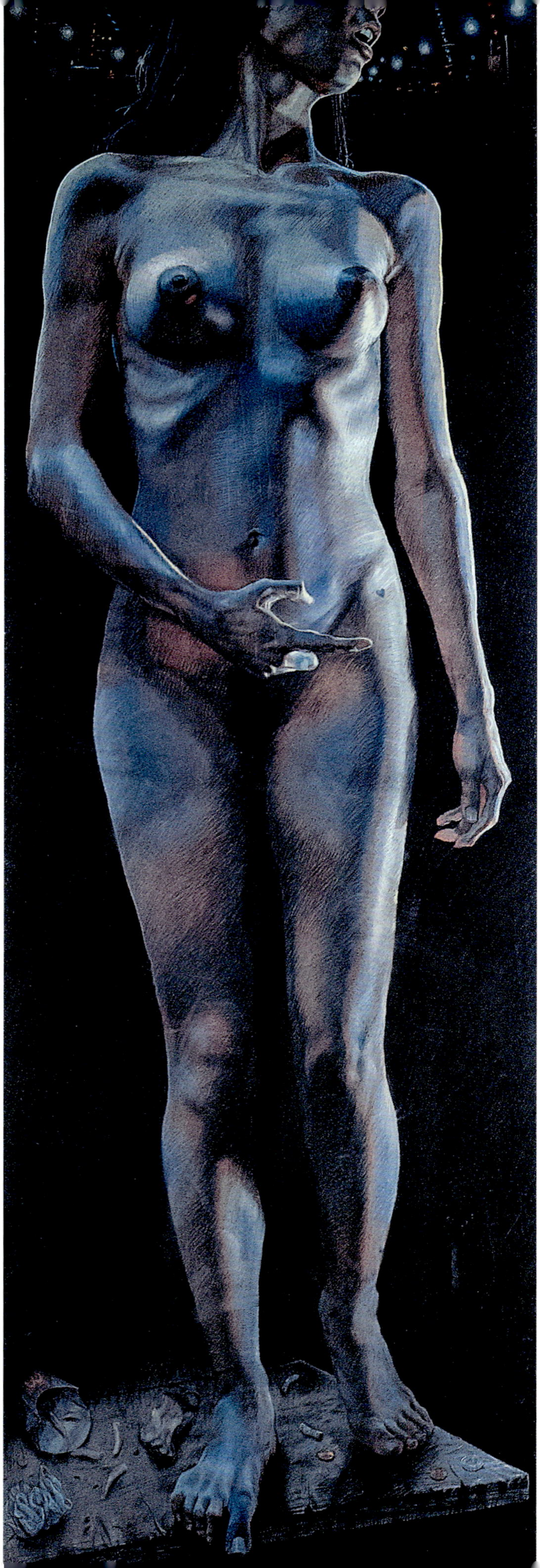

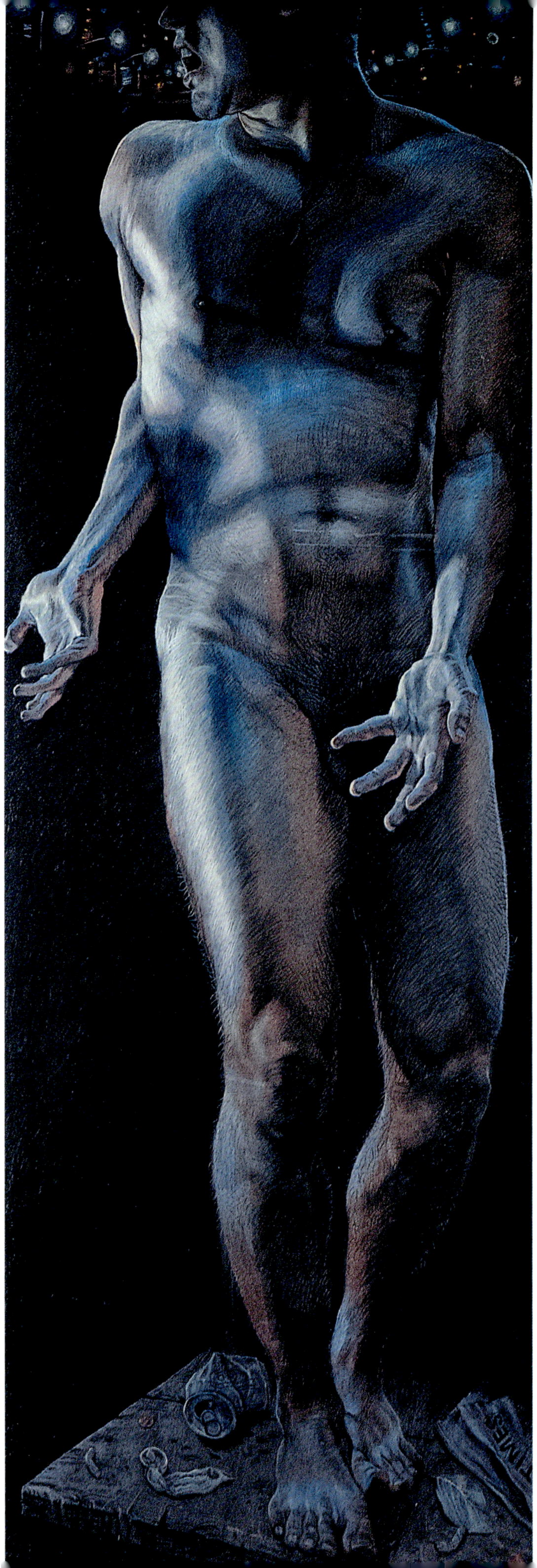

Expulsion from the Great City, 2002
Pastel on paper
Photo: Blaffer Art Museum

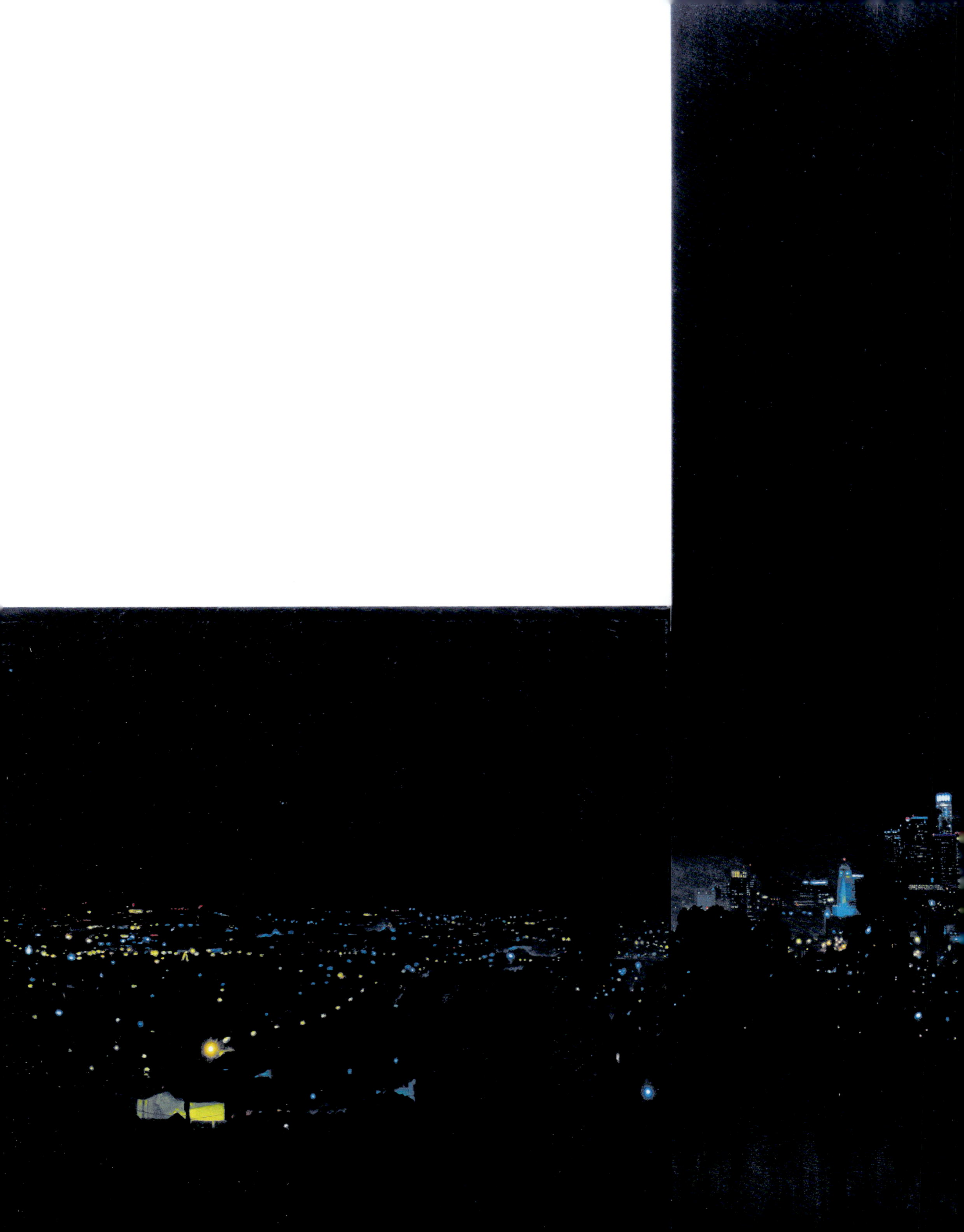

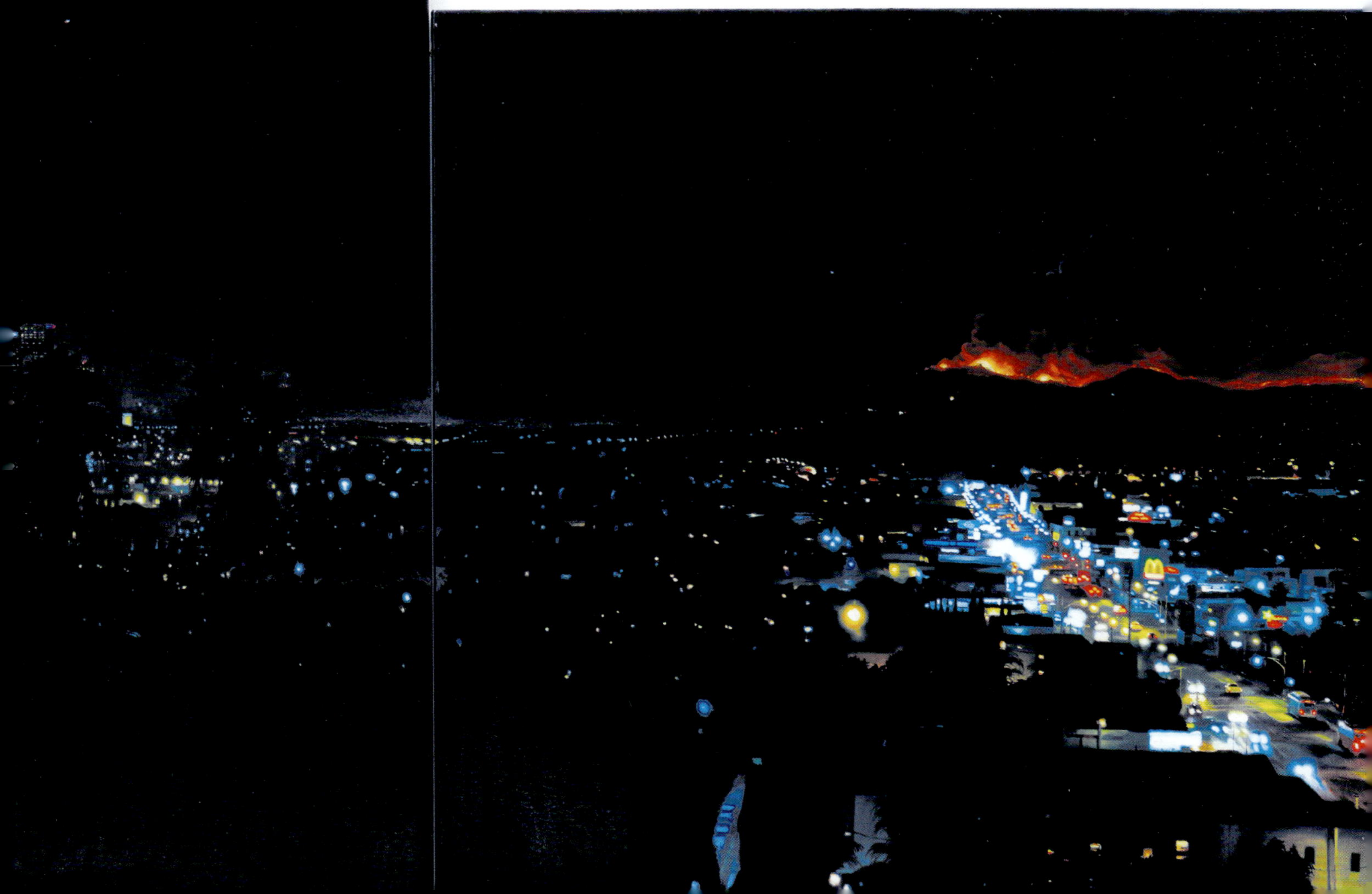

***Burn Baby Burn*, 2009**
Oil on canvas
Photo: Elon Schoenholz

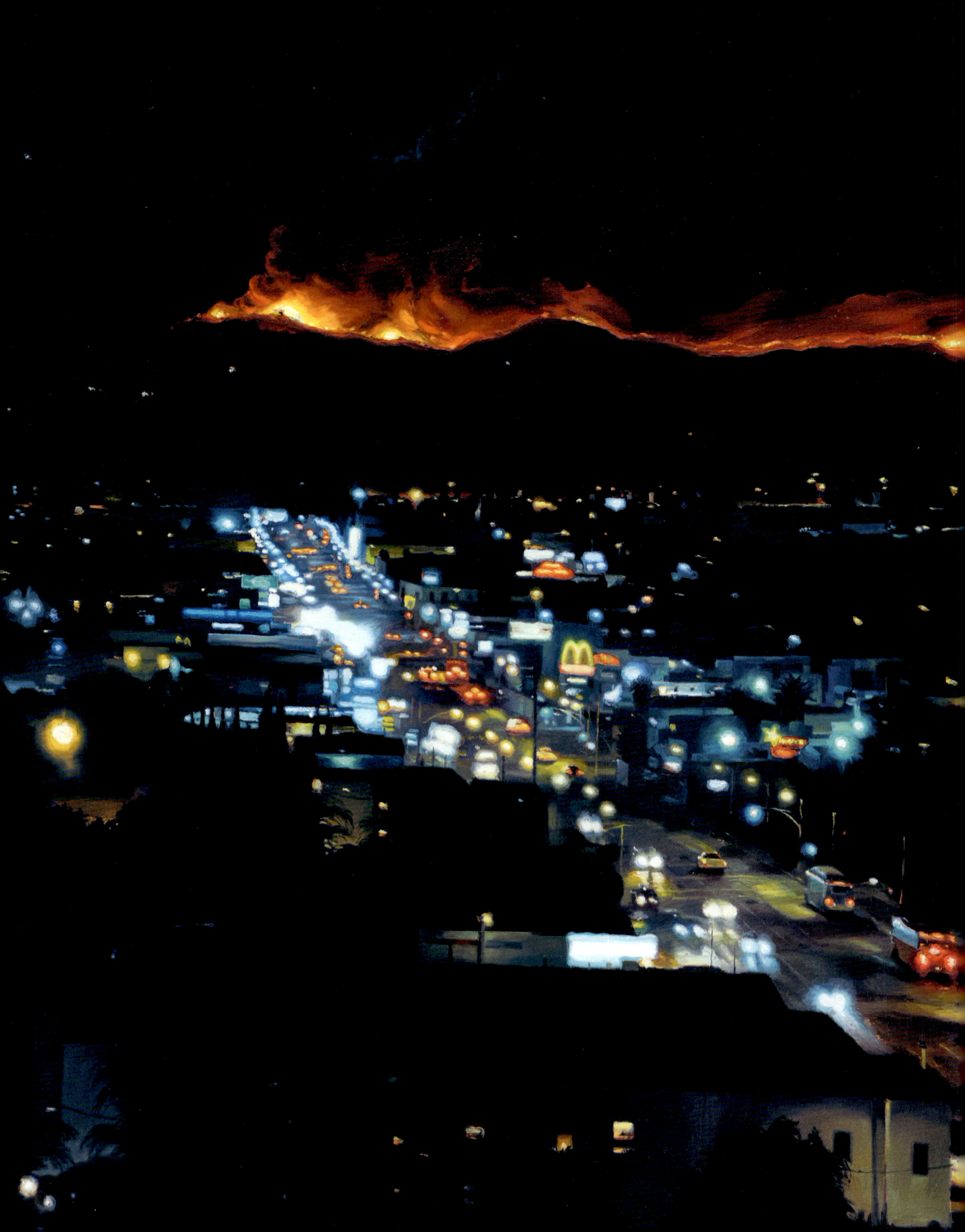

When I was seventeen
It was a very good year
When I was twenty one
It was a very good year
When I was thirty five
It was a very good year

—**FRANK SINATRA**
excerpt from "It Was a Very Good Year" (1965)

Somewhere in South Texas

EVAN GARZA

We didn't cross the border, the border crossed us. I don't mean this as hyperbole or an example of immigrant rights activist rhetoric (which it is), I mean it actually happened. In 1848, the Treaty of Guadalupe Hidalgo brought an end to the Mexican–American War and created the greatest territorial expansion in American history.[1] The agreement declared the United States' annexation of fifty-five percent of Mexico's territory, including all land north of the Rio Grande River, which the Treaty established as the new US–Mexico border. Norteños, or citizens of the regions of northern Mexico, were free to migrate to Mexico's new territory south of the river or to remain and be accorded American citizenship, thereby likely making this mid-nineteenth century land-grab the single greatest wholesale granting of naturalization to native Mexicans in American history.[2]

My parents were born and raised in the border town of Laredo, Texas, in the 1950s, and both were fourth-generation Americans whose fathers had worked their way up from the bottom to become successful real estate and banking executives, respectively. My mother, Celina, the eldest of ten children, grew up on a bone-dry ranch named for her father Isauro and his sons just five miles east of the border. Each of my parents' families were native to Laredo and the territory north of the river for centuries before the annexation of Texas. Therefore, my norteño ancestors and thousands of other families in what is now South Texas became Americans either by default or by force. The geographic inheritance of the region is one of perpetual contestation.

Vincent Valdez's work is not only a product of South Texas, it couldn't exist without it. The unflinching incisiveness of his practice—its sharpness, immediacy, and the simultaneous intoxication and revulsion his work inspires in its viewers—is made of the same stuff as South Texas: its climate hot and unpredictable, its terrain expansive, unforgiving, and wrought with historical legacies of violence, defeat, and resilience. The region comprises the territory from San Antonio to the US–Mexico border and extends to the Lower Rio Grande Valley, the verdant territory where the river meets the Gulf of Mexico. South Texas is the geographic and historical rudder of Texas, having guided her from the Indigenous sovereignty of the bands of Coahuiltecan, Karankawa, Caddo, Comanche, Lipan Apache, and Kiowa tribes to Spanish colonial rule, the Republic of Texas, and her subsequent annexation by the United States in its imperial expansion west to the Pacific Coast. Not unlike Valdez's work, the historical character of South Texas is its ongoing debate about who belongs and who doesn't, who has a claim to this land and who is forbidden, and the violence that befalls those who are told they don't belong.

There is a complicated duality about both the border region and Tejanos themselves which most Americans will never know, much less understand. It is something akin to being a part of two distinct and overlapping worlds, like living at the center of a Venn diagram, and never belonging to either group entirely. We are Mexican and American, and simultaneously neither. Like most forms of cultural inheritance rooted in displacement and discrimination, this is both a unique source of pride as well as a wound. This anxiety is manifest in Valdez's candid work *Somewhere In South Texas* (2015–2020), a series of seventeen drawings which combine illustrated scenes often seen in the border region with the historical anticipation of brutality and the contemporary specter of government surveillance.

Despite their quick and inexact renderings in ink and their relative compositional restraint, the picture Valdez paints of the US–Mexico border region is one of incredible accuracy. Individual scenes from the series—eighteen-wheelers flanked by palm trees, grackles gathering on a radio tower, a liquor store with a man on horseback in its drive-thru—conjure defining cultural and sensorial textures straight out of South Texas. Particularly for viewers from the border region, the sensations these drawings recall are rich and real. Standing before these works, I can practically smell the dry mesquite trees and the scent of diesel gas. For a series entirely devoid of chromatic hue, the *Somewhere In South Texas* works are colored by an unsettling conflation of xenophobia, surveillance, lived experience, and dignity.

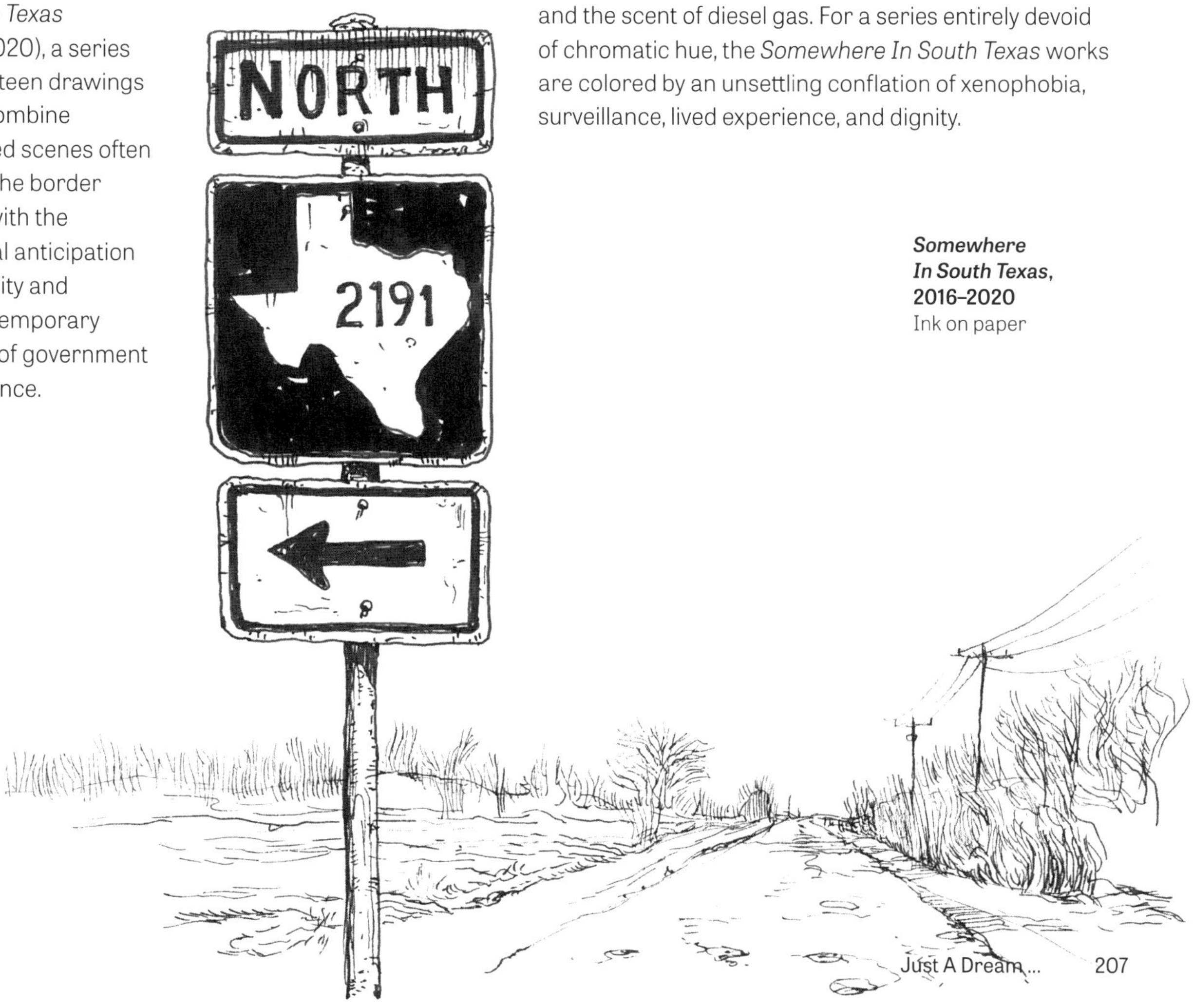

***Somewhere In South Texas*, 2016–2020**
Ink on paper

Valdez produced the drawings at a moment of remarkable cultural and demographic shifts in Texas and the United States, at a time when national perceptions of Hispanics and Latines are more xenophobic and politically polarizing than at perhaps any other time in modern American history.[3] Each work was drawn from observation during a trip through South Texas with a group of high school students from the School of the Americas. The series was later printed at Hare & Hound Press in San Antonio in early 2020 for *No Man's Land*, a group show at Houston's Station Museum that closed almost immediately after opening in the early days of the pandemic. The exhibition sought to explore legacies of colonialism and forced displacement, largely invisible contexts which Valdez's works make palpable. The series was later exhibited at the San Antonio Museum of Art as part of the 2021 *Texas Biennial*, a multi-museum project co-curated by this author that explored complicated historical legacies in the midst of tremendous global change.

In recent years, human rights abuses and injustice at the US–Mexico border, ICE raids, and the abject failure of US immigration law to protect migrants, asylum seekers, and their children have intensified national debates about the legality—and the very humanity—of Latinx, Latin American, and Brown people on what is now American soil. Families have been forcibly separated, kids placed in cages, floating barbed buoy barriers placed in the Rio Grande. At the time of this writing, razor-wire fences and walls of shipping containers await migrants along the river in Eagle Pass, Texas, across the street from a golf course.[4] If this weren't enough, Governor Greg Abbott recently announced, much to the chagrin of the federal government, that the state is building an 80-acre base camp here for Texas National Guard soldiers who are deployed for Operation Lone Star, the $10 billion state effort to deter people from immigrating into Texas illegally.[5] More than 175 years since the annexation of Texas from Mexico, the debate—if it can be called that—about who has jurisdiction and control of the land continues to rage and enrage.

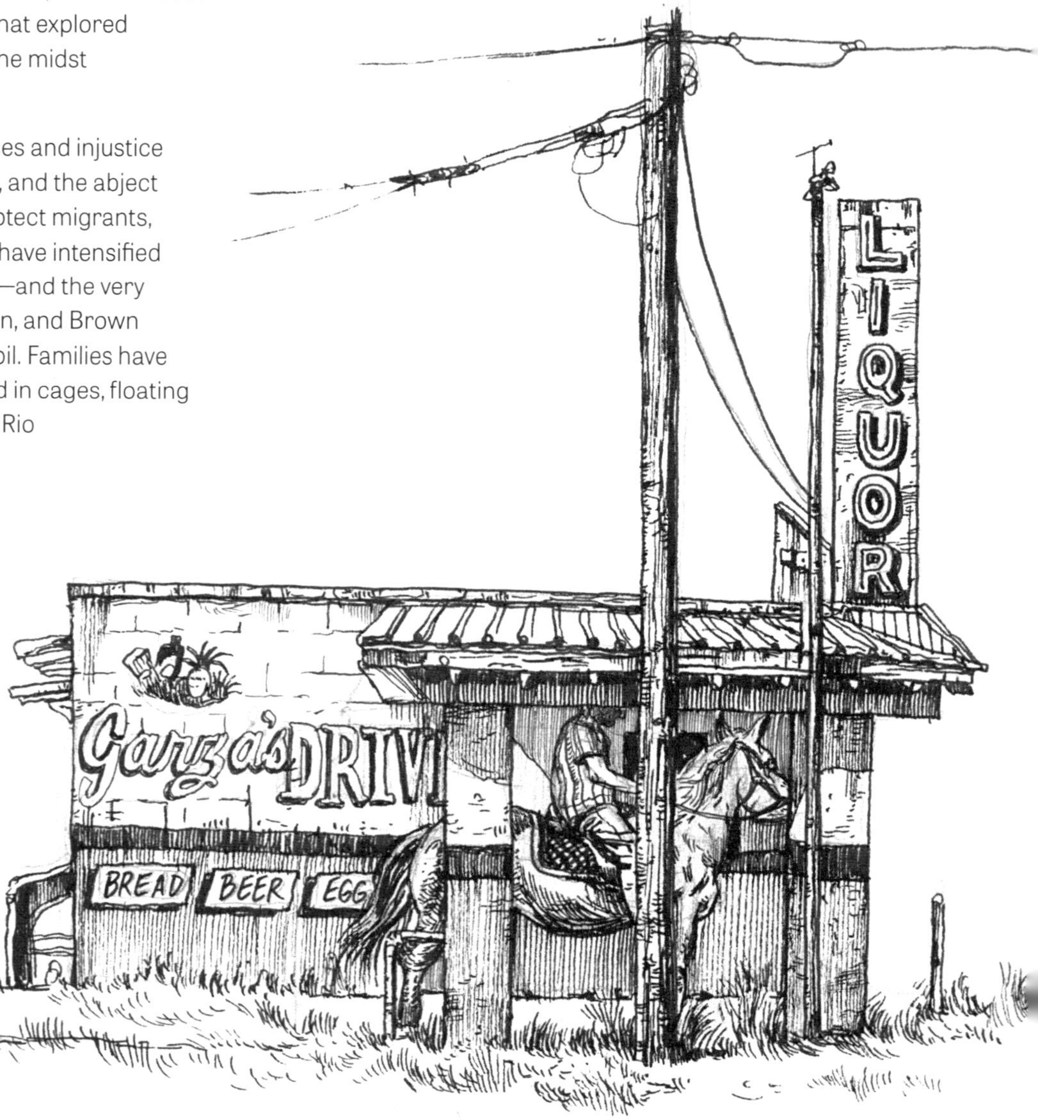

A drawing in the series features a US Border Patrol bicycle unit cycling above a serene and verdant river scene; a caption in the corner reads, "BORDER AGENTS ON THE RIO GRANDE." The water is remarkably still. The tension of implied movement permeates the entire composition. The riverbanks are lined with plant life which, on the left bank, seems to billow upwards like smoke or lilting flames. By contrast, in the hinterland across the river a vertical pattern of incomplete inorganic lines appears to faintly whisper the threat of a fence. Is the view of the center of the river from the perspective of a migrant or a security camera? The tranquility that might otherwise define this riparian scene is disturbed by the threat that literally and figuratively hangs over the Rio Grande.

Other works in the series are less subtle. One drawing depicts the ferocious head of a snarling dog captured mid-bark, whose large fangs send saliva in all directions. Its furry ears seem transformed into makeshift horns. The canine's ferocity is matched only by the aggressive negative space around it, forcing the viewer to confront the sheer terror of the beast and leaving us to question what might have provoked it. The dog's breed is commonly used by the US Customs and Border Patrol (CBP) Canine Program, whose express purpose is "terrorist detection and apprehension," language that openly camouflages an intent to racially profile.[6] As we've seen throughout American history, the use of canines by law enforcement is an extension of a consistent and deeply racist practice of subjecting Black and Brown communities to physical violence. Perhaps we might understand the dog's terrifying growl as concealing the very fear that motivates the State to patrol Brown bodies.

Another work illustrates the tall steel beams and chain-link of the US–Mexico border wall at a point of entry on US territory. A law enforcement vehicle bridges the divide created by the wall's open gate. Outside the vehicle, an officer stands with a darker figure whose arms appear to be behind their back. Above them, towering poles with high-intensity lighting and security cameras survey the surrounding terrain. Despite its depiction as a landscape, the work also functions as a portrait of America's southern border in the twenty-first century. As such, the work is also a portrait of a polarizing political issue, to say nothing of what the border wall represents in the lives of those who choose to cross it. The threat of arrest and legal peril continues from the scene to a note inscribed by the artist in the bottom right of the work: "NO PHOTOGRAPHY ALLOWED, WILL BE PROSECUTED."

Language is at the interpretive center of several works in *Somewhere In South Texas*, either as subject, within the composition, or in short blurbs of contextual information Valdez has selectively included. The languages at work are not only limited to textual readings, they also operate figuratively. One drawing in the series features a descending group of people depicted in the figural language of universal symbols, the kind you'd find outside a public restroom, only the figures are either armed with weapons or visibly pained and distraught.

Another work features the serif text, "If it's not right for you, leave," illustrated above the ominous white cloud of a petrochemical exhaust chimney. These flare stacks, which burn off excess natural gas, have come to increasingly disfeature the landscape of the South Texas plains since the dawn of the "shale boom" in the mid-2000s,[7] when landowners increasingly began fracking on properties along the Eagle Ford Shale.[8] The quote was made by a border agent to Valdez's students in describing his own failed attempts at becoming a cop.[9] However, this message carries an additionally sinister significance. "If it's not right for you, leave," is a uniquely American sentiment historically directed at foreigners, immigrants, and anyone from somewhere else, a toxic byproduct of xenophobia and coloniality.

Spanish language is featured on highway signs for a clothing and mattress store in one work, on others it appears hand-drawn on jugs and buckets of water. In another, a sign welcoming children and mothers to a refugee center reads "Bienvenidos Amigos," or "Welcome, Friends," above a map of the United States and a children's smiling toy train. Arrows superimposed on the map present paths from regions of northern Mexico to various corners of America. Despite the sign's well-meaning text, the image's subtext is not welcoming. Valdez has emphasized this apprehension by imagining the toy locomotive as spewing dark fumes of thick black smoke into the air, obscuring the letters that spell "America." The conceptual exercise at work lays bare how the routine emptiness of language can obscure historical and ongoing trauma.

It must be said that there are also brilliant glimmers of pride among these drawings, like cactus flowers bursting with color and the promise of life despite the threat of thorns. The scene of one such work in particular could only be found in South Texas: a man on horseback waiting patiently under the awning of a small liquor store drive-thru. The physical structure is no bigger than a storage shed, and signs advertising the sale of bread, beer, and eggs are posted on the brick wall of "Garza's Drive-In." (No relation to this author that I'm aware of, but verifiable proof that my people are from the borderland.) A wooden utility pole and power lines bring energy to the vertical "LIQUOR" sign above the drive-thru window. This is a scene of considerable disjunction—so is South Texas—and yet it's real. In the lower corner of the work, Valdez acknowledges the viewer's disbelief: "SOUTH TEXAS. YES. I REALLY SAW THIS."

With these sixteen works, Valdez draws connections between historical trauma, present day politics, and the land on which these events have played out. His insistence on depicting cultures and conditions as they are here reveals a region fraught with contrasts and contestations, certain fears and uncertain futures. The vast expanse of Texas would be almost hazardously open to interpretation were it not fenced in by history. In Valdez's hands, the searing and complicated reality of this place is just as open, just as wild and unending as the South Texas landscape.

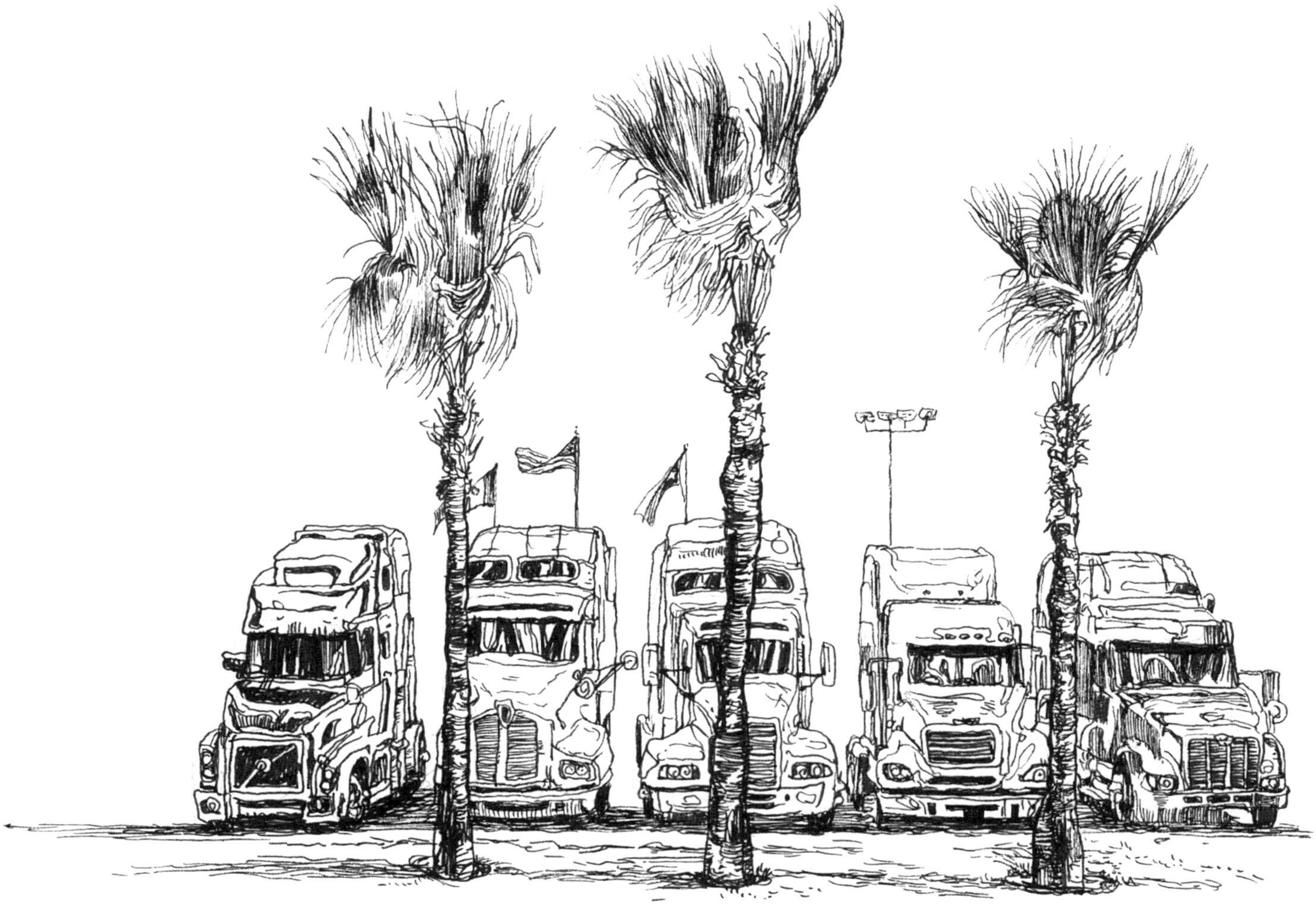

[1] US Department of State, Office of the Historian, "The Annexation of Texas, the Mexican-American War, and the Treaty of Guadalupe-Hidalgo, 1845–1848," https://history.state.gov/milestones/1830-1860/texas-annexation.

[2] National Archives, "Treaty of Guadalupe Hidalgo (1848)," https://www.archives.gov/milestone-documents/treaty-of-guadalupe-hidalgo.

[3] Trent Ollerenshaw and Ashley Jardina, "The Asymmetric Polarization of Immigration Opinion in the United States," *Public Opinion Quarterly* 87, no. 4 (December 1, 2023), pp. 1038–53. https://doi.org/10.1093/poq/nfad048.

[4] Uriel J. García, "In Eagle Pass, a tense border standoff between Texas and the federal government is reaching a crescendo," *The Texas Tribune*, January 22, 2024, https://www.texastribune.org/2024/01/22/texas-border-patrol-immigration-enforcement-eagle-pass-park.

[5] Uriel J. García and Davis Winkie, "Texas to build 80-acre base in Eagle Pass for National Guard troops," *The Texas Tribune*, February 16, 2024, https://www.texastribune.org/2024/02/16/texas-border-national-guard-base-eagle-pass.

[6] US Customs and Border Protection, "Canine Program," December 21, 2023, https://www.cbp.gov/border-security/canine-program.

[7] Robert Rapier, "How the Shale Boom Turned the World Upside Down," *Forbes*, April 21, 2017, https://www.forbes.com/sites/rrapier/2017/04/21/how-the-shale-boom-turned-the-world-upside-down/?sh=6640613f77d2.

[8] Texas Commission on Environmental Quality, "Eagle Ford Shale Geological Area," April 27, 2023, https://www.tceq.texas.gov/airquality/eagleford.

[9] In the artist's words: "The text 'If it's not right for you, leave' was spoken by a Homeland Security agent to the students, after describing to them how he arrived in the Valley from Boston. After failing to get hired by his local police department, a friend encouraged him to join the agency down south as hiring standards were low and the demand was high. The students were inspiringly quick to react to his contradictions and hypocrisy about seeking a change for a better life, his statements about leaving home, as well as his comments about not feeling it necessary to attempt to learn Spanish as a requirement for his line of work."

Vincent Valdez

SOLO UN SUEÑO ...

VINCENT VALDEZ: NUEVA PLEGARIA ESTADOUNIDENSE[1]

Por Denise Markonish

"El futuro es oscuro, y creo que eso es, en general, lo mejor para el futuro".
—Virginia Woolf[2]

"Solo quienes tienen esperanza pueden sacar provecho de las lágrimas. Cuando terminan de llorar, se sienten mejor. Pero quienes no tienen esperanza, cuya angustia es básica y permanente, nada bueno consiguen con llorar. Nada cambia para esas personas. En general, lo saben, pero aun así no pueden dejar de llorar".
—Nathanael West[3]

El futuro parecía oscuro, y las lágrimas se sentían calientes. Era el 9 de noviembre de 2016, un día en el que muchas personas se despertaron con una noticia que cambiaría el rumbo de Estados Unidos. Esa mañana amanecí en San Antonio, Texas, donde me alistaba para abrir un trío de exposiciones en Artpace. Mientras me quedaba dormida la noche anterior, pensaba: "Tal vez salga todo bien". Cuando miré mi teléfono a las tres de la mañana, me di cuenta de que mi pensamiento estaba muy alejado de la realidad. Así que, con los ojos empañados, a punto de llorar y, en general, aturdida, me dirigí al estudio de Vincent Valdez. Había conocido a su compañera Adriana Corral (una artista increíble por mérito propio) un año antes, y cuando llegué a la estación de bomberos reformada donde vivían y trabajaban, lo primero que vi fue un enorme dibujo sobre el piso. La imagen en blanco y negro con la que me encontré era la de un águila americana tendida sobre el dorso, sin vida, pero con sus plumas suaves todavía un poco animadas, como si acabara de exhalar su último aliento. Por suerte estaba enmarcada, porque si no, mis lágrimas hubieran manchado la superficie.

Al ver *este* dibujo en *ese* momento sentí como si Vincent me hubiera quitado una terrible ilusión. Presentar, después de una elección trágica, una imagen de nuestro país vulnerable y moribundo, parecía muy difícil de soportar. A lo largo de los años Vincent y yo nos hemos convertido en grandes colaboradores, amigos y colegas, razón por la cual, en este ensayo, verán inusualmente un cambio del "Vincent" personal al "Valdez" profesional. Esto refleja la profunda interrelación que existe entre artistas y curadores. La imagen, titulada *Réquiem*, en honor a los rituales que honran la muerte, perdura casi ocho años después. En 2019, invité a Vincent y a Adriana a presentar una nueva versión de esta pieza para la exposición *Sufro de realidad* del Massachusetts Museum of Contemporary Art (MASS MoCA). Para esta otra presentación, el águila se fundió en bronce con una pátina de negro carbón hecha con cenizas de papeles quemados. Los papeles contenían historias que los dos artistas recolectaron de 243 estadounidenses (el número hace referencia a la edad que cumplía Estados Unidos ese año). Entre las personas que contribuyeron, había artistas, personas en prisión, activistas, docentes, personas sin hogar, abogados de inmigración, asistentes sociales, ambientalistas, músicos, trabajadores industriales, niñeros, conductores de autobús, inmigrantes, curanderos, cajeros de tiendas, budistas, periodistas, trabajadores civiles, enfermeros, historiadores, jardineros, custodios, abogados de derechos humanos, soldados, etc. Cada entrada incluía una fecha y una descripción de un momento personal o histórico importante, y en conjunto contaban la historia del pueblo de Estados Unidos. El águila fue llevada en procesión por las galerías antes de recostarla para que descansara frente a una pared en la cual Adriana había grabado meticulosamente estas fechas. El silencio reinaba en la habitación, excepto por la triste música lúgubre que tocaban los músicos de la zona del sur de Texas, a los que Vincent se unió como trompetista.

El Testigo

"Pero ¿cómo podemos ser testigos de un mundo que va hacia su propia ruina con los ojos vendados y el rostro cubierto, de una república que colapsa sin lucidez ni orgullo, temerosa y humillada? La ceguera es lo más desesperante, porque los condenados creen que pueden dirigir su propio naufragio, juran que pueden mantener todo bajo control técnicamente, que no se necesita un nuevo dios o un nuevo cielo, solo prohibiciones, expertos y médicos. Pánico y engaño". —
Giorgio Agamben[4]

Esta inquietante evocación del estado de ánimo del momento me llevó a creer que Vincent era una especie de vidente mágico; ya que el dibujo no se había terminado esa mañana y se había estado trabajando en él mucho antes de que las cosas colapsaran. Sin embargo, Vincent no tiene nada de sobrenatural. Solo es testigo del mundo, no tiene miedo de quitar el velo, de prestar profunda atención ni de comprender que la historia sucede en el momento en que la captamos. Sabe que el pasado es un fantasma que nos hostiga en el presente. Afirma: "Soy un observador. Soy testigo. Me comprometo a registrarlo. A testificar. Elijo enfrentar al mundo en lugar de mirar hacia otro lado".[5] Como los cuatro jinetes del Apocalipsis, Vincent revela lo que sabemos que es verdad: es difícil encontrar esperanza en un mundo en llamas. Pero, al mismo tiempo, debemos tratar de visualizar aquello de lo que parece demasiado doloroso hablar —y más doloroso aún enfrentar— y tratar de combatirlo.

Hay valentía en desnudar el mundo, decirnos que no debemos mirar para otro lado. Susan Sontag hablaba a menudo de esta urgencia por ver la verdad. Primero, en *Ante el dolor de los demás*, escribe: "Debemos permitir que las imágenes atroces nos persigan. Aunque solo se trate de muestras, y posiblemente no podamos abarcar la mayor parte de la realidad a que se refieren, cumplen una función esencial. Las imágenes dicen: 'Esto es lo que los seres humanos son capaces de hacer y, tal vez, lo que se ofrezcan a hacer con entusiasmo, convencidos de que es lo justo'. No lo olvides".[6] Esta compulsión por mirar hacia lo que sucede en lugar de hacia otro lado es lo que convierte a Vincent en el artista más hábil para imaginar su época. Igual que Goya —de quien Sontag habla en este libro—, no evita el horror, sino que lo saca a la luz para que nosotros y nosotras tampoco podamos evitarlo. Usar la pintura como tablero de mensajes es complejo, dado que se trata de un medio esencialmente mudo; no obstante, Vincent sabe que puede hablar sin palabras, con un silencio ensordecedor. En *Estética del silencio*, Sontag aborda esta necesidad de arte que puede ser silencioso con estas palabras: "El arte tradicional invita a mirar. El arte silencioso engendra la necesidad de fijar la vista". Y continúa: "Quizás, el acto de fijar la vista sea el punto más alejado de la historia, y el más cercano a la eternidad, al que puede llegar el arte contemporáneo".[7] Este llamado al silencio es también un llamado a detener el tiempo y ofrecernos la posibilidad de observar. Es la oportunidad de ver las plumas suaves del águila panza arriba y preguntarnos cómo llegamos hasta este lugar y adónde podríamos ir después.

Lo extraordinario, y también inquietante, es que, desde pequeño, Vincent ya comprendía su responsabilidad de velar por un mundo que a menudo permanece ciego. Comenzó su carrera muy joven —como queda demostrado en un video de 1987—, siempre dibujando e incluso metiéndose en problemas por hacer la tarea de arte de otros niños en la escuela. Cuando Vincent tenía nueve años participó en el proyecto de mural organizado por Alex Rubio, artista público y mentor de artes de su San Antonio natal. Rubio se dio cuenta muy rápido de que Vincent no era como cualquier otro niño, y muy pronto el joven artista ya pintaba junto con su mentor. En el video, vemos la entrevista de un noticiero local a los niños y niñas que trabajaban en el mural original patrocinado por la escuela. La reportera escucha a una niña que pinta escenas idílicas de flores, hogares armoniosos, mascotas y mariposas... lo normal para cualquier persona de diez años. Luego, se encuentra con Vincent, quien pinta la siguiente escena: un campo de trabajadores recogiendo la cosecha mientras aviones de combate estadounidenses caen en picada por encima de ellos, con un cartel que dice "Hagan comida, no la guerra", todo ante un cielo que parece reflejar las consecuencias de lluvias nucleares. La mira a los ojos y le dice: En el futuro, ¿quedará algún animal, alguna flor o aire para respirar? ¿Estaré aquí todavía?". Vemos cómo la reportera retrocede y busca rápidamente a algún niño que esté pintando un cachorrito, en un intento desesperado por salvar su historia y su alma. Pero ella no comprendió que Vincent no hacía referencia a una aniquilación completa, sino que buscaba advertirnos de que no fuéramos complacientes porque nos enfrentamos a un futuro incierto.

Con esta incertidumbre, Vincent nos ofrece una nueva plegaria estadounidense, una que no se basa en la religión, sino en un optimismo cauteloso, una plegaria que revela las verdades que la historia ha oscurecido. ¿Qué significa rezar por algo en lo que no sabemos si creemos? ¿Existen personas parecidas que están enfermas y cansadas y afligidas? ¿Vemos los ojos de las demás personas que están al otro lado de la habitación, ligeramente rojos? ¿Nuestros compatriotas responden a nuestro llamado y nos aseguran que no estamos solos? ¿Nos confirmamos unos a otros que, como escribió Langston Hughes, "Oh sí, lo digo claro, América nunca fue América para mí, y aun así pronuncio este juramento: '¡América lo será!'?".[8] Es en este lugar, y solamente aquí, el lugar de esta plegaria, el de las creencias a pesar de las probabilidades, donde las pinturas de soldados y las de cachorritos coexisten y deben coexistir. Este foco en la ambigüedad y la desolación, mezcladas con esperanza, es lo que hace que la obra de Vincent sea tan humana y, me atrevo a decir, esperanzadora, porque nos recuerda que aún estamos vivos y que debemos abrirnos paso entre los escombros del hongo nuclear.

La Pelea

"Celebrar mientras aún estamos peleando es quizás lo que representa el comportamiento de este país más que cualquier otra cosa. Ser testigos de tanta muerte que tranquilamente podría ser la nuestra es presionar para redefinir el 'país' hasta que se vuelva un lugar donde haya orgullo Y seguridad... Entonces la comunidad se alimenta más de sí misma, pero no se olvida de celebrar, y no se olvida de cantar". —Hanif Abdurraqib[9]

No sorprende que Valdez, en general, represente esta pelea con imágenes de boxeadores. En *Del boxeo*, Joyce Carol Oates escribe sobre el deporte como una metáfora de la humanidad. Afirma: "Considerado en abstracto, el cuadrilátero de boxeo es una especie de altar, uno de esos espacios legendarios donde las leyes de una nación quedan suspendidas: cuerdas adentro, en el transcurso de un round de tres minutos regulado de manera oficial, un hombre puede morir a manos de su contrincante, pero no puede ser asesinado legalmente. El boxeo habita un espacio sagrado anterior a la civilización; o, para citar a D. H. Lawrence, anterior a que Dios fuera amor. Si ello sugiere una ceremonia salvaje o un rito expiatorio, también sugiere la futilidad de tales gestos. Pues, ¿qué posible expiación es el combate librado si ha de ser en breve librado otra vez... y de nuevo una vez más? El combate de boxeo es la mismísima imagen —y tanto más aterradora por ser tan estilizada— de la agresividad colectiva de la humanidad, de su continua demencia histórica".[10] Y nos volvemos a encontrar con un lugar de adoración, pero este imita el mundo mediante sus eternos ciclos de violencia real y actuada. Entre 2001 y 2004, Valdez creó la serie *Estaciones*, en la que narra la última pelea de un boxeador, sus esperanzas, sueños y posibilidades, pero también el fin último de su realidad. Los trece carboncillos de gran escala se refieren a las estaciones del vía crucis, la tradicional imagen del ciclo de Jesucristo el día de la crucifixión. A lo largo de la historia del arte, las estaciones han sido representadas muchas veces, desde Giotto hasta Picasso; no obstante, la versión que más resuena asociada a Valdez es la interpretación que hace Barnett Newman de este tema, creada entre 1958 y 1966. Las pinturas de Newman están hechas completamente en blanco y negro, con sus característicos zips (cierres) de pintura en sentido vertical. La paleta es similar a la de los carboncillos de Valdez; pero también lo es la abstracción de Newman con respecto a este tema, que para el artista se trata de una reflexión sobre la humanidad y un homenaje a las víctimas del Holocausto, del mismo modo que Valdez pone el foco en el boxeo como símbolo de la lucha por la dignidad y la supervivencia.

En *Estaciones* de Valdez, como destaca Oates, el cuadrilátero de boxeo es el escenario; transitamos imágenes que pasan por la euforia, la derrota y, finalmente, la desesperación. *Estaciones: El hombre más fuerte del mundo es el que camina solo* muestra a nuestro protagonista ingresando al estadio, con la capucha de la bata puesta y expresión de determinación. Es el que lleva las de perder, pero aun así camina frente a los fanáticos de su oponente sin notar las cámaras que apuntan a su cara. Prácticamente podemos escuchar la estridencia de la multitud, tan fuerte como el sonido de la sangre que bombea en la cabeza del boxeador mientras se prepara para subir al cuadrilátero. En este momento, no hay signos de que le espere la derrota, y como buen luchador, da por sentada la victoria. Asimismo, en *Estaciones: Evento principal* se ve a nuestro boxeador de pie, alto sobre el cuadrilátero, listo para pelear. A partir de aquí, se desata la tragedia. *Estaciones: Buen desempeño de nuestro ganador esta noche* lo muestra en el suelo, chorreando sangre de la cabeza mientras personas del público lo atienden. *Estaciones: Entonces cayó una vez más* es una vista aérea de la derrota: brazos y piernas abiertos, un tatuaje fantasmagórico de Jesús en el pecho del boxeador. La pieza es precursora de *Estaciones IX: Noqueado*, en la que el boxeador descansa estirado sobre una camilla (¿o es, acaso, un altar?). Es difícil saber si está vivo o muerto, y Valdez no revela la respuesta.

Casi veinte años después, Valdez pintó *Solo un sueño (En Estados Unidos)* (2020-2021). La pintura de ocho pies de alto (dos metros y medio) muestra a un boxeador sentado en un banco, con los brazos pesados a los costados, abierto de piernas. Tiene la cara muy golpeada. Aquí Valdez rompe la monocromía de grises de la pintura y agrega toques de rojo alrededor de los ojos, las rodillas y la cara maltrecha. A sus pies, encontramos los residuos de basura del evento: billetes de dólar, monedas, latas aplastadas, bollos de papel, palomitas de maíz desparramadas, un balde, etc. Es imposible saber si estamos en el medio del combate o si este ya terminó, pero queda claro que, a pesar de la actitud de derrota y el cuerpo destrozado, el boxeador sigue con los ojos abiertos y no se ha rendido. Cuesta no pensar en la película *Toro Salvaje* (1980) de Martin Scorsese, que muestra el ascenso y la caída del boxeador Jake LaMotta. La representación de Valdez recuerda la conmovedora interpretación que hace Robert De Niro de este luchador ya entrado en años. Valdez transmite aún más gravedad a su pintura: en lugar de fijarse a la pared como se hace tradicionalmente, el lienzo está sobre un conjunto de ladrillos, lo que hace que el peso del sujeto se desplace aún más hacia el suelo. Detrás de la pintura emana suavemente el sonido de la canción de 1958 "Solo un sueño" de Jimmy Clanton. La letra alegre de los años cincuenta habla de la pérdida de un amor, y adopta un contexto metafórico más amplio cuando se une a la pintura de Valdez, que agrega la frase "En Estados Unidos" a su título. Clanton canta: "Sé que lo nuestro no hubiera durado / No logramos que durara en el pasado / Es solo un sueño que sueño en vano / Contigo solo podía sufrir".[11] Pero queda claro que Valdez no está hablando de amor, ni siquiera de boxeo, sino del sueño destrozado de Estados Unidos, un país derrotado, pero que todavía no está listo para rendirse. Porque, como vuelve resumir Oates: "El boxeador hace visible algo que en nosotros es invisible, y en consecuencia, nos define, y se define a sí mismo, en una simple acción consagrada".[12]

Los boxeadores de Valdez representan un tipo diferente de masculinidad, desgastada y vulnerable. Este antiheroísmo es evidente en el retrato *John* (2010–12). El subteniente John R. Holt Jr. era el mejor amigo de Valdez; después de servir como médico de combate en Irak, perdió la batalla contra el trastorno de estrés postraumático en 2009. La pintura en tamaño real de Valdez muestra a John en el campo de batalla, envuelto en humo y escombros. A diferencia de la mayoría de las imágenes de guerra, John parece temeroso y ausente a la vez, como si lo viéramos observándose a él mismo en una pesadilla. Aquí no hay gloria, especialmente si vemos la pintura junto con *Fragmentos para John* (2012), una serie de pinturas al óleo de escala íntima que muestra la secuencia de un cortejo fúnebre militar. El ataúd envuelto en una bandera es la única imagen clara, todo lo demás se disuelve en la bruma. Estos dibujos representan la ausencia, el ocultamiento no solo del ataúd, sino de la brutal realidad de la guerra y del trastorno de estrés postraumático. Valdez explica lo siguiente sobre la serie: "Los efectos apagados, disolventes y alucinatorios de estas pinturas son mi intento de traducir lo que experimenté la mañana de su funeral. Me sentí entumecido por la lluvia helada y por un sentimiento de rendición emocional".[13]

Los bordes difuminados de *Fragmentos para John* son una elección estilística que recorre gran parte de las obras de Valdez. La suavidad difumina la figura y el fondo, como si se fusionaran la memoria y la realidad. Esta característica se hace evidente en los dibujos de *Amnesia* (en desarrollo desde 2023). Estas obras, en su mayoría realizadas en lápiz de un solo color sobre papel (aunque a veces en rojo y azul juntos), presentan figuras apenas visibles y líneas tanto precisas como difuminadas. Los rostros se manifiestan justo antes de desvanecerse en el papel. Los cuerpos apenas aparecen, como si los personajes desaparecieran ante nuestros ojos. Es como la escena de *Volver al futuro* (1985) en la que Marty McFly —interpretado por Michael J. Fox— toca la guitarra en el baile de graduación luego de viajar en el tiempo hasta el momento en que sus padres se conocieron. En riesgo de afectar negativamente al futuro, las manos de McFly empiezan a desvanecerse mientras interpreta "Johnny B. Goode", de Chuck Berry. Debe volver a su tiempo antes de desaparecer frente nuestros ojos. En su libro *Esperanza en la oscuridad* (2004), Rebecca Solnit escribe sobre el poder de la amnesia. La autora afirma: "La otra aflicción que trae la amnesia es la falta de ejemplos de cambio positivo, de poder popular, pruebas de que podemos hacerlo y de que lo hemos hecho. George Orwell escribió: 'Quien controla el pasado controla el futuro. Quien controla el presente controla el pasado'. Para controlar el pasado, primero debemos conocerlo; las historias que contamos sobre quiénes fuimos y qué hicimos inciden en lo que podemos hacer y lo que haremos".[14] Y como con las manos de McFly y los retratos de Valdez, deseamos que los seres humanos que se desvanecen vuelvan a manifestarse en su totalidad; para evitar que desaparezcan, debemos permitirles contar sus historias, como hizo Valdez con John.

Así como no podemos comprender realmente los efectos de la guerra sin haberla vivido, tampoco podemos comprender los matices de la experiencia personal. Para acercarnos a esa comprensión, Valdez infunde una hermosa empatía en sus retratos de personas que suelen ser incomprendidas: el boxeador no es un salvaje, es falible; el héroe de guerra está atormentado; y el pandillero es amable y contemplativo. *Hasta pronto, Mary Ann* (2019) muestra una figura anónima sin camiseta de la cintura para arriba. El joven tiene la cabeza rapada y está cubierto de tatuajes en los brazos, el pecho y la cara, y tiene también un aire gentil. Tiene las manos entrelazadas a la altura del pecho y nos mira con ojos compasivos; está delante de una perfecta puesta de sol difuminada en azul, rosa y morado. Como en un Vermeer, la figura resplandece en un momento de reflexión interna. Si vemos el cuadro de cerca, observamos cicatrices en su pecho y el nombre "Mary Ann" tatuado en sus nudillos, en referencia a la canción de Leonard Cohen de 1967 de la que el cuadro toma su nombre. En la canción, Cohen le canta a un amor perdido: "Porque ahora necesito tu amor oculto Estoy frío como una hoja de afeitar / Te fuiste cuando te dije que tenía curiosidad / Nunca dije que fuera valiente / Hasta pronto, Marianne, es hora de que comencemos / A reír y llorar, a llorar y reír de todo eso de nuevo".[15] Casi podemos oír cómo resuena el estribillo en la cabeza del sujeto de Valdez y, aunque no conozcamos su historia, sí sabemos cómo se sienten la pérdida y el desamor, y eso lo acerca más a nuestras experiencias y a la empatía.

Los Recuerdos

"No siento que mis recuerdos hayan sido arrancados de raíz. Aunque se desvanezcan, algo queda. Como pequeñas semillas que podrían volver a germinar si llueve. Y aunque la memoria desaparezca por completo, el corazón retiene algo. Un pequeño estremecimiento o dolor, un poquito de alegría, una lágrima". —Yoko Ogawa[16]

La empatía y la amnesia son fuerzas opuestas, y la única manera de alcanzar la primera y erradicar la segunda es contando las historias de las personas olvidadas. Esta es la misión de Valdez. En sus primeras obras, como *¡Maten al pachuco malnacido!* (2001) y *El Chavez Ravine* (con Ry Cooder, 2005–7), la narrativa es potente y clara: se trata de la violencia y la expulsión de personas mexicanas y mexicoestadounidenses de Los Ángeles. Valdez es un narrador que revela historias que se suelen ignorar; y es por ello que sus obras nos llevan a considerar el lugar en el que nos encontramos hoy: un Estados Unidos profundamente dividido y en desacuerdo sobre quién merece sentirse parte de la ciudadanía. Como dijo el escritor, humanitario y superviviente del holocausto Elie Wiesel en su discurso de aceptación del Premio Nobel de 1986: "Sin memoria, nuestra existencia sería estéril y opaca, como una celda de prisión en la que no penetra la luz; como una tumba que rechaza a los vivos... si algo puede salvar a la humanidad es la memoria. Para mí, la esperanza sin memoria es como la memoria sin esperanza".[17] Oír estas historias, como la Wiesel o Valdez, nos renueva la esperanza de que la verdad pueda superar a la banalidad del mal y de que, como consecuencia, podamos esforzarnos por vivir en lugar de limitarnos a desesperar.

¡Maten al maldito pachuco malnacido! hace referencia a los Disturbios del Zoot Suit de 1943. Entre el 3 y el 8 de junio, un grupo de militares estadounidenses apostados en el sur de California chocaron con jóvenes latinos en el centro y el este de Los Ángeles. Esto provoco lo que, en esencia, fue un motín racial. Apenas un año antes, la Junta de Producción de Guerra había promulgado normas sobre el uso de la lana con el fin de conservar recursos durante la Segunda Guerra Mundial. Un estilo popular entre la comunidad latina de la época era el traje zoot, que incluía voluminosos pantalones anchos y los característicos estampados a rayas. Muchos militares estadounidenses se encontraban de licencia en Los Ángeles a principios de los años cuarenta y, al ver a los latinos, o pachucos, con los trajes zoot los enfureció el desprecio a los valores de guerra estadounidenses y empezaron a atacarlos en calles y en bares.

El conflicto más grande sucedió el 3 de junio, cuando se unieron incluso los agentes de la policía de Los Ángeles que no estaban de servicio. Milagrosamente, nadie murió, pero cientos de personas resultaron heridas y fueron detenidas. No sorprende que haya habido que esperar hasta 2023 para que la ciudad pidiera disculpas públicamente por los disturbios, a pesar de que apenas una semana después del incidente, la entonces primera dama Eleanor Roosevelt condenara los hechos y se pronunciara al respecto: "La cuestión va más allá de los trajes. Es una protesta racial. Hace tiempo que me preocupa la situación racial mexicana. Se trata de un problema que se originó hace mucho tiempo, y no siempre afrontamos estos problemas como deberíamos".[18] Los dichos de Roosevelt fueron recibidos con indignación. La llamaban comunista por abordar la discordia racial.

La composición de la pintura de Valdez es tan caótica como la historia que representa. Un suelo a cuadros rojos y blancos se inclina en una perspectiva surrealista y forzada, mientras un tumulto de figuras aparece dispersa por el salón. En primer plano, un hombre vestido con traje zoot, pantalones anchos a rayas, una cadena de oro que cuelga del cinturón, camiseta de tirantes y sombrero de fieltro, empuja con su mano la cara de un oficial de la marina que revolea una botella rota. A la derecha, otro agente está violando a una mujer; y a la izquierda, un pachuco recibe un golpe rápido en el estómago. La escena recuerda a pintores como Peter Saul y Ed Paschke, cuyo surrealismo pop y colores vivos distorsionan y exageran sus figuras. En el caso de Valdez, esta alusión estilística se presenta en la perspectiva de la habitación, el machismo exagerado de las figuras y su piel enfermiza en tonos verdosos. La pintura también hace referencia a artistas de tradición chicana, como Luis Jiménez, John Valadez, Esther Hernández, César Martínez y Gaspar Enríquez. Pero es al realista estadounidense George Bellows a quien nos remite con más claridad esta obra. Puede parecer extraño mencionar a Bellows aquí y no en relación con Estaciones, ya que era reconocido por pintar boxeadores. Pero hay algo del caos en *¡Maten al maldito pachuco malnacido!* que, a pesar de su surrealismo, representa la realidad de la pelea en un bar, hasta tal punto que podemos sentir el olor de la sangre. Las pinturas de Bellows también contenían este caos, el movimiento de los boxeadores y la multitud dentro una habitación descarnada y cargada de violencia.

El Chavez Ravine describe un panorama más amplio de las tribulaciones a las que se enfrentaron las personas mexicanas y mexicoestadounidenses en Los Ángeles en los años 40 y 50. La historia de Chavez Ravine es una historia de supresión. En la década de 1950, la zona albergaba a la mayor comunidad latina de Los Ángeles. Sin embargo, sus habitantes fueron expulsados a la fuerza cuando la ciudad cedió los terrenos para construir el Dodger Stadium. La apropiación de terrenos trajo consigo la promesa de la urbanización de Elysian Hills, un desafortunado sueño idílico que se truncó en 1958 cuando la ciudad abandonó su desarrollo. De hecho, la construcción del Dodger Stadium sepultó a la comunidad que alguna vez hiciera de la región un lugar tan animado. De 1951 a 1961, los legítimos propietarios lucharon en vano por salvar sus hogares; y dejaron tras de sí una historia que ahora se cierne tan grande como el estadio.

En 2004, el músico Ry Cooder se comunicó con Valdez y lo llevó a Los Ángeles. Cooder le pidió que colaborara en un proyecto para acompañar su siguiente disco *El Chavez Ravine*. El álbum rinde homenaje al barrio con letras como: "Chavez Ravine bloqueado / Bunker Hill derrumbado / Las mezcladoras de cemento difundiendo la palabra / Esta de aquí es mi ciudad / Es mi ciudad".[19] Para ilustrarlo, Valdez no creó un pintura convencional; sino que Cooder adquirió un carro de helados Good Humor (que significa 'buen humor') de 1953 restaurado por los padrinos del lowriding, Duke's Car Club, y Valdez lo convirtió en el guion gráfico de una historia. Valdez pintó cada centímetro del camión con las imágenes del dueño de los Dodgers, Walter O'Malley, del exjefe de la policía de Los Ángeles, William H. Parker, de J. Edgar Hoover y de las familias desplazadas. La palabra "Elysian" (Elíseo) aparece junto a planos de urbanización, y hay grafitis y guiños a la cultura *lowrider*. El dolor de la gentrificación aparece en toda la superficie, y el carro de helados, un símbolo de alegría, se contrarresta con el conflicto. La presencia del "buen humor" desplazado nos remite a la resiliencia frente a la injusticia. Tal como escribe Mike Davis en *Ciudad de cuarzo*, "Los Ángeles es... la representación del capitalismo en general. La principal relevancia —y singularidad— histórico–mundial de Los Ángeles es que ha llegado a tener el doble papel de utopía y distopía para el capitalismo avanzado. Como destacó [Bertol] Brecht, el mismo lugar simboliza tanto el cielo como el infierno".[20]

Los Estados Unidos De América

"Estados Unidos, te lo he dado todo y ahora no soy nada". —Allen Ginsberg[21]

Parece imposible escribir un ensayo sobre Valdez sin mencionar *El principio está cerca (una trilogía estadounidense), capítulo uno: La ciudad, La ciudad I* (2015–16). Se trata de una pintura de 30 pies (9 metros) de figuras del Ku Klux Klan ante un fondo con luces de ciudad y pilas de basura, todo iluminado por los faros de una camioneta de caja abierta. Es probable que, de toda la carrera de Valdez, sea la obra sobre la que más se ha escrito y discutido, y la más controversial, que ha suscitado comparaciones con Philip Guston. La contraria que hay en mí dejará muchas cosas sin decir sobre esta obra, pero lo que sí diré es que crear una pintura épica del Ku Klux Klan en el siglo XXI es un movimiento audaz, pero necesario. Asumimos, muy ingenuamente, que estas figuras encapuchadas pertenecen al pasado, pero si la insurrección del 6 de enero de 2021 en el edificio del Capitolio de Estados Unidos nos confirma algo, es que estas fuerzas del mal todavía operan con orgullo en Estados Unidos. En 1980, Gil Scott–Heron escribió "El Klan," cuya letra decía: "Quien anda con el Klan / No es un hombre, sino un demonio / Pues debajo de su blanco disfraz / He visto sus ojos".[22] Y si hay algo que nos permite hacer *La ciudad* I es mirarlos a los ojos; porque cuando nos paramos delante de la pintura, nos encontramos con las figuras que nos miran fijamente mientras nosotros les devolvemos la mirada, de ese modo se aseguran de que sepamos que el mero hecho de que no lleven capuchas, no significa que no existan. Valdez contrarrestó *La ciudad* con la serie titulada *(El principio está cerca (una trilogía estadounidense) capítulo tres: Los nuevos estadounidenses)* (en desarrollo desde 2021). Estas obras rinden homenaje a personas que tratan de generar un cambio: las artistas Adriana Corral y Teresita Fernández, los músicos Wynton Marsalis y Flaco Jiménez, y las figuras sociopolíticas Mr. Checkpoint (creador de AFTP —Always Film the Police [Filma siempre a la policía] y Always for the People [Siempre para el pueblo]— con el fin de crear ciudades más seguras compartiendo información y ofreciendo apoyo[23]) y al abogado de derechos civiles Juan Cartagena. Estos retratos de tamaño casi natural representan a sus protagonistas de frente y con dignidad. Nos miran fijamente, y nosotros también los miramos a ellos con gusto; sabemos que a pesar de los males del mundo la esperanza aún existe.[24]

Al situar las dos obras dentro de la misma serie, Valdez nos advierte que no debemos acercarnos ciegamente a la esperanza. Hanif Abdurraqib nos recuerda "el valor del optimismo mientras las ciudades arden, mientras la gente teme por su vida y la de sus seres queridos, mientras el discurso se reduce a reír a través de un coro de ansiedad".[25] Las complicaciones de este coro son fundamentales en la novela de Kurt Vonnegut *Matadero cinco* (1969), en especial cuando se le pregunta sobre la guerra al protagonista Bill Pilgrim. Mientras este piensa superficialmente en su respuesta, se da cuenta de que el epitafio perfecto para su lápida sería: "Todo era hermoso y nada dolía".[26] Por supuesto, esto no podría estar más alejado de la realidad. Durante la novela, Pilgrim, un prisionero de guerra, usa con frecuencia la frase “así son las cosas”, como si se dijera a sí mismo, y a quien esté leyendo, que debemos seguir adelante, a pesar de las realidades de la vida. Las similitudes entre el libro de Vonnegut y la misión de Valdez se hacen evidentes cuando el autor escribe: “Y me pregunté por el presente: cuán amplio era, cuán profundo era, cuánto me pertenecía y debía conservar”.[27] En la obra de Vonnegut, Pilgrim es un viajero en el tiempo que afirma haber sido abducido por una raza alienígena del planeta Tralfamadore que lo obliga a viajar a través del tiempo, lo que hace que deje de sentir miedo porque puede ver el futuro. Casualmente, los habitantes de Tralfamadore ven a través de los ojos que tienen en las manos, casi como un pintor, de la misma manera que se manifiesta el testimonio de Valdez. Pilgrim es entonces un vidente, como Valdez, por lo que resulta oportuno que el artista haya creado hace poco veinte dibujos para ilustrar la edición de 2024 de *Matadero cinco* junto con la editorial Arion Press de San Francisco.[28]

Valdez siempre se sintió atraído por este libro, por los motivos antes mencionados, pero también por razones personales. El ensayo introductorio de la edición de Arion Press dice: “Vonnegut celebró su vigésimo segundo cumpleaños vistiendo el uniforme de soldado y recién alistado en el Ejército de los Estados Unidos. Pronto fue enviado a Francia, en los últimos meses de la Segunda Guerra Mundial, a tiempo para verse envuelto en la feroz contraofensiva lanzada por la 1.ª División Panzer alemana en diciembre de 1944, conocida como la batalla de las Ardenas. El soldado Vonnegut, asignado a la 106.ª División de Infantería de los Estados Unidos como explorador de inteligencia, quedó aislado de su batallón en medio del caos reinante. Fue capturado el 19 de diciembre luego de deambular solo detrás de las líneas enemigas durante once días”.[29] Este es el telón de fondo de la experiencia de Pilgrim. Sin embargo, también es una historia que Valdez escuchó de niño, porque su tío abuelo, Ernest Valdez, fue, igual que Vonnegut, capturado por los alemanes durante la batalla de las Ardenas y retenido como prisionero de guerra. El estuche militar antiguo recreado en el que viene el libro se inspira en los objetos de la guerra que le pertenecieron a Ernest y en la última carta que envió a su familia antes de que se lo considerara desaparecido en combate. Los descarnados dibujos en tinta de Valdez ilustran varias escenas del libro, siempre con un toque diferente: la máquina de optometría se convierte en un dispositivo de viaje en el tiempo o de control estatal; un vagón de mercancías toma un giro siniestro cuando se convierte en un transporte para prisioneros de guerra; un relicario con la palabra del Señor aparece solo en la página, apartado de su dueño muerto, y una lápida cubierta por un ángel contiene el epitafio “Todo era hermoso y nada dolía”. Sin embargo, hay un dibujo que se destaca: la silueta de una mujer en tinta punteada que pareciera que está desapareciendo, como los dibujos de Valdez en *Amnesia*. La mujer tiene la cabeza vuelta hacia nosotros, y lo único que vemos con claridad son sus ojos, que nos miran a nosotros. El texto de Vonnegut que acompaña a la imagen dice lo siguiente: “Y a la mujer de Lot, por supuesto, se le dijo que no mirara hacia atrás, donde habían estado todas aquellas personas y sus hogares. Pero ella sí miró hacia atrás. Y yo la amo por eso, porque fue algo muy humano. Se convirtió en una estatua de sal. Así son las cosas. Las personas no deben mirar atrás. Ciertamente, yo ya no lo haré. Ya terminé mi libro de guerra. El próximo será divertido. Este es un fracaso. Tenía que serlo, ya que fue escrito por una estatua de sal”.[30]

Valdez nunca dejará de mirar atrás. Aún no se ha convertido en una estatua de sal, así que parece que el uso que hace de los viajes en el tiempo es el adecuado por ahora. Utiliza la reflexión para interrogar y revelar lo que hace que Estados Unidos sea el país que es. Este es el tema de las obras que están en progreso en su estudio: *Una procesión estadounidense* y *Fue un gran año* (en proceso desde 2024) Ambas comienzan con imágenes reconocibles que muchas personas recordarán haber visto por primera vez, gracias a la llegada de la cultura televisiva. En *Sobre la tiranía: veinte lecciones que aprender del siglo XX* (2017), Timothy Snyder explica cómo la literatura predijo nuestra actual cultura saturada de medios de comunicación: “Hace más de medio siglo, las novelas clásicas acerca del totalitarismo nos advertían sobre el dominio de las pantallas, la supresión de los libros, la disminución del vocabulario y las consiguientes dificultades de pensamiento. En *Fahrenheit 451*, de Ray Bradbury, publicada en 1953, los bomberos buscan y queman libros mientras la mayoría de la ciudadanía mira la televisión interactiva. En *1984*, de George Orwell, publicada en 1949, los libros están prohibidos y la televisión es bidireccional, lo que permite al gobierno observar a las personas en todo momento”.[31] Para ambas series, Valdez analizó sus propios recuerdos en busca de imágenes relevantes basadas principalmente en los medios de comunicación, aunque no las experimentara directamente él mismo. *Una procesión estadounidense* se centra en reuniones, movimientos, desfiles, etc. A Valdez le atrajo la idea de la procesión porque transmite la sensación de avanzar constantemente, algo que el artista considera que se refleja en la política estadounidense, tanto para bien como para mal. Las pinturas de esta serie incluyen la persecución del Bronco blanco de O. J. Simpson mientras huía de la policía (1994); la caravana de John F. Kennedy en Dallas el día de su asesinato (1963); el bombardeo de Dresden, Alemania, en la Segunda Guerra Mundial (1945), y una reunión del Ku Klux Klan en Washington, D. C. (1925).

En *Fue un gran año* —una referencia a la canción homónima de Frank Sinatra, de 1966— estos temas se manifiestan en forma de imágenes sobre acontecimientos importantes que ocurrieron durante la vida de Valdez y que se han quedado congeladas en el tiempo. Igual que muchas personas de nuestra generación, el artista vivió el desarrollo de estos momentos a través imágenes en movimiento en la pantalla: televisión, teatro y películas caseras. Por lo tanto, la serie es tanto una cronología de la vida de Estados Unidos como de la de Valdez. Entre otros temas, se incluyen las audiencias por el caso Irán–Contra de Oliver North (1987), la noche de la toma de posesión en que Reagan le pasó el bastón a George H. W. Bush (1989), la dinastía Bush (1989–2009), la invasión de Panamá (1989), la explosión del transbordador espacial Challenger (1986), el incendio del cabello de Michael Jackson mientras filmaba un comercial de Pepsi (1984), el desafío a la gravedad de Michael Jordan en el concurso de clavadas (1988), etc. Las pinturas en múltiples paneles representan estos temas casi en tamaño real: salen de la pantalla y ocupan un espacio como objetos independientes colocados espalda con espalda, y crean una estructura similar a la de un laberinto. En una de las duplas vemos al teniente coronel Oliver North prestando juramento durante las audiencias por el caso Irán–Contra. Este escándalo político se desató porque la administración de Reagan negoció un acuerdo ilegal para vender armas a Irán con el fin de financiar a los contras, un grupo rebelde antisandinista de Nicaragua. Alegaron que su objetivo era facilitar la liberación de rehenes estadounidenses que Hezbolá, un grupo conectado con irán, mantenía en el Líbano. North testificó acerca de la destrucción de documentos relacionados con el escándalo. En la pintura de Valdez, la boca de North está cerrada, como silenciada por su propio delito. En el lado opuesto aparece una ascensión para contrarrestar la solidez de North: Michael Jordan compitiendo en un concurso de clavadas, justo un año antes de que North subiera al estrado como testigo. En esta imagen, Jordan desafía la gravedad y nos demuestra que, si nos esforzamos, podemos detener el tiempo. Hanif Abdurraqib afirma lo siguiente sobre un concurso de clavadas de 1985 en el que participó Jordan: “Comenzó en un extremo del Market Square Arena en Indianápolis, corrió, se catapultó por sus propios medios desde la línea de tiros libres [sí, ¡desde la línea de tiros libres real!]

y permaneció suspendido y estirado por un tiempo que, hasta el día de hoy, parece una hora gloriosa. Una hora sublime. La hora que sueñas con volver a vivir desde que sus últimos granos de arena rozaron la montaña de la parte inferior del reloj. ¿Ha estado tanto tiempo en el aire que sus pies empezaron a enamorarse de la nueva superficie invisible y familiar sobre la que seguramente caminaba? Porque esa superficie tiene que existir, si no, no hay otra forma de describir el milagro que lo mantiene flotando. ¿Cuánto tiempo ha pasado en suspensión en un lugar que le ama con la misma ferocidad y la misma libertad con la que podría hacerlo el suelo, la tumba...?".[32] En esta pintura, ambas figuras contemplan las estrellas: en el caso de North, las de la bandera estadounidense, y en el caso de Jordan, son las luces del estadio; ambos tienen la mano derecha levantada, como si estuvieran haciendo su propio juramento al sueño estadounidense de idealización, excepcionalidad e inmortalidad.

En una dupla que aún no comenzó, Valdez planea llevar la serie a un territorio más profundamente personal: de un lado, piensa pintar la explosión del Challenger, y del otro, una silueta de su madre en la playa, con él en sus brazos cuando tenía un año. A quienes crecimos en la década de los ochenta, la historia del Challenger nos resulta cercana, ya que era la primera vez que se invitaba a bordo a una civil: la maestra de escuela Christa McAuliffe. Colocaron televisores en las aulas para que pudiéramos ver el suceso.[33] El cohete explotó poco después de su lanzamiento, y murieron las siete personas a bordo. La mayoría de las personas que estábamos mirando, aún podemos ver la icónica forma de la explosión, y seguimos sintiendo el horror y lo inexplicable de la experiencia. Valdez incluso hizo un dibujo de la tripulación y del transbordador tan solo una semana después de la explosión. Al unir esto con una imagen tan personal de él con su madre (quien falleció en 2020), Valdez nos pega donde más nos duele, y nos trae el recuerdo de la pérdida de la inocencia. De este modo, mientras observamos los lienzos de Valdez, experimentamos las dicotomías entre el paraíso y el infierno, la alegría y el dolor, la corrupción y la habilidad de volar.

El Principio De...

"Para ser honesta, espero el apocalipsis, o busco el mal, la indiferencia y el sufrimiento internacionales, y trabajo para vencerlos, siempre que no me sienta aturdida por las probabilidades, o me encuentre temporalmente paralizada por la repulsión y la dolorosa desesperación. Pero la vida misma obliga a ser optimista". — June Jordan[34]

Como esta es una historia de ciclos, me encuentro de nuevo en el estudio de Vincent, esta vez en Los Ángeles, el 23 de enero de 2024. Siento que es un *déjà vu*, ya que volvemos a enfrentarnos a la posibilidad de otra elección para Trump. La exposición de Vincent *Solo un sueño...* se inaugura en Houston, Texas, justo una semana después de las elecciones presidenciales de 2024. Volveremos a encontrarnos en Texas, ocho años después, y aunque espero no tener que volver a lamentarme por el resultado, el miedo es inevitable. Pero, como siempre, Vincent se está preparando. Su más nueva y profética visión está en proceso. No es un águila. Esta vez reinventa la fundación de Estados Unidos mediante la imagen de George Washington cruzando el río Delaware. En 1776, durante la guerra de Independencia, las fuerzas hessianas —tropas alemanas auxiliares del ejército británico— fueron atacadas por sorpresa en la batalla de Trenton, Nueva Jersey. Este momento ha sido retratado a lo largo de la historia del arte. Tal vez la versión más icónica sea *Washington cruzando el Delaware* (1861), de Emanuel Leutze, una pintura histórica de Washington al frente del barco en el que se agita con heroísmo la bandera de Estados Unidos. La versión de 1965 de Peter Saul es una obra maestra del arte pop; su composición tecnicolor está en un rosado carnoso, y Washington está representado como un bufón en un barco que se hunde, con una pequeña bandera en la mano. Por su parte, Robert Colescott, en la obra *George Washington Carver cruzando el Delaware: página de un libro de historia estadounidense* (1975), pone al mando al héroe y científico afroamericano George Washington Carver, rodeado de estereotipos raciales previos a la era de los Derechos Civiles, por ejemplo, Aunt Jemima. Tanto Saul como Colescott deciden no considerar como verdad absoluta lo que narran los libros de historia, ni tampoco la pintura histórica, y lo mismo hace Valdez, cuya versión del tema es la más delirante de todas.

Este pequeño dibujo (que pronto se convertirá en un lienzo a gran escala) se titula *Hola, América* (2024), y está inspirado en la novela del mismo nombre escrita por J. G. Ballard en 1980, y presenta a Mickey Mouse como Washington. Delante de él está Davy Crockett con su sombrero de piel de mapache, agitando una bandera con la frase "Denme la libertad o denme la muerte" y la imagen de la serpiente de "No me pisoteen" en su superficie; asimismo, hay filas del Pato Donald junto a Crockett y, detrás de ellos, aparece Cristo cargando la cruz, que es también un mástil. Abordo hay, además, espectadores: paparazzi, celebridades anónimas, una banda de marcha, agentes de seguridad tipo Blackwater y un veterano condecorado, pero olvidado. El artista tiene planeado incorporar algunos detalles más en la obra: el bote remolcará un montón de bombas mientras, en el horizonte, se ven restos del brazo y la antorcha de la estatua de la libertad caída, alcanzando una "tierra prometida" de rascacielos, carteleras y alambres de púa. Cuando observo esta composición, la cabeza se me inunda de pensamientos: la escena en que Elaine Benes de Seinfeld le dice a su futuro jefe J. Peterman, "¡Por Dios! Lo siento. Ni siquiera sé a dónde voy". Y él le responde: "Esa es la mejor manera de llegar a un lugar en el que nunca has estado".[35] O tal vez es así como llegaron los insurgentes al Capitolio el 6 de enero. Pero, sobre todo, pienso en el libro de Ballard. *Hola, América* ocurre después de que el estrecho de Bering ha sido contenido y Estados Unidos se convierte en un basurero. Se emprende una expedición a Las Vegas conducida por un equipo, entre quienes se encuentra el candidato político Wayne. Allí se encuentran con la civilización y con un hombre que se llama a sí mismo Charles Manson, el 45.o presidente de Estados Unidos. Manson le dice constantemente a Wayne que, juntos, pueden "Hacer a Estados Unidos grande de nuevo", un lema que usaba Reagan en aquella época y, antes de eso, los fascistas en la década de 1930. En una escena, Wayne se despierta en un pasillo de presidentes robóticos. Ballard escribe:

"Ahora todos gritaban a la vez, atropellándose alrededor de Wayne como si trataran de ganar su voto, un alboroto de voces protestantes que hacían eco en los miles de asientos vacíos del estadio.

'...tanques, armas, aviones...'
'...estadounidenses mestizos...'
'...seguridad para la democracia...'
'...demasiado orgullo para pelear...'
'...*Ich bin ein Berliner*...'
'...lo único que tenemos que temer es...'
—Wayne gritaba".[36]

Ballard y Valdez nos demuestran que los fantasmas del pasado están vivos, y revelar sus debilidades es realmente la forma de hacer que Estados Unidos vuelva a ser grande. "Vengan, reúnanse, porque los tiempos están cambiando", nos invita Bob Dylan, o quizás el cambio va a venir, pero es difícil verlo entre el humo de la destrucción. Luego recuerdo la pintura *Velocidad de Dios* (2019). Representa otro barco, aparentemente sin pasajeros, que está siendo tragado por un mar rabioso. El único signo de humanidad es una bengala en el cielo, un faro y un grito de esperanza. Claro que Washington llegó a la otra orilla, ¿pero podrá hacerlo Estados Unidos? ¿Se nos ofrecerá a nosotros, su ciudadanía, lo mismo? Con Valdez en el timón, creo que podríamos.

El Fin

"SUBDOSIFICACIÓN HISTÓRICA: Vivir en una época en la que parece que nada sucede. Algunos de los síntomas principales son

adicción a los periódicos, las revistas y los programas de televisión sobre las noticias. SOBREDOSIFICACIÓN HISTÓRICA: Vivir en una época en la que parece que ocurren muchas cosas. Algunos de los síntomas principales son adicción a los periódicos, las revistas y los programas de televisión sobre las noticias". —Douglas Coupland[37]

Tanto Vincent como yo somos productos de la generación X, nacidos en la década de 1970 y criados con MTV. Crecimos con un actor que se convirtió en presidente, con las mejillas manchadas de rímel de Tammy Faye Bakker, con Michael Jordan desafiando la gravedad, con los rizos de Michael Jackson en llamas, con Oliver North, con "este es tu cerebro bajo los efectos de las drogas" frito en una sartén, con la explosión del Challenger y con el vestido azul de Monica Lewinski, todo eso con la banda de sonido Run–DMC, Madonna, Milli Vanilli, Duran Duran, y la desolación del grunge que inspiró "Sueña cariño sueña" de Suicide. Huele a espíritu adolescente aquí. ¿Pero cómo se espera que analicemos la diferencia entre verdad, fantasía y realidad cuando crecimos frente a una televisión llena de imágenes artificiales?: "¿quién le disparó a JR?", travestismo para conseguir una vivienda más barata en *Amigos del Alma: Bosom Buddies*, y Alf, el alienígena favorito de la hora central que comía gatos. Entonces, no sorprende que, cuando llegamos a los años de Trump, las noticias falsas parecieran normales. Nos habíamos desgastado por la hipernormalización[38] de Estados Unidos… mejor dicho, del mundo. Tratamos de leerle los labios a Bush, pero los impuestos seguían llegando; no lográbamos entender por qué su hijo no podía pronunciar la palabra "nuclear", pero los aviones igual se estrellaron contra las torres gemelas; y todos los "desconocidos que desconocemos" que Donald Rumsfeld nos arrojó a la cara eran, en realidad, conocidos, porque Estados Unidos era el arma de destrucción masiva. Por eso, cuando se nos convocó a "Hacer a Estados Unidos grande de nuevo", ya lo habíamos escuchado antes, pero del presidente estrella de cine, no del presidente del reality show. Aun así, indiferente como se cree que es esta generación holgazana, practicamos un optimismo oscuro, no dejamos que nos arrastre, todavía tenemos esperanza. Sabemos que el fuego quema, pero también renueva. Nos reconocemos unos a otros porque, como escribió Wisława Szymborska, "Somos hijos de nuestra época, / una época política. / Todo el día y toda la noche, / todos los asuntos —los suyos, los nuestros, los de ellos— / son asuntos políticos. / Nos guste o no, / nuestros genes tienen un pasado político; / nuestra piel, un tono político; / nuestros ojos, un aspecto político. / Lo que digas resuena, / lo que callas habla por sí mismo. / Hagas lo que hagas, hablas de política".[39]

Voy a dejar una última dupla de imágenes que podría convertirse en pintura alguna vez: dos visitas improbables a la Casa Blanca. En 1991, el rapero Eazy–E de N.W.A recibió una carta de Bill Graham, senador de Texas, en la que lo invitaba a participar de una comida del círculo íntimo de la élite republicana con George H. W. Bush. Eazy declaró acerca de los 1,250 dólares por plato que pagó ese 18 de marzo: "Querían invitarme al Partido republicano. No soy ningún maldito republicano, pero fuimos, y cuando nos bajamos del avión, estaban CBS, CNN y todos esos medios que exageran diciendo: 'el pandillero y traficante de drogas Eazy–E vino al almuerzo con el presidente'. Básicamente, lo que hice fue pagar 1,200 dólares por una publicidad que cuesta un millón"[40]. Resultó ser que los organizadores habían enviado la invitación por error, pero Eazy solo podría haber tenido ganas de asistir en la era post–Reagan, en la que los políticos se habían convertido en un entretenimiento. Dos años más tarde, Vincent Valdez ganó un concurso nacional de arte, que incluía una excursión a la Casa Blanca, esta vez, con Bill Clinton. Hay una fotografía de la ocasión. En ella, Henry Cisneros, director designado del Departamento de Vivienda y Desarrollo Urbano (HUD, por sus siglas en inglés) y exalcalde de San Antonio, presenta a Vincent a una revista, mientras que, detrás de él, se ve un retrato de Clinton sonriente. Pero lo que más se destaca es la expresión de Vincent: pura desconfianza. Quizás estaba pensando en la hamburguesa que había pedido, o en el mural de soldados caídos que había pintado, o tal vez, incluso a los dieciséis, alcanzó a ver la fachada de Estados Unidos. Una parte de mí desea que él y Eazy hubieran ido el mismo día, solo para sentir la actividad sísmica de la supernova.

Vincent Valdez es un narrador que quita el ruido blanco y congela a la humanidad para que no podamos mirar para otro lado. Su obra es un uróboro, un collage, un recuerdo, un delirio febril, pero es real, igual que la llegada a la luna o el lanzamiento de un transbordador que no pudo ser para una maestra. El Estados Unidos de Vincent no fue hecho por Stanley Kubrick en un estudio de sonido, sino que ocurre en una nueva sala de operaciones, una que permite la lucha productiva, libre del doblepensar y la quema de libros. La sala de operaciones de Vincent es su estudio, y si bien es posible que el mundo nunca sea nuestro, un resplandor engalanará el cielo oscuro. Seguimos queriendo a nuestra MTV y sabemos que la revolución verdadera no se televisará. No sabemos si los animales seguirán estando allí, pero oímos el distante sonido de los pájaros: pío, pío, pi. Así son las cosas.

[1] El título del ensayo es un guiño a una pieza hablada de Jim Morrison, "Una plegaria estadounidense". The Doors compuso la música para esta pieza después de la muerte de Morrison y la grabó para el álbum homónimo de 1979. Una parte significativa de la letra afirma: "Nos hemos reunido en el interior de este teatro antiguo y delirante / Para propagar nuestra sed de vida y huir de la sabiduría abrumadora de las calles".

[2] Rebecca Solnit, *Esperanza en la oscuridad: la historia jamás contada del poder de la gente* (Chicago: Haymarket Books, 2016), pág. 1.

[3] Nathanael West, *Miss Lonelyhearts: El día de la langosta*, (Cambridge: New Direction, 1933), pág. 103.

[4] Giorgio Agamben, *Cuando la casa se quema*, trad. Kevin Attell (Londres: Seagull Books, 2022), págs. 3–4.

[5] Declaración que el artista envió a la autora.

[6] Susan Sontag, *Ante el dolor de los demás* (Londres: Picador, 2004), pág. 115.

[7] Susan Sontag, "Estética del silencio", Aspen no. 5+6, 1967, pág. 6.

[8] Langston Hughes, "Que América vuelva a ser América", *Recopilación de poemas de Langston Hughes* (Nueva York: Vintage Books, 1994), pág. 189.

[9] Hanif Abdurraqib, *No pueden matarnos hasta que nos matan* (Columbus: Two Dollar Radio, 2017) pág. 165.

[10] Joyce Carol Oates, *Del boxeo* (Nueva York: Harper Perennial Modern Classics; Reedición, 2006), págs. 20–21.

[11] Jimmy Clanton and His Rockets, "Solo un sueño", Ace Records, 1958.

[12] Oates, pág. 170.

[13] Vincent Valdez, "Vincent Valdez en "Fragmentos para John" en Hogar—Tan Diferente, Tan Atractivo", *Unframed*, May 29, 2017, https://unframed.lacma.org/2017/05/29/vincent-valdez-%E2%80%9Cexcerpts-john%E2%80%9D-home%E2%80%94so-different-so-appealing.

[14] Solnit, pág. xx.

[15] Leonard Cohen, "Hasta pronto, Marianne", de *Canciones de Leonard Cohen*, Columbia Records, 1967.

[16] Yoko Ogawa, *La policía de la memoria*, trad. Stephen Snyder (Nueva York: Pantheon Books, 2019), pág. 81.

[17] Elie Wiesel, "Esperanza, desesperación y memoria" (Discurso de aceptación del Premio Nobel, 11 de diciembre de 1986). https://www.nobelprize.org/prizes/peace/1986/wiesel/lecture/.

[18] "Los Angeles Disturbios de Zoot Suit, 1943", Los Angeles Almanac, accessed June 27, 2024, https://www.laalmanac.com/history/hi07t.php.

[19] Ry Cooder, "En mi ciudad" de *Chavez Ravine*, Nonesuch Records, 2005. Bunker Hill hace referencia a otra área de Los Ángeles que se demolió para llevar a cabo el desarrollo urbano.

[20] Mike Davis, *Ciudad de Cuarzo* (Londres/Nueva York: Verso Books, 1990), pág. 15.

[21] Allen Ginsberg, "Estados Unidos", 1956, https://www.poetryfoundation.org/poems/49305/america–56d22b41f119f.

[22] Gil Scott–Heron, "El Klan" de *Real Eyes (Ojos reales)*, Arista Records, 1980.

[23] El acrónimo AFTP es una referencia a la canción de 1988 "A la mierda la policía" (FTP) del álbum de N.W.A *Recién salido de Compton*.

[24] *La ciudad* es el capítulo uno de *El principio está cerca (una trilogía estadounidense)*; y *Los nuevos estadounidenses* es el capítulo tres. En esta serie también se incluyen las trece pinturas del capítulo dos, *Sueña, cariño, sueña* (2015–16), que representa a los deudos de Muhammad Ali.

[25] Abdurraqib, *No pueden matarnos*, pág. 77.

[26] Kurt Vonnegut, *Matadero cinco* (Nueva York: Dial Press, 1999), pág. 155.

[27] Vonnegut, pág. 23.

[28] Arion Press une artistas y literatura para crear libros de edición limitada hechos a mano.

[29] Kurt Vonnegut, Jr., *Matador cinco, o— La cruzada de los niños: una danza de deber con la muerte*, (San Francisco: Arion Press, 2023), p. 2, https://static1.squarespace.com/ static/5c5b11c1bfba3e4a2e2cbe3a/t/6578b15f26605c4e125224e7/1702408544852/ Arion.S5+prospectus.pdf.

[30] Vonnegut, pág. 28.

[31] Timothy Snyder, *Sobre la tiranía: veinte lecciones que aprender del siglo XX* (Nueva York: Crown, 2017), pág. 61.

32 Hanif Abdurraqib, *Siempre tenemos este año: sobre la ascensión en el básquetbol* (Nueva York: Penguin Random House, 2024), págs. 17–18.

33 Ese día estaba enferma, me quedé en casa y miré el acontecimiento sola. Escribí sobre esa fecha para la obra *Réquiem* de Valdez y Corral.

34 June Jordan, "Introducción", *Algunos de nosotros NO morimos: ensayos nuevos y seleccionados* (Nueva York: Civitas Books, 2003), pág. 4.

35 Del episodio "El reemplazo", 1995.

36 J. G. Ballard, *Hola, América*(Londres: W. W. Norton & Co, 1981), págs. 169–70.

37 Douglas Coupland, *Generación X: cuentos para una cultura acelerada* (Nueva York: St. Martin's Griffin, 1991), pág. 7.

38 El documental de Adam Curtis *Hipernormalización* de 2016 toma su título del libro de Alexei Yurchak's *Todo era para siempre hasta que no lo fue más: la última generación soviética* de 2006. Yurchak sostiene que la máquina de propaganda soviética fue tan eficaz que normalizó la corrupción. La película de Curtis lleva eso a los años de Trump.

39 Wisława Szymborska, "Hijos de nuestra época" de *vista con un grano de sal: poemas selectos*, trad. Stanisław Barańczak y Clare Cavanaugh (Boston: Harcourt Books, 1995), pág. 149.

40 Jay Quad, "Cena con el presidente: el almuerzo infame de Eazy-E con George H.W. Bush" Rock the Bells, March 21, 2022, https://rockthebells.com/articles/eazy-e-lunch-with-george-bush/.

HAY UN LADO POSITIVO EN ALGUNA PARTE...

De Patricia Restrepo

París, 1922. Ernest Hemingway se encuentra en una situación bastante desagradable. Le robaron su colección completa de manuscritos, empaquetados en maletas junto con sus copias. Solo sobrevivieron dos de sus manuscritos. Por ese entonces, Hemingway intercambiaba lecciones de boxeo por consejos sobre escritura con Ezra Pound. Pound respondió al dolor y al agotamiento de Hemingway a causa del robo de esta manera: "Si el centro, es decir, la FORMA, de la historia está bien, uno debería poder reconstruirla de memoria... Si la cosa tambalea y no se puede volver a armar... entonces nunca hubiera funcionado".[1]

Hemingway, perturbado por este consejo elíptico, escribió ese mismo año *Fuera de temporada*, un cuento en el que lanzaba su "teoría del iceberg". La historia relata un día de pesca de una pareja de expatriados junto con un guía italiano borracho. Su narrativa en capas aborda temas de alienación y fragilidad masculina. Hemingway omite detalles narrativos fundamentales de manera deliberada, en lo que constituye un enfoque tremendamente experimental para la época. Compara la historia con un iceberg y su forma escrita con el pico visible, y afirma que "la dignidad del movimiento de un iceberg se debe a que solo una octava parte de él está sobre el agua",[2] con lo cual anticipa la capacidad del lector para identificar verdades veladas en el subtexto de palabras no dichas.

Hemingway puede parecer un punto de partida curioso para pensar en la evolución de la obra de Vincent Valdez. Ambos, innovadores en sus respectivas disciplinas, caracterizan la vida estadounidense. El escritor y el artista comparten incluso la afinidad por el boxeo. Su similitud también radica en el uso de la elipsis como estrategia narrativa. Este recurso léxico consiste en omitir palabras de manera convencional e insinuar fragmentos no dichos. Walt Whitman utilizaba con regularidad este gesto gramatical para presentar pausas pronunciadas, una señal para reducir la velocidad. Sus primeras obras contenían elipsis dispersas de diferentes longitudes: con frecuencia incluía cuatro puntos, en lugar de los tres habituales. "Las elipsis de Whitman no indican lo que se ha omitido, sino todo lo que, en principio, se podría incluir".[3]

El título de la exposición de Valdez, de aparente levedad en su longitud, pero de efecto contundente, introduce una elipsis. *Solo un sueño...* hace referencia a su pintura *Solo un sueño (En Estados Unidos)* (2020–21), en la que presenta a un boxeador fatigado. En el centro de su práctica, Valdez responde a las censuras pasadas por alto o motivadas por cuestiones políticas en nuestro país —las elipsis de nuestra sociedad— que ejemplifican la dualidad entre lo que se ve y lo que no se ve, que es tan elemental para la obra del artista.

A diferencia de lo escrito, la forma elíptica de Valdez no trunca verdades; más bien, llena el espacio entre su obra y los ojos de las personas espectadoras con una invitación a mirar las historias no contadas. A su vez, podemos imaginar la trayectoria de sus figuras y, quizás, de la sociedad en su conjunto. Como público, podemos llenar los vacíos narrativos. Si bien la obra de Valdez está cargada de referencias reveladas con atención y tiempo, sus elipsis son una extensión física de sí mismo, que impregnan su obra de una generosidad construida mediante la convergencia de su vida y sus antiguas preocupaciones sociopolíticas. "Lo personal es político" resuena a través de las décadas de carrera de Valdez.

Valdez pone el foco principal en la cuestión fundamental del poder: quién lo recibe y a quién se le niega. Al artista le resulta difícil celebrar a los Estados Unidos a ciegas, ya que, muchas veces, el país obtuvo sus victorias a un costo inmenso para otros. En sus obras, con regularidad hace referencia al abuso de poder, con preocupaciones persistentes en torno a la violencia y la discriminación racial consentida por el estado. Basándose en las reflexiones del filósofo Michel Foucault sobre el "discurso valiente"[5] o el deber moral de decir la verdad a pesar del riesgo consecuente, la obra de Valdez sirve como antídoto frente al acto de ignorar el trato injusto. Similar a los dibujos de redes políticas del artista Mark Lombardi, Valdez identifica tejidos que conectan constelaciones de poder y declara: "Ahogan a la gente. Ahogamos sus presupuestos. Vean lo rápido que se curan su pérdida de audición y amnesia. Sindicatos y departamentos de policía, megaiglesias, redes de medios, bancos, desarrolladores, políticos, instituciones y empresas. Conecten los puntos. Solo fichas de dominó".[6]

Valdez encarna la verdad al poder y nos induce con urgencia a buscar la veracidad mediante sus escenas estilizadas. Nos recuerda que "mentir es nuestro pasatiempo nacional"; el artista confronta verdades distorsionadas y los mitos que las sustentan. Esta desestabilización provoca malestar y aborda la brecha entre un relato fantástico de la historia de este país y su situación actual. Sus pinturas exploran las dinámicas de poder autoritario y, a la vez, recuerdan vidas dejadas de lado por los poderes establecidos, que luego Valdez vuelve a poner en primer plano con sus pinceladas. Su obra tiene un poder magnificador, que apela a la conciencia pública y que les recuerda a las personas espectadoras su propio poder de acción. Esa fusión de lo político y lo personal es evidente a lo largo de este texto, que despliega la evolución de la práctica de Valdez no sólo para trazar su obra a través de una lente biográfica, sino para abrir portales de comprensión o elipsis que nos inviten a reflexionar.

Hagan comida, no la guerra 1987-93

La trayectoria artística de Valdez precede a su nacimiento. El artista recuerda su primera experiencia de "museo" a los cuatro o cinco años: cuando contemplaba decenas de pinturas de José María Valdez, su bisabuelo, colgadas con orgullo en la casa de sus abuelos. Una pieza particularmente impactante era un Cristo representado de manera clásica, que miraba hacia arriba a través de su corona de espinas, pintado a fines de la década de 1890. El joven Valdez quedó cautivado por las imágenes y su poder tangible. La obra de su bisabuelo fue tan imborrable que Valdez se hizo un tatuaje con dicha pieza en el antebrazo izquierdo como recordatorio de sus inicios.

José María Valdez esperaba que sus hijos continuaran con actividades artísticas similares. A fin de imprimir en su memoria la importancia de la tradición muralista mexicana, llevó a su hijo, Arthur Valdez, al Palacio de Bellas Artes en la Ciudad de México a ver el monumental mural *Nueva Democracia* de David Alfaro Siqueiros; esto fue alrededor de 1964. A pesar de que no llegó a verlo con vida, Valdez sentía que conocía a su bisabuelo a través del conjunto de imágenes que había dejado. Si bien los miembros de su familia de otras generaciones no se convirtieron en artistas, sí comprendieron la importancia de documentar historias.

Es gracias a la inclinación de los Valdez a registrar y conmemorar momentos que, de otro modo, se perderían en el tiempo, que conocemos las primeras actividades artísticas de Valdez. Comenzó a dibujar cuando tenía alrededor de tres años; uno de sus primeros dibujos fue el del patito feo. Décadas más tarde, el artista identificó esta imagen como un autorretrato adecuado: el de un desvalido o un marginado. Aprendió a dibujar a partir de libros con imágenes fotográficas, donde trazaba figuras antes de colorearlas, y luego recurrió a cómics y enciclopedias en busca de imágenes originales. Sin embargo, Valdez no sostuvo un pincel hasta que aprendió a pintar murales en 1987.

Ese año, Valdez se encontró codo a codo, en sentido figurativo, con artistas chicanos con conciencia política en su ciudad natal de San Antonio. Alex Rubio, nueve años mayor que él, le trató de igual a igual y reconoció su gran talento y su insaciable deseo de pintar. Rubio le causaba intriga a Valdez, con su cigarrillo colgando y su cabello largo recogido con un pañuelo. Se convirtieron en estrechos colaboradores y amigos y trabajaron juntos todos los sábados creando murales en toda la ciudad para el programa Artes Culturales de la Comunidad. Se conocieron en el antiguo sitio del Esperanza Peace and Justice Center, donde Valdez y sus compañeros de quinto grado comenzaron un proyecto de mural sobre la paz mundial que se llevó a cabo durante un mes. Mientras sus compañeros pintaban figuras de palos, arcoíris y corazones, la escena de Valdez mostraba aviones de combate que lanzaban napalm sobre los trabajadores del campo con un texto decorado en el cielo que decía "hagan comida, no la guerra".

Rubio le enseñó a Valdez las técnicas básicas de la pintura: "Cómo sostener y limpiar los pinceles, cómo sacar la pintura de su lata, cómo mezclar colores, cómo sostener una paleta, cómo considerar la composición, cómo generar luces y sombras". Debido a que Valdez era demasiado joven para subir a lo alto del andamio, a menudo dividían la pared, y Valdez se encargaba de la parte inferior. Desde 1987 hasta 1993, Rubio y Valdez pintaron murales en toda la ciudad de San Antonio: llamaban la atención sobre la crisis del sida, conmemoraban a los veteranos de la guerra de Vietnam y rendían homenaje a la Virgen de Guadalupe. En una escena más fantástica, representaron un partido de fútbol ficticio entre un guerrero azteca y un jugador moderno, un tributo al legado histórico del fútbol en América; pintado en la pared del gimansio de la escuela secundaria de Valdez.

Este trabajo intensivo y centrado en la comunidad tuvo un profundo impacto para Valdez, quien además comenzó a verse a sí mismo como parte de las tradiciones artísticas chicanas. Los murales fueron un espacio donde el joven artista se sintió reflejado y conectado con el mundo que lo rodeaba. También se vio empoderado por su capacidad para narrar relatos alternativos a los que encontraba en sus libros de texto. Estos relatos se centraban en los guerreros de la comunidad cultural, en lugar de enfocarse en figuras estadounidenses como Nelson Rockefeller y Davy Crockett. Después de todo, el muralismo era un camino para excavar historias que destacaban a las comunidades de color y clases socioeconómicas diversas. Incluso a una temprana edad, Valdez comprendió el poder de los contramonumentos para comunicarse con las masas mediante mensajes críticos de resistencia. También aprendió a tener en cuenta al público, ya que trabajaba al aire libre y, con frecuencia, quienes pasaban por allí se detenían para hablar de la obra o preguntar sobre su progreso. En muchos sentidos, este tipo de pintura presagió el arco de una carrera reconocida por elaborar una práctica artística accesible, centrada en la inmediatez de la imagen y la claridad de su voz.

Otro lugar donde Valdez encontró comunidad a través del arte fue en una de las organizaciones chicanas más antiguas del país: el Guadalupe Cultural Arts Center (GCAC) de San Antonio. El GCAC le proporcionó numerosos recursos, gracias a sus mentores, los artistas Alex Rubio y Kathy Vargas. Allí se encontró con la obra de artistas chicanos como Luis Jiménez, José Luis Rivera y César Martínez, que luego estudió intensamente. Valdez comenzó a comprender el legado del grabado político: muchas imágenes originales presentaban una paleta de colores en negro y rojo, que se convirtió en su elección predominante durante varios años. A través del GCAC, también cobraron un rol fundamental en la vida del artista la música y su impacto cultural, que le hacían rememorar sus viajes semanales a las tiendas de discos junto con Vargas. Conoció a sus eternos favoritos, incluidos Leonard Cohen, Bob Dylan, The Doors, Jimi Hendrix e importantes músicos de Tex-Mex/conjunto, como el Flaco Jiménez, a quien más tarde representaría en su serie en curso *El principio está cerca (una trilogía estadounidense), capítulo tres: Los nuevos estadounidenses, Veteranos nro. 1 (Flaco)* (2024).

Además de su experiencia con la pintura mural, el joven Valdez quedó cautivado por el espectáculo de las pantallas de cine y televisión. En 1987, quedó atónito viendo la famosa clavada televisada de Michael Jordan, donde el ángulo bajo de la cámara permitía que se apreciaran hazañas aparentemente imposibles del atletismo humano. En su juventud, detenía las películas en la videocasetera y copiaba la imagen congelada. La televisión se convirtió en su maestra de anatomía y expresión humanas, así como de composición. A Valdez también le fascinaba la experiencia colectiva del cine, donde su atención se desplazaba entre la película y la mirada de los demás espectadores. El artista atribuye su deseo de cautivar al público con imágenes a su experiencia mirando la película *Pelotón* (1986) cuando tenía ocho o nueve años. En la sala repleta, mientras otros estaban sentados mirando la pantalla, él se centraba en el silencio del público y su concentración en la imagen proyectada.

Valdez también le atribuye al cine la influencia en su enfoque del retrato, que lo llevó a recrear una sensación cinematográfica en gran parte de su trabajo, mediante una iluminación dramática y una energía palpable. Muchas de sus pinturas, representadas con hábiles claroscuros, incluyen una fuente de luz en el interior de la obra, ya sean faros de camión, soles radiantes o flashes de cámaras. Los lienzos panorámicos alargados, característicos del artista, también recuerdan el formato de pantalla ancha del cine. Por mucho que le ofreciera, la pantalla era a la vez un espacio que hacía que Valdez se sintiera invisible. En aquella época, la comunidad latina estaba aún menos representada en los anuncios, las series de televisión o los relatos cotidianos del ser "estadounidense". Esta falta de representación llevó al joven Valdez a preguntarle a su madre sobre su propia identidad estadounidense. Una persistente sensación de otredad lo haría preguntarse quiénes son él y su país hasta el día de hoy.

Peso mosquito 1997 & 2001-2

En 1997, Valdez dejó Texas tras recibir una beca completa para la Rhode Island School of Design (RISD) en Providence. Comenzó a estudiar ilustración, pero las limitaciones del trabajo para clientes lo disuadieron. En su tercer año, como no podía regresar a casa, se quedó en el campus para el Día de Acción de Gracias. Allí, a través de la pintura, encontró una conexión con su familia. Recuerda de ese momento: "estaba completamente aislado en el estudio con una buena provisión de sándwiches y cereales. Entonces, escuché canciones de mi hogar y pensé en mi familia: la cocina de mi abuela y mi abuelo en su patio trasero, después de un largo día de estar cortando el césped con el calor sofocante de Texas. Pinté día y noche, de forma ininterrumpida, durante dos semanas. Estos recuerdos personales, junto a la letra de una canción de conjunto (el estilo musical), despertaron mi imaginación: me senté a la mesa, suspiré y pensé en cómo solían ser las cosas".

El resultado de eso, *Recuerdo* (1999), retrata a su abuelo Gabriel, sentado en el patio de su casa al anochecer, fumando, rememorando y tocando el acordeón después de un duro día de trabajo. El cigarrillo que le cuelga de la boca de manera graciosa e inverosímil se comba como si estuviera mojado, pero sus brasas rojas afirman lo contrario. El sol se pone al fondo mientras el protagonista reflexiona sobre el ocaso de su propia vida. Más de veinte velas aparecen distribuidas en el fondo, mientras que una veladora central (o vela de oración) proyecta sombras dramáticas sobre el rostro del hombre y sus nudillos anudados. Se percibe una brisa, ya que la ropa colgada levanta vuelo. Una de las prendas es increíblemente fantasmal, mientras que las otras se pueden reconocer como sarapes y calcetines. A pesar del potencial juerguista de la obra con instrumentos e iluminación ceremonial, hay una energía sombría representada en una pequeña cruz de cementerio.

Al conectarse con su familia en *Recuerdo*, a pesar de los miles de kilómetros que los separan físicamente, Valdez encontró en la pintura una herramienta para trascender el espacio y el tiempo extrayendo imágenes de la memoria. En ese momento, aprovechó su singular capacidad para contar historias, contó lo siguiente: "Esta pintura representa un momento importante para mí: fue el momento en que me di cuenta por completo de en qué se estaban por convertir mi voz y mi visión como pintor".

Esta obra nos recuerda una pintura posterior que también rinde homenaje a la familia de Valdez, *Personas del sol (abuela y abuelo Santana)* (2019). La tierna pieza rinde homenaje a los abuelos del artista, que pasaron más de setenta años juntos: Gabriel, representado en *Recuerdo*, y Carmen Santana. En la obra, encontramos objetos que hablan de una vida ya vivida: una radio AM antigua, un vigoroso cactus del suroeste, una vasija pintada con iconografía del códice azteca. Esta alusión a los aztecas, que se llamaban a sí mismos "el pueblo del sol", honra al sol como una fuerza de vida fundamental. Podemos ver otros signos de su existencia llena de sol en la forma de "las manos curtidas, la piel de mi abuelo quemada tras toda una vida de trabajo bajo el sol de Texas, y las sábanas levitadas de mi abuela que sirven como escudo y protección". La sábana que protege a sus abuelos, como un telón de fondo detrás de ellos, es reflejo de la ropa tendida en el fondo en *Recuerdo*. El linaje familiar de Valdez está sostenido por estos significantes, envueltos en una protección simbólica.

La estatura y el orgullo de los abuelos de Valdez los convierten en una presencia amorosa y formidable en el lienzo y en el mundo más allá de la imagen. Personas del sol de Valdez nos recuerda a *Gente en el sol* (1960) de Edward Hopper, que presenta a un grupo melancólico y aislado de personas que toman sol. Sin embargo, para Valdez, lo más importante es que *Personas del sol* "sirve como testimonio visual de la presencia histórica de los mexicoestadounidenses y del suroeste de Estados Unidos, con frecuencia no reconocida dentro del canon de la historia estadounidense, tanto pasada como presente. Nuestra historia es una parte innegable de la historia épica y en desarrollo de Estados Unidos". En su búsqueda por conmemorar lo personal, Valdez representa cada vez más a sus familiares y amistades desde una mirada introspectiva, que se aleja de la fría distancia que puede verse en la pintura de Hopper.

Mientras estaba en la RISD, Valdez se interesó en el boxeo, un tema común en gran parte de su obra hasta el presente. En su último año, se inscribió en un gimnasio y se mofaba de sí mismo pensando que podría ser coronado campeón de "peso mosquito". Finalmente les dio vida a estos sueños en el papel, con la representación de un boxeador por primera vez ese mismo año. Este maltratado luchador de ojos verdes, que perdió un diente y, probablemente, la pelea, se recupera dentro del cuadrilátero.

Los boxeadores de Valdez contradicen las representaciones habituales de hombres poderosos e invulnerables. Por el contrario, suelen mostrar cicatrices físicas y emocionales. Los luchadores, en conflicto no con enemigos temibles sino consigo mismos, se autoinfligen heridas psicológicas tal vez superiores a las lesiones físicas. Estos atletas están al borde del colapso, y luchan por pararse en el cuadrilátero y seguir adelante. Simbolizan una lucha por la supervivencia. Valdez relaciona estas figuras con el *Frankenstein* (1818) de Mary Shelley: inventado, creado y utilizado por una sociedad solo para ser activado y descartado. Las imágenes de boxeadores de Valdez exceden su connotación literal; son un análogo de nuestros intentos diarios de persistir a pesar de las presiones cotidianas y apelan a los desafíos internos emocionales, físicos y mentales que enfrentamos en nuestros respectivos cuadriláteros.

Los boxeadores, entonces y ahora, representan en última instancia la lucha, que toma muchas formas en la obra y la vida de Valdez. Por ejemplo, Valdez experimentó un choque cultural cuando estudiaba en la RISD, un paisaje y un entorno muy alejados de Texas. También encontró una falta de representación en sus libros de texto de historia del arte, y empezó a considerar enfoques y métodos que pudieran contrarrestar estos preocupantes patrones. En su último año en la RISD, comenzó a buscar en línea material sobre los Disturbios del Zoot Suit, un capítulo importante, pero pasado por alto, de la historia estadounidense. Durante un período de cinco días en 1943, militares y civiles estadounidenses golpearon a los pachucos o jóvenes mexicoestadounidenses en público por usar trajes zoot. Estos llamativos trajes, populares entre los jóvenes afroamericanos, latinos y filipinos de los Estados Unidos, fueron demonizados como antipatrióticos debido a su uso excesivo de tela que durante la guerra estaba mal visto debido al racionamiento. Sin embargo, Valdez nos recuerda que "la violencia tenía más que ver con la tensión racial que con la moda".

La consecuente pintura, *¡Maten al pachuco malnacido!* de 2001, se presentó por primera vez en la exposición de finalización de estudios. Valdez visualiza una versión estilizada del conflicto; una truculenta pelea en un bar entre los militares y los pachucos: un juego de cartas interrumpido mientras vuelan botellas por el aire, rostros aplastados, ropas rasgadas, un perro rabioso que lucha con el uniforme de un marinero, y militares borrachos que orinan y dejan una estela de destrucción en el fondo. El suelo de baldosas rojas camufla la sangre derramada. La compleja escena está marcada por el hábil manejo de los cuerpos contorsionados por parte de Valdez, y por su dominio sobre los matices del juego de luces y las fuentes de iluminación, incluidas las luces policiales apenas visibles. La escena es escalofriante, y se vuelve aún más terrible por el hecho de que Valdez fue el modelo físico de todas las figuras representadas, para lo cual encarnó una multiplicidad de identidades y posturas. *¡Maten al pachuco malnacido!* enfrentó resistencia, ya que varios integrantes del cuerpo docente de Valdez criticaron este tipo de obra por considerarla desagradable, además de que se equivocaron al pensar que tendría una carrera corta. Sin embargo, el actor y coleccionista Cheech Marin vio la obra y la compró al año siguiente. Aquí fue cuando Valdez empezó a comprender de verdad su propia lucha e inició un compromiso de décadas, cuyo objetivo sería enfrentar la violencia pasada por alto mediante el uso de detalles llamativos y el dominio técnico que captaran la atención de la persona espectadora. Si bien esta pintura representa una fotografía sangrienta y violenta en el medio de una pelea, más tarde Valdez evoluciona y va de una representación abierta a rastros más alusivos e insidiosos, como elipsis que delimitan la culminación de la violencia: invisible, pero inquietante.

Yo Soy-ee Blaxican 2000-3

Tras graduarse en la RISD en el 2000, Valdez regresó a Texas, donde comenzó a desarrollar una paleta que reflejaba la luz que se observa en los paisajes físicos, históricos y políticos del suroeste de Estados Unidos. Le recordó a un día de verano, dominado por violetas intensos, naranjas sanguíneos y rojos fuego, cuando el sol colgaba en su estado de purgatorio separando la noche y el día. Los detalles de los orígenes de Valdez no han recibido suficiente reconocimiento en análisis previos de su obra, que con frecuencia se centraron en el cuerpo. Sin embargo, al observar la obra de Valdez, queda claro que el escenario se convierte en el estado psicológico y simbólico de los sujetos representados, lo que hace imposible separarlos.

Este profundo enfoque en el paisaje se traduce en la intensidad del color evidente en obras como *Yo Soy–ee Blaxican* (2003). En el centro de la composición, intercambiamos miradas con un joven con la cabeza de lado, una gorra hacia atrás y la barbilla levantada. La pose confiada de la figura nos asegura que su presencia es innegable. El sol enrojece el espacio detrás de él en forma electrizante. La paleta roja y negra de la pintura, símbolo de resistencia, rinde homenaje a los gráficos políticos, en particular, los del movimiento de derechos civiles, que Valdez había estudiado en su juventud. El enfoque estilístico de *Yo Soy–ee Blaxican* también es un reconocimiento a la comunidad de artistas chicanos de Texas a quienes Valdez admiraba, como César Martínez, famoso por sus retratos de mexicoestadounidenses sobre fondos de colores vibrantes.

En *Yo Soy–ee Blaxican*, Valdez representa una identidad estadounidense híbrida central para el siglo XXI. Cuando regresó a Texas, Valdez tuvo una conversación formativa con su hermano menor Daniel,[7] que entonces estaba en la escuela secundaria. El artista le preguntó con qué categoría racial se identificaba a la hora de rellenar los formularios de los exámenes académicos oficiales y de identificación personal. Su hermano respondió entre bromas que “nunca había estado en México, no sabía qué era un chicano, se encogía de hombros ante el término “latino” y no hablaba español”. En su lugar, besó dos de sus dedos, los lanzó al aire en conmemoración del rapero recientemente fallecido Tupac Shakur y exclamó: “Soy blaxicano”. Valdez se dio cuenta de que la fusión de culturas de Daniel abría las puertas a un nuevo enfoque sobre la formación de identidad. “Blaxicano” era la forma que tenía su hermano de hacer espacio y crear un lugar en su mundo, uno que reflejara su propio entorno complejo mientras Estados Unidos “regurgita su propia identidad, muta, evoluciona y se adapta indefinidamente”.[8]

A principios de la década del 2000, Valdez amplió su arquetipo del boxeador, fusionando la lucha de un personaje por la supervivencia con la tensión subyacente de algo que estaba a punto de suceder.[9] Esto derivó en la obra de cuatro paneles de la serie *Hombres hechos* (2002). Para crear esta serie, Valdez actuó como director de cine, poniendo en escena modelos vivos en su estudio. Las cuatro figuras fatigadas, que se representan en forma individual, están producidas en cinco tonos de pastel, medio que Valdez llama su “viejo amigo”. Cada una de ellas parece mirar hacia algo que está más allá del papel; lucen esculturales, pero vislumbrando su destino de derrota. A pesar de la sensación de que sus partidos están arreglados, de que su juego está amañado, se mantienen desafiantes. Las figuras de esta serie no son solo boxeadores; se basan en arquetipos masculinos heroicos que se encuentran en la mitología y la historia occidentales: guerreros, mártires, gladiadores, chicos de barrio contemporáneos. Siguen siendo los antihéroes en sus círculos de lucha, en las zonas de guerra y en las calles estadounidenses de hoy en día.

Las pequeñas irrupciones de luz brillantes que encierran la parte superior de la cabeza de las figuras son simbólicas. El boxeador con un ojo casi cerrado por una lesión ve las proverbiales estrellas antes de desplomarse. Lo sigue una figura que se asemeja a Cristo, que ve las estrellas fugaces como la luz que precede a su muerte o las profecías del fin de los tiempos. El soldado que luce sus placas de identificación podría estar reviviendo los estallidos de la guerra. El cuarto es el hermano de Valdez, Daniel. En esta imagen, las farolas urbanas apenas iluminan un camino oscuro mientras el personaje reflexiona sobre los retratos anteriores, tal vez cavilando sobre las pocas opciones y caminos que tiene él.

La serie *Hombres hechos* también incluye el díptico *Expulsión de la gran ciudad* (2002), la obra más grande de Valdez en ese momento. La escala de los dibujos en pastel, de catorce pies de altura, evoca su pasado como muralista. Las figuras masculina y femenina están desnudas y recortadas desde las fosas nasales hasta los dedos de los pies, y discuten desde sus respectivos lienzos. Esparcidos a sus pies se ven colillas de cigarrillos desechadas, envases de comida rápida y periódicos arrugados. La postura de los cuerpos exhibe tensión, se ve un dedo que señala y la forma de las bocas muestra disgusto, todo lo cual da indicios de una incapacidad para encontrar puntos en común. Están parados en una acera que termina de manera abrupta, que al parecer los llevaría al borde de la tierra, mientras la base debajo de sus pies es inestable. Los dedos de sus pies cuelgan precariamente. Frente a otra elipsis, decidimos su destino.

Encontrar su vuelta a casa 2004 & 13

En 2004, el icónico músico estadounidense Ry Cooder llamó a Valdez con una oportunidad que desafiaba el género y que consistía en renovar el poder. Cooder estaba buscando un artista para abordar un sueño novedoso: pintar un carro de helados de 1953 con una interpretación alegórica de la historia del Chavez Ravine. El músico se convenció de que Valdez era el artista adecuado cuando vio *¡Maten al pachuco malnacido!* en el catálogo de la exposición *Visiones chicanas: Pintores estadounidenses al límite* (2002) de Cheech Marin.

Para desentrañar esta historia centrada en la región, Valdez se trasladó a Los Ángeles durante dos años para completar la gigantesca tarea de *El Chavez Ravine* (2005-7). Aunque Chavez Ravine está ubicado en un lugar más allá de donde nació Valdez, sus trasfondos de gobierno descontrolado, la eliminación de comunidades históricas de color y la resistencia del pueblo a esas fuerzas ya estaban presentes en su trabajo. Con respecto a la ciudad, Norman Klein manifiesta: “Los Ángeles es una ciudad que ha prosperado durante mucho tiempo gracias a la recreación continua de [su] propio mito”,[10] lo que Valdez ve como una declaración paralela a todo Estados Unidos.

A lo largo de la superficie del carro, Valdez representa la evolución del barrio Chavez Ravine durante la década de 1950. Fusiona dos formas de arte tradicional mexicoestadounidense: los murales y la personalización de automóviles. El amplio panorama está representado en colores que reflejan la puesta de sol de California. Hay referencias visuales a la historia de acaparamiento de tierras que eliminó el histórico vecindario latino, incluida la adquisición de dominio eminente por parte de la ciudad para abrir paso a las viviendas públicas, el desalojo forzoso de los antiguos residentes y la construcción del Dodger Stadium encima de los escombros de las casas arrasadas. También se ven imágenes de las casas originales del barrio, junto a políticos intrigantes cuya piel es inquietantemente roja, lo que evoca la histeria anticomunista de la era McCarthy o del temor rojo.

Esta colaboración con Cooder en *El Chavez Ravine* consolidó el uso de la pintura por parte de Valdez como homenaje e intento de escribir nuevos futuros. Si bien la esperanza se orienta hacia el futuro, el territorio fértil para la producción de esperanza exige que se haga memoria. Valdez se acercó a este concepto en *Fragmentos para John* (2012). El amigo de toda la vida del artista, el subteniente John R. Holt Jr., un médico de combate que prestó servicio en Irak, falleció en 2009. John no murió en una zona de combate, sino durante su regreso a los Estados Unidos, donde se convirtió en una estadística del trastorno de estrés postraumático. Valdez expresa que "*Fragmentos para John* es un tributo para aquellos que no pueden encontrar el camino a casa".[11] A lo largo de seis paneles, el desarrollo confuso y monocromático de la procesión fúnebre militar resulta conmovedor. Como expresó Susan Sontag: "Recordar es un acto ético, tiene valor ético en sí mismo. La memoria es, dolorosamente, la única relación que podemos tener con los muertos".[12] El video *Hogar* (2012), que acompaña las pinturas, sigue el ataúd de John, cubierto con una bandera, flotando sin ningún soporte visible, navegando por San Antonio como un lowrider, bajo y lento, para llegar a su lugar de descanso final. La centralidad del ataúd aborda la elíptica supresión en la conciencia estadounidense respecto de esta crisis que atraviesan los veteranos, dada una prohibición de dieciocho años de fotografiar ataúdes cubiertos con banderas que regresaban a los Estados Unidos, que no fue revocada hasta 2009.

En 2012, pensando en otras historias condenadas al olvido y en las vidas asociadas por las que no se derramaron lágrimas, Valdez comenzó a investigar los linchamientos de mexicoestadounidenses en Texas desde fines de la década de 1880 hasta la década de 1930. En casi la totalidad de las dos décadas que precedieron al inicio del siglo XX, la cantidad de linchamientos superó la de ejecuciones legales.[13] Y, sin embargo, la historia de linchamientos de mexicanos y mexicoestadounidenses en el país sigue siendo poco conocida. Los linchamientos, una "institución distintivamente estadounidense", aclaran los escritos de Judith Butler sobre la "capacidad de duelo" o la valoración perniciosa de algunas vidas por encima de otras. Ella afirma: "Una forma de plantear la cuestión de quiénes somos 'nosotros' en estos tiempos de guerra es preguntándonos qué vidas se consideran valiosas, qué vidas se lloran y qué vidas no se consideran dignas de ser lloradas".[14]

Valdez se enfurece ante la idea de la historia como un registro fiel y ve, en cambio, la oportunidad de revertir lo olvidado reclamando la representación del pasado. Para tal fin, realizó *La fruta más extraña* (2013) como un antídoto para el olvido deliberado en nuestro país de la violencia ignorada por el estado. La serie muestra a diez hombres mexicoestadounidenses contemporáneos, contorsionados y suspendidos desde sogas invisibles. Sus cuerpos giran colectivamente alrededor de un eje central. Reconocemos que son contemporáneos a nuestro tiempo sobre todo por la ropa: jeans, una camiseta de baloncesto de los Houston Rockets, sudaderas y calzado Nike.

Estas figuras han sido extraídas de su entorno y flotan en el espacio. El vacío simboliza relatos olvidados de violencia racial. Las imágenes de Valdez, si bien están ancladas en estas historias, también hablan de nuestro momento presente. Respecto de la serie, el artista afirma: "Exponer este tema histórico en un contexto contemporáneo me permite presentar la soga como una metáfora y sugerir que la amenaza está latente".[15] Valdez sostiene que nuestro país se fundó sobre la violencia y que el racismo quedó incrustado en nuestro ADN nacional. Esta injusticia sistémica se manifiesta en formas menos evidentes: violencia económica, planificación urbana, políticas corporativas predatorias, encarcelamiento masivo, discriminación racial, sistemas educativos y de justicia no equitativos y políticas de inmigración.

En *La fruta más extraña* Valdez utilizó como modelos a amigos y familiares (reconocemos a Daniel otra vez), convirtiendo a la serie en algo muy personal. La serie omite la violencia gráfica, pero analiza, en cambio, la violencia residual de la sociedad. Las figuras están atrapadas en un limbo ambiguo: es nuestra tarea, como personas espectadoras, determinar si están ascendiendo pacíficamente o hundiéndose en el olvido.

Pertenecer aquí 1993 & 2015-16

Valdez a menudo sentía que la discriminación le mantenía al margen de la vida estadounidense, pero tenía un fuerte deseo de entender la política como una forma de actuar en este país. Esto se hizo muy evidente un día cuando, a los dieciseis años, salía de trabajar del cine AMC al lado de Alamo en el centro de San Antonio. Sin darse cuenta, se encontró en medio de una concentración nacionalista blanca y vio cara a cara a un grupo de miembros del Klan que caminaban en círculos. Recuerda una figura encapuchada que sostenía una bandera estadounidense sobre su hombro y que hizo contacto visual con él, se inclinó hacia adelante y le susurró: "No perteneces aquí".

Años más tarde, en 2015, Valdez vio la pintura *Los límites de la ciudad* (1969) realizada por Philip Guston; que estaba en la exposición *Testigo: arte y derechos civiles en la década de 1960* en el Blanton Museum de Austin, Texas. La pintura de Guston, que parece un dibujo animado, muestra un automóvil con tres miembros encapuchados del Ku Klux Klan apretados en su interior, todo ello con un paisaje urbano como telón de fondo. *Los límites de la ciudad* despertó en Valdez las ganas de abordar una visión que había albergado durante varios años, basada en el recuerdo de su encuentro con la concentración del poder blanco cuando era adolescente. Condujo rápidamente a su estudio para trazar un esbozo de lo que se convertiría en su pintura épica: *El principio está cerca (una trilogía estadounidense), capítulo uno: La ciudad* (2015-16). Esta obra de dos paneles fusiona la experiencia de la vida y la referencia histórica del arte. Valdez reflejó su progreso de esta manera: "Primero, una sensación. Luego, una visión. A continuación, una idea. Luego, una realidad".

Catorce miembros encapuchados del Ku Klux Klan encuentran nuestra mirada incómoda en el primer panel de más de treinta pies (nueve metros) de largo, *La ciudad I* de 2015–16. Hemos interrumpido su reunión como la persona visitante no invitada. El grupo está formado no solo por adultos, sino también por un niño pequeño, cuyo dedo acusador es una referencia inquietante al anuncio de reclutamiento del tío Sam en la Primera Guerra Mundial, representado como un cartel dentro del bar de *¡Maten al pachuco malnacido!* más de una década atrás. Valdez consideró si incluir al niño o no, ya que reconocía que podría ser un punto álgido de controversia. Sin embargo, sostiene que el racismo y sus ideologías persistentes se enseñan y se transmiten de generación en generación.

En *La ciudad I*, los miembros del Klan se han reunido en un acantilado con vista a una metrópolis nocturna. Valdez se refiere al paisaje urbano circundante como "la base que une toda la imagen".[16] Hace a un lado la tendencia del público a centrarse solo en las figuras y combina *La ciudad I* con un panel complementario: *La ciudad II*. Una vez más, el paisaje reclama nuestra atención. La pintura, desprovista de figuras humanas, muestra una pila de colchones acompañados de basura en una representación simbólica de *La ciudad I*.

Valdez desdibuja la distinción entre pasado y presente mediante una paleta de blanco y negro para recordarnos que el racismo es persistente: el presente está siempre repleto de posibles actos de violencia. Este racismo cotidiano evoca los escritos de Hannah Arendt sobre el mal, en los que separa la naturaleza maligna de los crímenes y las personas comunes responsables.[17] Su término "banalidad" es análogo a las señales visuales de Valdez, ya sea la lata de cerveza Budweiser o el radiante iPhone. Estos detalles alteran las representaciones tradicionales del mal como excepcional o demoníaco, y las convierten en algo común y rutinario. Como expresó James Baldwin: "Siempre ha sido mucho más fácil (porque siempre ha parecido mucho más seguro) darle un nombre al mal exterior que localizar el terror interior".[18] Valdez advierte que la intolerancia no debe historizarse ni exteriorizarse: el potencial para el odio se encuentra en todos nosotros. En el mismo sentido, Guston afirmó que sus figuras encapuchadas eran autorretratos, reconociendo así su complicidad con los males sociales.

Un aspecto clave de *La ciudad I* es que los ojos de las figuras encapuchadas se encuentran a la misma altura que la de los espectadores. "Presentarlas atrapadas en actos mundanos y corrientes fue mi manera de despojarlas de su poder". ¿Cómo funcionan estas obras que rememoran el trauma en un momento tan inundado de imágenes de violencia? Valdez sostiene que cumplen una función necesaria: invita a su imagen a dejar un residuo psicológico, mientras el espectador lidia con la yuxtaposición de la banalidad con el mal. Las imágenes de Valdez perduran, como fantasmas. Sobre este fenómeno, el escritor Andrew Gallix observa: "Cuando lo piensas, todas las formas de representación son fantasmales. Las obras de arte son fantasmales, no solo por las formas ideales de las que son instancias imperfectas, sino también por lo que escapa a la representación".[19] Lo que escapa a la representación es también la parte sumergida del iceberg.

Esta obra fue profética en su presagio sobre la normalización del discurso intolerante durante las elecciones de 2016 y a partir de ese momento. Como temía Valdez, su arte y la situación política exterior se fusionaron. Mientras Estados Unidos se presentaba a sí mismo como una sociedad posracial después de la presidencia de Barack Obama, Valdez sintió que se estaba formando una reacción opresiva y advirtió que nos habíamos vuelto demasiado complacientes en nuestra negación.

La ciudad, se convirtió en el primer capítulo de una serie de tres partes, seguida de *El principio está cerca (una trilogía estadounidense), capítulo dos: Sueña, cariño, sueña* (2018). El título de la serie alude a la encrucijada del futuro de los Estados Unidos que comenzó en 2016 y se extiende hasta el presente. El 3 de junio de 2016, mientras Valdez completaba el panel final de *La ciudad I*, murió el venerado boxeador Muhammad Ali. El artista vio la cobertura televisiva del funeral de Ali desde su estudio y quedó conmovido por la diversidad y la armonía de los oradores y oradoras invitados, una verdadera representación de los Estados Unidos del siglo XXI. *Sueña, cariño, sueña* está compuesta por doce paneles monocromáticos que representan a personas compungidas de pie ante un par de micrófonos y un fondo de arreglos florales funerarios. Vemos el rostro de la viuda de Ali ocultado por un sombrero de ala grande, un trío de nativos americanos, un rabino judío, un político y un poeta musulmán. Nos encontramos con otro momento elíptico: las personas que hablarán, están listas para hacerlo, pero permanecen en silencio. Incluso una de las imágenes de la serie aparece como un podio vacío.

Los rituales funerarios de *Sueña, cariño, sueña* marcaron una rara ocasión en la que Estados Unidos lamentó la muerte de un manifestante desafiante, un musulmán devoto, un activista contra la guerra, un estadounidense negro. En diversos idiomas y provenientes de una variedad de orígenes culturales, el grupo de panegiristas homenajeó a un individuo comprometido con la promoción de opiniones políticas a menudo poco populares en el avance hacia el progreso. Ali cuya figura no aparece como el iceberg de Hemingway, está representado a través de quienes lo lloran, es un retrato del extraordinario luchador a través de quienes reconcilian "la vida y el legado de Ali con la incipiente aprensión, la ansiedad, la división y la desilusión que surgieron y que resonaron en todo el país, de pantalla en pantalla".[20] La última obra de esta serie, y la única pintura vertical, muestra la corona funeraria de Ali, en la que aparece un lazo con este texto escrito: "Mantén los sueños ardiendo para siempre...", citando la canción de 1979 de Suicide, *Sueña, cariño, sueña*. La referencia lírica de Valdez enfatiza las elipsis como un espacio para que el público imagine nuevos finales posibles para este tiempo bifurcado de la historia de nuestra nación. ¿Es esta la pérdida o el renacimiento de un sueño estadounidense?

Esperando ser determinado 2018-19

En diversas obras de 2018 y 2019, Valdez experimentó con la fragmentación como estrategia visual para representar el declive político. Estas obras fueron creadas en un período marcado por la batalla por la confirmación de Brett Kavanaugh en la Corte Suprema, la separación de familias de inmigrantes en la frontera entre Estados Unidos y México y los intentos generalizados de supresión de votantes. *Devorados* de 2018–19 es una alegoría del camino destructivo de la codicia con un insólito protagonista central. Un cerdo glotón descansa indigestado en medio de un entorno posapocalíptico, que evoca el páramo de *La ciudad II*. Hay desechos cotidianos (anteojos, billetes de dólar arrugados, un reloj, un cigarrillo humeante, un insecto muerto, un libro mordido) desparramados por el lienzo. La mano y el pie de un ser humano sobresalen por debajo del cuerpo hinchado del cerdo, lo que recuerda a las pinturas de Théodore Géricault de miembros amputados del cuerpo masculino partido en pedazos y luego vuelto a unir. Los rasgos físicos del cerdo provienen de rostros estadounidenses familiares de personas que han moldeado las políticas exterior e interior y la vida cotidiana de nuestro país: las orejas de Robert McNamara, exsecretario de Defensa de los Estados Unidos y arquitecto de la estrategia militar para la guerra de Vietnam; los ojos de J. Edgar Hoover, director del FBI durante casi medio siglo, y la piel de Steve Bannon, fundador de Breitbart News. El cerdo, que nos mira directo a los ojos, ha devorado todo y a todos a su paso, sin un final a la vista.

Desde 1977 (2019), de la misma época que *Devorados*, contiene meras sugerencias de los rasgos físicos de políticos estadounidenses. Con ocho dibujos, Valdez representa los retratos de los siete presidentes que ocuparon el cargo desde el año de su nacimiento, como se referencia en el título de la obra. Esta serie presenta retratos políticos y un autorretrato poco convencionales. Las imágenes son como fotogramas congelados de las figuras del poder estadounidense que Valdez ha observado a lo largo de su vida. Como "el rostro es el lugar de la política",[21] estas figuras prominentes están reducidas a la parte superior de su cabeza, en particular, a sus peinados icónicos, ojos furtivos y frentes emotivas. Son palpables sus emociones humanas básicas, como la vergüenza, el orgullo, la codicia y la ansiedad (así como la insolencia). Casi que los vemos como simples hombres, despojados de su poder mediante un encuadre orquestado. Esta serie complementa la anterior *Expulsión de la gran ciudad*, donde apreciamos los cuerpos completos de las figuras, salvo los ojos y la parte superior del rostro.

La historiadora de arte Linda Nochlin equiparó ese recorte de la figura con un dolor modernista por la pérdida de una plenitud utópica. Sostiene que la representación artística de un cuerpo humano fragmentado surgió a fines del siglo XIX a partir de "esa sensación de fragmentación social, psicológica e incluso metafísica que parece caracterizar la experiencia moderna: una pérdida de la plenitud, una ruptura de la conexión, una destrucción o desintegración".[22] Las cabezas fragmentadas de los que ocupan cargos ejecutivos en el poder en Desde 1977 descienden en forma gradual cada vez más, con lo cual insinúan un constante declive a medida que pasa el tiempo. Como conclusión de la obra, Valdez propone "un vacío parecido a un abismo, que espera a ser determinado por ustedes, el pueblo estadounidense".

Brilla fuerte 2020-24

En 2020, Valdez se trasladó a New Haven, Connecticut, para iniciar una residencia de estudio. Debido al brote de COVID-19, la residencia de un año de Valdez se alargó a dos. Este período, marcado por el aislamiento y la incertidumbre para la mayoría de las personas, no fue diferente para el artista, quien se encontró en un nuevo entorno lejos de sus familiares y amistades. En este contexto, creó obras muy personales, como dibujos diarios de "mi entorno inmediato" para marcar cada uno de los días. Valdez comenzó la serie *Amnesia* imaginando a colegas de la residencia seguidos de jóvenes boxeadores aficionados que entrenaban en el centro comunitario de al lado. Experimentó con una expresión más inmediata y con limitaciones de tiempo más reducidas, lo cual se pone de manifiesto en sus marcas gestuales. Estos pilares de apoyo colgaban en su estudio como una presencia optimista en una época cada vez más incierta. La serena determinación de las figuras contrarresta la ansiedad y la inquietud palpables en sus obras anteriores, y aborda con confianza los rostros desolados de los boxeadores de *Hombres hechos*.

La especificidad del retrato vista en los dibujos de *Amnesia* se repite en las obras más recientes de Valdez, y se consolida así su creencia en los individuos ante todo. En un principio, el artista pretendía concluir *El principio está cerca* con *Sueña, cariño, sueña*, pero en cambio consideró urgente terminar con una nota personal y poderosa con *El principio está cerca (una trilogía estadounidense), capítulo tres: Los nuevos estadounidenses* (en curso desde 2021). Aquí, como Valdez se centra en un solo individuo por panel, el formato panorámico de los dos primeros capítulos ahora es vertical y en color. En 2021, Valdez se comprometió a pintar a veintiún estadounidenses del siglo XXI que siguen dando "la buena batalla" dentro de sus comunidades. Estos monumentos retratan anclas personales para Valdez, incluidas las artistas Teresita Fernández y Adriana Corral, así como los activistas Mr. Checkpoint (#AFTP) y Juan Cartagena (fundador de Latino Justice PRLDEF). Valdez, dice: "*Los nuevos estadounidenses* son para mí un simple recordatorio de que el futuro, incluso en su hora más oscura e incierta, aún puede brillar con fuerza".

Asimismo, este conjunto se convierte en una especie de autorretrato de Valdez, una crónica personal de las personas que lo han inspirado y animado a seguir adelante. En celebración de los objetivos diferentes pero nobles de las personas retratadas, cuya motivación va más allá de la fama o el beneficio propio, estas obras tienen una escala monumental y miden casi ocho pies (dos metros) de alto, haciendo a los sujetos más grandes que en la vida real. Aparecen de pie, desafiantes, y en una amplia gama de colores; "un pulso obstinado en un latido moribundo".[23] Cada modelo eligió su respectivo fondo como participante activo de su retrato. Por ejemplo, Fernández está en el verdoso jardín de su casa en Brooklyn, un elemento muy relevante para su práctica artística, ya que se dedica a desenterrar historias arraigadas en el paisaje. Por su parte, Mr. Checkpoint mira desde la intersección frente al departamento de policía de Santa Mónica, donde fue detenido y encarcelado injustamente en 2012. Los capítulos anteriores de la trilogía que cuestionaban la injusticia y la ineficacia política dan un giro en *Los nuevos estadounidenses*, y se transforman en retratos de amor y fortaleza. Estos testimonios afirman que las personas estamos conectadas a través de la acción colectiva. Valdez nos recuerda: "Incluso cuando tengan pocas posibilidades y les jueguen sucio, la justicia, la verdad y la humanidad deben prevalecer. Mantengan la cabeza bien en alto".

El principio está cerca aborda las dualidades —agitación y contemplación, tensión y paz— para encender tanto nuestra empatía como nuestra aprensión. Esta dicotomía se hace evidente en *Ascenso* de 2019. En esta obra, Valdez pone en primer plano un enorme montículo de piedras, el sol, en tanto, se oculta en el horizonte. ¿Son bloques de construcción o los restos de un colapso? El montículo está iluminado por un sol resplandeciente, una referencia ambigua, ya que puede ser el amanecer o el atardecer; es un cielo en transición. En este entorno desorientador, el tiempo queda suspendido, es incierto. Una bruma lo cubre todo. El principio parece cercano, también el final.

Esta obra, una señal de esperanza que emerge de la desesperación, alude a la letra de *Hay un lado positivo en alguna parte,* de Ry Cooder:

Pues hay un lado positivo en alguna parte

Hay un lado positivo en alguna parte

Y no descansaré hasta encontrarlo

Hay un lado positivo en alguna parte

Y hay más amor en alguna parte

Y hay más paz en alguna parte

No descansaré hasta encontrarlos

Hay un lado positivo en alguna parte[24]

En contraste con el "lado positivo", las obras de Valdez pueden parecer sombrías. Sin embargo, quizás sea mejor una definición alternativa de elíptico: oscuro. La oscuridad puede significar lo no visto, lo desconocido y lo no descubierto. Abre posibles futuros, en lugar de insinuar pesimismo. En ese mismo sentido, no podemos reducir la obra de Valdez a una connotación unidimensional de oscuridad, porque durante los últimos veinticinco, a partir de su rechazo a la tentación de ignorar el pasado, nos ha ofrecido un testimonio visual. Identificar la esperanza frente a la incertidumbre es lo que mejor sabe hacer Valdez; lo vemos una y otra vez: en el vacío del último panel de *Desde 1977* o en el resplandeciente sol de *Ascenso*. Valdez nos recuerda que todavía hay muchas cosas por las que merece la pena luchar. Esta audacia de imaginar una alternativa no nace de la ingenuidad, sino que tiene su origen en una evaluación crítica.

Valdez construye un legado emancipador y desorientador para revelarnos un nuevo horizonte en el que no hay ninguna brújula que nos ayude a guiarnos. Consideremos su autorretrato *En busca de una nueva tierra* (2018), donde se representa a sí mismo mirando hacia una tierra estéril, un Estados Unidos que aún no se ha construido o que fue devastado. Cuál de las dos, no lo sabemos. Sin embargo, él sigue buscando. Por medio de esta imagen, Valdez nos invita a acompañarlo en la búsqueda de nuevas figuras para celebrar: un vecino o una vecina, una persona luchadora que sigue en pie, el sentido del yo y, quizás, una nueva tierra...

[1] Paul Smith, "1924: El equipaje de Hemingway y el año milagroso" en *Complemento de Cambridge para Ernest Hemingway*, editado por Scott Donaldson (Cambridge: Cambridge University Press, 1966), pág. 41.

[2] Charles M. Oliver, *Ernest Hemingway de la A a la Z: la referencia esencial a la vida y la obra* (Nueva York: Facts on File, 1999), pág. 322.

[3] Seamus Perry, *Estados Unidos es un poema en nuestros ojos* (Times Literary Supplement, número 6127, septiembre de 2020), pág. 4.

[4] El título de Valdez proviene de la canción de 1958 de Jimmy Clanton and His Rockets.

[5] Michel Foucault, *El discurso valiente*, ed. Joseph Pearson (Los Ángeles, Semiotext(e), 2001).

[6] Todas las citas del artista provienen de una serie de entrevistas con el autor durante 2023 y 2024, a menos que se indique lo contrario.

[7] Daniel aparece varias veces en la obra de Valdez, también se lo ve en *Hombres hechos: Juro que veo mi reflejo* (2003), y como el boxeador central en *Estaciones* (2002–04).

[8] *Vincent Valdez: En conversación*, Museum of Fine Arts Boston, 7 de mayo de 2022, 24:54.

[9] Entrevista oral de historia con el artista y educador Vincent Valdez, entrevistado por Brookes Ebetsch, Universidad de Notre Dame, IN, 2005, 28:00.

[10] Norman Klein, *Una historia de olvidos* (Londres: Verso Books, 1997), copia de portada.

[11] *Vincent Valdez: Fragmentos para John* por Walley Films, 2012.

[12] Susan Sontag, *Ante el dolor de los demás* (Nueva York: Farrar, Straus and Giroux, 2003), pág. 115.

[13] Richard Hofstadter, "Reflexiones sobre la violencia en Estados Unidos", *The Baffler Magazine*, nro. 28, 2015, pág. 28.

[14] Judith Butler, *Marcos de guerra: las vidas lloradas)*(Londres y Nueva York: Verso Books, 2010), pág. 38.

[15] Juan Cartagena, "La soga, la sudadera y el estado" en *Vincent Valdez: La fruta más extraña* (Waynesboro, VA: McClung Companies, 2015), pág. 39.

[16] Andrea Lepage, *Entrevista con Vincent Valdez: EL principio está cerca*, folleto, 2016, pág. 3.

[17] Hannah Arendt, *Eichmann en Jerusalén: un estudio sobre la banalidad del mal* (Nueva York: Penguin Books, 1992), pág. 287.

[18] James Baldwin and Richard Avedon, *Nada personal* (Colonia: Taschen, 2017), pág. 17.

[19] Andrew Gallix, "Espectrología: una manifestación crítica no muy nueva. La nueva moda en la teoría literaria está impregnada de ideas anteriores" *The Guardian*, 17 junio de 2011.

[20] Ian Alden Russell, *Sueña, cariño sueña*, folleto para David Shelton Gallery, Houston, TX, 2018.

[21] Giorgio Agamben, *Cuando la casa se quema: desde el dialecto del pensamiento* (Chicago: University of Chicago Press, 2022), pág. 8.

[22] Linda Nochlin, *El cuerpo en pedazos: el fragmento como metáfora de la modernidad* (Londres: Thames & Hudson, 2001), pág. 56.

[23] *Vincent Valdez: Las tardes de los martes con el ciclo de conferencias modernas*, Modern Art Museum of Fort Worth, 8 de marzo de 2022, 54:04.

[24] Ry Cooder, *Mi nombre es Buddy*, Nonesuch Records, 2007.

DEL BOXEO

Joyce Carol Oates

¿Por qué te has hecho boxeador?, le preguntaron al irlandés Barry McGuigan, campeón peso pluma. Él respondió: "No puedo ser poeta. No sé contar historias...."

Cada combate de boxeo es una historia, un drama sin palabras, único y sumamente condensado. Incluso cuando no sucede nada sensacional: entonces el drama es "meramente" psicológico. Los boxeadores están ahí para establecer una experiencia absoluta, una rendición pública de cuentas sobre los límites máximos de su propio ser. Ellos saben, como pocos podríamos saber acerca de nosotros mismos, qué poder físico y psíquico poseen, es decir hasta dónde son capaces de llegar. Entrar al *ring* medio desnudo y arriesgar la propia vida es hacer de su público una especie de *voyeur*... el boxeo es tan íntimo. Es salirse de la conciencia de la cordura para entrar en otra, difícil de nombrar. Es arriesgarse, y a veces alcanzar, la agonía (cuya raíz proviene del griego "agón", que significa "contienda").

En el cuadrilátero de boxeo hay dos actores principales, observados por un sombrío tercero. El ceremonial toque de campana es un llamamiento a la vigilancia total para los dos boxeadores y para los espectadores. Pone en marcha, además, la autoridad del tiempo.

Los boxeadores pondrán en el combate todo lo que son, y todo quedará expuesto, incluso secretos que ni ellos mismos pueden advertir del todo. Y además, el yo físico, o bien la virilidad, que subyace en el "yo". Hay boxeadores poseídos por una intuición tan extraordinaria, una clarividencia tan misteriosa, que podría pensarse que, de algún modo, están recordando sus peleas, y no luchando en ese momento que presenciamos. Hay boxeadores que actúan con destreza, pero mecánicamente, que no pueden improvisar para responder al cambio de estrategia del otro; hay boxeadores que, mientras actúan al máximo de su talento, advierten, en mitad del combate, que no será suficiente; hay boxeadores, incluso grandes campeones, cuyas carreras terminan abrupta e irrevocablemente ante nuestras miradas. Ha habido al menos un boxeador poseído por una conciencia extraordinaria e inquietante, no solo de cada movimiento actual y anticipado de su contrincante, sino también de los más sutiles cambios de ánimo del público, de los cuales parece haberse sentido personalmente responsable: Cassius Clay/Muhammad Ali, por supuesto. "La dulce ciencia de magullar" celebra la naturaleza física de los hombres aun cuando dramatiza las limitaciones, a veces trágicas, y sobre todo conmovedoras, de lo físico. Si bien el espectador masculino se identifica con los boxeadores, no hay boxeador que actúe como un hombre "normal" cuando está en el ring, y no hay combinación de golpes que sea "natural". Todo es estilo.

Todo talento debe desplegarse en la lucha. Así habla Nietzsche del pasado helénico, la historia de la "contienda" atlética, y de otra índole mediante la cual los jóvenes griegos eran educados en la ciudadanía griega. Sin la ferocidad de la competición, incluso sin "envidia, celos y ambición" en la contienda, la ciudad helénica, al igual que el hombre helénico, se degeneró. Si la muerte es un riesgo, la muerte es también el premio... para el atleta vencedor.

En el cuadrilátero de boxeo, incluso en nuestros muy humanizados tiempos, la muerte es siempre una posibilidad, lo cual explica por qué algunos preferimos mirar películas o cintas de combates ya pasados, ya definidos como historia. O, en algunos casos, como arte. (Si bien mientras me preparaba para escribir este ensayo de estilo mosaico miré las grabaciones de dos infames y recientes combates "mortales": el de 1982 entre los pesos gallo Lupe Pintor y Johnny Owen, y la pelea de los pesos ligeros Ray Mancini y Duk Koo-Kim del mismo año. En ambos casos los boxeadores murieron como consecuencia de su pasmosa resistencia y energía inagotable: "su corazón", como se dice en los círculos pugilísticos). En la mayoría de las ocasiones, sin embargo, la muerte en el cuadrilátero es extremadamente improbable; una rara posibilidad estadística, como tu posible muerte mañana a la mañana en un accidente automovilístico o en el próximo siniestro aéreo que reseñen los periódicos del mes que viene o en algún oscuro accidente que entrañe una caída por las escaleras o en la bañera, una fractura de cráneo, una hemorragia subaracnoides. En los combates "mortales", los espectadores suelen sostener que lo que sucedió pareció suceder, sencillamente... de manera imprevisible, en cierto sentido, por accidente. Solo en retrospectiva aparece la muerte como algo que fue inevitable.

Si un combate de boxeo es una historia, es siempre una historia caprichosa, una en la que cualquier cosa puede suceder. Y en cuestión de segundos. ¡En fracciones de segundos! (Muhammad Ali se jactaba de poder lanzar un puñetazo a mayor velocidad de la que el ojo podía seguirlo, y es posible que tuviera razón). En ningún otro deporte pueden ocurrir tantas cosas en un lapso de tiempo tan breve, ni de modo tan irrevocable.

Que el combate de boxeo sea una historia sin palabras no significa que no tenga texto ni lenguaje, que sea, de algún modo, una historia "bruta", "primitiva", "inarticulada"; lo que ocurre es que el texto se improvisa en la acción; el lenguaje es un diálogo de la más refinada especie entre los boxeadores (podría decirse que tanto neurológico como psicológico: un diálogo de reflejos detonados en fracciones de segundos), en una respuesta conjunta a la misteriosa voluntad del público, que es siempre que el combate valga la pena para que la cruda parafernalia del escenario: cuadrilátero, luces, cuerdas, la lona manchada, los mismos y atentísimos observadores quede borrada, olvidada. (Como en el teatro o en la iglesia, el escenario queda borrado, idealmente, mediante la acción trascendente). Los anunciadores de la primera fila le dan al mudo espectáculo una unidad narrativa; sin embargo, en tanto que actuación pública, el boxeo es, con toda claridad, más afín a la danza o la música que a la narrativa.

Pasar de una pelea preliminar ordinaria a un "combate del siglo" como aquellos entre Joe Louis y Billy Conn, Joe Frazier y Muhammad Ali, Marvin Hagler y Thomas Hearns, es como pasar de escuchar, o de escuchar a medias, un punteo perezoso en una guitarra a escuchar *El clave bien temperado* de Bach perfectamente ejecutado, y eso también es parte del misterio de la historia: ocurre tanto tan rápidamente y con tal sutileza de infarto que no puede asimilarse sino para saber que algo profundo está sucediendo y que está sucediendo más allá de las palabras.

Trato de darle a mi adversario en la punta de la nariz porque intento hundirle el hueso en el cerebro.—MIKE TYSON

El boxeo pretende ser superior a la vida en la medida en que es, en el mejor de los casos, superior a todo accidente. Nada contiene que no sea del todo intencionado.

El boxeador se enfrenta a un contrincante que es una distorsión onírica de sí mismo en el sentido de que sus debilidades, posibilidad de error y de ser gravemente herido, sus desaciertos intelectuales, todo, puede ser interpretado como fortalezas que pertenecen al Otro; los parámetros de su ser íntimo no son más que las ilimitadas afirmaciones de la personalidad del Otro. Esto es sueño, o pesadilla: mis fortalezas no son del todo las mías, sino las debilidades de mi adversario; mi fracaso no es totalmente el mío, sino el triunfo de mi adversario. Él es mi yo-sombra, no mi (mera) sombra. El combate de boxeo, tan "serio, completo y de cierta magnitud" —para emplear la definición aristotélica de la tragedia— es un evento que necesariamente subsume a ambos boxeadores, del mismo modo en que cualquier ceremonia subsume a sus participantes. (Lo cual explica que se pueda decir, por ejemplo, que el mejor combate de la carrera de Muhammad Ali fue uno de los pocos que perdió: su primera y heroica pelea con Frazier).

El viejo adagio del boxeo —sin duda falso— según el cual no te pueden dejar *noqueado* si ves venir el golpe, y si *te propones* que no te dejen *noqueado*, tiene un significado más sutil e intimidador: nada de lo que le suceda al boxeador en el *ring*, incluso la muerte —su muerte— es ajeno a su voluntad o al fracaso de esta. Lo que se sugiere es un modelo de mundo en el que somos humanamente responsables no solo de nuestros propios actos sino también de aquellos ejecutados contra nosotros.

Ello explica que el boxeo, aunque se desprende de la vida, no es una metáfora de esta sino un mundo único, cerrado y autorreferencial, indirectamente afín a esas religiones severas para las cuales el individuo es a la vez "libre" y "determinado", en un sentido poseído por una voluntad equivalente a la de Dios, y, en otro, totalmente indefenso . La sensibilidad puritana habría entendido una boca que se llena de sangre, un ojo expulsado de su órbita: el castigo a un instante de negligencia.

Se dice que la tarea más difícil de un entrenador de boxeo es convencer a un boxeador joven de que se levante y siga peleando después de haber sido derribado. Y si el boxeador ha sido derribado por un golpe que no vio venir —lo cual suele ocurrir— ¿cómo puede abrazarse a la esperanza de evitar que lo derriben una y otra vez? El golpe invisible es, al fin y al cabo, invisible.

Resultaría insoportable, profundamente vergonzoso, contemplar una conducta "normal" en el *ring*, pues los seres "normales" comparten con todas las criaturas vivientes el instinto de preservación, como decía Spinoza, en su propio ser. El boxeador ha de aprender de algún modo, mediante algún esfuerzo de voluntad que los no boxeadores seguramente no podrían intuir, a inhibir su propio instinto de supervivencia; debe aprender a ejercer su "voluntad" sobre sus impulsos meramente humanos y animales, no solo a eludir el dolor sino también a eludir lo desconocido. En términos psíquicos esto suena a magia. Levitación. La cordura puesta del revés, la "locura" revelada como una forma más elevada y pragmática de la cordura.

En el cuadrilátero, los luchadores están sujetos al tiempo —nada debe ser tan dolorosamente largo como un asalto de tres minutos ferozmente disputado— pero la lucha en sí es atemporal. En cierto sentido se convierte en todas las luchas, del mismo modo en que los boxeadores son todos los boxeadores. Por medio de las películas, las grabaciones y las fotografías, todo se convierte, muy rápido y ante nuestros ojos, en historia, incluso, a veces, en arte. El tiempo, al igual que la posibilidad de muerte, es el adversario invisible del cual los boxeadores y el árbitro, los ayudantes, los espectadores son profundamente conscientes. Cuando un boxeador es noqueado no significa, como suele pensarse, que haya quedado sin sentido, o incluso incapacitado; significa, en un sentido más poético, que ha sido sacado del tiempo. (El dramático conteo hasta diez que entona el árbitro constituye una especie de paréntesis metafísico a través del cual el boxeador debe introducirse si pretende continuar en el tiempo). Hay, de alguna manera, dos dimensiones del tiempo que operan de forma abrupta: mientras el boxeador que permanece en pie está *en el tiempo*, el boxeador caído *está fuera del tiempo*. Concluido el conteo hasta diez, se le da "por muerto", en simbólico remedo de la antigua tradición deportiva según la cual el combatiente estaría con toda probabilidad muerto. (Aunque, conforme recordamos, los astutos romanos se reservaban, como espectadores, el golpe de gracia que habría de traer la muerte propiamente dicha: el gladiador vencedor estaba obligado a esperar una orden que provendría de fuera de la arena antes de acabar con su adversario).

Si el boxeo es un deporte, es el más trágico de todos, pues consume, más que cualquier otra actividad humana, la mismísima excelencia que saca a relucir: su drama es precisamente esta consumación. Consumirse librando la pelea más grande de la carrera es iniciar, por necesidad, la curva de descenso que podría la próxima vez ser un hundimiento, una abrupta caída en el abismo. *Soy el más grande*, dice Muhammad Ali. *Soy el más grande*, dice Marvin Hagler. "Siempre piensas que vas a ganar", señaló irónicamente Jack Dempsey en su vejez, "de otro modo, no podrías pelear". El castigo —al cuerpo, al cerebro, al espíritu— que un hombre debe soportar para llegar a ser un boxeador más o menos bueno es inconcebible para la mayoría de los que asociamos la idea del riesgo personal con el ego o lo emocional. Pero cuando el castigo empieza a revelarse, incluso en un boxeador joven y vigoroso, es atentamente observado por sus rivales, que esperan su descuido. (Después de que Aaron Pryor, campeón de peso superligero, ganara una mediocre pelea el año anterior, un joven boxeador de su misma categoría, entrevistado junto al cuadrilátero, dijo con una sonrisa: "Se me hace agua la boca". También está la cruda declaración de Billy Costello cuando dijo, a sus veintinueve años: "Si no puedo derrotar a un viejo [de treinta y tres años], más vale que me retire", poco antes de su combate con Alexis Argüello, en el que fue noqueado en uno de los primeros asaltos).

En el *ring*, los boxeadores viven una extraña especie de tiempo "lento"—los aficionados nunca pelean más de tres asaltos, y para la mayoría esos nueve minutos son agotadores— mientras que fuera del cuadrilátero viven en un tiempo alarmantemente acelerado. Un boxeador de veintitrés años ya no es joven en la medida en que lo es un hombre de treinta y tres años; uno de treinta y cinco años es francamente viejo. (Y es por eso que Muhammad Ali cometió un trágico error cuando decidió continuar con su carrera después de haber perdido su título por segunda vez y salió de su retiro a los treinta y ocho para pelear con Larry Holmes ; y por ese mismo motivo Holmes cometió un error parecido, ya que años después se expuso sin necesidad alguna a graves lesiones y a situaciones profesionalmente vergonzosas cuando se enfrentó con el campeón de los pesos semipesados Michael Spinks. La victoria de Jersey Joe Walcott, de treinta y siete años, sobre Ezzard Charles, de treinta, por el título de los pesos pesados en 1951, es *sui generis*. Y Archie Moore es *sui generis*). Todos los atletas envejecen muy rápido, pero ninguno lo hace tan veloz y tan visiblemente como el boxeador.

Así las cosas, la experiencia de observar a grandes boxeadores del pasado es en extremo diferente a verlos actuar cuando eran campeones reinantes. Jack Johnson, Jack Dempsey, Joe Louis, Sugar Ray Robinson, Rocky Marciano, Muhammad Ali, Joe Frazier: como espectadores, sabemos no solo cómo termina un combate sino también una carrera. No solo la trayectoria de diez o quince asaltos sino también la de toda una vida...

Todo cuanto el hombre estima dura un momento o un día. El placer del amor a su amor aleja, el pincel del pintor consume sus sueños; el grito del heraldo, el paso del soldado agotan su gloria y su poder: todo cuanto flamea sobre la noche ha alimentado el resinoso corazón del hombre.—WILLIAM BUTLER YEATS, de *La resurrección*

Odio decirlo, pero es verdad: sólo me gusta más cuando viene el dolor. — FRANK "THE ANIMAL" FLETCHER, antiguo contendiente de peso medio.

No pretendo justificar que el boxeo es un deporte porque nunca lo he considerado como tal.

No hay nada fundamentalmente lúdico en él; nada que parezca pertenecer a la luz del día, al placer. En sus momentos de mayor intensidad parece contener una imagen de la vida tan completa y potente —belleza de la vida, vulnerabilidad, desesperación, coraje incalculable y a veces autodestructivo— que el boxeo es la vida, y es muy difícil que pueda ser un simple juego. Durante un combate pugilístico de altura (Ali-Frazier I, por ejemplo), nos sentimos profundamente conmovidos por la comunión del cuerpo consigo mismo a través de la intransigente carne de otro. El diálogo del cuerpo con su yo-sombra o bien con la Muerte. El béisbol, el fútbol, el baloncesto: esos pasatiempos tan norteamericanos por excelencia son deportes de fácil reconocimiento porque implican jugar, es decir, son juegos. *Se juega* al fútbol, pero no se *juega* al boxeo.

Cuando observamos deportes en equipo, equipos de hombres adultos, podemos ver cómo los hombres son niños en el sentido más dichoso de la palabra. Pero el boxeo, en su ferocidad elemental, no puede asociarse con la niñez. (Si bien es real que hay hombres muy jóvenes que boxean, incluso profesionalmente, y muchos campeones mundiales se iniciaron en el boxeo en los primeros años de su adolescencia. Cuando tenía dieciséis años, Jack Dempsey, desarraigado y a la deriva en el Oeste, peleaba por pequeñas sumas de dinero en salas de boxeo sin árbitro, en las que, siguiendo el orden natural de las cosas, podría haber encontrado la muerte). Los espectadores de juegos públicos obtienen gran parte de su placer al recrear las emociones colectivas de la niñez, pero los espectadores de los combates de boxeo reviven la infancia homicida de la raza. De ahí el salvajismo ocasional de las masas de aficionados al boxeo —la multitud, en su mayoría hispana, que lanzó gritos de júbilo cuando el galés Johnny Owen perdió el sentido a manos del campeón de peso gallo, el mexicano Lupe Pintor, por ejemplo— y la excitación que se produce cuando un hombre empieza a sangrar en serio.

Cuando habla de sangre, Marvelous Marvin Hagler habla de la suya, por supuesto.

Considerado en abstracto, el cuadrilátero de boxeo es una especie de altar, uno de esos espacios legendarios donde las leyes de una nación quedan suspendidas: cuerdas adentro, en el transcurso de un asalto de tres minutos regulado de manera oficial, un hombre puede morir a manos de su contrincante, pero no puede ser legalmente asesinado. El boxeo habita un espacio sagrado y depredador de la civilización; o bien, para emplear la frase de D. H. Lawrence, un tiempo “antes de que Dios fuera amor”. Si ello sugiere una ceremonia salvaje o un rito expiatorio, también sugiere la futilidad de tales gestos. Pues, ¿qué posible expiación es el combate librado si ha de ser en breve librado otra vez... y de nuevo una vez más? El combate de boxeo es la mismísima imagen —la más aterradora, por ser tan estilizada— de la agresividad colectiva de la humanidad, de su continua demencia histórica.

Hace años, a principios de la década de 1950, cuando mi padre me llevó por primera vez a un campeonato de boxeo Golden Gloves (Guantes de Oro) en Buffalo, Nueva York, le pregunté por qué esos chicos querían pelearse entre ellos, por qué estaban dispuestos a salir heridos. Como si fuera una explicación, mi padre dijo: “Los boxeadores no sienten el dolor igual que nosotros”.

El dolor, en el contexto adecuado, es algo distinto al dolor.

Consideremos: la única derrota de Gene Tunney durante una carrera de trece años de grandes distinciones, ocurrió frente a un afamado boxeador, Harry Greb, quien parece haber sido, a juzgar por el saber pugilístico, el boxeador más sucio de la historia. Greb era infame por sus faltas —golpes bajos, empujones, agarrones, restregar los cordones contra los ojos del adversario, manoteos— además de un frenético estilo de boxeo en el que los golpes eran lanzados desde cualquier dirección. (De ahí su mote de “el Molino de Viento Humano”). Greb, que murió joven, fue campeón mundial solo durante tres años, pero su presencia en los círculos pugilísticos fue muy notoria durante largo tiempo. Después del primero de sus muchos combates contra Greb, Tunney, de veintidós años, quedó tan malherido que tuvo que pasar una semana en cama; había perdido casi dos litros de sangre durante el combate de quince asaltos. No obstante, años más tarde, Tunney dijo:

Greb me dio una paliza terrible. Me rompió la nariz, quizás de un empujón. Me cortó los ojos y las orejas, tal vez con sus cordones... Me dejó la mandíbula hinchada desde la sien derecha hasta la mejilla, por debajo del mentón y parte del otro lado. El árbitro y también el ring estaba lleno de sangre... Pero fue en ese primer combate, en el que perdí mi título nacional de peso semipesado, cuando supe que había encontrado la forma de derrotar a Harry en un futuro. La verdad es que fui afortunado. Si el boxeo de aquella época hubiese padecido a los médicos de las comisiones que tenemos hoy —que están siempre metiendo la nariz en el ring para examinar heridas superficiales— el primer combate con Greb habría sido suspendido antes de que yo descubriera cómo derrotarlo. Es posible, incluso probable, que de haber pasado eso no se hubiera oído hablar de mí nunca más.

En otras palabras, la carrera de Tunney se construyó sobre el dolor. Sin él, nunca habría ascendido a la categoría de Dempsey.

Tommy Loughran, campeón de los pesos semipesados desde 1927 hasta 1929, fue un maestro del boxeo muy admirado por otros boxeadores. Abordaba el boxeo como una ciencia —al igual que Tunney— estudiaba el estilo de sus adversarios y trazaba estrategias de desplazamientos en el cuadrilátero para cada combate, tal como suelen hacerlo los boxeadores y entrenadores de la actualidad. Loughran instaló espejos en su sótano para poder mirarse mientras entrenaba, porque, como él decía, ningún boxeador se ve a sí mismo tal como lo ve su contrincante. Él ve a su contrincante, pero no se ve a sí mismo como contrincante. El secreto de la carrera de Loughran era que la mano derecha se le rompía con mucha facilidad, así que estaba obligado a usarla una sola vez por combate: para el golpe del nocaut o nada. “Si después de dar un golpe el tipo se volvía a levantar, el dolor me hacía más daño”, decía Loughran. Cualquiera al que le metiera un gancho de izquierda caería de bruces, pero nunca correría el riesgo, porque si me estropea la mano izquierda, estoy acabado.

Tanto Tunney como Loughran dejaron el boxeo mucho antes de que los obligaran a retirarse... una interesante lección. Tunney se convirtió en un próspero hombre de negocios, y Loughran, en exitoso broker del azúcar en el mercado de valores de Wall Street. (Esto para recordar que los boxeadores no son invariablemente estúpidos, analfabetos o borrachines).

¡Luego llegó Carmen Basilio!, adorado por su audaz estilo en el ring, su método de golpear y ser golpeado. Basilio fue campeón mundial de pesos medios y semimedios entre 1953 y 1957; un boxeador estoico, decidido y agresivo, dispuesto a dejarse golpear con el objetivo de propinar fuertes contragolpes. Los observadores se maravillaban ante el castigo que Basilio parecía absorber, si bien él insistía en que no era golpeado como la gente creía. Y cuando era golpeado, duramente golpeado...

La gente no se da cuenta de cómo te afecta un golpe de nocaut cuando te pegan en la barbilla. Todo pasa en los nervios. No hay una verdadera contusión en el cerebro. Yo recibí un golpe en la punta de la barbilla [en un combate contra Tony DeMarco en 1955]. Fue un gancho de izquierda que me pegó en la punta derecha del mentón. Lo que sucede es que te desencaja la mandíbula por el lado derecho y la empuja hacia el izquierdo, y el nervio que hay allí me paralizó todo el lado izquierdo del cuerpo, sobre todo las piernas. Se me dobló la rodilla izquierda y casi me vengo abajo, pero cuando volví a mi rincón, en la planta del pie sentía como si tuviera agujas de quince centímetros de largo, y lo que hice fue dar pisotones en el suelo, tratando de despertarlo. Cuando sonó la campana, ya estaba bien.

Basilio pertenece a la desenfrenada época de LaMotta, Graziano, Zale, Pep, Saddler, Gene Fullmer, Dick Tiger, Kid Gavilán, época en que si dos querían pelear sucio, era probable que el árbitro les autorizara, o al menos no interfiriese.

De la época de plenitud de Muhammad Ali, Norman Mailer señaló: “Parecía trabajar sobre la premisa de que había algo obsceno en que lo golpearan”. Pero en posteriores combates de su carrera, como el que libró contra George Foreman en el Zaire, hasta Muhammad Ali se mostraba dispuesto a ser golpeado, y resultar herido, con el propósito de cansar a su adversario. Los boxeadores camorreros —aquellos con "coraje", como Jake LaMotta, Rocky Graziano, Ray Mancini— no tienen mucha más opción que la de recibir terribles castigos a cambio de obtener alguna ventaja (que no siempre se da). Y sin duda es cierto que algunos boxeadores (véase la obra autobiográfica *Toro salvaje*, de Jake LaMotta) propician la lesión como medio para mitigar la culpa, en un intercambio, al estilo Dostoievski, de bienestar físico por tranquilidad de espíritu. El boxeo se trata más de ser golpeado que de golpear, del mismo modo en que se trata más de sentir dolor, cuando no una devastadora parálisis psicológica, que de ganar. Se ve con claridad, por las "trágicas" trayectorias de una enorme cantidad de boxeadores, que en el cuadrilátero prefieren el dolor físico antes que la ausencia de dolor, que es condición ideal de una vida común. Si no se puede golpear, por lo menos se puede ser golpeado, y saber que todavía se está vivo.

Podría decirse que con el boxeo se pretende, sobre todo, mantener un cuerpo con la capacidad de entrar en combate contra otros cuerpos en buenas condiciones. No es el espectáculo público, ni el combate en sí, sino el período de riguroso entrenamiento que conduce a él lo que exige la mayor disciplina, y se cree que es la causa principal de las dolencias físicas y mentales de los boxeadores. (A medida que el boxeador envejece, sus parejas de entrenamiento son más jóvenes, el juego en sí se vuelve más desesperado).

El artista percibe cierta afinidad, aunque indirecta y parcial, con el boxeador profesional en este aspecto del entrenamiento. La fanática subordinación del ser a un destino deseado. Podría compararse el espectáculo público de un combate de boxeo, limitado en el tiempo (que podría ser tan breve como de unos ignominiosos cuarenta y cinco segundos: ¡tiempo récord para una pelea por un título!), con la publicación del libro de un escritor. Lo "público" no es más que la fase final de un largo, arduo, agotador y a menudo desesperante período de preparación. En efecto, una de las razones de la habitual atracción de escritores serios por el boxeo (desde Swift, Pope y Johnson, hasta Hazlitt, Lord Byron, Hemingway y Norman Mailer, George Plimpton, Ted Hoagland, Wilfrid Sheed, Daniel Halpern, y otros) es el sistemático cultivo del dolor de ese deporte en aras de un proyecto, de una meta vital: la voluntaria trasposición de la sensación que conocemos como dolor (físico, psicológico, emocional) a su polo opuesto. Si eso es masoquismo —y dudo que lo sea, o que sea simplemente eso— es también inteligencia, astucia, estrategia. Es un acto de autodeterminación consumada: el restablecimiento constante de los parámetros de nuestro ser. No solo aceptar, sino además propiciar lo que la mayoría de los seres sanos evitan —dolor, humillación, pérdida, caos— es experimentar el momento presente como algo, en cierto sentido, ya pasado. *Aquí y ahora* no son sino parte de la construcción del *allí y entonces*: dolor ahora, pero control, y en consecuencia triunfo, después. Y el propio dolor es milagrosamente traspuesto por obra de su contexto. Ciertamente, podría decirse que el "contexto" lo es todo.

El novelista George Garret, boxeador aficionado de hace algunas décadas, recuerda su período de entrenamiento:

Aprendí algo... acerca de la hermandad de los boxeadores. La gente se dedicó a esta actividad brutal y a menudo autodestructiva por una amplia variedad de razones, casi todas amargamente antisociales y rayanas en lo psicótico. La mayoría de los luchadores de los que supe algo eran personas heridas que sentían una urgencia profunda y poderosa de herir a otras a riesgo de herirse verdaderamente. Al principio, lo que sucedía era que en casi todos los casos se exigía tanta disciplina y destreza, tantas otras cosas en las que concentrarse además de las propias motivaciones originales, que estas pasaban a tornarse borrosas y vagas, a menudo olvidadas, perdidas por completo. Muchos luchadores buenos y experimentados (como ha sido frecuentemente observado) se vuelven afables y simpáticos... Están acostumbrados a dejar sus peleas en el ring. E incluso allí, en el ring, resulta peligroso invocar demasiada rabia. Puede ser un estimulante, pero es muy oneroso en energía. La mayoría de las veces resulta poco práctico encolerizarse.

De todos los boxeadores, parece haber sido Rocky Marciano (que sigue siendo el único campeón estadounidense invicto de los pesos pesados) quien se entrenaba con la más monástica devoción; sus métodos de entrenamiento se han vuelto legendarios. A diferencia de boxeadores atolondrados como Harry Greb, "el Molino de Viento Humano", que se mantenía en forma porque no paraba de boxear, Marciano deseaba alejarse del mundo, incluso de su mujer y su familia, hasta tres meses antes de un combate. Aparte de la agotadora y rigurosa prueba física de ese período y de la obsesiva preocupación por la dieta, el peso y el tono muscular, Marciano se concentraba en una sola cosa: el combate por venir. Cada minuto de su vida estaba definido en términos del instante en que se inicia el combate. En su campo de entrenamiento, jamás se mencionaba el nombre de su adversario en presencia de Marciano, y tampoco se hablaba de boxeo. Llegado el último mes, Marciano no escribía cartas, pues las cartas pertenecían al mundo exterior. Durante los últimos diez días antes del combate no miraba su correspondencia, no recibía llamadas telefónicas, no se encontraba con nuevas amistades. La última semana anterior al combate se abstenía de dar la mano; no viajaba en coche, por corto que fuera el trayecto. ¡Nada de nuevos alimentos! ¡Nada de soñar con la mañana siguiente a la pelea! Pues todo lo que no fuera el combate tenía que ser excluido de la conciencia. Cuando Marciano entrenaba con un saco de boxeo veía a su contrincante frente a él, cuando corría veía a su adversario correr junto a él, sin duda cuando dormía lo "veía" sin cesar: como el monje o la monja enclaustrados deciden, por un acto de fanática voluntad, "ver" solo a Dios.

¿Es demencia —o mera disciplina— esta subordinación absoluta del ser? Comoquiera que sea, a Marciano le dio resultado.

EN ALGÚN LUGAR DEL SUR DE TEXAS

Evan Garza

Nosotros no cruzamos la frontera, la frontera nos cruzó a nosotros. Y no lo digo a modo de hipérbole ni como ejemplo de la retórica activista por los derechos de las personas migrantes (que, de hecho, lo es), sino porque realmente pasó. En 1848, se firmó el Tratado de Guadalupe Hidalgo, que puso fin a la guerra méxico–estadounidense y dio lugar a la expansión territorial más grande de la historia de Estados Unidos.[1] El acuerdo estableció que Estados Unidos anexaría el cincuenta y cinco por ciento del territorio mexicano, incluidas todas las tierras al norte del Río Grande, que en el Tratado se establecieron como la nueva frontera entre México y Estados Unidos. Los norteños, es decir, aquellas personas que vivían en las regiones del norte de México, eran libres de migrar al nuevo territorio mexicano, al sur del río, o de permanecer en su lugar y que se les considerara ciudadanos y ciudadanas estadounidenses. Ese hecho convierte a esta toma de tierras de mediados del siglo XIX en la única vez que se naturalizó a personas nativas mexicanas de forma masiva en la historia de Estados Unidos.[2]

Mi padre y mi madre nacieron y se criaron en la ciudad fronteriza de Laredo, Texas, en la década de 1950, ambos pertenecían a la cuarta generación de estadounidenses; sus padres habían empezado desde abajo y trabajado arduamente para convertirse en un ejecutivo inmobiliario y en un ejecutivo bancario, respectivamente. Mi madre, Celina, la mayor de diez hermanos, creció en una zona totalmente seca, en un rancho llamado Isauro en honor a su padre y sus hijos, a solo cinco millas (ocho kilómetros) al este de la frontera. Tanto la familia de mi padre como la de mi madre eran nativas de Loredo y del territorio al norte del río desde muchos siglos antes de la anexión de Texas. Por lo tanto, mis antepasados norteños y miles de otras familias de lo que ahora es el sur de Texas se convirtieron en estadounidenses, ya sea de forma automática o por la fuerza. La herencia geográfica de la región está en eterna disputa.

La obra de Vincent Valdez no solo es un producto de la región del sur de Texas, sino que no podría existir sin ella. La imperturbable lucidez de su práctica —con su agudeza, su inmediatez, y los sentimientos simultáneos de excitación y rechazo que despierta su obra en el público— está hecha de la misma materia que el sur de Texas: su clima ardiente e impredecible, y su amplio terreno implacable, forjado con legados históricos de violencia, derrota y resiliencia. La región abarca el territorio comprendido entre San Antonio y la frontera entre México y Estados Unidos, y se extiende hasta el valle del Río Grande, el territorio verde donde el río se encuentra con el golfo de México. El sur de Texas, el timón geográfico e histórico de Texas, ha guiado a esta región desde la soberanía indígena con las bandas de los pueblos coahuilteco, karankawa, caddo, comanche, lipán, apache y kiowa hasta el gobierno colonial español, la República de Texas y la posterior anexión a Estados Unidos durante su expansión imperial al oeste de la Costa del Pacífico. Igual que la obra de Valdez, el sur de Texas se caracteriza históricamente por el continuo debate sobre quién pertenece y quién no, quién tiene derecho a esta tierra y quién tiene prohibido entrar, y por la violencia que recae sobre aquellas personas a quienes se les dice que no pertenecen al lugar.

Existe una dualidad compleja tanto acerca de la región fronteriza como de la comunidad tejana que vive allí, complejidad que la mayor parte de estadounidenses nunca llegará a conocer, y que mucho menos entenderá. Se trata de algo parecido a formar parte de dos mundos diferentes y superpuestos; es como vivir en el centro de un diagrama de Venn y nunca terminar de identificarse por completo con ningún grupo. Somos personas mexicanas y estadounidenses y, a la vez, no somos ni una cosa ni la otra. Como la mayoría de las formas de herencia cultural arraigada en el desplazamiento y la discriminación, esta situación es un motivo singular de orgullo y, al mismo tiempo, una herida. Esta ansiedad se manifiesta en la obra sincera de Valdez *En algún lugar del sur de Texas* (2015–2020), un conjunto de diecisiete aguafuertes en los cuales combina escenas ilustradas que suelen verse en la región fronteriza con la anticipación histórica de la brutalidad y el espectro contemporáneo de vigilancia por parte del gobierno.

A pesar de sus representaciones rápidas e inexactas en tinta y su relativa moderación compositiva, la imagen que Valdez pinta de la región fronteriza entre México y Estados Unidos es de una precisión increíble. Las escenas individuales de esta serie —camiones con una hilera de palmeras delante de ellos, zanates reunidos en torno a una antena de radio, una tienda de bebidas alcohólicas con un hombre a caballo en la ventada de atención a vehículos— evocan texturas culturales y sensoriales muy características del sur de Texas. Para el público de la región fronteriza en particular, las sensaciones que despiertan estos dibujos son ricas y reales. Cuando veo estas obras, casi que puedo sentir el aroma de los mezquites secos y el diésel. Si bien es una serie de aguafuertes totalmente desprovistos de tonalidad cromática, las obras de *En algún lugar del sur de Texas* están teñidas de una inquietante combinación de xenofobia, vigilancia, experiencias vividas y dignidad.

Los dibujos fueron realizados en una época de importantes cambios culturales y demográficos en Texas y Estados Unidos, cuando las percepciones nacionales de las personas hispanas y latinas generan más xenofobia y polarización a nivel político, tal vez más que nunca antes en la historia moderna de Estados Unidos.[3] Valdez obtuvo la inspiración para estas obras durante un viaje por el sur de Texas que hizo junto a un grupo de estudiantes de secundaria de la Escuela de las Américas. El conjunto de obras luego se imprimió en Hare & Hound Press en San Antonio, a principios del 2020, para *Tierra de nadie*, una exposición grupal en el Station Museum de Houston que cerró casi inmediatamente después de abrir, durante los primeros días de la pandemia. La exposición tenía como fin explorar los legados del colonialismo y el desplazamiento forzado, contextos que en su mayor parte han sido invisibilizados y que los aguafuertes de Valdez ponen en evidencia. Luego, el conjunto de aguafuertes se expuso en el San Antonio Museum of Art como parte de la *Bienal de Texas* 2021, un proyecto que fue organizado entre varios museos y en el cual este autor participó como curador adjunto y que exploró complejos legados históricos en medio de un cambio global extraordinario.

En los últimos años, los abusos contra los derechos humanos y las injusticias en la frontera entre México y Estados Unidos, las redadas del Servicio de Control de Inmigración y Aduanas de los Estados Unidos (ICE, por sus siglas en inglés) y el rotundo fracaso de las leyes de inmigración estadounidenses para proteger a las personas inmigrantes o refugiadas y a sus hijos e hijas han intensificado los debates nacionales sobre la legalidad —y la propia humanidad— de las personas latinas, latinoamericanas y marrones en lo que ahora es suelo estadounidense. Se han separado familias por la fuerza, se han puesto niños y niñas en jaulas, se han colocado barreras de boyas con púas en el Río Grande. En el momento en que se escribe este texto, cercos de alambre de púas y muros de contenedores esperan a las personas migrantes a lo largo del río en Paso del Águila, Texas, frente a un campo de golf.[4] Por si esto fuera poco y para disgusto del gobierno federal, el gobernador Greg Abbott anunció recientemente que, en este lugar, el estado está construyendo un campo base de 80 acres (32 hectáreas) destinado a los soldados de la Guardia Nacional de Texas desplegados para la Operación Estrella Solitaria, la iniciativa a la que el estado destinó 10 billones de dólares con el objetivo de desalentar la inmigración ilegal a Texas.[5] Han pasado más de 175 años desde la anexión de Texas a Estados Unidos, y el debate —si es que se le puede llamar así— acerca de quién tiene jurisdicción y control de la tierra sigue provocando furia.

Uno de los dibujos de Valdez presenta una unidad de biciagentes de la Patrulla Fronteriza de los Estados Unidos en la serenidad y el verdor de una escena ribereña; una leyenda en la esquina dice: "BORDER AGENTS ON THE RIO GRANDE" (Agentes de la frontera en el Río Grande). El agua está notablemente quieta. La tensión del movimiento implícito impregna toda la composición. Las riberas están cubiertas con vegetación que, del lado izquierdo, parece elevarse como si fuera humo o llamas danzantes. En contraste, en el interior, al otro lado del río, un patrón vertical de líneas inorgánicas e incompletas parece susurrar suavemente la amenaza de un cerco. ¿La vista desde el centro del río es la perspectiva de una persona migrante o la de una cámara de seguridad? La tranquilidad que, en otras circunstancias, definiría esta escena ribereña se ve perturbada por la amenaza que, en sentido literal y figurado, se cierne sobre el Río Grande.

Otras obras del conjunto son menos sutiles. Un dibujo muestra la feroz cabeza de un perro gruñón, captado justo en el momento en que ladra; sus largos colmillos despiden saliva para todos lados. Sus orejas peludas parecen haberse transformado momentáneamente en cuernos. La ferocidad del can solo se ve igualada por la agresividad del espacio negativo que lo rodea, lo que obliga al público a tener que enfrentarse con el terror de la bestia, y nos deja con la duda de qué fue lo que provocó su reacción. La raza del perro es la que suele usarse en el programa canino de la Oficina de Aduanas y Protección Fronteriza de Estados Unidos. El objetivo expreso de esta oficina es la "detección y detención de terroristas", frase que esconde abiertamente el intento de discriminar por motivos de raza.[6] Como hemos visto a lo largo de la historia estadounidense, el uso de canes por parte de las fuerzas de seguridad es la extensión de una práctica racista constante y arraigada de someter a las comunidades negras y marrones a la violencia física. Tal vez podríamos comprender el gruñido de terror del perro como el encubrimiento del mismo miedo que motiva a los Estados a vigilar a los cuerpos marrones.

Otra obra ilustra las vigas de acero altas y el cerco alambrado del muro que está en la frontera entre México y Estados Unidos en un punto de acceso al territorio estadounidense. Un vehículo de las fuerzas de seguridad está sobre la línea divisoria que se formó al abrir el portón del muro. Fuera del vehículo, un oficial aparece de pie junto a una figura más oscura con los brazos detrás de la espalda. Por encima de ellos, unos postes altísimos con iluminación de alta intensidad y cámaras de seguridad vigilan el terreno circundante. A pesar de estar representada como un paisaje, la obra también funciona como un retrato de la frontera sur de Estados Unidos en el siglo XXI. Como tal, la obra también es un retrato de una cuestión política que polariza a la sociedad, por no hablar de lo que el muro de la frontera representa en la vida de quienes eligen cruzarlo. La amenaza de arresto y peligro legal se extiende desde la escena hasta una nota escrita por el artista en el extremo inferior derecho: "NO PHOTOGRAPHY ALLOWED, WILL BE PROSECUTED" (Prohibido tomar fotografías, se procesará a quien lo haga).

El idioma está en el centro interpretativo de muchas obras de *En algún lugar del sur de Texas*, ya sea como tema, dentro de la composición, o bien en forma de breves anuncios de información contextual que Valdez ha incluido de forma selectiva. Los idiomas de trabajo no se limitan solo a una lectura textual, sino que también funcionan en sentido figurado. Un dibujo del conjunto muestra a un grupo de personas ubicadas de manera descendente y representadas en el lenguaje figurativo de símbolos universales, como los que encontramos en la entrada de un baño público, solo que las figuras portan armas, o están visiblemente adoloridas o consternadas.

Otra obra presenta la frase "If it's not right for you, leave" (Si no está bien para ti, vete) escrita en la fuente serif y ubicada sobre la amenazante nube blanca de una chimenea de escape petroquímica. Estas chimeneas, que eliminan el gas natural residual, han llegado para distorsionar cada vez más el paisaje de las llanuras del sur de Texas desde que comenzó "el auge del gas de esquisto" a mediados de la década del 2000.[7] En esa época, los terratenientes comenzaron con la fracturación hidráulica en las propiedades que se encuentran a lo largo de Eagle Ford Shale.[8] La cita remite a las palabras que les dijo un agente fronterizo a estudiantes de Valdez mientras describía sus propios intentos fallidos para convertirse en policía.[9] Sin embargo, este mensaje tiene un significado adicional siniestro. "Si no está bien para ti, vete" es un sentimiento exclusivamente estadounidense dirigido históricamente hacia personas extranjeras, inmigrantes, y hacia a cualquiera que venga de otro lugar, un derivado de la xenofobia y el colonialismo.

En una obra, el idioma español aparece en los letreros de una tienda de ropa y colchones en una carretera; en otras, aparece dibujado a mano en jarras y cubetas de agua. En otra, un cartel que da la bienvenida a niños, niñas y madres a un centro de personas refugiadas dice "Bienvenidos Amigos" sobre un mapa de Estados Unidos y un sonriente tren de juguete. Las flechas superpuestas en el mapa representan caminos desde regiones del norte de México hasta diferentes rincones de Estados Unidos. A pesar del texto bienintencionado del cartel, el subtexto de la imagen no es acogedor. Para acentuar esta aprensión, la locomotora que incluye Valdez despide oscuras emanaciones de espeso humo negro que oscurecen las letras que dicen "América". El ejercicio conceptual pone de manifiesto cómo la falta rutinaria del lenguaje puede ocultar traumas históricos y actuales.

Debemos decir que también hay brillantes destellos de orgullo entre estos dibujos, como las flores de cactus que rebosan de color y la promesa de vida a pesar de la amenaza de las espinas. La escena de una de esas obras en particular solo puede encontrarse en el sur de Texas: un hombre a caballo espera con paciencia bajo el toldo de una pequeña tienda de bebidas alcohólicas con atención para vehículos. La estructura física no es mayor que el cobertizo de un almacén, y en la pared de ladrillo de "Garza's Drive-In" hay carteles que anuncian la venta de pan, cerveza y huevos (que yo sepa, no guardan relación con este autor, pero es una prueba de que mi gente es de la frontera). Un poste de madera y el tendido eléctrico le dan energía al cartel vertical que dice "LIQUOR" (licor) situado sobre la ventanilla de este drive-in. Se trata de una escena de considerable disyunción —al igual que el sur de Texas— que, sin embargo, es real. En la esquina inferior de la obra, Valdez reconoce la incredulidad del público: "SOUTH TEXAS. YES. I REALLY SAW THIS" (sur de Texas. Sí, de verdad vi esto).

Con estas diecisiete obras, Valdez establece una conexión entre el trauma histórico, la política actual y la tierra en la que se han desarrollado estos acontecimientos. Su insistencia en retratar las culturas y las condiciones tal y como son permite dar visibilidad a una región plagada de contrastes y disputas, ciertos temores y futuros inciertos. La vasta extensión de Texas estaría casi peligrosamente abierta a la interpretación si no estuviera cercada por la historia. En manos de Valdez, la dolorosa y complicada realidad de este lugar es tan abierta, tan salvaje e interminable como el paisaje del sur de Texas.

[1] Oficina del Historiador del Departamento de Estado de Estados Unidos, "La anexión de Texas, la guerra mexicana-estadounidense y el Tratado de Guadalupe Hidalgo, 1845-1848", https://history.state.gov/milestones/1830-1860/texas-annexation.

[2] National Archives, "El tratado de Guadalupe Hidalgo (1848)", https://www.archives.gov/milestone-documents/treaty-of-guadalupe-hidalgo.

[3] Trent Ollerenshaw y Ashley Jardina, "La polarización asimétrica de la opinión sobre la inmigración en Estados Unidos", *Public Opinion Quarterly, volumen 87, nro. 4 (1 de diciembre de 2023)*, págs. 1038-53. https://doi.org/10.1093/poq/nfad048.

[4] Uriel J. García, "En Paso del Águila, un tenso enfrentamiento por la frontera entre Texas y el Gobierno federal llega a su punto más álgido", The Texas Tribune, 22 de enero de 2024, https://www.texastribune.org/2024/01/22/texas-border-patrol-immigration-enforcement-eagle-pass-park.

[5] Uriel J. García and Davis Winkie, "Texas construirá una base de 80 acres en Paso del Águila para las tropas de la Guardia Nacionals", *The Texas Tribune*, 16 de febrero de 2024, https://www.texastribune.org/2024/02/16/texas-border-national-guard-base-eagle-pass.

[6] Oficina de Aduanas y Protección Fronteriza de Estados Unidos, "Programa canino", 21 de diciembre de 2023, https://www.cbp.gov/border-security/canine-program.

[7] Robert Rapier, "Cómo el auge del gas de esquisto puso el mundo al revés", Forbes, 21 de abril de 2017, https://www.forbes.com/sites/rrapier/2017/04/21/how-the-shale-boom-turned-the-world-upside-down/?sh=6640613f77d2.

[8] Texas Commission on Environmental Quality, "Área geológica de Eagle Ford Shale", 27 de abril de 2023, https://www.tceq.texas.gov/airquality/eagleford.

[9] Explicación del artista: "Un agente de Seguridad Nacional dijo la frase 'Si no le parece bien, márchese' a los estudiantes después de contarles cómo llegó al Valle desde Boston. Después de fracasar en su intento de conseguir trabajo en el departamento de policía local, un amigo lo animó a unirse a la agencia del sur, ya que las condiciones de contratación eran menos exigentes y había más demanda de personal. Los estudiantes reaccionaron con rapidez y de forma inspiradora a sus contradicciones e hipocresía respecto de la búsqueda de un cambio para tener una vida mejor, y también a sus declaraciones sobre el hecho de haber tenido que abandonar su hogar y a sus comentarios sobre que no sentía la necesidad de aprender español como requisito para hacer su trabajo".

Exhibition Checklist

All dimensions h x w x d in inches unless otherwise noted
All artworks courtesy of the artist unless otherwise noted

***Recuerdo (Remembering)*, 1999**
Oil on wood
60 x 20
Collection of Joe A. Diaz, San Antonio, TX

***Kill the Pachuco Bastard!*, 2001**
Oil on canvas
48 x 72
Collection of Cheech Marin and The Cheech Marin Center for Chicano Art & Culture of the Riverside Art Museum, CA

***Expulsion from the Great City*, 2002**
Pastel on paper
168 x 42 each, two panels
Collection of Mollie Middleton, Houston, TX

***Made Men: They Say Every Man Must Need Protection*, 2002**
Pastel on paper
61 ⅝ x 48 ⅖
Collection of the Modern Art Museum of Fort Worth, TX, Gift of the Estate of Edmund W. Schenecker II in Memory of Anne Marion

***Made Men: They Say Every Man Must Fall*, 2002**
Pastel on paper
61 ⅝ x 48 ⅖
Collection of the Modern Art Museum of Fort Worth, TX, Gift of the Estate of Edmund W. Schenecker II in Memory of Anne Marion

***Made Men: Yet I Swear I See My Reflection*, 2002**
Pastel on paper
61 ⅝ x 48 ⅖
Collection of the Modern Art Museum of Fort Worth, TX, Gift of the Estate of Edmund W. Schenecker II in Memory of Anne Marion

***Made Men: Any Day Now, I Shall Be Released*, 2002**
Pastel on paper
61 ⅝ x 48 ⅖
Collection of the Modern Art Museum of Fort Worth, TX, Gift of the Estate of Edmund W. Schenecker II in Memory of Anne Marion

***Stations IX: Laid Out*, 2001–4**
Charcoal on wove paper
45 ½ x 96
Museum of Fine Arts, Houston, TX, Museum purchase funded by the Vaughn Foundation Fund, Ilene and Donald Kramer, Leslie and Jack S. Blanton, Jr., and Bridget and Patrick Wade, 2016.35

***Stations: Main Event*, 2001–4**
Charcoal on paper
92 x 42
Collection of Mike Loya, Houston, TX

***Stations: The Strongest Man in the World is He Who Walks Alone*, 2001–4**
Charcoal on paper
42 x 92
Collection of Mike Loya, Houston, TX

***Stations: Weigh In: Coming in at 140 lbs 8 oz*, 2001–4**
Charcoal on paper
72 x 42
Collection of Mike Loya, Houston, TX

Vincent Valdez and Ry Cooder
***El Chavez Ravine*, 2005–7**
Oil on 1953 Chevy Good Humor ice cream truck
72 x 156 x 60
Collection of Los Angeles County Museum of Art, CA, gift of Ryland Cooder (M.2021.16)

***Burn Baby Burn*, 2009**
Oil on canvas
94 x 144
Collection of Suzanne K. Klein and Edna Meyer-Nelson, Houston, TX

***America's Finest*, 2012**
Graphite on paper
40 x 26 each, 6 panels
Collection of the Fairbanks Family, Houston, TX

***Black Flag*, 2012**
Lithographic crayon on folded canvas, pedestal, and lucite vitrine
11 ½ x 22
Collection of Elisabeth and Alex Tynberg, Austin, TX

***Excerpts for John*, 2012**
Oil on canvas
24 x 36 each, 6 panels
Collection of the Lucas Museum of Narrative Art, Los Angeles, CA

***Home*, 2012**
HD video: color, sound
TRT: 9:16 min
Smithsonian American Art Museum, Washington, DC, Museum purchase through the Frank K. Ribelin Endowment, 2019.37
Director: Vincent Valdez
Videographer: Jim Mendiola
Editor: Faith Radle

***The Strangest Fruit*, 2013**
Oil on canvas
90 x 55 each, 9 panels
Collection of Blanton Museum of Art, The University of Texas at Austin, Promised gift of Jeanne and Michael Klein, 2016 (#1 and #5); Collection of Candice Taylor-Horvath and Dan Horvath, Chicago, IL (#2); Collection of David Hoberman, Malibu, CA (#3); Museum of Fine Arts, Houston, TX, Museum purchase funded by the Latin Maecenas, 2016.170 (#4) Collection of El Museo del Barrio, New York. Gift of the Jacques and Natasha Gelman Foundation, 2021 (#7)

***The Beginning is Near (An American Trilogy) Chapter One: The City The City I*, 2015–16**
Oil on canvas
74 x 360
Blanton Museum of Art, The University of Texas at Austin, Purchase through the generosity of Guillermo C. Nicolas and James C. Foster in honor of Jeanne and Michael Klein, with additional support from Jeanne and Michael Klein and Ellen Susman in honor of Jeanne and Michael Klein, 2017

***The Beginning is Near (An American Trilogy) Chapter One: The City The City II*, 2016**
Oil on canvas
74 x 90
Blanton Museum of Art, The University of Texas at Austin, Purchase through the generosity of Guillermo C. Nicolas and James C. Foster in honor of Jeanne and Michael Klein, with additional support from Jeanne and Michael Klein and Ellen Susman in honor of Jeanne and Michael Klein, 2017

***The Beginning is Near (An American Trilogy) Chapter Two: Dream Baby Dream*, 2018**
Oil on paper
42 x 72 each, 11 panels
72 x 42, one panel (#12)
Collection of Ellen Spencer Susman, Houston, TX (#3); Collection of Javier & Monica Mora, Miami, FL (#6); Collection of Benjamin and Sophia Abram, Durham, NC (#7, #9, #10); Collection of Sarah Labowitz and Peter Molick, Houston, TX (#8)

***The Rope (After Marsden Hartley)*, 2018**
Oil pastel on paper
42 x 28
Collection of Lisa Rich and John McLaughlin, Houston, TX

***Eaten*, 2018–19**
Oil on canvas, and bronze
63 x 190
Collection of David Hoberman, Malibu, CA, promised gift to the Hammer Museum, Los Angeles, CA

***Godspeed*, 2019**
Oil on canvas
52 x 84
Collection of Brent Barry, Hermosa Beach, CA

***It Was Never Yours*, 2019**
Oil on paper
42 x 60
Collection of William Leung, New York

***People of the Sun (Grandma & Grandpa Santana)*, 2019**
Oil on canvas
62 x 46
Collection of Alexa Pooter Brundage, San Antonio, TX

***Rise*, 2019**
Oil on canvas
42 x 58
Private Collection, Los Angeles, CA

***Since 1977*, 2019**
Lithography crayon on paper
24 x 18 each, 9 panels
Collection of Ric Whitney and Tina Perry–Whitney, Los Angeles, CA

***So Long, Mary Ann*, 2019**
Oil on canvas
63 x 96
Private Collection, Chicago IL

***Torn*, 2019**
Oil on linen
16 x 12
Private Collection, Los Angeles, CA

***Just a Dream (In America)*, 2020–21**
Oil on canvas, audio component, and bricks
95 x 63
Williams College Museum of Art, MA, Museum purchase, Kathryn Hurd Fund, M.2021.5, Williamstown. Song credit: "Just a Dream," 1959, by Jimmy Clanton. Audio editor: Justin Boyd

***The Beginning is Near (An American Trilogy) Chapter Three: The New Americans The New Americans #2 (Mr. Checkpoint)*, 2021**
Oil on canvas
95 x 63
Collection of Beth Rudin DeWoody, Palm Beach, FL

***The Beginning is Near (An American Trilogy) Chapter Three: The New Americans The New Americans #3 (Juan)*, 2021**
Oil on canvas
95 x 63
Collection of the Marquez Family, Miami, FL

***The Beginning is Near (An American Trilogy) Chapter Three: The New Americans Study for The New Americans #4 (Teresita)*, 2021**
Color pencil on paper
50 x 38
Private Collection, New York

***Study for American Procession #1*, 2021**
Oil on wood
20 x 24
The Scantland Collection, Columbus, OH

***Amnesia*, 2024**
Color pencil on paper
42 x 30
Two works from the Collection of Charles and Judy Tate, Houston, TX

***Sharif*, 2024**
Color pencil on plaster
20 x 18
Paola Creixell Collection, Houston, TX

***The Beginning is Near (An American Trilogy) Chapter Three: The New Americans The New Americans #1 (Adriana)*, 2024**
Oil on canvas
95 x 63

***The Beginning is Near (An American Trilogy) Chapter Three: The New Americans The New Americans #5 (Wynton)*, 2024**
Oil on canvas
96 x 63

***The Beginning is Near (An American Trilogy) Chapter Three: The New Americans Veteranos #1 (Flaco)*, 2024**
Oil on canvas
95 x 63

***SUPREME*, 2024**
Oil on canvas
80 1/2 x 80 1/2

***Look What You Created (1992)*, 2024**
From the series *It Was a Very Good Year*, 2024–ongoing
Pencil on bronze
14 x 14

***Untitled (#2)*, 2024**
From the series *Notes for a Future*, 2024–ongoing
Pencil on bronze
8 ½ x 11

***Hello America*, 2024**
Ink and pencil on paper
24 x 30
Collection of David Hoberman, Malibu, CA

MASS MOCA Only

***Red Ear (Twenty One Years)*, 1999**
Oil on canvas
18 x 24

***Stations: A Fine Performance by Our Winning Fighter Tonight*, 2001–4**
Charcoal on paper
42 x 72
Collection of Mike Loya, Houston, TX

***Stations: Collect 'Em All*, 2001–4**
Charcoal on paper
72 x 42
Collection of Mike Loya, Houston, TX

***Stations: Get Outta There!, Kill 'Im!, No Mercy!, Finish Him!*, 2001–4**
Charcoal on paper
36 x 42 each, 4 panels
Collection of Mike Loya, Houston, TX

***Stations: They Say Every Man Must Fall*, 2001–4**
Charcoal on paper
Collection of Jorge Elizondo

***Nothing to See Here, Keep on Movin'*, 2008**
Lithograph crayon on paper
42 x 60
Private Collection

***Somewhere in South Texas*, 2016**
Etchings on paper
11x 14, 16 works
Edition of 2, printed at Hare & Hound Press

***Siete Dias*, 2022**
Serigraph on synthetic material
Printed by Gary Lichtenstein Editions
48 x 72, 21 works

***The Slaughterhouse Five Drawings*, 2023**
Ink and pencil on paper
11 x 17, 23 works
Courtesy of the artist and Arion Press

CAMH Only

***The Hole (In Memory) The Cops*, 2024**
Pencil on bronze
13 x 13

***The Hole (In Memory) The Portrait*, 2024**
Pencil on bronze
8 ½ x 11

***The Hole (In Memory) The Testimony*, 2024**
Pencil on bronze
8 ½ x 11 each, twelve parts

***Study for It Was a Very Good Year (1987, 1988)*, 2024**
Ink on paper
30 x 41 each, two parts

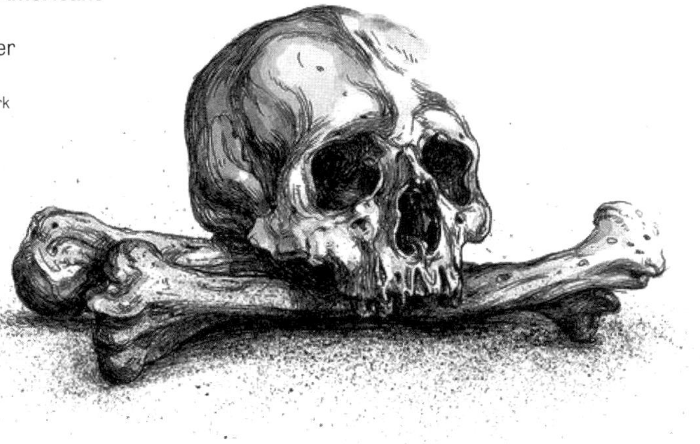

***The Slaughterhouse Five Drawings*, 2023**
Ink and pencil on paper, published by Arion Press

VINCENT VALDEZ

CURRICULUM VITAE

American, b. 1977
Lives and works in Los Angeles and Houston

EDUCATION

2000, BFA; Rhode Island School of Design, Providence

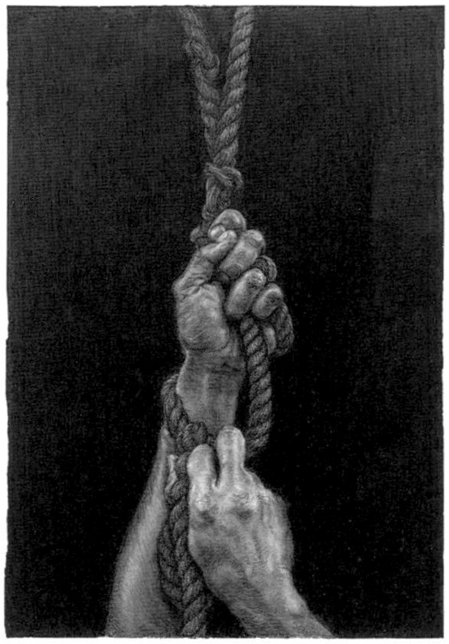

***The Rope (After Marsden Hartley)*, 2018**
Oil pastel on paper
Photo: Peter Molick

SELECTED SOLO EXHIBITIONS

2024-5

Just A Dream…
CAMH, TX, and MASS MoCA, North Adams, MA

2024

Ordinary People: Photorealism and the Work of Art since 1968, MOCA Grand Avenue, Los Angeles, CA

2023

Vincent Valdez and Ry Cooder: El Chavez Ravine, Los Angeles County Museum of Art, CA

The Slaughterhouse Five Drawings, The Drawing Center, New York

Texas Artist of the Year, Houston Art League, TX; traveled to Artpace, San Antonio, TX

2022

Land of the Free: En Memoria (In Memory), Mana Contemporary, Jersey City, NJ

2021

The New Americans, Art Basel Miami, FL, with Matthew Brown Gallery Los Angeles, CA

2019

It Was Never Yours, Matthew Brown Gallery Los Angeles, CA

2018

The Beginning Is Near, An American Trilogy, Chapter Two: Dream Baby Dream, David Shelton Gallery, Houston, TX

The Beginning Is Near, An American Trilogy, Chapter One: The City, Blanton Museum of Art, The University of Texas at Austin

2016

The Beginning Is Near, An American Trilogy, Chapter One: The City, David Shelton Gallery, Houston, TX

2015

Till Then: Window into Houston, Blaffer Art Museum, The University of Houston, TX

2013

The Strangest Fruit, David Winton Bell Gallery, Brown University, Providence, RI; traveled to Artpace, San Antonio, TX (2014); and Staniar Gallery, Washington and Lee University, Lexington, VA (2015)

2012

Excerpts for John, McNay Art Museum, San Antonio, TX

2011

America's Finest, Texas Contemporary Art Fair, with David Shelton Gallery, Houston, TX

2010

Flashback, Southwest School of Art, San Antonio, TX

Stations, Mesa Contemporary Arts Center, AZ

2009

Burn, Federal Art Projects, Los Angeles, CA

Vincent Valdez and Ry Cooder: El Chavez Ravine, San Antonio Museum of Art, TX

2008

Without End, Gallery at UTA, The University of Texas at Arlington

2007

Pride of the Southside, Museo Alameda Smithsonian, San Antonio, TX; O'Kane Gallery, University of Houston–Downtown, TX

Winner's Circle, Western Project, Los Angeles, CA

2005–6

Stations, Snite Museum of Art, University of Notre Dame, South Bend, IN; Texas A&M International University, Laredo; Richard E. Peeler Art Center, DePaul University, Greencastle, IN; Islander Art Gallery, Texas A&M University, Corpus Christi

2004

Stations, McNay Art Museum, San Antonio, TX

Made Men, Finesilver Gallery, San Antonio, TX

Two to Watch: Vincent Valdez & Oscar Casares, Artpace, San Antonio, TX

TX Mix! Series: Vincent Valdez, Dallas Contemporary, TX

SELECTED GROUP EXHIBITIONS

2023

Hidden Histories, Museum of Fine Arts, Houston, TX

Strike Fast, Dance Lightly, Flag Art Foundation, New York

Something Beautiful: Reframing La Colección, El Museo del Barrio, New York

Paper Trail, Matthew Brown Gallery, Los Angeles, CA

Estampas de la Raza: Contemporary Prints from the Romo Collection, Delaware Museum of Art, Wilmington; traveled to Crocker Museum of Art, Sacramento, CA; Oglethorpe University Museum of Art, Atlanta, GA

Refined Reflections into the Formidable: Contemporary Latino Art from the Joe Diaz Collection, Russell Hill Rogers Galleries, The University of Texas at San Antonio

2022

The Outwin 2022: American Portraiture Today, National Portrait Gallery, Washington, DC

Cheech Collects: Inaugural Exhibition, The Cheech Marin Center for Chicano Art & Culture of the Riverside Art Museum, CA

Black Indians from New Orleans, Musée du quai Branly—Jacques Chirac, Paris, France

2021

Texas Biennial: A New Landscape, A Possible Horizon, San Antonio Museum of Art, TX

Shattered Glass, Jeffrey Deitch, Los Angeles, CA

Undoing Time, ASU Art Museum, Arizona State University, Tempe; traveled to Berkeley Art Museum and Pacific Film Archive, UC Berkeley, CA (2022); Contemporary Arts Center, New Orleans, LA (2023)

Carriers: The Body as a Site of Danger and Desire, Blaffer Art Museum, The University of Houston, TX

Día de Muertos: A Time to Grieve and Remember, National Museum of Mexican Art, Chicago, IL

2020

Hockney to Warhol: Contemporary Drawings from the Collection, McNay Art Museum, San Antonio, TX

2019

Charles White and the Legacy of the Figure, Christian Green Gallery, The University of Texas at Austin

Between Play and Grief: Selections from the Permanent Collection, Museum of Fine Arts, Houston, TX

Suffering from Realness, MASS MoCA, North Adams, MA

2018

Occupying the Third Space: Representations of Cultural Hybridity and Identity in the Southwest, Kansas City Art Institute, MO

WE THE PEOPLE: Contemporary American Figurative Art, Mesa Arts Center, AZ

Texas, Philip Martin Gallery, Los Angeles, CA

Los Tejanos: Chicano Art from the Collection of Cheech Marin, Art Museum of South Texas, Corpus Christi

2017

Barrio Logos: Displacement and Vanishing Iconography, curated by Oscar Magallanes in conjunction with Pacific Standard Time, LA Residency Art Gallery, Inglewood, CA

From Out Under, Philip Martin Gallery, Los Angeles, CA

Home—So Different, So Appealing, part of *Pacific Standard Time*, Los Angeles County Museum of Art, CA; traveled to Museum of Fine Arts, Houston, TX (2017–18)

The Face of Battle: Americans at War, 9/11 to Now, National Portrait Gallery, Washington, DC

State of the Art: Discovering American Art Now, Frist Art Museum, Nashville, TN

2016

Tastemakers & Earthshakers: Notes from Los Angeles, 1943–2016, Vincent Price Art Museum, East Los Angeles College, Monterey Park, CA

Northern Triangle, Threewalls, Chicago, IL; traveled to Staniar Gallery, Washington and Lee University, Lexington, VA (2017); and Blue Star Contemporary, San Antonio, TX (2018)

Contemporary Portraiture, Gallery at UTA, The University of Texas at Arlington

2015

American Art: It's Complicated, Minnesota Museum of American Art, St. Paul

Hidden Histories in Latin American Art, Phoenix Art Museum, AZ

Back from Berlin, Blue Star Contemporary, San Antonio, TX

2014

State of the Art: Discovering American Art Now, Crystal Bridges Museum of American Art, Bentonville, AK

Parallel Myths, David Shelton Gallery, Houston, TX

Estampas de La Raza: Prints for the People, The Romo Collection, North Carolina Museum of Art, Raleigh

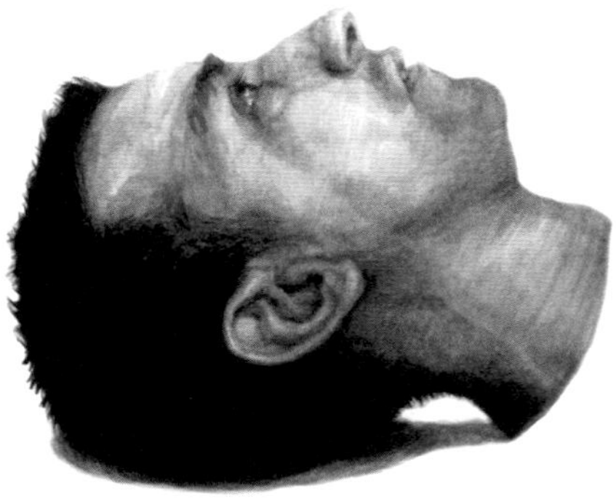

Head, 2010
Ink on paper
Photo: Pete Galindo

The Slaughterhouse Five Drawings, **2023**
Ink and pencil on paper, published by Arion Press

2013

Face to Face: Artists' Self Portraits from the Jackye and Curtis Finch Collection, Arkansas Arts Center, Little Rock

Legend Tripping, Masters & Pelavin, New York

Changing Perceptions of the Western Landscape, Albuquerque Museum of Art, NM

2012

Prelude, David Shelton Gallery, Houston, TX

Pride, Protest & Plains, Red Arrow Contemporary, Dallas, TX

ICONS: RISD, Woods–Gerry Gallery, Rhode Island School of Design, Providence

Represent LA, Vincent Price Art Museum, East Los Angeles College, Monterey Park, CA

2011

Silver: 25th Anniversary Exhibition, Gallery at UTA, The University of Texas at Arlington

Arte Tejano: de Campos, Barrios y Fronteras, Fundacion Osde, Buenos Aires, Argentina Muertes, National Museum of Mexican Art, Chicago, IL

Works on Paper, David Shelton Gallery, San Antonio, TX

2010

Roadshow: Houston, David Shelton Gallery at Inman Annex, Houston, TX

Foretopia, David Shelton Gallery, San Antonio, TX

El Grito: The Cry for Independence, University of Arkansas, Little Rock

2009

Western Project: The First Six Years, Western Project, Los Angeles, CA

West/Southwest, Albuquerque—Los Angeles Exchange, 516 Arts, Albuquerque, NM, and LA Art Core, Los Angeles, CA

2008

Angelenos: Painters of Los Angeles, Los Angeles County Museum of Art, CA

American Realism, Fort Wayne Museum of Art, IN

In the Land of Retinal Delights: The Juxtapose Factor, Laguna Art Museum, Laguna Beach, CA

Beyond the Border, National Museum of Mexican Art, Chicago, IL

2007

La Vida Lowrider: Cruising in the City of Angels, Petersen Automotive Museum, Los Angeles, CA

The Sirens' Song: Contemporary Narrative Painting, Arthouse at the Jones Center; Austin, TX

2006

Swallow Harder, Frye Art Museum, Seattle, WA

Drawing Conclusions on the Wall, Chapman University, Orange County, CA

2005

Latitude, Te Whare Wananga o Awanuiarangi, Whakatane, New Zealand

2004

A Timeless Montage of Conflict and Being, Parsons New School of Design, Paris, France

Selections from the Joe A. Diaz Collection, Art Museum of South Texas, Corpus Christi; traveled to National Hispanic Research Center, Albuquerque, NM; San Jose Museum of Art, CA; and National Museum of Mexican Art, Chicago, IL

2003

Likeness and Presence, Self Help Graphics, Los Angeles, CA

Treinta: 30 Years of Chicano Printmaking and Justice, Self Help Graphics, Los Angeles, CA

Larger Than Life, Leisure Club Mogadishni, Copenhagen, Denmark

2002

Chicano Visions: American Painters on the Verge, from the Collection of Cheech Marin, San Antonio Museum of Art, TX; traveled to National Museum of Mexican Art, Chicago, IL; Weisman Museum of Art, University of Minnesota, MN; Smithsonian Museum, Art and Industries Building, Washington, DC; Museum of Contemporary Art San Diego, La Jolla, CA; Los Angeles County Museum of Art, CA; O'Kane Gallery, University of Houston–Downtown, TX

Contemporary Drawing in Texas, McNay Art Museum, San Antonio, TX

17th Annual New American Talent, Arthouse at the Jones Center, Austin, TX
Contemporary Figurative Works on Paper, Blue Star Arts Center, San Antonio, TX

The Power of Place, Finesilver Gallery, San Antonio, TX

RESIDENCIES

2023

Arion Press King Residency, San Francisco, CA

2020–21

NXTHVN Fellowship, New Haven, CT

2018

Joan Mitchell Center (AIR), New Orleans, LA

2014

Künstlerhaus Bethanien, Blue Star Contemporary Berlin Residency Program, Germany

2011

Vermont Studio Center, Johnson

2005

Skowhegan School of Painting & Sculpture, ME

2003

SALA: SA Meets LA Exchange Program, CA

AWARDS

2024

Houston Arts Alliance Artist & Creative Individuals Grant

2023

Houston Arts Alliance Let Creativity Happen Grant

Texas Artist of the Year Award

2022

Mellon Foundation Latinx Artist Fellowship

2019

Artadia Artist Grant

2015

Joan Mitchell Foundation Grant, Painters and Sculptors Program

Texas Commission on the Arts, State Visual Artist

2006

Artist Foundation of San Antonio, Visual Art Grant

2005

Artpace Travel Grant, San Antonio

SELECTED PUBLICATIONS

Slaughterhouse Five, a novel by Kurt Vonnegut, Jr., artwork by Vincent Valdez (San Francisco: Arion Press, 2024).

Vincent Valdez: In Memory; texts by Denise Markonish, Roberto Tejada, and Rufus Wainwright (Santa Fe: Radius Books, 2023).

Lost [In Translation] (New York: Common Practice, 2022).

Vincent Valdez: The Strangest Fruit (Lexington: Staniar Gallery, Washington and Lee University, 2015).

Ry Cooder/Vincent Valdez: El Chavez Ravine (San Antonio: San Antonio Museum of Art, 2009).

Vincent Valdez: Stations (San Antonio: McNay Museum, 2004).

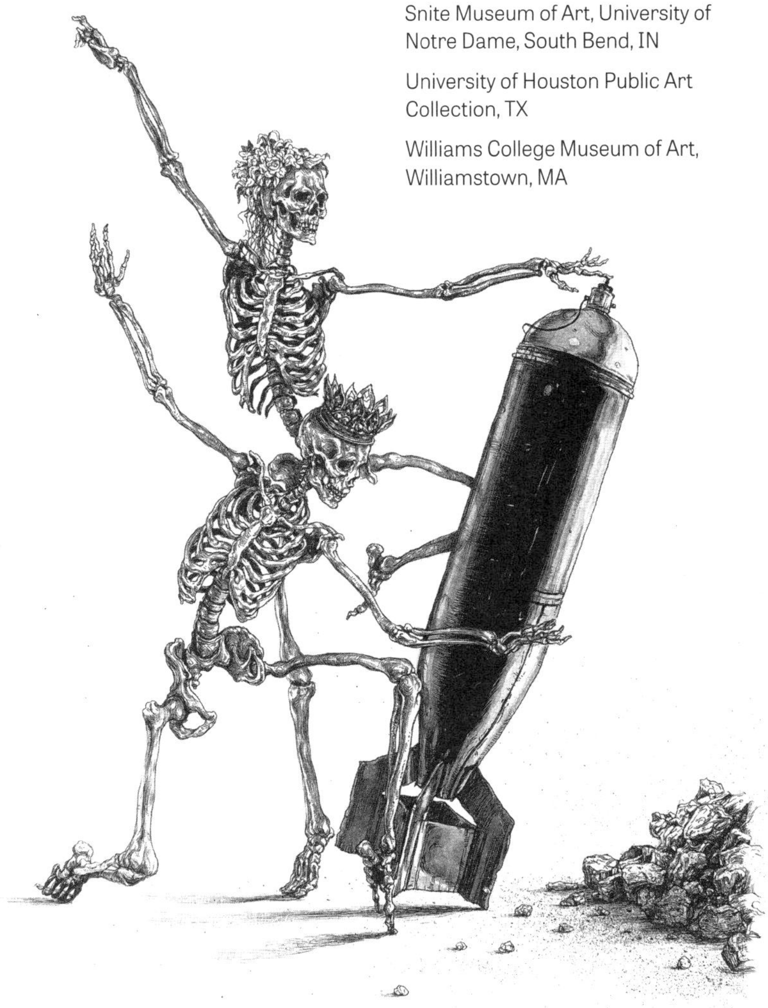

SELECTED COLLECTIONS

Blanton Museum of Art, The University of Texas at Austin

David Winton Bell Gallery, Brown University, Providence, RI

El Paso Museum of Art, TX

Ford Foundation, New York

Frye Museum of Art, Seattle, WA

The Hammer Museum, Los Angeles, CA

The Los Angeles County Museum of Art, CA

The Lucas Museum of Narrative Art, Los Angeles, CA

McNay Art Museum, San Antonio, TX

Modern Art Museum of Fort Worth, TX

Museum of Fine Arts, Houston, TX

National Museum of Mexican Art, Chicago, IL

The National Portrait Gallery, Washington, DC

San Antonio Museum of Art, TX

The Smithsonian Museum of American Art, Washington, DC

Snite Museum of Art, University of Notre Dame, South Bend, IN

University of Houston Public Art Collection, TX

Williams College Museum of Art, Williamstown, MA

CONTEMPORARY ARTS MUSEUM HOUSTON

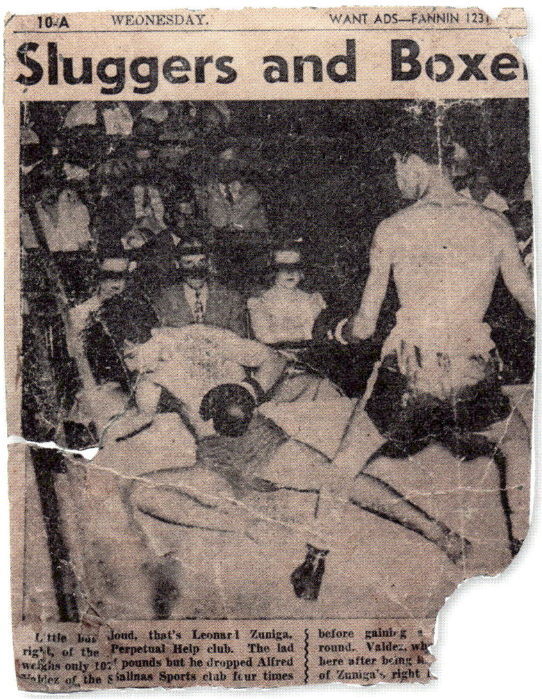

10-A WEDNESDAY. WANT ADS—FANNIN 123

Sluggers and Boxe

L'ttle bas Joud, that's Leonard Zuniga, right, of the Perpetual Help club. The lad weighs only 10 pounds but he dropped Alfred Valdez of the Salinas Sports club four times before gaining round. Valdez, wh here after being k of Zuniga's right

Newspaper clipping on Valdez's grandfather's boxing match, c. 1942
Photo: Abdurrahman Danquah

Contributors

DENISE MARKONISH

Denise Markonish is the Chief Curator at MASS MoCA. Her exhibitions include *Jeffrey Gibson: POWER FULL BECAUSE WE'RE DIFFERENT*; *Joseph Grigely: In What Way Wham?*; *Amy Yoes: Hot Corners*; *Marc Swanson: A Memorial to Ice at the Dead Dear Disco* (MASS MoCA and Thomas Cole National Historic Site, Catskill, NY); *Lily Cox-Richard: Weep Holes*; *Amy Hauft: Terra, Luna, + Sol*; *Glenn Kaino: In the Light of a Shadow*; *Suffering from Realness*; *Trenton Doyle Hancock, Mind of the Mound: Critical Mass*; *Nick Cave: Until* (co-organizers Carriageworks, Sydney, Australia, and The Momentary, Bentonville, AK; traveled to Tramway, Glasgow, Scotland); *Explode Every Day: An Inquiry into the Phenomena of Wonder*; *Teresita Fernández: As Above So Below*; *Oh, Canada* (traveled to Alberta, New Brunswick, and Prince Edward Island); *Nari Ward: Sub Mirage Lignum*; *These Days: Elegies for Modern Times*; and *Badlands: New Horizons in Landscape*. She has worked on long-term projects with Laurie Anderson and has commissioned works by Sarah Oppenheimer, Stephen Vitiello, Julianne Swartz, Mark Dion, and many others. Markonish has produced numerous exhibition catalogues and has guest edited the books *Teresita Fernández: Wayfinding* (DelMonico) and *Wonder: 50 Years of RISD Glass*, and co-edited *Sol LeWitt: 100 Views* (Yale University Press). She has taught at Williams College and the Rhode Island School of Design, was a visiting curator at Artpace, San Antonio, and Haystack School of Craft, Deer Isle, Maine.

EVAN GARZA

Evan Garza is a curator at MASS MoCA. They were awarded the 2021–2022 IMMA Fulbright US Scholarship at the Irish Museum of Modern Art and a visiting research fellowship in History of Art and Architecture at Trinity College Dublin, where they researched Irish contemporary art, protest movements, and Ireland's anticolonial history of rebellion. Garza has organized several exhibitions and projects internationally and was artistic director of the 2021 *Texas Biennial*, co-curated with Ryan N. Dennis. Garza is the former director of Rice Public Art at Rice University in their native Houston, and previously was Assistant Curator of Modern and Contemporary Art at the Blanton Museum of Art at the University of Texas at Austin. Garza was co-founder of Fire Island Artist Residency (FIAR), a New York nonprofit and the first residency program in the world exclusively for LGBTQ+ artists, where they served as assistant director until 2015. Their writing on the work of global contemporary artists has been published in several books and monographs and by *Flash Art*, *ART PAPERS*, and *Artforum*. Garza earned their MA from the Williams Graduate Program in the History of Art at the Clark Art Institute, and recently curated the exhibition *Steve Locke: the fire next time*, at MASS MoCA..

JOYCE CAROL OATES

Joyce Carol Oates was born in Lockport, New York, in 1938. She has published more than seventy books of fiction, poetry, and essays. Her novels include *Night. Sleep. Death. The Stars.* (2020); *The Book of American Martyrs* (2017); *The Accursed* (2013); *The Gravedigger's Daughter* (2007); *Blonde* (2000), winner of the National Book Award; *We Were the Mulvaneys* (1996); *Because It Is Bitter, and Because It Is My Heart* (1990); *You Must Remember This* (1987); *Bellefleur* (1980); and *them* (1969), winner of the National Book Award. She is also the author of the story collections *Beautiful Days* (2018) and *Dis mem ber* (2017). Her short stories and essays have appeared in the *New York Times*, the *Washington Post*, *The Atlantic*, and *Harper's*, and have been widely anthologized. Oates has also published numerous books of poetry, including *American Melancholy* (2021), *Tenderness* (1996), *The Time Traveler* (1989), *Love and Its Derangements* (1970), and *Women In Love and Other Poems* (1968). She has been a professor at Princeton University since 1978, and was the founding editor of *The Ontario Review*. She has been a finalist for the Pulitzer Prize multiple times, received the National Book Award for *them* (1969) and for *Blonde* (2000), and received the National Humanities Medal in 2010 for her lifetime achievement in literature.

PATRICIA RESTREPO

Patricia Restrepo is the Curator at CAMH. She commissioned the site-specific sculptural landscape *Olivia Erlanger: If Today Were Tomorrow* (2024), accompanied by a catalogue (Hatje Cantz) with texts by Lydia Kallipoliti, Chris Kraus, and Mark von Schlegell. She co-curated *Slowed and Throwed: Records of the City through Mutated Lenses* (2020 and 2021), a transhistorical exhibition addressing DJ Screw's process of material manipulation, featuring artists Jamal Cyrus, Shana Hoehn, Tomashi Jackson, and Sondra Perry; and curated *Will Boone: The Highway Hex* (2019–20), the artist's first solo museum exhibition. Restrepo explored CAMH's seventy-year history of championing performances by artists such as Laurie Anderson, James Lee Byars, Joan Jonas, Autumn Knight, and Robert Rauschenberg in *Stage Environment: You Didn't Have to Be There* (2018). She coordinated the Museum's presentations of *Troy Montes Michie: Rock of Eye* (2022) and *The Dirty South: Contemporary Art, Material Culture, and the Sonic Impulse* (2021–22), and has managed CAMH's artist-centric publications and their digitization. Restrepo previously worked at the Institute of Aesthetic Research (Instituto de Investigaciones Estéticas) of the Universidad Nacional Autónoma de México (UNAM). She is a PhD candidate in Art History at Rice University and holds a Master's degree from Katholieke Universiteit Leuven, Belgium, and Bachelor's degrees from Rice University.

Acknowledgments

Both institutions and the artist would like to thank the lenders who made this survey exhibition possible. We know how painful it is for them to be separated from the works for two years. We also thank the generous funders who made *Just a Dream...* a reality; your generosity is unparalleled.

Just as no man is an island, no exhibition or book can be tackled alone. I would like to thank my colleagues at MASS MoCA, without whom I would get absolutely nothing done. My curatorial team of Susan Cross, Allie Foradas, and Meghan Clare Considine are continual pillars of support and inspiration. You have been hearing me talk about Vincent Valdez's work for years, and I'm glad I finally get to share this exhibition with you; thank you for your advice and time. Thank you to the entire visual arts team: Spencer Byrne-Seres, Andy Slemenda, Martin Gonzalez, Zoe Berg, Tavish Costello, Ren Rennick, Dylan Bean and Rory Coyne—you make magic happen every day, and your unflagging support of curators and artists is truly an inspiration, especially as you are wonderful artists in your own right. Our Buildings and Grounds and Custodial teams are also our keen collaborators in the galleries. Ellen Beck, Elizabeth Smith, and Paige Bartels worked tirelessly with me on raising the funds for this exhibition; Jen Falk on the marketing; Amy Chen on the amazing graphic design; and so many more. MASS MoCA is like a huge living organism, or a ship that functions best when we all work together, with our director, Kristy Edmunds, at the helm.

Thank you to my co-curator at CAMH, Patricia Restrepo, and to her team there. Patricia, you always bring a positive outlook to every meeting and task; your dogged enthusiasm for Vincent's work means that our collaboration has been a wonderful partnership—and thanks for always knowing how to find the best restaurants.

Special thanks to Teresita Fernández, who first introduced me to Vincent and his partner Adriana Corral, and to Riley Robinson, director of Artpace in San Antonio, for not only bringing me to Texas—where I would fall in love with the art scene—but for driving me to Vincent's studio for the first visit. Both of you knew Vincent and me well enough to understand that this would be a match made in heaven.

This book would not have happened without some great co-conspirators: fellow authors Evan Garza, a member of MASS MoCA's Curatorial Exchange Initiative and now curator at the Museum, who wrote a beautiful essay about West Texas from a personal point of view; and Patricia, who enlivened Vincent's biography by weaving together his life and work. Plus, I am honored to present excerpts from Joyce Carol Oates' *On Boxing*, approved by Joyce herself (thank you to Ted Gioia for making that connection). Thank you to Jane Calverley for always understanding everyone's voice; and to Paulette Wein for finding every typo when the rest of our eyes have looked too many times. I feel so lucky to have a partner in X Artists' Books—Alexandra Grant and Addy Rabinovich; you two are the absolute best, I want to publish every book with you forever. I know, for Vincent, this book is a true manifestation of how he sees the world and his work within it—Bob Faust, you make dream books. You listen, you see things that no artist or curator can, because you too are an artist; I love working with you, my dear friend.

And last, but certainly not least, I want to thank Victor . . . whoops, Vincent! . . . Dude, you are like the brother that I never knew existed until we met in 2016, and then, bam!, wonder twin powers activate—together we can either rule the world or bring it down, depending on the day. Your unflinching ability to image the United States with love, despite all its peril and pride, inspires me every day. I feel honored to put this book and show into the world. You, Adri, and Weens are such an important part of my life, and maybe together we can have a dream where the hamburger is eating us!

DENISE MARKONISH
Chief Curator, MASS MoCA

I am privileged to work at CAMH, a nimble non-collecting institution that prioritizes supporting living artists like Vincent Valdez. Vincent is both a singular human and imagemaker, his inimitable vision matched by inimitable skill. In 2016, a half-mile walk led me to David Shelton Gallery, where I was left awestruck by Vincent's first chapter of *The Beginning is Near*. While I am continuously amazed by the artistic strength in the Houston region, I was moved to find ways to support Vincent's practice as robustly as possible. I have treasured the opportunity to be in dialogue with Vincent over the four years leading up to *Just a Dream...*, our conversations regularly leaving me pulsating and energized.

The exhibition was forged through the first co-organizing partnership between CAMH and MASS MoCA, where Denise Markonish spearheads curatorial efforts. MASS MoCA was an ideal collaborator for CAMH and for this exhibition, as the institutions share an artist-centered approach and experimental ethos. I relish the opportunity to engage in multi-vocal curatorial efforts, as the additional eyes add texture and dynamism to an exhibition. Denise is a powerhouse, and I have absorbed countless insights from watching the way she moves through our field and champions artists. I am grateful to Denise for her careful and considerate oversight of this catalogue, which is an innovative and exquisite accompaniment to extant scholarship about Vincent.

At CAMH, we focus our platform on tackling projects that might not be possible or supported in other spaces within Houston's rich cultural ecosystem. My passionate and visionary colleagues made this exhibition richer and accessible to more audiences. Our team's enthusiastic support of *Just a Dream...* started with our director, Hesse McGraw, who was committed to making this presentation a reality from the first day of his tenure, when I burst into our meeting itching to pitch this exhibition idea. The rest of our leadership team—Felice Cleveland, Naomi B. Crawford, Ryan N. Dennis, Troy Jasmin, Melissa McDonnell Luján, and Rebecca Matalon—have identified critical ways to amplify the scope of this show. Our Facilities and Exhibitions colleagues played an invaluable role in preparing our space to host this significant survey: Tim Barkley, Marcelina Guerrero, Michael Reed, and Jeff Shore. CAMH's Development department solicited the support of generous funders; thanks to Lorielle Anderson, Faye Hosein, Kate Kendall, Dawn J. Malone, and Joshua Pierre. Quincy Berry, Kenya Evans, Autumn Johnson, Jack Morillo, Shavon Morris, Phillip Pyle, II, Michael Robinson, and YET Torres, CAMH's Learning and Engagement crew, pursued exciting ways to draw in audiences. Our Partnerships team, Charonda Johnson and Mich Stevenson, were supportive of expanding the reach of *Just a Dream...*

I have also had the support of two CAMH Curatorial Fellows. First, Ginevra Bria's input always made for engaging dialogue about Vincent's work. Frances Bolger, most recently, provided key research assistance while also conceiving of and orchestrating the audio guide accompaniment for the exhibition as her major fellowship project. Felice Cleveland helped bring to life CAMH's Program Advisory Committee, which supports the community-centered focus of this exhibition. The committee members—Alberto Careaga, Will Davison, Theresa Escobedo, Sean Fitzpatrick, Sarah Labovitz, Roberto Tejada, and Michelle Tovar—have been invaluable collaborators.

On a personal level, I am thankful to my parents, as well as my former colleague Dean Daderko, for supporting my early vision for this presentation.

PATRICIA RESTREPO
Curator, CAMH

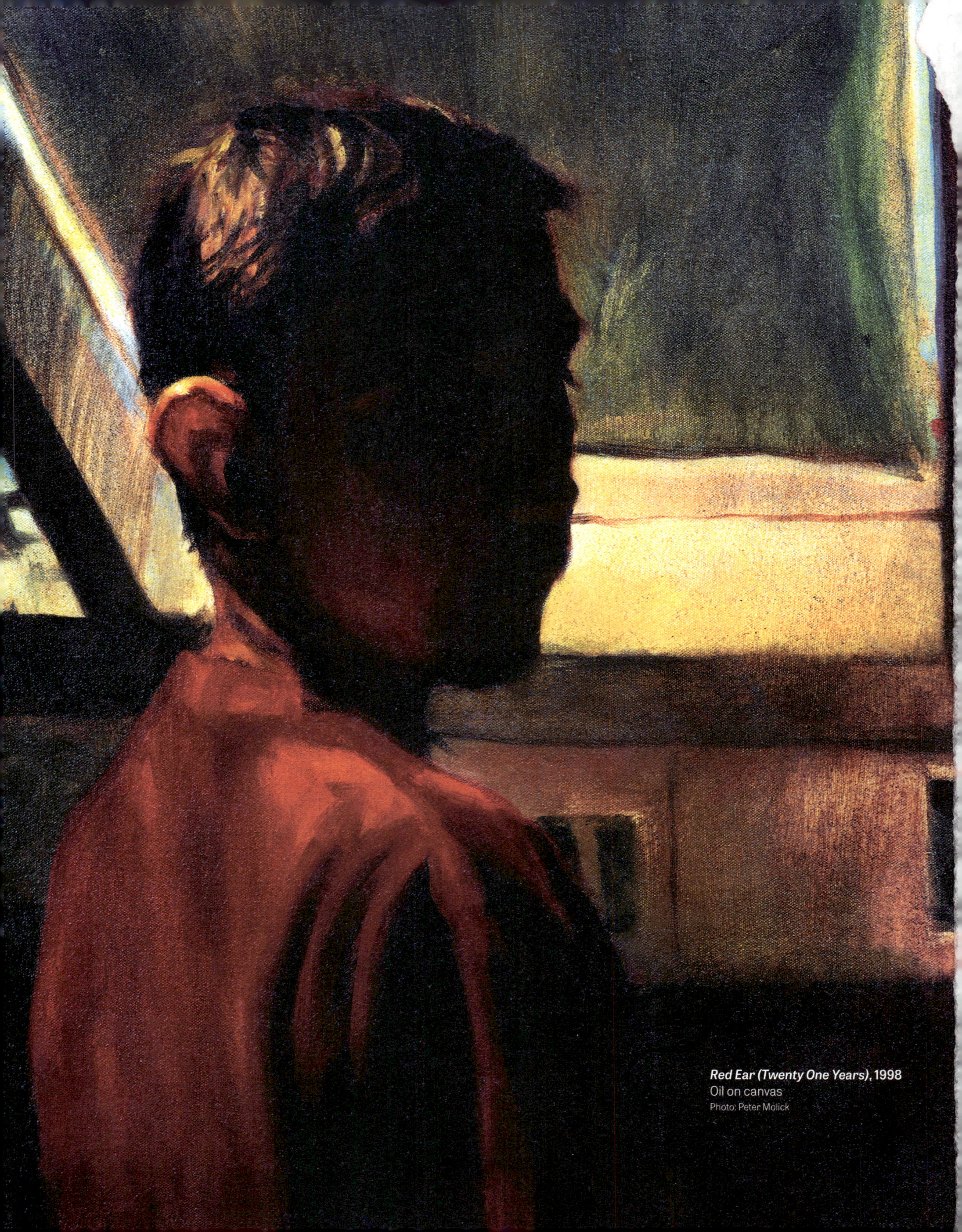

***Red Ear (Twenty One Years)*, 1998**
Oil on canvas
Photo: Peter Molick

A HALF MAST ?
FOR THE COUNTLESS DEAD?
BODIES, BONES, SCATTERED SHOES.

AN AMERICAN DREAM?
THE AMERICAN NIGHTMARE.
I WAS TOLD THE HALF MAST IS FOR
JUSTICE SCALIA; A REAL AMERICAN.

X FEBRUARY 19, 2016 X

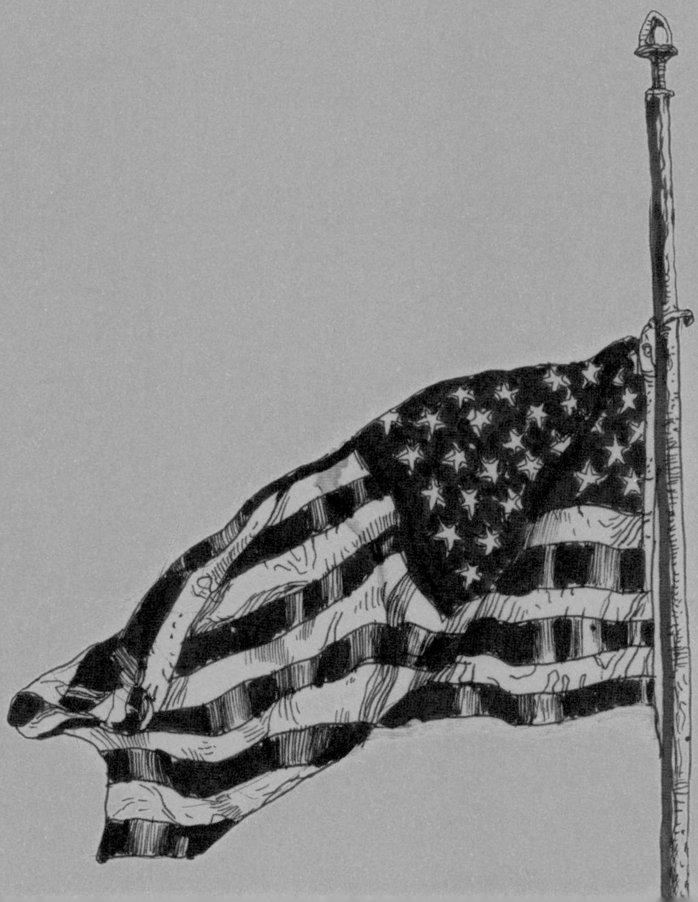

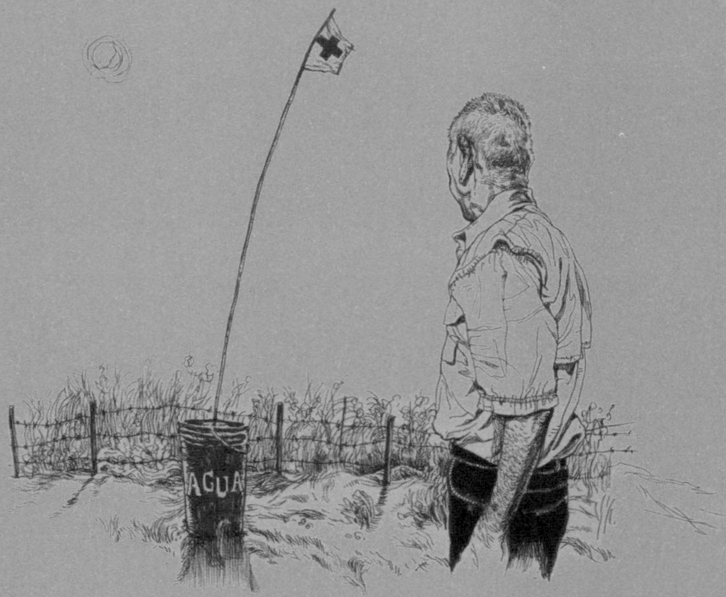
AGUA

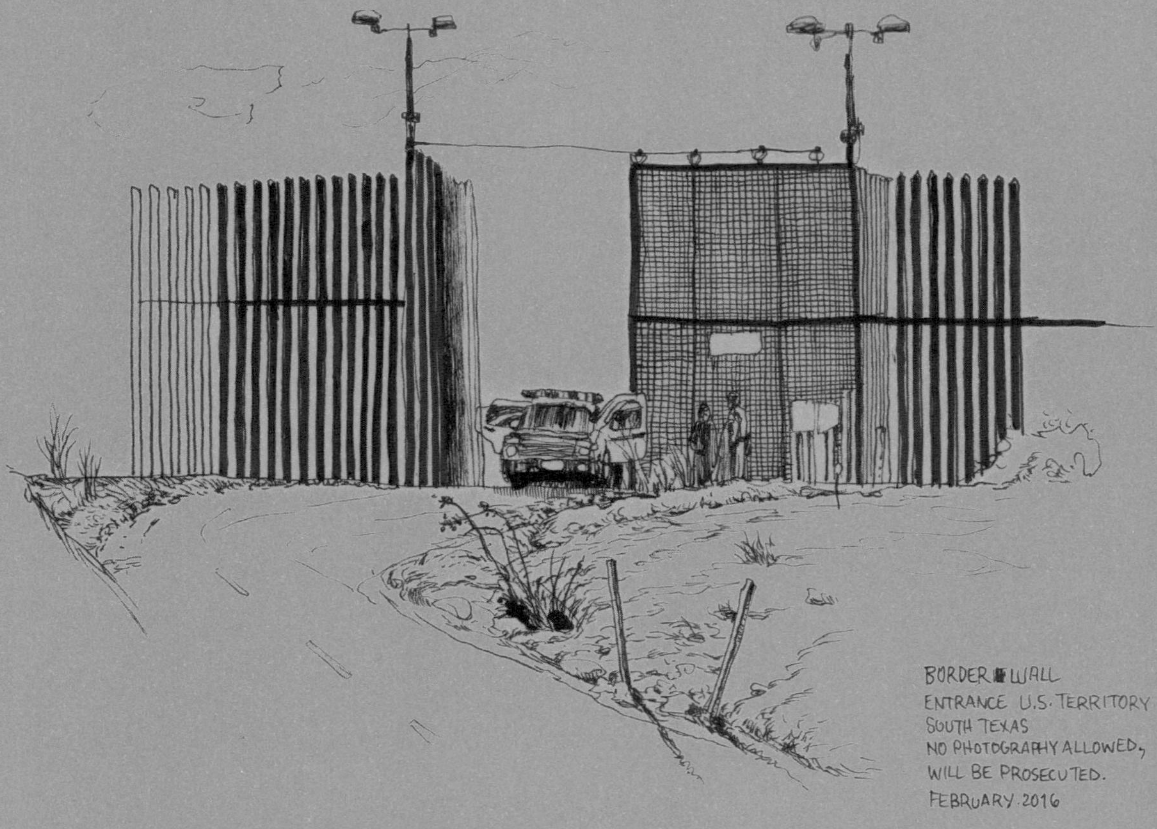
BORDER WALL
ENTRANCE U.S. TERRITORY
SOUTH TEXAS
NO PHOTOGRAPHY ALLOWED,
WILL BE PROSECUTED.
FEBRUARY 2016